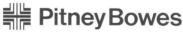   

America's Greatest Brands ©

AN INSIGHT INTO MORE THAN 70 OF AMERICA'S STRONGEST BRANDS

VOLUME 2

America's Greatest Brands, Inc.©

Editor-in-Chief
Stephen P. Smith

Associate Publishers
F. W. Pete McCutchen
Peter Richardson

Managing Editor
Bob Land

Design Director
Jack Huber

Published by America's Greatest Brands, Inc.
350 Theodore Fremd Avenue
Rye, New York, 10580

Telephone (914) 921-3300
Facsimile (914) 931-3330
e-mail pm@americasgreatestbrands.com
www.americasgreatestbrands.com

Special thanks to Amber Bagstad, Gene Bartley, Cheryl
Berman, Jonathan Bond, Rich Hamilton, Rich Jernstedt, Keith
Newton, Keith Reinhard, Hal Riney, Kevin Roberts, Clay
Timon, Bob Tomei, Marcel Knobil, Bill Colegrave, Richard
Thomas, Peter Ledbetter, Eamonn Sadler, Duncan Whitehead,
Kelvin and Ray, May Yap, Chris, Carmen and Aruna, Robert
and James Brown, John, Nick, Chris, Caron and Lily-Rose,
Jean, Sara, Peter, Tammy, Rob, Mark Hofer, Maura Toller,
Gerard Wilson, Jake Wilson, Annie Richardson, Blair
Hamilford, Jilly, Soraya, Kara, Elizabeth Smith, Kevin Boland,
Angela Pumphrey, Bruce Connolly, David Goldschmidt,
Edwin Fabiero, Ferdi Stolzenburg, Ray Barnes, Jack Maisano,
Jeff Palfreyman, Noel Derby, Paul Gregory, Craig Hines,
Russell Yu, Steve Moss, Peter Brack, Paul Ashby, Lindsay
Birley, Victor Jeffery, Bruce Johnston, Chris Mooney,
Christine, Brendon, Kevin, Kerrie Lindsay, Peter Ryall,
Neville Young, Agnes, Jason, Peter, Daniel, Sally, Jack,
William, Sam, Espie, Alexander, Georgina, Anne, Alix,
Louise, Lisa, Callie, Kendra, Dick, Tere, Mitchell, and Harry.

ISBN 0-9706860-1-3

America's Greatest Brands ©

AN INSIGHT INTO MORE THAN 70 OF AMERICA'S STRONGEST BRANDS
VOLUME 2

This book is dedicated to the men and
women who build and protect
America's greatest brand assets.

www.americasgreatestbrands.com

CONTENTS

ABC
ABC, Incorporated
500 South Buena Vista Street
Burbank, CA 91521

Aetna
Aetna, Incorporated
151 Farmington Ave.
Hartford, CT 06156

American Red Cross
American Red Cross
431 18th Street NW 5th Floor
Washington, DC 20006

Andersen Windows and Doors
Andersen Windows, Inc.
100 Fourth Avenue North
Bayport, MN 55003

Avery Dennison
Avery Dennison Corporation
150 N. Orange Grove Boulevard
Pasadena, CA 91103

Avis
Cendant Corporation
6 Sylvan Way
Parsippany, NJ 01054

Bank of America
Bank of America Corporation
Bank of America Corporate Center
100 N. Tryon St.
Charlotte, NC 28255

Buick Motor Division
General Motors Corporation
100 Renaissance Center 32nd Floor
Detroit, MI 48265-1000

Callaway Golf
Callaway Golf
2180 Rutherford Road
Carlsbad, CA 92008

Carlsberg
Labatt USA
101 Merritt 7
Norwalk, CT 06856

Carrier
Carrier Corporation
1 Carrier Place
Farmington, CT 06034

Caterpillar
Caterpillar Inc.
100 N.E. Adams Street
Peoria, IL 61629

Century 21
Century 21 Real Estate Corporation
One Campus Drive
Parsippany, NJ 07054

Chiquita
Chiquita Brands International, Inc.
250 East 5th Street
Cincinnatti, OH 45202

Club Med
Club Med Sales, Incorporated
75 Valencia Avenue
Coral Gables, FL 33134

Coca-Cola
The Coca-Cola Company
One Coca Cola Plaza
Atlanta, GA 30313

Comcast
Comcast Cable Communications,
Incorporated
1500 Market Street
Philadelphia, PA 19102

Crest
The Procter & Gamble Company
One Procter & Gamble Plaza
Cincinnati, OH 45202

Cunard Line
Cunard Line
6100 Blue Lagoon Drive
Miami, FL 33126

Domino's Pizza
Domino's Pizza LLC
30 Frank Lloyd Wright Drive
Ann Arbor, MI 48106

French's Foods
Reckitt Benckiser, Incorporated
1655 Valley Road
Wayne, NJ 07474

Fritos
Frito-Lay, Incorporated
7701 Legacy Drive
Plano, TX 75024

Gateway
Gateway, Inc.
14303 Gateway Place
Poway, CA 92064

Gatorade
The Gatorade Company
555 W. Monroe Street
Chicago, IL 60661

GEICO
GEICO Direct
1 GEICO Plaza
Washington, DC 20076

Guardsmark
Guardsmark, LLC
10 Rockefeller Plaza, 12th Floor
New York, NY 10020

GUESS?
GUESS?, Incorporated
144 South Alameda Street
Los Angeles, CA 90021

Hanes
Sara Lee Branded Apparel
475 Corporate Square Boulevard
Winston-Salem, NC 27105

Honeywell
Honeywell
101 Columbia Road
Morristown, NJ 07962

Hoover
The Hoover Company
101 E. Maple Street
North Canton, OH 44720

Huggies
Kimberly-Clark Corporation
351 Phelps Dr.
Irving, TX 75038

Hush Puppies
Wolverine World Wide, Incorporated
9341 Courtland Drive
Rockford, MI 49351

IBM
IBM Corporation
New Orchard Road
Armonk, NY 10504

IKON
IKON Office Solutions, Inc.
70 Valley Stream Parkway
Malvern, PA 19355

ITT Industries
ITT Industries, Incorporated
4 West Red Oak Lane
White Plains, NY 10604

Jockey
Jockey International, Incorporated
2300 60th Street
Kenosha, WI 53140

Kellogg's
Kellogg Company
1 Kellogg Square
Battle Creek, MI 49016

KeyBank
KeyCorp
127 Public Square
Cleveland, OH 44114

Lennox
Lennox International Inc.
2140 Lake Park Blvd.
Richardson, TX 75080

M&M'S
Masterfoods USA
800 High Street
Hackettstown, NJ 07840

McDonald's
McDonald's Corporation
One Kroc Drive
Oak Brook, IL 60521

Meow Mix
The Meow Mix Company
400 Plaza Drive 1st Floor
Secaucus, NJ 07094

Moen
Moen Incorporated
25300 Al Moen Drive
North Olmsted, OH 44070

New York Stock Exchange
New York Stock Exchange, Inc.
11 Wall Street
New York, NY 10005

OshKosh B'Gosh
OshKosh B'Gosh, Inc.
112 Otter Ave.
Oshkosh, WI 54901

Panasonic
Matsushita Electric Corporation of
America
One Panasonic Way
Secaucus, NJ 07094

Pitney Bowes
Pitney Bowes Inc.
1 Elmcroft Road
Stamford, CT 06926-0700

Polaroid
Polaroid Corporation
1265 Main Street
Waltham, MA 02451

Roadway Express
Roadway Express, Inc.
1077 Gorge Boulevard
Akron, OH 44310

Royal Doulton
The Royal Doulton Company
Sir Henry Doulton House Forge Lane
Etruria
Stoke-on-Trent, England ST1 5NN

Saturn
The Saturn Corporation
100 Renaissance Center
Detroit, MI 48265

SBC
SBC Communications, Inc.
175 East Houston Street
San Antonio, TX 78205

Scott Tissue
Kimberly-Clark Corporation
351 Phelps Dr.
Irving, TX 75038

Scotts
The Scotts Co.
14111 Scottslawn Road
Marysville, OH 43041

Simmons
Simmons Company
1 Concourse Pkwy., Ste. 800
Atlanta, GA 30328

Sony
Sony Electronics Inc.
One Sony Drive
Park Ridge, NJ 07656

Sprint
Sprint Corporation
6200 Sprint Parkway
Overland Park, KS 66251

Stanley
The Stanley Works
1000 Stanley Drive
New Britain, CT 06053

State Farm
State Farm Insurance Companies
1 State Farm Plaza
Bloomington, IL 61710

Swanson
Pinnacle Foods Corporation
1 Old Bloomfield Road
Mt. Laes, NJ 07046

TBS Superstation
TBS Superstation
1050 Techwood Drive NW
Atlanta, GA 30318

The New York Times
The New York Times Company
229 W. 43rd Street
New York, NY 10036

3M
3M Company
3M Center
Saint Paul, MN 55144-1000

TNT
Turner Network Television
1050 Techwood Drive NW
Atlanta, GA 30318

Toys "R" Us
Toys "R" Us, Incorporated
461 From Road
Paramus, NJ 07652

United States Marine Corps
United States Marine Corps
3280 Russell Road
Quantico, VA 22134

U.S. Bank
U.S. Bancorp
225 South 6th Street
Minneapolis, MN 55402

Vaseline
Unilever
33 Benedict Place
Greenwich, CT 06830

Verizon
Verizon, Incorporated
1095 Avenue of the Americas
New York, NY 10036

Yellow
Yellow Corporation
10990 Roe Avenue
Overland Park, KS 66211

Zenith
Zenith Electronics Corporation
2000 Millbrook Drive
Lincolnshire, IL 60069

FOREWORD

Stephen P. Smith
Publisher
Chairman, The American Brands Council

When we published the first edition of *America's Greatest Brands* in 2001, we had no idea how successful the concept would be. Just about everyone in advertising, marketing, brand management, and the media industry wanted a copy. Even consumers with no direct involvement in branding issues were fascinated by the information provided, and they bought thousands of copies of *America's Greatest Brands*. This should not have been a surprise, because the brands featured in our publication were, and are, an integral part of all of our lives.

Publication of the second edition of *America's Greatest Brands* was a challenge in ways we never could have anticipated. Between editions, the American landscape changed — emotionally, economically, fiscally, and from a marketing perspective. Thrust into world events in a most unexpected and cataclysmic manner, Americans and American brands faced a scenario that few long-range corporate strategists would ever have considered. Because of the events of one late summer morning in 2001, marketing campaigns changed, business plans were overhauled or discarded, movies shelved, and concepts deemed taboo, at least for a time.

In such an environment, American citizens — indeed, people the world over — look for comfort. Everyone finds comfort in the familiar, and for Americans, few images and concepts are as comfortable and familiar as those represented by the brands on the following pages. Whether it's the shape of a bottle or the forlorn look in a hound-dog's eyes, continuity and safety take on added importance in times like these.

The companies and the brands featured in the second edition of *America's Greatest Brands* are indeed an integral part of our lives, sources of comfort and strength, signifiers that the American way of life persists. More than a maker's mark, a great brand is almost an heraldic symbol, carrying with it a whole web of positive associations — and at certain times, positive associations are just what people need.

Leading companies have long recognized that their brands are powerful assets. Recent surveys indicate that brands may account for 50 to 70 percent of a company's total value, perhaps worth billions of dollars. Studying the way these brands began, developed, and grew into trusted household names is not only vital for anyone interested in the way the modern marketplace functions; it is also fascinating and often fun.

This book contains many informative brand stories and offers some fascinating insights into the creation and development of many of America's brand icons. Worldwide, our organization has researched and presented over 1,200 of the strongest brands in 20 countries.

In the following pages, we present comments from members of The American Brands Council — some of the United States' most eminent media and communications executives — about the importance and influence of brands. As you read this book, please consider along with them: What makes a brand one of America's Greatest Brands? What creates the awareness, desirability and power that a great brand has? With the help of the Council and the companies themselves, we have compiled for you the stories of some of America's, and the world's, greatest brands and attempted to capture the innovation and prestige that surround them.

"More than a maker's mark, a great brand is almost an heraldic symbol, carrying with it a whole web of positive associations — and at certain times, positive associations are just what people need."

WHAT MAKES A GREAT BRAND?

BY THE AMERICAN BRANDS COUNCIL

Gene Bartley
President, FCB Worldwide

Rather than give you some dry, precise definition of a brand in terms only an adman or woman would love, let's have some fun with this. Let's play a game that gets at the heart of what great brands are really about. I'll mention three things sequentially; you try and guess the brand they bring to mind.

Adventure, the great outdoors, and an all-terrain vehicle. You guessed it: Jeep. Fantasy, fun, and big ears. Did I hear Disney? If so, you're right on the money. And finally, Coney Island, cotton candy, and hot dogs. That's right: Nathan's hot dogs. (How could we talk about American brands without touching on hot dogs?)

When a brand delivers, like the three knockouts above, you don't have to spend a lot of time figuring out how or why. They mean something very specific to anyone who has ever encountered them. They elicit feelings of warmth and confidence, a comfort level that's usually reserved for family or friends. That's what great brands and successful advertising are all about.

Jonathan Bond Co-Chairman, Kirshenbaum Bond & Partners

Brands used to be all about finding that one unique rational product attribute and hammering away at it. Today the great brands have meaningful relationships with their customers that go far beyond a single attribute.

Great brands are complex matrices of attributes, features, experiences, values, and emotions that bind the customer to them on a variety of levels. However, each strand of the brand is weak and easily broken by a competitive offer. That's why uni-dimensional brands are vulnerable. Look at each "connection" to the consumer as a single weak and fragile thread. Taken together, though, all of these threads can weave a strong fabric, binding the brand to the customer in a way that is all but unbreakable.

The great brands of today are diverse, yet consistent. Like a great actor who can take on many roles while maintaining the essence of who he or she is, a great brand is consistent, yet extendable; complex, yet universally understandable. A brand that does all of these things — a mega-brand — is the ultimate business weapon in today's world.

Keith Newton Branding Manager, Young and Rubicam Advertising

A brand is a set of differentiating promises that link a product to its customers.

The brand assures the customer of consistent quality plus a superior value (both functional and emotional) for which the customer is willing to give loyalty and pay a price that brings a reasonable return to the brand.

Great brands that retain their vitality have one more important ingredient: owners who acknowledge that their brands are their business, not just a marketing mark. These owners' brands always have a clear and enduring belief: a common belief that finds its way into the minds of many groups.

All good brands support their owners on the everyday battleground for revenue and profit. But great brands truly transcend this, and create powerful, intangible value on the balance sheet.

Keith Reinhard Chairman, DDB Worldwide

The twentieth-century Spanish philosopher Jose Ortega y Gasset counseled, "The first act of any society is the selection of a point of view." And so it is for brands. A great brand is distinguished by a passionately held point of view, from which evolves a relevant and compelling promise — the combination of which is conveyed with a distinctive style and personality.

McDonald's point of view is that eating out is about more than food. It therefore promises a good time every time, always with a style that is warm and human. Volkswagen's point of view is that automotive excellence should be available to everyone. It is therefore expanding its line in order to promise the unique Volkswagen driving experience to people of all economic classes . . . but always with the same special style that launched the Beetle in 1959.

A well-selected point of view, a compelling promise stated or implied, and a winning personality. These are the key elements of a great brand.

Hal Riney Chairman and Chief Executive Officer, Publicis & Hal Riney

A great brand must first and foremost be familiar to a substantial portion of its consumers. But familiarity alone is of little value unless the brand, whether a product or service, has been consistently responsive to consumer interests and needs over a substantial period of time. These two qualities — familiarity and historic satisfaction — are the primary components of brand strength: the ability to survive competitive threats or even to thrive through periods where the brand's actual qualities may not actually be equivalent to those of a competitor. The result of brand strength is brand value: the difference between what the consumer will consistently pay for a brand that is comforting and familiar, and a brand that isn't.

Cheryl Berman Chairman and Chief Creative Officer, Leo Burnett U.S.A.

Brands live and breathe. They flourish, prosper, stumble, and gasp. Brands get sick and brands get well. Brands grow tired and old, and sometimes a brand dies right before our eyes.

They need love and passion and loyalty to survive. But most of all, to become a great brand, they need belief — a potent, active belief by consumers that their brands are the ones they can trust. Their brands always deliver on promises made. Their brands even reflect the consumer's own self-image, as all of our collective brand choices work together, to inform what I like to think of as a person's own brand.

Great brands know who they are and behave as such, consistently delivering their promise, yet constantly evolving to stay relevant and meaningful to their believers. Grand brands never sit still. They have coverage because they make choices that others hesitate to make. They thrive by embedding themselves in their culture.

So, no matter what we may read or hear, a great brand can never be owned by some company — it is, and always will be, owned by the people.

Rich Hamilton Chief Executive Officer, Zenith Media Services, Inc.

Great brands have a life of their own. They are immortal; they stand for something.

They are durable, simple, and elegant in design. They inspire loyalty. People pay more to buy them. Why? Because it's worth it!

Who are they in America?

They are brands like Cheerios, M&M'S, Sony, Oreo, Coca-Cola, Ford, Disney, and Kellogg's. There are many more.

The companies that own these brands work to protect and indeed build them through innovation in product development, distribution and sales efforts, and all forms of marketing.

Mars Inc., owner of M&M'S, conducted a sweepstakes which let consumers select the next new color of M&M'S. Consumers picked purple! A great example of leadership and consumer-focused marketing from the owner of a true brand icon.

Rich Jernstedt Chief Executive Officer, Golin/Harris International

Great brands are distinguished from good ones by the "magic contradiction" — the ability to transform constantly while remaining true to core values. Too often, brands with stellar pedigrees grow stale and dynamic brands flicker out.

But in the contradiction, you must see opportunity. The secret is to develop and maintain trust in your brand.

A great brand is a trusted brand.

A trusted brand meets expectations of excellence, integrity, and fidelity. Customers, employees, investors, and neighbors can count on it. The one constant for every trusted brand is commitment: not just making a promise, but delivering on it. Not just once, but always and in all ways.

The Golin/Harris Trust Survey reveals that approximately 70 percent of Americans are experiencing a crisis of trust in business. They said, "I just don't know whom to trust anymore."

They are sending a message. Great brands get it — and they are doing something about it.

Kevin Roberts Chief Executive Officer Worldwide, Saatchi & Saatchi

Brands are running out of juice. Even great brands are being squeezed hard by a number of mounting factors: the erosion of premium pricing, the struggle to maintain differentiation, the rapid imitation of innovation, and more and more competition.

Brands were invented for kinder times with growing markets and eager customers. But some brands can still win. Such brands have evolved into something so different they need a new name. We call them Lovemarks.

Quality, performance, and all the rest have become table-stakes. Only Lovemarks know that long-term relationships are based on three human fundamentals: the thrill of mystery, the immediacy of sensuality, and the trust of intimacy.

Lovemarks are the future for America's great brands. Some have made it. The direction is clear. Product to trademark. Trademark to brand. Brand to Lovemark. Lovemarks are super-evolved brands that make deep emotional connections with consumers, great brands that inspire loyalty beyond reason.

Clay Timon Chairman, President, and Chief Executive Officer, Landor Associates

At Landor, we know through our BrandAsset™ Valuator (BAV) research that great brands build on four fundamentals.

- Differentiation. If a brand is not differentiated from its competition, it has no reason for being.
- Relevance. Without relevance, one might build a niche brand, but if the brand is not relevant to a sufficiently large audience, it will not become one of the world's great brands.
- Esteem — The regard customers have for a brand.
- Knowledge — Customers who are able to actually describe what they believe the brand stands for. In the end, customers will look at themselves as BMW drivers, not merely automobile drivers; as a Coke or Pepsi drinker, not a soda drinker.

The brands that achieve the highest levels across all four fundamental building blocks become the world's greatest brands.

Bob Tomei Chief Marketing Officer, AC Nielsen

A great brand is best defined by the equity and positioning it holds in the marketplace. Brand equity is defined by the price/value relationship it maintains among a specific target audience. Once a brand's equity is established in the market, its positioning and image must reinforce that price/value relationship over and over again. It is critical to maintain a consistent message over time that reinforces those attributes of a brand that consumers value.

A brand should also not extend beyond its defined equity and positioning. A great brand must deliver on its stated commitment to responsibly fulfill a specific consumer need or desire. The brand's packaging, promotion, advertising, and positioning in the market need to support that commitment. While it's relatively easy to "refresh/update" a brand using repackaging or close-in line extensions, the real challenge lies in making it relevant over time to your target consumer.

THE MARKET

Although television viewing remains America's number-one leisure time activity, the fight for viewers has become increasingly competitive. With four major networks, two smaller "weblets" and local independent stations, targeted cable networks, satellite delivery systems, and digital recording devices, this highly competitive marketplace also faces the continued growth of the Internet and new technologies, VCRs, DVDs, movies, video games, MP3s, and land-based and satellite-delivered radio.

For the networks, this continued fragmentation of the audience represents a problem and a challenge. For some, defining and narrowing their audience has been the answer. For ABC, this present-day climate has created an opportunity to differentiate and reposition its brand as the one offering the broadest, most wide-reaching, and most accessible of choices — a brand whose programming mix brings people and families back together to watch television.

ACHIEVEMENTS

ABC remains one of America's broadest and most innovative television brands because of the combined growth of its diverse and distinctive programming, and a patient, successful brand strategy. This year, ABC reaches its milestone 50th year in

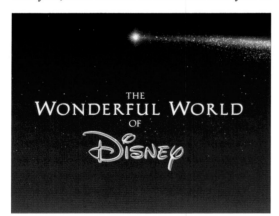

providing a quality mix of news, sports, and entertainment programs.

That success has deep roots. ABC developed groundbreaking program partnerships like those in the 1950s with The Walt Disney Company, with shows like *Disneyland* and *The Mickey Mouse Club*, and Warner Brothers, who produced action westerns like *Cheyenne*, *Kings Row*, and *Wyatt Earp*.

In the 1960s, ABC achieved incredible success with aggressive risk-taking and pioneering broadcast and technological innovations like the

establishment of the first-ever separate AM and FM broadcast radio divisions. ABC created new program styles in the 1970s like made-for-television movies and multi-part mini-series, like *Rich Man, Poor Man* and the unprecedented eight-day television event, *Roots*.

ABC also changed the way people watched television with program innovations like *Monday Night Football*, *The Wide World of Sports*, and late night's *Nightline*. And with the success of *Who Wants to Be a Millionaire*, ABC reinvigorated the primetime game show and spawned a new wave of reality programming.

HISTORY

In its rich 50-year history, ABC has broadcast some of the most popular shows on television, like *The Lone Ranger*, *Leave It to Beaver*, *Batman*, *Marcus Welby, M.D.*, *The Untouchables*, *Happy Days*, *Laverne and Shirley*, *The Love Boat*, *The Brady Bunch*, *Charlie's Angels*, *Dynasty*, *thirtysomething*, *The Wonder Years*, *Roseanne*, *Home Improvement*, *Twin Peaks*, *NYPD Blue*, *The Drew Carey Show*, *The Practice*, *Alias*, and more.

The network began in 1943, when businessman Edward Noble of Rexall Drugs bought NBC's Blue Radio Network for $8 million after the U.S. government

ordered NBC to sell one of its two networks. Noble named his new entity the American Broadcasting Company. It was owned by United Paramount Theatres, and then by Capital Cities Communications, before its present owner, The Walt Disney Company, acquired it in 1996 for $19 billion.

After early years of struggling, ABC eventually overtook its competitors in the mid- to late 1970s, thanks to a string of successful urban, contemporary series like *Happy Days*, *Laverne & Shirley*, *Charlie's Angels*, and *Family*, as well as the development of *Monday Night Football*, still television's number-one sports franchise.

Further success in ABC Sports and ABC News under the leadership of Roone Arledge brought the network to even greater prominence.

THE PRODUCT

The ABC Television Network is the broadcast network division of ABC Inc., a division of The Walt Disney Company. Other ABC Inc. properties include cable networks such as ESPN, the Disney Channel, ABC Family, Toon Disney, and SoapNet; syndicated TV programmer, Buena Vista Television; Touchstone Television; ABC Radio, the ABC Radio Network, and Radio Disney; Walt Disney Television International; and Hyperion, Disney's trade publishing division.

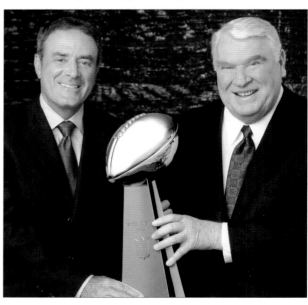

ABC-TV's products appeal to all demographics and every member of the family. The ABC Entertainment lineup boasts such top-rated audience favorites as *The Wonderful World of Disney*, *NYPD Blue*, *The Practice*, *My Wife and Kids*, *According to Jim*, and *Alias*. ABC's Daytime offers popular serial dramas *General Hospital*, *All My Children*, and *One Life to Live*, as well as *The View*.

ABC News features the most informative and most respected journalists in broadcasting with Peter Jennings, Ted Koppel, Barbara Walters, Diane Sawyer, Charles Gibson, and more. Programs

more provocative dramas and hard-hitting newsmagazines at 10:00 p.m.

ABC News has experienced a resurgence in popularity, acclaim, and growth. *Good Morning America* has increased its audience by double digits. *World News Tonight with Peter Jennings* experienced greater total audience growth than both of its competitors combined. Newsmagazines *20/20* and *Primetime* are revitalized and experiencing continued success.

ABC Daytime marked its unparalleled 25th year as the number-one network in Daytime television with women 18–49.

In Late Night, ABC announced the debut of the highly anticipated *Jimmy Kimmel Live*, immediately following *Nightline*.

ABC Sports began its unprecedented streak of championship event broadcasts that features the Super Bowl, NBA Finals, the Stanley Cup, the Bowl Championship Series, and more.

ABC developed a revolutionary approach towards promoting both horizontally and vertically across the week. With traditional television promotion mostly focused on keeping viewers watching through the night (vertical approach), ABC has added a promotional strategy for their "family friendly" shows that air every weeknight at 8:00 p.m. This concept was introduced as ABC's "Happy Hour" promotion that "claims ownership" of the 8:00 p.m. hour, establishing a horizontal block across the week.

Finally, ABC's new programming philosophy, a return to the family-friendly brand it stood for years ago, will strike an emotional connection with an American culture looking for a return to a sense of community and family.

BRAND VALUES

For 50 years, ABC has been a network that is real, broad, accessible, diverse, fun, smart, reflective, and inviting. The programming is a genuine reflection of that brand attitude and of the diverse population that tunes in each day. In its 50th anniversary year, the brand is now looking back as much as it is looking ahead in delivering audiences

include *Good Morning America*, *World News Tonight*, *Nightline*, *20/20*, *Primetime*, and Sunday's political forum, *This Week*.

ABC Sports features an unrivaled schedule of season-long sports coverage and big championships that include *Monday Night Football* and *The Super Bowl*; the *NBA Finals*; *NCAA College Football* and *Bowl Championship Series*; *NCAA Basketball*; *The British Open*; the *Indianapolis 500*; *NHL Hockey* and *Stanley Cup*; the *U.S. and World Figure Skating Championships*, and more.

And in ABC's popular entertaining and educational children's programming, the *ABC Kids* lineup offers animated character-based programs and fun interstitial programming that reaches millions of American children.

RECENT DEVELOPMENTS
ABC Entertainment's newly invigorated primetime programming philosophy in its 50th anniversary year is rededicated towards the brand's historical strength — strong, smart, inclusive comedies targeted towards young adults, but that the entire family can watch, beginning at 8:00 p.m.; more adult comedies and escapist dramas at 9:00 p.m.; and

PROMOTION
Distinctive promotion, marketing, and branding, in concert with programming, have proven to be the drivers of the ABC brand.

The focus of ABC's promotional efforts starts with its own on-air and paid media. Much of that promotion will work even harder this year with the broadcast of television's top-rated *Super Bowl* and the *Academy Awards*.

Great strides have been taken in leveraging the synergistic opportunities afforded by their corporate parent, The Walt Disney Company. This association has resulted in an enormous array of added media exposure, reaching viewers through theme parks, hotel rooms, and retail store promotional events; radio, cable, home video, and DVD cross-promotion; magazine and direct mail; and Internet partnerships.

ABC has also developed countless successful cross-promotional partnerships with advertisers and sponsors, with shared extended media exposure for ABC shows through unique consumer promotions, innovative integrated product placement, and program entitlement opportunities.

the kind of programs that struck a chord with its viewers throughout its history. The ABC brand prides itself on producing the best storytelling and delivering the highest-quality programming.

Photos: ©2002 ABC Photography Archives

THE MARKET

Health care in America today is a focal point of enormous economic, social, and political stresses. Americans spent more than $1.4 trillion on health care in 2001 and enjoy arguably the best health care system in the world; yet, costs are rising at double-digit levels, more than 41 million Americans are uninsured, and recent reports from the Institute of Medicine have questioned the quality and safety of health care in America.

The growing concerns regarding the cost and quality of health care, along with a rising tide of consumerism, are leading to an end to the paternalism and consumer passivity that has characterized the U.S. health care system. In its place, a more consumer-oriented approach is emerging, in which individuals take more control of their health coverage and care decisions.

Aetna is leading the development of innovative consumer-directed products that provide consumers with incentives to be more conscious of their health care spending as they are aided in making more informed decisions. This approach should lead to a more efficient system with better outcomes for patients.

ACHIEVEMENTS

In 2003, Aetna proudly celebrates its 150th anniversary, a milestone that few companies reach. Throughout its history, Aetna has remained a leader by helping people protect against the risks and uncertainties of life, promising to be there when they need it most. Aetna's long-term leadership has required constant change, while holding true to enduring values.

Today, Aetna helps employers, individuals, and families meet their comprehensive health-related benefits needs. Aetna also takes the larger view of a responsible corporate citizen. The company considers part of its mission to be a leader, cooperating with doctors and hospitals, employers, patients, public officials, and others to build a stronger, more effective health care system.

Aetna is taking significant actions to improve the system, including:
• Working to eliminate disparities in health care status that exist for racial and ethnic minority and economically disadvantaged populations with programs to increase access to quality care for members of these populations.
• Proposing health insurance industry guidelines for coverage of genetic testing to promote disease

prevention and management, while respecting members' privacy. Aetna believes that a small investment in testing today can prevent or mitigate human suffering, while saving on future health care costs.
• Urging government action to improve access to health coverage for the uninsured, including

government support programs, tax credits, and some coverage mandates. In addition, Aetna offers streamlined, cost-efficient plans that make it easier for small businesses to provide coverage for their employees.

Further, Aetna has created a culture of caring, supporting initiatives that improve the quality of life where Aetna's employees and customers work and live. Since 1980, the Aetna Foundation has contributed more than $250 million in grants, scholarships, and social investments.

Aetna also has an outstanding record on diversity issues and is considered a leading employer, frequently appearing on lists of the top places to work for minorities and women.

HISTORY

Aetna Life Insurance Company was established in 1853, amidst burgeoning industrial development in Hartford, Connecticut. The company entered into the accident-coverage market in 1891, initiating a 30-year transformation from a mono-line to a multi-line insurer. The company entered health in 1899, commercial liability and workers collective in 1902, auto in 1907, fidelity and surety in 1911, group and homeowners in 1913, and inland/ocean marine in 1916.

In the 1980s, Aetna began to reevaluate its lines of businesses and identified unprofitable markets. In 1990, Aetna dropped its individual health lines; in 1991, the company pulled out of the auto market in 22 states and out of homeowners in several

others, and in 1996, Aetna sold its remaining property-casualty operation to Travelers.

The reversal of Aetna's century-old multi-line philosophy marked the end of an era, but also a promising opportunity to focus and strengthen the business. By 1996, the company had determined that its nucleus would be health care. In an $8 billion deal that year, Aetna merged with U.S. Healthcare. It acquired the health insurance businesses of New York Life in 1998 and Prudential in 1999. In 2000, Aetna sold its financial services and international businesses to ING, completing its transformation to a company singularly dedicated to health care and health-related group benefits.

THE PRODUCT

Aetna offers a wide range of health benefits choices with a variety of health plans, pharmacy, behavioral health and dental benefits, as well as long-term care policies, disability coverage, and group life insurance.

Aetna members enjoy access to expansive nationwide networks of physicians, hospitals, pharmacies, and other health professionals — more than 552,000 as of December 31, 2002. Broad, national presence enables Aetna to serve large, multi-site corporations as well as small employers.

The ability to meet employers' needs is important, because Aetna's products reach individuals at the workplace as employment benefits. Employers generally subsidize these programs, and in many cases, the employer must make difficult decisions, balancing complex options that result in different plan designs and costs.

Increasingly, many employers are interested in integrated solutions that employ health, pharmacy, and disability data that Aetna is uniquely able to provide. With access to transaction data from millions of members, Aetna analyzes information to help employers design programs that respond to the specific health and financial needs of their employees.

While working closely with employers, Aetna also is becoming more focused on the needs of individual members and their families.

RECENT DEVELOPMENTS

In September 2001, the company introduced Aetna HealthFund™, the first consumer-directed health benefit plan offered by a national health benefits company. Aetna HealthFund is now evolving into a family of products designed to better serve the unique and varied needs of individuals and their families.

Aetna HealthFund gives individuals more control of their health care dollars, while allowing them to become more involved in coverage and care decisions. Members get helpful tools and customized information, delivered in language they can understand, so they can make informed choices, along with their physicians.

For consumer-directed care to be most effective, the core financial incentives should be cou-

pled with approaches that increase the likelihood that members will access cost-effective, high-quality physicians and hospitals and use patient care management programs when needed. Patient care management strategies include disease management programs, lifestyle interventions, information therapy, and hospital care management programs that support effective clinical decision-making.

The success of these programs depends upon good information sharing between the health plan, the physician, and the consumer. Aetna is committed to respect and work effectively with doctors and hospitals by establishing efficient processes and providing prompt claims payments and useful information that helps them provide safe, affordable, high-quality health care.

PROMOTION

Aetna's advertising has reflected both the historic shifts in American society and changes in Aetna's products and services. During the first half of the 20th century, Aetna's advertising helped to establish the need for insurance protection, not only building Aetna's business, but also the category generally.

In the late 1980s, Aetna developed an innovative new campaign with the theme, "A Policy To Do More." The campaign addressed pressing national issues and featured a "straight talk" approach that appealed to both common sense and higher values.

After 1996, when Aetna exited the property-casualty business and became more focused on health care, Aetna's advertising began to focus on how Aetna helps people with information to make the right choices about "What Matters Most" — health care and financial security.

Today, the Aetna name, already well known and highly regarded in the marketplace, remains the same, but Aetna's fresh, new logo embodies a robust vision. It reflects the duality of the Aetna brand: strong and stable, yet human, approachable, and empowering. It is the new face of the new Aetna.

Aetna's advertising reaches consumers, employers, brokers, and consultants with messages that focus on Aetna's innovative approaches to consumer-directed health care, promoting Aetna HealthFund and emphasizing open-access plans and easy-to-understand information that helps customers make more informed choices.

BRAND VALUES

Aetna today is dedicated to helping people achieve health and financial security by providing easy access to safe, cost-effective, high-quality health care and protecting their finances against health-related risks.

To fulfill this mission, Aetna provides employers advice, cost-effective benefits choices, and value-added programs that protect the finances and improve the health status and productivity of their work forces. It also gives individuals affordable coverage choices, helpful service, and information so they get the right care and coverage for themselves and their families.

The Aetna brand stands for easily accessible and relevant information that's customizable to the customer's unique needs and results in better outcomes. More choices, smarter decisions, better results.

Aetna is the brand name for products and services provided by one or more of the Aetna group of subsidiary companies.

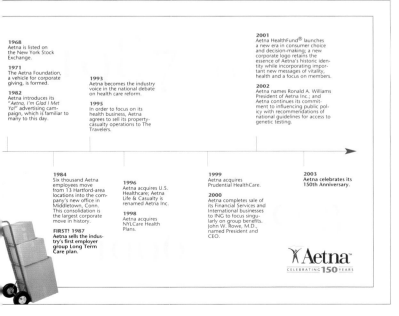

1968
Aetna is listed on the New York Stock Exchange.

1971
The Aetna Foundation, a vehicle for corporate giving, is formed.

1982
Aetna introduces its "Aetna, I'm Glad I Met Ya!" advertising campaign, which is familiar to many to this day.

1993
Aetna becomes the industry voice in the national debate on health care reform.

1995
In order to focus on its health business, Aetna agrees to sell its property-casualty operations to The Travelers.

2001
Aetna HealthFund® launches a new era in consumer choice and decision-making; a new corporate logo retains the essence of Aetna's historic identity while incorporating important new messages of vitality, health and a focus on members.

2002
Aetna names Ronald A. Williams President of Aetna Inc.; and Aetna continues its commitment to influencing public policy with recommendations of national guidelines for access to genetic testing.

1984
Six thousand Aetna employees move from 13 Hartford-area locations into the company's new office in Middletown, Conn. This consolidation is the largest corporate move in history.

FIRST! 1987
Aetna is the industry's first employer group Long Term Care plan.

1996
Aetna acquires U.S. Healthcare; Aetna Life & Casualty is renamed Aetna Inc.

1998
Aetna acquires NYLCare Health Plans.

1999
Aetna acquires Prudential HealthCare.

2000
Aetna completes sale of its Financial Services and International businesses to ING to focus singularly on group benefits. John W. Rowe, M.D., named President and CEO.

2003
Aetna celebrates its 150th Anniversary.

✕ Aetna™
CELEBRATING 150 YEARS

American Red Cross

Together, we can save a life

Sharon Burnett/American Red Cross

THE MARKET

Through a network of almost 1,000 local chapters in virtually every market, the American Red Cross links people with critical needs together with caring people who want to help. People committed to ensuring the safety of their families and their communities work through their local Red Cross to provide disaster relief; reliable information on preparing for and preventing emergencies; the latest training in first aid, CPR, and defibrillator use; classes in water safety and lifeguarding; meaningful volunteer opportunities, and more.

As the supplier of half of the nation's blood supply, the American Red Cross works with corporate and civic groups to sponsor local blood drives that offer people the opportunity to give the gift of life.

The American Red Cross actively seeks both local and national partnerships with corporations and other organizations to share in its mission of helping people prevent, prepare for, and respond to emergencies.

ACHIEVEMENTS

In 2002, in collaboration with millions of committed supporters, the American Red Cross met the urgent needs of the victims of almost 72,000 disasters, from hurricanes to house fires. Local chapters trained nearly 12 million people in lifesaving skills such as first aid, CPR, and water safety, making every community a safer place to live.

More than half a million families separated by military service received help from the Red Cross in exchanging vital information about family emergencies, and Red Cross workers deployed with U.S. service members to locations around the world. About 3,000 hospitals from coast to coast relied on the American Red Cross to supply them with blood and blood products.

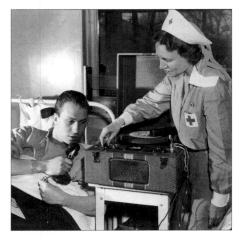

Beyond these well-recognized services, many local Red Cross chapters provide additional services geared specifically toward the needs of their own communities, such as transportation services for elderly or handicapped individuals and food programs.

The key to this high level of community service is the 1.2 million people who proudly call themselves American Red Cross volunteers and millions more who support the American Red Cross with their financial gifts and blood donations.

HISTORY

In 1862, Swiss businessman Henry Dunant wrote of witnessing 40,000 troops killed or wounded and left without help on a battlefield in Northern Italy. His conviction that he could provide lifesaving help by enlisting the aid of other concerned individuals ultimately led to the birth in 1863 of the International Committee of the Red Cross (ICRC) and, later, to the Geneva Conventions, a series of international treaties designed to protect victims of war and armed conflict. Dunant was a co-recipient of the first Nobel Peace Prize in 1901.

During the American Civil War, the visionary Clara Barton cared for the wounded on the battlefield. Later, while working in relief efforts for civilians during the Franco-Prussian War, she learned about the Red Cross movement. Upon her return to the United States, Barton received assurance that the U.S. government would sign the Geneva Conventions. She founded the American Red Cross on May 21, 1881.

Among Barton's unique contributions to the growing worldwide Red Cross Movement was mobilizing volunteers and donors to help disaster victims. In 1910, the Red Cross extended this powerful idea to address a rash of industrial accidents by instituting first-aid training; four years later, the soaring number of accidental drownings prompted introduction of programs in water safety and swimming.

During World War I, the Red Cross raised more than $400 million in supplies and donations to support its services. As the United States entered World War II, under the direction of Dr. Charles Drew, a pioneer in the development of plasma, the Red Cross laid the groundwork for its national blood program.

As new emergencies have arisen, the American Red Cross has developed programs to meet the critical needs of people confronting them. Over the years, the American Red Cross has worked in local communities across the country to combat emerging crises, from influenza epidemics to tuberculosis to HIV and AIDS. To the list of natural disasters to which the Red Cross responds have been added transportation accidents such as airline crashes, manmade disasters such as chemical spills, and catastrophic events such as the Oklahoma City bombing and the terrorist attacks of September 11, 2001.

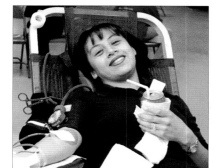

THE PRODUCT
The best-known product of the Red Cross is its disaster services. Red Cross disaster workers use donated resources to meet immediate disaster-caused needs, such as shelter, food, and health and mental health services. If needed, the Red Cross helps with such necessities as groceries, clothing, temporary housing, emergency home repairs, transportation, essential household items, medicines, and occupational tools. Disaster victims needing long-term recovery assistance can also turn to the Red Cross when all other resources — including insurance benefits, community and personal resources, and government assistance — have been exhausted. Assistance is based on verified disaster-caused needs.

Red Cross disaster workers feed disaster victims and emergency workers, handle inquiries from concerned family members outside the disaster area, and help those affected by disaster access other community resources. The Red Cross also provides blood and blood products to disaster victims as needed.

RECENT DEVELOPMENTS
The American Red Cross welcomed a new president and CEO in August 2002. Before coming to the Red Cross, Marsha Johnson Evans served for 29 years in the U.S. Navy, retiring as rear admiral, and went on to become executive director of the Girl Scouts USA.

Evans is working to create during these uncertain times a greater understanding of the vital role Red Cross chapters and Blood Services regions play in preparing local communities. Her priorities include initiatives to better inform donors about how their contributions are used, updating systems for response to major disasters, showcasing the contributions of Red Cross volunteers, and establishing partnerships with civic, business, and governmental organizations that share the Red Cross mission.

Under her leadership, the Red Cross is also working closely with governmental organizations and other blood banking groups to encourage blood donation and to continue to improve both the safety and availability of blood and blood products.

PROMOTION
With almost 1,000 local chapters, 36 Blood Services regions, stations at U.S. military bases around the world, and 1.2 million volunteers, the American Red Cross comprises an unparalleled grassroots network of caring individuals, poised to respond to emergencies at a moment's notice. Linked by their own internal Web site, local units and volunteers are able to keep constantly updated about emerging crises.

The American Red Cross's much-visited public Web site, *www.redcross.org*, is widely recognized as one of the best sources of safety and preparedness information on the Internet and was a pioneer in online fund raising. Visitors to the site can also receive information on disaster response in the United States and around the world and see who is working with the Red Cross to make their communities safer.

The Red Cross creates award-winning multimedia advertising campaigns to promote its brand to the public. Like many nonprofits, the Red Cross relies on public service advertising for most of its placements, but also works to obtain sponsored advertising. Further media exposure is gained through cooperation with media production companies, which know that a Red Cross poster or prop, or technical assistance, can effectively set the stage and add authenticity and credibility.

Over the years, celebrities from Shirley Temple to Jane Seymour have lent their names and images to American Red Cross efforts. The Red Cross recently formalized these arrangements by creating a Celebrity Cabinet made up of well-known personalities — from actors and musicians to sports stars and authors — who commit to giving time for one year to help the American Red Cross.

Always on the lookout for innovative ways to partner with groups that share its mission, the Red Cross pairs with others on an array of local and national initiatives. Many corporations find Red Cross support an effective way to demonstrate to customers, employees, and shareholders that they are committed to safety and compassion.

Target Corporation and Federal Express are among the founding members of the Annual Disaster Giving Program, in which companies make substantial leadership contributions to the Red Cross Disaster Relief Fund. This reserve fund gives the Red Cross the financial means to move people and equipment immediately to the sites of major disasters, without regard to eventual fund-raising potential.

Many retailers, including Lowe's Home Improvement Warehouse, 7-Eleven and Food Lion, invite their customers to donate to local chapters and to national disaster relief efforts when making a purchase. CoinStar has programmed its machines to accept contributions.

Other companies, such as AT&T Wireless, share their products and technical expertise with the Red Cross. Online companies including Yahoo!, eBay, and AOL have found innovative ways to work with the Red Cross to help people. The organization recently launched an affinity credit card with Capital One Services, Inc. and MasterCard International, Inc. The robust and innovative card program is designed to strengthen core support for local chapters while recruiting the next generation of Red Cross supporters.

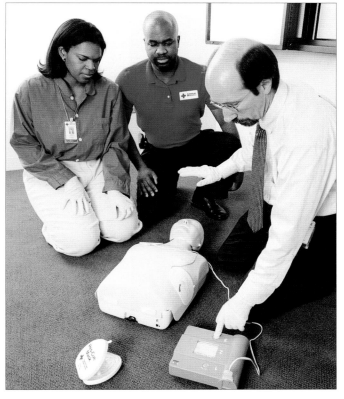

BRAND VALUES
The American Red Cross brand stresses people and partnership in providing lifesaving services in every community. The slogan, "Together, we can save a life," emphasizes the feeling of accomplishment and satisfaction individuals and organizations receive by joining in the Red Cross mission by volunteering their time, their financial support, and their blood.

THINGS YOU DIDN'T KNOW ABOUT THE AMERICAN RED CROSS

○ Ninety-two percent of the disasters to which the Red Cross responds are house and apartment fires.

○ Every Red Cross chapter is a locally supported institution with its own volunteer board of governors.

○ Only 5 percent of people who are eligible to give blood actually donate.

THE MARKET

No place is more important to people than their homes. As a result, the home products industry has always been competitive.

That's especially true today, as the number of new home construction and remodeling projects is growing. Every year, more than 1.5 million new homes are built in the United States and over 4 million remodeling projects include windows and doors.

In the window and door category, amid competition from national companies and small regional manufacturers, one brand has stood as the leader for 100 years. One brand is the most widely used and recognized. One brand is looked to more often to help create the places people call home. Andersen.

ACHIEVEMENTS

From the start, three underlying principles have motivated every Andersen innovation: To make homes more comfortable, beautiful, and able to withstand the test of time.

In 1905, when on-site window construction was the norm, company founder Hans Andersen invented the "two-bundle" method of making standardized window frames. Horizontal and vertical frame parts were bundled separately, yet they combined in multiple ways in only 10 minutes without cutting. As a result, builders could more efficiently create the windows people wanted and dealers could stock the parts at a lower cost.

By 1932, Andersen eliminated the need for on-site assembly altogether with the industry's first fully manufactured window unit, the Andersen® master casement.

Andersen has always believed that to be a source of comfort, a home should be worry proof and time proof. Andersen's 1966 invention of Perma-Shield® cladding all but guaranteed this result. Perma-Shield protects the exterior wood and virtually eliminates maintenance.

From the 1970s to the 1990s, Andersen continued to bring window performance to new levels. With advancements in energy-efficient design and Low-E glass technology, Andersen became the first national window manufacturer whose standard product

Can windows actually make coffee taste better?

A cup of espresso. An inspiring view. And Andersen® windows. For nearly 100 years, Andersen has been helping create stunning home settings. We craft beautiful windows and patio doors in virtually any style. They're built, backed and serviced like no other. What better way to make your home worryproof, timeproof. Call 1-800-426-4261, ref.®0000, or visit andersenwindows.com LONG LIVE THE HOME®

line met ENERGY STAR® Window criteria across the country.

The passion for innovation continues today, as evidenced by the invention of Fibrex™ material. A revolutionary composite made of reclaimed wood fiber and vinyl, Fibrex material exhibits some of the best thermal and low-maintenance qualities of both its source materials. As an extruded material, its custom applications are virtually limitless.

HISTORY

Danish immigrant Hans Andersen, along with his wife Sarah and their two sons, began the business as a lumberyard in 1903.

The Andersens positioned their original building along the St. Croix River in Hudson, Wisconsin. From this location, they could use the river to transport logs directly to the site. Andersen soon specialized in window frames, selling over 100,000 in 1909 alone. In 1913, Andersen moved across the river to Bayport, Minnesota, where its headquarters and main manufacturing facility are still located.

Today the parent company and its subsidiaries employ over 7,500 people with manufacturing facilities operating in Minnesota, Wisconsin, Iowa, Virginia, and Ontario.

THE PRODUCT

Andersen® products have come a long way since the two-bundle system of 1905. Yet the objective has remained steadfast: To create functional, timeless beauty that endures.

Andersen windows and doors are now available in virtually limitless shapes and sizes — all with low-maintenance exteriors and beautiful wood interiors that can be painted or stained to complement any décor.

A broad and ever-expanding product offering ensures that builders and homeowners have what they need for any project. Andersen® 400 Series products are a premium line with a full array of options and accessories. Andersen® 200 Series products offer the most popular sizes, styles, and options at a truly uncommon value.

More than products, however, have built the Andersen brand. Andersen has a fervent belief that customer service must work hand-in-hand with products. For this reason, Andersen backs their windows and patio doors with one of the industry's most comprehensive after-sales packages, including a 20-year limited warranty on the glass, 10-year limited warranty on non-glass parts, plus hundreds of trained service providers across the country.

One way to insulate.

The way to insulate with a view.

RECENT DEVELOPMENTS

The last five years have seen the company respond as never before to a rapidly changing marketplace. Andersen now offers an expanded portfolio that complements a more diverse range of building, remodeling, and replacement projects, and the brand now competes strongly where it has never competed before.

Recent additions to the Andersen family of companies include KML Windows, Inc., and EMCO Enterprises, Inc. With KML by Andersen™ architectural window and door products, the company now caters to more tastes and styles with custom products not readily available from most

manufacturers. EMCO, a leading manufacturer of all-season doors, fits with the Andersen tradition of product performance and gives the company more ways to offer solutions throughout the home.

As important as home is to Andersen, so, too, is community. For nearly a century, Andersen Corporation has been committed to giving back to the communities in which Andersen employees live and work. This dedication results in company support of a wide variety of community-based charitable organizations, and is demonstrated through significant product donations and employee volunteer efforts aiding Habitat for Humanity.

As a leading manufacturer, Andersen understands its unique responsibility to monitor and adjust its environmental impact. Therefore, the concept of sustaining, preserving, and protecting natural resources forms one of the cornerstones of the company's mission. The Environmental Protection Agency recognizes Andersen as a charter member of the National Environmental Performance Track for its commitment to sound environmental management, public outreach, and community involvement.

PROMOTION

Throughout the years, Andersen has built its promotional strategies around the changing role of the home, the company's heritage, and the emotional appeal of its products.

In the 1930s and 1940s, the home was understood to be an investment in the American Dream. Andersen urged consumers to add value to their investments with the proclamation that "Only the Rich Can Afford Poor Windows.®"

The 1950s saw homeowners become more brand conscious. Andersen responded by asking people to look for builders who choose Andersen products, as an indication of the quality the builder would put into the rest of the home.

Enter the 1960s, the era of remodeling, and Andersen Perma-Shield® windows. As people replaced old windows, what could be more valuable or timely than windows and patio doors that required little or no maintenance?

By the 1970s, with the emergence of the first real energy crisis, homeowners became energy conscious. Families battled for control of thermostats. With the message, "The Beautiful Way to Save Fuel,®" Andersen emphasized that the home can be both beautiful and energy efficient.

In the 1980s, television advertising was the king of marketing mediums. At this time Andersen became the first window company to advertise on television, with the theme, "Come Home to Quality, Come Home to Andersen."

By the 1990s, as Baby Boomers showed signs of burnout from the stress of the workplace, they looked to their homes as an escape. By inviting people to "Come Experience Andersen Light," Andersen was able to leverage the idea of home as an appealing cocoon.

Today, Andersen knows that people are looking at their homes in new ways. No longer are homes the passive, safe havens they were in the 1990s.

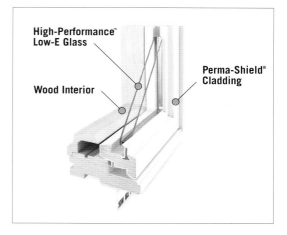

High-Performance™ Low-E Glass

Wood Interior

Perma-Shield® Cladding

They are now a place where people proactively blend style with technology and self-expression. Andersen's current communications capture this new point of view with "Long Live the Home.™"

BRAND VALUES

For 100 years, Andersen has embodied the very spirit of home and the belief that home is more than a physical place.

This belief has helped create the longevity of the Andersen brand, because love of and pride in the home ring true across all generations. While times may change and values may shift, one thing has endured throughout time: Home is the center of life.

THINGS YOU DIDN'T KNOW ABOUT ANDERSEN

○ During World War II, Andersen contributed to the war effort by reducing the use of scarce metals by 97 percent and by manufacturing nearly 5 million ammunition boxes.

○ Builders choose Andersen windows in the homes they build for themselves three times more than any other brand. Remodelers choose Andersen windows and patio doors for their projects nearly two-to-one over the closest competitor.

○ Andersen introduced the first wood gliding patio door in 1964 and is the largest manufacturer of patio doors today.

○ In 1914, Andersen Corporation created one of the very first employee profit-sharing programs. This vision continues today in a progressive attitude of sharing the rewards of success with employees, as demonstrated through substantial employee ownership of the company.

○ Andersen has been on the leading edge of mass production and customization technologies since it first began mass production in 1904 — a full nine years before Henry Ford put the automobile on an assembly line.

THE MARKET

From the corners of the 50 states to around the world, consumers are organizing, printing, archiving, gluing, communicating, identifying, marking, presenting, meeting, mailing, writing, personalizing, promoting, and designing with Avery® products. Whether it's an office worker mailing packages with shipping labels, a mother printing her daughter's soccer game photos on digital photo paper, or a college student highlighting notes with a highlighter, Avery brand products provide what you need for all of these functions.

Avery Dennison Worldwide Office Products — the company that markets products under the well-known Avery brand name — is the world's leading manufacturer of self-adhesive labels for laser and ink-jet printers, labeling software, binders, sheet protectors, index and tab dividers, and other office-, home-, and school-related supplies. Avery brand products are a common part of life for consumers.

ACHIEVEMENTS

As a result of the rapid growth of personal computing, PC software, and desktop printing technology, Avery Dennison has become a global office products leader in today's automated offices, homes, and schools. The company's philosophy is to provide high-quality, innovative products that make it easy for consumers to

achieve impressive results with their projects. That's what the company's slogan — "Great Results Begin with Avery" — is all about.

HISTORY

Avery Dennison Office Products — recognized worldwide for innovation and technological advancement — is part of the larger Avery Dennison Corporation, which was founded and built upon a single, revolutionary concept: the self-adhesive label.

Avery Dennison was founded in 1935 by R. Stanton Avery, who not only invented the world's first self-adhesive label, but pioneered an industry. In fact, the growth and development of the self-adhesive industry would set the stage for the introduction of Avery brand office products and the growth of a dynamic, global, office products business.

Until the late 1960s, Avery Dennison distinguished itself primarily as an industrial self-adhesive business. But as the pressure-sensitive industry grew and spread, the company began to concentrate on specific markets, segmenting different lines of business into specialized categories, such as office products.

In 1968, in partnership with Xerox Corporation, Avery Dennison developed the Xerox-brand copier

label, the first "office automation label." Two years later, Avery Dennison entered the office products industry, introducing its own line of copier labels and quickly becoming the market leader in the field.

By the early 1980s, personal computers were replacing typewriters in the office, and Avery Dennison began manufacturing and marketing a broad line of office products for use with personal computers and desktop printers, beginning with labels for dot-matrix printers. As personal printing technology began to evolve rapidly, so did Avery Dennison's innovation in providing more and more products and solutions for personal printing. With the advent of laser printing technology, Avery Dennison developed and launched the first desktop laser printer labels, and Avery Laser Printer labels quickly became the market leader. Avery Dennison teamed up with Microsoft® to put templates in Microsoft software — to make it easy for consumers to design and print their own labels and other printable supplies. The company eventually developed relationships with many of the leading software manufacturers, such as Microsoft, Corel, Borland, and Lotus. During the 1990s, easy-to-use templates for Avery brand products began to be featured in leading word processing, spreadsheet, and database software.

Avery Dennison also forged relationships with leading printer manufacturers, such as Hewlett-Packard and Canon. The company established a Printer Lab to test all its printable supplies with a wide range of desktop printers. Avery Dennison also conducted joint marketing promotions with its printer manufacturer partners.

Meanwhile, Avery Dennison moved forward to meet the needs of PC users by developing its own software. The company entered the software business in 1988 with Avery® LabelPro™, providing PC users with the ability to easily design and print Avery labels and other products. The program was developed for all operating platforms: DOS, Macintosh, and eventually Microsoft® Windows.

In 2000, the company launched Avery Print from the Web, a free application that enabled consumers with access to the Internet the ability to format and print Avery products directly from the Web with no special software needed.

In addition to Avery brand office products, Avery Dennison develops, manufactures, and markets a wide range of products for consumer and

industrial markets, including Fasson-brand self-adhesive materials, automated retail tag and labeling systems, peel-and-stick postage stamps, reflective highway safety products, and specialty tapes and chemicals. In 2001, Avery Dennison's sales were $3.8 billion. The corporation employs more than 17,300 men and women in more than 200 manufacturing facilities and sales offices in 39 countries around the world.

Avery Dennison ranked 430 on the Fortune 500 list of largest U.S. industrial and service companies in the year 2000.

THE PRODUCT

Avery Dennison manufactures and markets more than 6,000 Avery brand products. There's hardly an application in the office that isn't made a little easier or a little better thanks to an Avery brand product. From mailing labels to markers and from CD labeling products to sheet protectors, Avery Dennison offers a broad array of products for the office.

The name "Avery" is practically synonymous with the word "self-adhesive label." Avery brand labels are so well-known by consumers that some of them know Avery labels by their product numbers, such as 5160™. The company is the world's leading manufacturer of self-adhesive labels and provides a wide array of labeling solutions for consumers in the area of mailing and shipping, organization and filing, electronic media, and identification. From promotional labels in neon colors to return address labels in metallic foil, Avery Dennison provides consumers with a multitude of choices for almost every occasion.

Avery Dennison takes great pride in the quality of its products. All of its products come with a product guarantee and provide consumers with a number of unique, patented innovations and solutions. For instance, Avery Dennison has introduced mailing labels that are guaranteed not to jam laser printers. The company has also developed highlighters that are guaranteed not to smear.

RECENT DEVELOPMENTS

Avery Dennison continues to be the leader and innovator in the office products industry. Some recent examples:
- The blank CD media market is experiencing explosive growth as consumers turn to CDs for everything from personalized music CDs to digital photo albums to data storage. Avery Dennison is the leading provider of CD labeling and application products, which make it easy for consumers to customize and organize their CDs.
- Digital cameras will soon overtake analog cameras as the most popular camera in families' homes. However, despite their popularity, consumers are frustrated by a "chain of pain" that makes it difficult to edit and print their own digital photos. To help solve the problem, Avery Dennison has teamed together with Microsoft, and the companies are co-marketing new Avery Digital Photo Paper with Microsoft photo editing software in every package. The Avery paper features a patented technology to make photos "snap out" easily with no perforations for a sharp, professional look.
- Avery Dennison is taking this same "quick and clean" technology to the office with its line of

Clean Edge Business Cards. Now anyone can easily customize and print his or her own professional-looking, smooth-edge business card that snap out of the sheet with no perforations. With Avery Clean Edge Business Cards, printing your own cards is easier than going to a professional printer, but your results will still look professional.
- Sometimes even small innovations make a big difference. Avery Dennison is a leader and innovator in the divider category. As anyone who has burned the midnight oil before a big

Great results begin with Avery!™

presentation knows, putting together multiple sets of presentations can be time-consuming. Thanks to Avery Index Maker® Dividers with "Easy Apply" labels, labels for all sections of a set of dividers can be applied one at a time, saving a lot of time and hassle.

PROMOTION

Avery products can be purchased from office superstores, office products dealer catalogs and Web sites, mass merchandisers, wholesalers, computer retailers, warehouse clubs, electronics retailers, mail order services, and drug and grocery stores.

Avery Dennison works with several leading software manufacturers to ensure that Avery templates are available in most popular software titles. For instance, more than 450 templates for Avery products (more than any other brand) appear in the latest version of the number-one word processing software program, Microsoft® Word.

Avery Dennison also offers consumers its own software, Avery® DesignPro™, making it easy for them to do everything from format a project to merge a mailing list. The software is sold in Avery

Dennison's traditional sales channels, and limited versions are available for free on the company's Web site, *www.avery.com.* The Web site also offers another free service, Avery® Print from the Web, which allows consumers to print directly from the Web without the need for special software.

Keeping the consumer "top of mind" is an important component of the company's business strategy, and Avery Dennison maintains a toll-free customer service line to respond to consumer questions about its products.

BRAND VALUES

Avery Dennison makes achieving great results with office, home, and school projects easy by providing a broad range of products and the tools to do the job. From easy and free downloadable templates from the Web to software, Avery Dennison provides tools that make it simple for consumers to format and print their projects.

Office professionals the world over know the Avery brand. For them, the brand represents a "trusted friend" who works hard for them and helps them portray a professional image. The rapid pace of technological change affects everybody. Avery Dennison is helping consumers harness the power of that change by making technology easier to use and helping them be more productive and empowered.

THINGS YOU DIDN'T KNOW ABOUT AVERY DENNISON

○ Company founder Stan Avery invented the self-adhesive label in 1935.

○ More than 400 easy-to-format Avery product templates appear in Microsoft® Word and hundreds of other popular software titles.

○ *Avery.com* features free downloads of software, clip art, templates, and product information about thousands of Avery products.

AVIS ®

THE MARKET

With almost $20 billion in revenues and a fleet of nearly two million vehicles, the auto rental market is a significant player in the business of getting Americans where they need to go. Car rental activity is also integrally tied to a variety of key segments of the U.S. economy, including business and leisure travel in general, the airline industry specifically, auto insurance, and vehicle manufacturing and resales. Given its link to airline travel, much of rental car demand is driven by business travel.

In this hotly competitive market, Avis is both a pioneer and a leading player. Because of its historic strength in providing premium personalized customer service, the company has long been a leader in the demanding commercial segment, deriving about 65 percent of its revenue from these business travelers. Avis Rent A Car System, Inc. and its subsidiaries operate the world's second-largest general-use car rental business, providing business and leisure customers with vehicles from more than 1,700 locations in the United States, Canada, Australia, and New Zealand, and in the Latin American/Caribbean region.

With over 19,000 employees, Avis is recognized as the industry leader in applying new technologies and is one of the world's top brands for customer loyalty. The company is a wholly owned subsidiary of Cendant Corporation and has marketing agreements with Avis Europe Plc that further extend the Avis brand through 3,050 Avis locations in Europe, the Middle East, and Africa. Cendant is primarily a provider of travel and residential real estate services, serving businesses and consumers in more than 100 countries.

ACHIEVEMENTS

A force in the industry for nearly 60 years, Avis revolutionized the automobile rental industry in 1972 with the introduction of Wizard®, the first real-time information management and reservation system. Today, Wizard technology is in place in over 50 countries and still remains the backbone of Avis' highly sophisticated rental operations. Numerous innovations, including the now-ubiquitous "Roving Rapid Return," followed over the ensuing years. More recently, Avis in 1996

became one of the first car rental companies to launch a Web site, *avis.com*.

Four years later, Avis InterActive hit the market in an important step that again defined the company's leadership in the commercial travel segment. Avis InterActive became the car rental industry's first Internet-based reporting system for corporate accounts.

But Avis is recognized for much more than just its technological innovation. In the last few years alone, Avis has garnered many accolades for its relationships with employees, customers, and the communities in which it operates.

For example, in the area of customer loyalty and satisfaction, out of 158 companies surveyed, Avis ranked as the number-one brand in the 2001 and 2002 Brand Keys® Customer Loyalty survey.

Additionally, in 2001, Avis tied for the #1 Car Rental Company for Customer Satisfaction Among Business Travelers, according to J.D. Power and Associates (2001).

Over the years, Avis has also won a number of awards for its employee and supplier relations.

- In 2001, Avis was named one of 11 "exemplary companies for workers over 50" by AARP.
- The Women's Business Enterprise National Council cited Avis as "One of America's Elite Eight Corporations for Women's Business Enterprises" in 2002 and 2003.

- *Fortune* magazine listed Avis as the "Most Admired Company" in the Automotive Retailing/Services Category (February 2001).
- In May 2001, *Asian Enterprise* magazine rated Avis one of the nation's top-10 companies for Asian Americans.

One of the core values Avis strives to embrace is diversity of ideas, cultures, ethnicities, and backgrounds for both employees and customers alike. In that spirit, The Foundation for Ethnic Understanding awarded Cendant its 2002 Corporate Diversity Award in recognition of Avis' work promoting understanding among different racial and ethnic groups.

HISTORY

Soon after returning home from service in World War II, Warren Avis opened the first Avis office in 1946 at Willow Run Airport in Detroit, Michigan. At that time, his fleet included only three cars, but Avis became the first-ever car rental company to operate out of an airport. Today travelers take for granted the quick walk or shuttle ride from the plane to the rental car, but until Avis no such service existed.

By 1953, Avis was the second-largest car rental company in the United States and had already expanded overseas, opening franchised operations in Mexico, Canada, and Europe. In 1963, the timeless "We Try Harder" campaign was launched and quickly set the company on a decades-long streak of profitability.

Following numerous technology innovations in the 1970s, Avis entered worldwide advertising and

marketing agreements with General Motors in 1979 and since then has featured GM cars in its worldwide fleet.

Popularity and business success do not necessarily equate to stability. In the first 41 years of its history, Avis was bought and sold many times over. The change in ownership slowed for a time when in 1987 the Avis Employee Stock Ownership Plan (ESOP) purchased the company for $750 million — making it one of the largest employee-owned companies in the United States.

On the technological front, the seeds of Avis' current ownership were also sown in 1996. In that year, HFS Incorporated, the world's largest franchiser of hotels and residential real estate brokerage offices (which later became Cendant), purchased Avis from the ESOP. In the next year, HFS took Avis public. Five years later in 2001, Cendant purchased all of the outstanding shares of Avis Group Holdings that it did not already own — a transaction valued at $937 million. Avis headquarters moved in that year from its 35-year home in Garden City, New York, to its current home with other Cendant companies in Parsippany, New Jersey.

THE PRODUCT

The Avis fleet averages over 200,000 vehicles and features a wide variety of GM and other fine vehicles with the most desired features for comfort and safety. Available vehicles include:

- Compact cars like the Pontiac Sunfire or Chevrolet Cavalier
- Intermediate cars like the Oldsmobile Alero
- Full-size cars like the two-door Chevrolet Monte Carlo or the four-door Buick Century
- Premium cars like the Buick LeSabre, often equipped with the OnStar system
- Luxury cars like the prestigious Cadillac Sedan de Ville
- Mini-vans and Sport utility vehicles like the Chevy Blazer

Many Avis vehicles come equipped with GM's "On Star" navigation and emergency response system as well as XM Satellite Radio. Other high-tech products, like dashboard GPS navigational systems and automated check-in systems, are regularly being tested and introduced.

To deliver on its promise of providing a stress-free rental experience, Avis offers its customers complimentary membership into its Preferred Service and Preferred Select programs. Once enrolled, members can bypass the counter by going

directly to their car where their rental documents await them.

RECENT DEVELOPMENTS

In November 2001, building on its Avis Cares® focus on safety, Avis became the first and only car rental company to adopt the LATCH system, the new federal standard for child-safety-seat installation. The company featured LATCH, as well as its new Avis Cares Package, in its 2002 advertising campaign, becoming the first company in any industry to feature a child passenger safety device in a television ad.

The company has also in recent years taken steps to expand well beyond its traditional business travel focus. From its comprehensive partnership with AARP, to an aggressive push in the off-airport market that includes an exclusive partnership with Sears, Avis has quickly become a leader in nearly all segments in which it operates.

Even on the partnership front, the company's approach embodies the "We Try Harder" spirit. Two examples: Avis is now the exclusive car rental partner of the Upromise college savings network, helping to make college more affordable for families. Avis also began an in-depth relationship with the Make-A-Wish Foundation in 2002. Through its "Trying Harder To Drive Wishes" program, Avis provides hundreds of thousands of dollars in free and discounted rentals to help bring joy and hope to seriously ill children.

the benefits of trying harder

Child Safety and LATCH

PROMOTION

In 1963, Avis was struggling with a 10 percent market share, compared to Hertz' 75 percent. The new management of the company launched a groundbreaking advertising campaign that proved crucial in turning its fortunes around. The slogan — "We're only Number Two. We try harder." — emphasized a commitment to customer service that to this day remains at the core of the brand and the company's entire philosophy.

The tagline was the brainchild of William Bernbach of the Doyle Dane Bernbach advertising agency. *Advertising Age* has called it one of history's 100 greatest advertising mottoes. Avis continues, as it has for the past 40 years, to use the motto as the centerpiece of its advertising.

In 1989, Avis launched the Avis Cares program, a driver safety and preparation program designed to ensure that Avis customers have a safe and stress-free trip to their destination.

Components of the Avis Cares Program include a local travel safety tip sheet, child safety and booster seats, Route Navigator® directions and other local maps, a six-day local weather forecast, and wireless phones. In 2002, Avis introduced new pocket-sized "Quick City Guides" to great restaurants, tourist attractions, and business services covering 25 cities.

Aside from attention to customer service and the quality GM product, Avis keeps its brand in the public eye through its commitment to both corporate and employee involvement in civic and charitable activities. As an international corporation — and as a local business in the communities where it operates — Avis strives to be a role model and business leader. In addition to its partnership with the Make-A-Wish Foundation, Avis supports groups like the Achilles Track Club, the Special Olympics, the NAACP, MADD, and Prevent Blindness America.

BRAND VALUES

Simply stated, Avis is in business to ensure a stress-free rental experience by providing safe, dependable vehicles and special services designed to win customer loyalty. The company's stated

values are Integrity, Quality, Value, Community Responsibility, Teamwork, and Respect for the Individual. It's been said that "We Try Harder" is synonymous with the Avis brand, and the motto certainly summarizes Avis' focus on premium service. With high-touch service personalized to each customer. The company relies on the "Avis Experience" to constantly reinforcing its position as the premium car rental brand.

THINGS YOU DIDN'T KNOW ABOUT AVIS

○ Cell phones, wallets, and eyeglasses are the three items most commonly left behind in Avis cars.

○ Avis reservation centers handled 22 million calls in 2002, and the company processes 17.1 million transactions annually.

○ Avis supplies roughly 50,000 child safety seats to customers each year.

○ Avis has 350,000 customers enrolled in its Preferred Select program because they rent from Avis at least 15 times per year.

○ More than 300,000 users are registered through *avis.com*, a site that averages 1.5 million unique users monthly.

Bank of America

THE MARKET

On any given day, approximately $38 trillion flows through the U.S. financial services industry.

This industry includes consumer, small business, middle-market, and corporate banking markets, as well as insurance, asset management, and investment banking. With more than $600 billion in assets, Bank of America operates in all of these specialized markets, providing service to customers and clients not only in the United States, but also in 150 countries around the world.

ACHIEVEMENTS

Bank of America is quickly becoming one of the world's most admired companies by fulfilling its brand promise: *to be the people who make banking work for customers and clients in ways it never has before.*

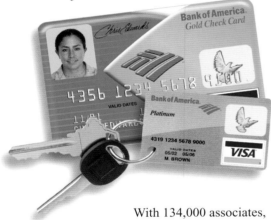

With 134,000 associates, offices in 30 countries, approximately 13,000 ATMs nationwide, more than 4,200 banking centers, and innovative telephone banking and online channels, Bank of America serves:
- 28 million consumer customers
- 2 million small-business clients
- More than 30 percent of all mid-sized companies within its franchise footprint
- Seventy-six percent of the Global Fortune 500
- Ninety-four percent of the U.S. Fortune 500
- More than 4 million active subscribers to Online Banking
- Clients in 150 countries

The company works to attract, retain, and deepen these relationships, improve processes, and drive internal growth.

Bank of America has helped shape the U.S. banking industry by:
- Installing the first nationwide ATM network, with approximately 13,000 ATMs, by far the largest proprietary network in the nation.

- Becoming the first major bank online and having currently the largest active online banking customer base in the world.
- Having the world's best consumer Internet bank site, according to a 2002 ranking from *Global Finance* magazine.
- Being a leading provider of comprehensive capital raising, advisory and working capital solutions, through its Global Corporate and Investment Banking (GCIB) group. (For example, in 2001, GCIB raised over $1.5 trillion in equity and debt capital for clients.)
- Being named the top lender in the country by the Small Business Administration.

Bank of America also leads the field as an employer-of-choice by:
- Being named one of the top companies for working mothers for over 12 consecutive years by *Working Mother* magazine.
- Being ranked as one of *Fortune* magazine's top 50 companies for minorities.

HISTORY

Throughout its 200-year history of predecessor organizations, Bank of America has been a community bank — originally established for immigrants and consumers from diverse cultural and economic backgrounds.

In 1805, a small group of farmers founded the Eastern Shore branch of the Farmer's Bank of Maryland, which later became Easton National Bank, the first bank in the country to pay interest on deposits.

In 1847, a businessman named George Knight Budd founded a bank for underserved riverboat workers in St. Louis called Boatmen's Bank, a place where "the average person can safely deposit a few dollars to earn interest."

In 1904, A. P. Giannini founded the Bank of Italy in San Francisco "to bring banking to the little fellow," Italian workers and shop owners whom other banks wouldn't serve. When the

Total Security Protection makes our cards safer.

earthquake and fire of 1906 destroyed much of San Francisco, Giannini set up a desk made of two barrels and a plank on the San Francisco waterfront and began making loans based only on a handshake.

This legacy of predecessor banks culminated in the 1998 merger of NationsBank in the east with BankAmerica in the west, creating Bank of America, the nation's first coast-to-coast bank.

THE PRODUCT

Bank of America delivers a comprehensive range of financial products and services.

For *consumers*, Bank of America offers core banking services such as checking and savings products, credit cards, Online Banking with Bill Pay, insurance, investments, loans, mortgages, home equity products, and other real estate services.

For *small businesses*, the company offers core banking services plus merchant card, treasury management, insurance, Online Banking, and value packages, to name a few.

For *commercial clients*, Bank of America offers creative solutions through its Commercial Banking, Real Estate Banking, and Business Credit groups — with services such as treasury management, investment banking, trade, credit and leasing, capital markets, and more.

For *clients of all types*, the Bank of America Asset Management Group serves as a trusted wealth advisor offering investment, securities, and financial planning services.

For *large corporations* and *institutional clients*, Banc of America Securities provides capital-raising solutions, advisory services, derivatives capabilities, equity and debt sales and trading, as well as traditional bank deposit and loan products, cash management, and payments services.

For *communities*, Bank of America Community Development Bank committed an unprecedented $350 billion — approximately $96 million a day and more than any other American company — to development efforts over 10 years (starting in 1998). By 2001, the company had created a total of 100,000 affordable housing units nationwide.

RECENT DEVELOPMENTS

Bank of America maintains an ongoing research and development project known as the Innovation and Development Market in Atlanta, a live testing environment of 31 banking and financial centers. Recent developments include:
• Digital check imaging that allows associates and customers to view digital images of checks and deposit slips online at *bankofamerica.com* or in banking centers, typically within a few seconds versus the old standard of at least three business days.

• Mobile Teller, a mobile computer device that allows banking center associates to move freely and quickly process deposits on-the-spot for customers who may be waiting in teller lines.
• The world's first Visa mini credit card — half the size of a regular credit card and attachable to a key chain.

Other company-wide developments include launching a Six Sigma quality and productivity program to improve processes, reduce error rates, increase efficiencies, and create a consistently outstanding customer experience.

PROMOTION

Bank of America invests in advertising programs and sponsorships that build brand awareness and consideration at a national level.

In 2002, to drive deposit growth and deepen customer relationships, Bank of America launched its largest ever general-market advertising campaign for its consumer products and delivery channels. One of the most successful ads in the series, titled "Love Letter," was nominated for a Grand Prix award at the Cannes Lion advertising competition.

Bank of America also launched its largest ever multicultural advertising campaign with television ads tailored to Asian-American, Hispanic, and African-American consumers.

Sponsorship marketing activities include a 2002 Olympic brand campaign with humorous ads to support the company's Olympic sponsorship. Most recently, Bank of America entered a four-year title sponsorship agreement with the PGA to host the Bank of America Colonial golf tournament in Fort Worth, Texas.

BRAND VALUES

Banks have not traditionally been perceived as having strong brands, but Bank of America is changing this perception. With a brand already valued at $21 billion, the company was ranked No. 55 in *BrandWeek*'s list of America's Top Brands for 2001, showing a strong upward trend from previous years' rankings of 123 and 427.

Within the highly competitive financial services market, the company is continually working to differentiate itself by bringing to life its brand promise: *to be the people who make banking work for customers and clients in ways it never has before*.

To further drive positive brand behavior, associates are rewarded for consistently demonstrating the company's five core values: trusting and teamwork, leadership, inclusive meritocracy, winning, and doing the right thing.

THINGS YOU DIDN'T KNOW ABOUT BANK OF AMERICA

❍ The Bank of America Foundation is one of the top five charitable givers in the country.

❍ Bank of America financed hundreds of popular movies, such as *Gone with the Wind, The Ten Commandments, Lawrence of Arabia, It's a Wonderful Life* and the world's first feature-length animated film, Walt Disney's *Snow White and the Seven Dwarfs*.

❍ Customers interact with Bank of America more than 3 billion times a year — or 116 times per second.

❍ During the Great Depression, when no other bank would put up the funds, Bank of America (as Bank of Italy) bought the $35 million in bonds that financed construction of San Francisco's Golden Gate Bridge.

❍ In the 1950s, Bank of America became the first bank to use computers by creating the Electronic Recording Method of Accounting, which automated the sorting of checks, debits, and withdrawal of funds. ERMA is now housed at the Smithsonian Institution.

BUICK

THE SPIRIT OF AMERICAN STYLE™

THE MARKET

Is any other product or industry as associated with the United States as the automobile? Whether studying emotional appeal or economic impact, to learn about cars is to learn about America, and vice versa. Americans love their cars, and a consumer's self-image is often reflected in the car he or she drives. And not only do Americans drive cars, but cars drive America. Industries whose fortunes are tied directly to a healthy automotive sector include textiles, metals, advertising, and professional sports.

The auto industry will likely sell in excess of 16.5 million vehicles this year, and to state that the U.S. auto industry is a trillion-dollar-a-year business may even underestimate the importance of the automotive market to the health of the American economy and psyche. The market features numerous new model introductions every year, and it has become driven by technology, innovation, and an eye to the future.

ACHIEVEMENTS

In this industry that holds so much importance for America, Buick is a standout brand and product. May 19, 2003, marks Buick's 100th anniversary, and a review of its first hundred years testifies to the influence of one of America's greatest brands. In the history of Buick's first 100 years, various names rise to the fore; however, none is greater than Harley Earl.

Harley Earl first brought the idea of the concept car to Buick in the late 1930s, forever changing the way automobiles would be designed and made. In Earl's thinking, the cars of the future could be built right then, and thus began the forward thinking for

which Buick is known, building on Earl's belief that innovation is an indelible part of the spirit of American style.

But even before Earl's influence on the brand, other people brought innovations to Buick that affected generations of Americans in myriad ways. In 1914, automotive pioneer Alanson P.

Brush — considered by some as the outstanding U.S. automotive engine expert of his era — moved the Buick driver's seat from the right- to the left-hand side, a change that originally brought protests from consumers. Buick President Ed Strong decided that the new 1928 Buicks would feature the latest electronics marvel: radio. Buick can also boast of many engineering and technological advances and innovations over its first 100 years. Brush's and Strong's contributions should resonate with any American who ever sat behind the wheel of a car.

HISTORY

Buick entered U.S. automotive history in a quiet fashion. On May 21, 1903, under the modest title of "Recent Incorporations" in *Motor World*, came the announcement: "Buick Motor Company, under Michigan laws, to manufacture automobiles, automobile equipment, power machinery, etc., capital $100,000. Incorporators: David Dunbar Buick, Thomas D. Buick and Emil D. Moessner." Four months later, the

publication announced that Buick was moving to a 200 by 65 feet brick building in Flint, Michigan. September 1903 also saw the first Buick advertisement. Needless to say, a lot has happened since then.

David Dunbar Buick was born in Scotland in 1854, and his family came to America two years later. In his adolescence and young adulthood, David Buick delivered papers, worked on a farm, and was a foreman at a company that made plumbing fixtures. He is credited with thirteen inventions in the 1880s, for items such as a lawn sprinkler, bathtubs, and a flushing device. Eventually, his interests turned toward the possibilities of the gasoline engine, and he organized a firm called the Buick Auto-Vim and Power Company. With the significant influence of his mechanical genius partner, Walter Lorenzo Marr — who perfected a four-cylinder gasoline motor wagon and developed a spark advance device — the first Buick was built around the turn of the century at Buick's shop in a barn behind his house.

Although originally scoffing at the invention of the automobile, William Durant was essentially responsible for the elevation of Buick from a local Flint manufacturer to worldwide icon. Durant had taken an interest in Buick in 1904–05, and in 1908 he created General Motors, quickly placing Buick under the GM umbrella. By 1908, Buick claimed U.S. car leadership with production of 8,820 vehicles. A scant fifteen years later, the company would build the one millionth Buick. Buick's commitment to innovation and forward thinking was evident early, with its 1911 advertising slogan, "When Better Automobiles Are Built, Buick Will Build Them."

During World War I, Buick built Liberty aircraft engines, mortar shells, ambulances, and experimental tanks to support the war effort. For World War II, Buick converted all of its Flint factories exclusively for war work. Sixty-five percent of

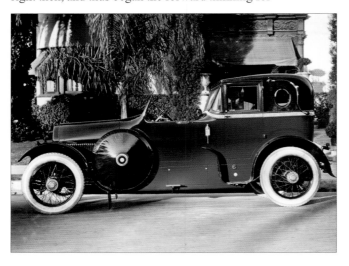

26

their automobile machine tools would be reworked or redesigned. Production lines were ripped out, and inspection stations and testing room equipment were all removed to storage. Aircraft engine parts, tanks, aircraft-gun mounts, and artillery shells took the place of automobile production.

The postwar years spawned a classic era of Buick styling and technical innovation. Throughout the mid-1950s, Buick's popularity soared with the development of features such as hard-top convertible styling, the Dynaflow automatic transmission, and the vertical bar-grille.

For 1962, the Buick Special was introduced, featuring the first U.S. mass-produced V6 engine. During the 1974–75 model year, Buick reintroduced the fuel-efficient V6. The 3.8-liter "3800" V6 would eventually become the premier engine in Buick's naturally aspirated, turbocharged, and supercharged versions.

In 1999, an era came to an end when the last of nearly 16 million Buicks were built in Flint, Michigan. The company has shifted manufacturing to various facilities located throughout North America. With nearly 37 million Buicks produced in its 100-year history, Buick looks toward the future now with its five established and distinct models and the 2004 model year introduction of the Rainier™, Buick's first full-frame SUV.

THE PRODUCT

Whether attracted to the style and elegance of Park Avenue®, the best-selling confidence and security of LeSabre®, the supercharged power of Regal®, the industry-leading quality of Century®, or the ingenious capability and functionality of Rendezvous®, Buick offers a car with a style that's right for just about every consumer.

Harley Earl was here.

For GM design guru Harley Earl, giving an automobile a feminine touch went way beyond the hood ornament. In 1943, he hired the industry's first female designers. These "Damsels of Design" soon brought a new sense of style to the American automobile.

BUICK
THE SPIRIT OF AMERICAN STYLE™

buick.com

RECENT DEVELOPMENTS

Buick has won many industry awards. Most recently, Century and LeSabre took the 2002 J.D. Power and Associates* highest ranking for initial quality, and *Kiplinger's*** magazine voted Park Avenue and LeSabre "First for Safety." In addition, *The Detroit News* recognized the 2002 Buick Rendezvous as its Truck of the Year, and *Autoweek* pegged Buick Bengal® as Best Concept Car for 2001.

PROMOTION

When Americans think of professional golf sponsorship, Buick is a top-of-mind company. Buick has been bringing PGA TOUR tournaments to the attention of the American public for over forty years.

Since its title sponsorship of the first Buick Open back in 1958, Buick's commitment to golf has been an integral part of the company's focus. Buick has raised more than $23 million for local charities through its multiple PGA TOUR events.

Over the decades, Buick's commitment to the sport has deepened and grown. The company now proudly claims title sponsorship of three major PGA TOUR events and the largest amateur golf event in the United States:
• The Buick Invitational, at Torrey Pines Golf Course in LaJolla, California
• The Buick Classic, at Westchester Country Club in Harrison, New York
• The Buick Open, at Warwick Hills Golf & Country Club in Grand Blanc, Michigan
• The Buick Scramble, with tournament finals in Orlando, Florida

Buick also has a sponsorship arrangement with numerous PGA TOUR professionals and coaches, including David Berganio Jr., Matt Gogel, Butch Harmon, and the world's number one–ranked player, Tiger Woods. Woods has been a member of the Buick team since 2000.

Aside from its involvement in the world of professional golf, Buick is a proud sponsor of the Primetime Emmy Awards. The auto manufacturer also utilizes state-of-the-art exhibit trailers that travel the country to provide potential Buick customers with the experience of Buick products in a fun, interactive environment.

BRAND VALUES

The Buick Motor Division is dedicated to manufacturing products that are gracefully styled, powerful, and effortlessly functional. These high-quality vehicles are built to give both drivers and passengers a feeling of confidence, pleasure, and well-being. Reflected in the spirit of the charismatic Harley Earl, the man who invented American automotive design, Buick offers the promise of great cars that capture the essence of American style.

* Study based on a total of 64,909 consumer responses indicating owner-reported problems during the first 90 days of ownership.

** Vehicles in the $23,000 to $30,000 range. Reprinted with permission from *Kiplinger's Personal Finance*, December 2001 issue.

THINGS YOU DIDN'T KNOW ABOUT BUICK

○ In 1906, a Model F Buick was the only car to complete a thousand-mile relay run from Chicago to New York.

○ During the postwar model years of 1946 and 1947, Buick offered — without charge — special driving controls to disabled World War II veterans.

○ Buick's presence in popular culture has a long history. C. B. Dixon, an enterprising manager of the Hollywood, California, Buick franchise back in the 1920s and 1930s, made sure that all the movie stars who came into the dealership had their pictures taken with a Buick, and the photos were then used in newspaper ads. Among the people featured were Cecil B. DeMille, Douglas Fairbanks, Clara Bow, and the Our Gang group.

○ Buicks have been prominently featured in some great Academy Award–winning American films: from Paul Newman in 1967's *Cool Hand Luke* being taken back to jail in a 1941 Special Estate® Wagon to Dustin Hoffman's claims of being an "excellent driver" of his family's 1949 Roadmaster® convertible in 1988's *Rain Man*.

○ The most famous of all Buick styling recognition devices were the VentiPorts® that initially appeared in 1949. The early '49 Roadmasters and Supers® had hoses attached to the ports that were used in engine ventilation. The hoses were soon removed, but the holes remained as decorative items. They returned in 2003 on Park Avenue® Ultra vehicles.

○ Bobby Allison won the 1988 Daytona 500 behind the wheel of a Buick Regal.

Callaway GOLF

THE MARKET

Some 20 years ago, Ely Callaway set out to build a company that would bring more fun and enjoyment to the average golfer. His vision changed the way the game is played. With the introduction of the friendly, forgiving Big Bertha Driver, the late founder of Callaway Golf Company turned the most feared club in a player's bag into the most loved. The innovation didn't stop there. From woods, irons, and putters to golf balls and golf accessories, Callaway Golf has consistently used ingenuity, quality construction, and technology to make premium products that are the most forgiving in the history of the sport. Other companies followed Callaway's lead, and a game once thought to be the province of a few has become the property of many.

Today, there are some 25 million golfers in the United States, and the majority of players say the pleasing sensation of a well-struck shot is the number-one reason they keep coming back. Ely Callaway believed all players should enjoy golf — whether they are young, old, man, woman, amateur, or professional — and Callaway Golf is now a global company bringing Demonstrably Superior and Pleasingly Different products to 107 countries, in 29 different languages, building more opportunities for more people to enjoy the game.

ACHIEVEMENTS

Simply put, Callaway Golf has changed the way the game is played. Golfers around the world have used the company's products to make the game more enjoyable. Perhaps the best example is Callaway Golf's Big Bertha line of metal woods. At one time, the driver was considered the most dreaded club in the bag for many golfers. But an ambitious attempt to create an oversize metal driver with increased forgiveness succeeded where other companies had failed, yielding the original Big Bertha Stainless Steel Driver in 1991. Ever since, Big Bertha and her progeny — including such current products as the Great Big Bertha II Titanium Driver and the Big Bertha Steelhead III Driver — have turned the driver from a symbol of fear to one of fun.

Callaway now designs and produces a complete line of drivers, fairway woods, irons, putters, and golf balls that share the same ideal, attempting to make the game more fun for golfers of all skill levels, from first-time golfers to tour professionals.

In fact, Callaway Golf products are among the most popular on the world's professional tours and have been used to set several scoring records and win hundreds of tournaments.

This success helped Callaway Golf become the world's largest manufacturer of golf clubs within five years of Big Bertha's launch, prompting major changes within the golf industry. Callaway Golf's success enabled it to become the first major golf company to go public, as shares of company stock began trading on the New York Stock Exchange in 1992, under the ELY ticker symbol.

HISTORY

Callaway's success story begins with a small, three-person golf company called Hickory Stick USA, which was founded in 1982 in Temecula, California. The company initially made wedges and putters that had unique shafts made of hickory with a steel core. These clubs caught the eye of Ely Callaway, who bought an interest in the company the following year. Mr. Callaway had already been a successful businessman in the fields of textiles and wine, and golf would become the third and most successful act in his entrepreneurial career. His business philosophy — that every product his company makes should be demonstrably superior and pleasingly different from every other product on the market — would cause a revolution in the golf world.

By 1988, the company had been renamed Callaway Golf and had shifted from trying to re-create classic clubs of the past to pioneering innovative design ideas. A series of engineering and production advancements led to the creation of the Big Bertha Stainless Steel Driver in 1991, a breakthrough product that lifted Callaway Golf to the top of the golf industry.

The company has continued to flourish. Callaway Golf bought putter manufacturer Odyssey Sports in 1996, and Odyssey Putters have become the number-one putters sold in the retail environment. In 2000, Callaway Golf entered the golf ball market and has become the number-two ball on tour in less than three years. Ely Callaway passed away in 2001, but his spirit lives on in every product that bears his name.

THE PRODUCT

Callaway Golf has an extensive line of golf clubs, balls, and accessories that are sold around the world. The company's driver and fairway wood products currently include the Great Big Bertha II Titanium Drivers and Fairway Woods, Great Big Bertha II Pro Series Titanium Drivers, and the Big Bertha Steelhead III Stainless Steel Drivers and

Fairway Woods. In irons, Callaway Golf products include Hawk Eye VFT Tungsten Injected Titanium Irons, Big Bertha Stainless Steel Irons, and Steelhead X-16 and Steelhead X-16 Pro Series Irons. The company also makes the classically styled Callaway Golf Forged Wedges. The company's golf ball line includes the HX Blue and Red golf balls, CTU 30 Blue and Red golf balls, HX 2-Piece Blue and Red golf balls, the CB1 Blue and Red golf balls, and Warbird golf balls. Callaway Golf also makes and sells Odyssey Putters, including the White Hot, TriHot, and DFX putters. In addition, the company offers a full line of golf accessories, including gloves, hats, and bags.

RECENT DEVELOPMENTS
Callaway Golf has the most advanced research and development department in the golf industry. Some of the groundbreaking new products to come out of the Richard C. Helmstetter Test Center include:
• The Great Big Bertha II Titanium Driver — which has proprietary hot-face technology that increases ball speed across a larger portion of the face than any previous Callaway Golf driver and is designed to create the potential for greater distance off the tee.
• The Steelhead X-16 Irons, which incorporate a new "Notch" weighting system to add even greater forgiveness to the X-series design that made the X-12 and X-14 Irons favorites with professional and amateur golfers around the world.
• The HX and HX 2-Piece golf balls, which feature the revolutionary Tubular Lattice Network, a series of interlocking tubes on the ball's surface that create improved in-flight aerodynamics compared with traditional golf ball dimple patterns.
• The Odyssey White Hot 2-Ball Putter, the best-selling putter in golf during 2002, which has a proprietary alignment aid system that can greatly increase putting accuracy and confidence.

PROMOTION
Led by the Big Bertha name, Callaway Golf is one of the world's most-loved and recognizable golf brands. The tech-savvy but friendly identity of the company resonates with players who are just as passionate about their golf game as they are about their fun, and is summed up in the Enjoy the Game tagline. One of the earliest company mantras still effectively describes the company's product line year after year: Demonstrably Superior and Pleasingly Different. On the tech side, the caricature of Sir Isaac Newton has been used to promote the science behind the company's products, with the line "You Can't Argue with Physics." Celebrity endorsers have included Microsoft CEO Bill Gates, rocker Alice Cooper, Motown legend Smokey Robinson, and singing sensation Celine Dion.

Over the years, Mr. Callaway appeared in only a few of the company's print and television advertisements. One of the most memorable found him bouncing a golf ball off the face of a driver in a hip, good-natured takeoff on Tiger Woods' popular television ad. "I understand they paid that fella a lot of money to do this," Mr. Callaway teased. "I agreed to do it for nothing. But I did make them put my name on the ball."

Richard C. Helmstetter, the company's tech guru, chief of new products, and father of the Big Bertha Driver, continues to be a figure in much of Callaway Golf's promotion in print and television and on its Web site at *www.callawaygolf.com*. With a snow-white beard and bespectacled smiling face, he's a popular and effective voice for the company's technical messages domestically and abroad — particularly in Japan, where he's fluent in the language and spent a good portion of his life before being lured away by founder Callaway in the company's early days.

And while amateur golfers around the globe find more fun and enjoyment with Callaway Golf products, it just so happens that pros have great results with them, too. Swedish superstar Annika Sorenstam, the world's best female player, has played Callaway Golf clubs since turning pro, and The King, Arnold Palmer, began using and playing Callaway Golf products a few years back after happening upon the Company's inaugural golf ball during a desert golf outing. Others include Johnny Miller, young golf sensation Charles Howell, and legends Gary Player and Seve Ballesteros.

BRAND VALUES
The global Callaway Golf brand stands for heritage, technology, quality, and leadership in the industry. "We are the golf equipment company that uses technology to put more enjoyment into the game our consumers are so passionate about," says Ron Drapeau, chairman, president, and CEO of Callaway Golf. "When we market, we don't promise greater distance or lower scores, but when we build equipment, we build equipment that is designed to deliver those things. Ultimately, what we're promising is more opportunity to experience more of those well-struck shots that make the game so much fun."

The promise of fun and forgiveness that Callaway Golf brought to Big Bertha Drivers has spread throughout the bag, from fairway woods and irons to putters, golf balls, and accessories. From the Hickory Stick beginnings to the titanium clubheads and HX golf ball aerodynamics of today, the company is the clear leader in finding new ways to make a very difficult game a little easier at times — and more enjoyable at all times.

THE MARKET

America is the largest beer market in the world, with roughly 17 percent of total global consumption. Domestic brewers have historically dominated the American market, but in recent years, international beers such as Carlsberg have steadily advanced. On the global scene, the beer industry is characterized by tight competition between a handful of international brands and hundreds of local brands.

ACHIEVEMENTS

Carlsberg is one of the best-known international beers and has an unrivaled reputation for quality. It enjoys an undisputed number-one position in Scandinavia and is currently the fifth-largest global brewer in terms of total volume. Carlsberg has sales in over 140 markets.

The Carlsberg brand is owned by the global brewer Carlsberg Breweries, which has 29,000 employees worldwide and an annual beer production of 5.25 million gallons, which breaks down to roughly 56 million bottles of beer per day. If a year's production of the beer produced by Carlsberg Breweries were bottled and laid end-to-end, the line would stretch around the world more than 100 times.

HISTORY

Carlsberg's founder, J. C. Jacobsen, laid the cornerstone of the modern brewing industry by focusing on and developing many of the analytical brewing skills that are still in use today around the world.

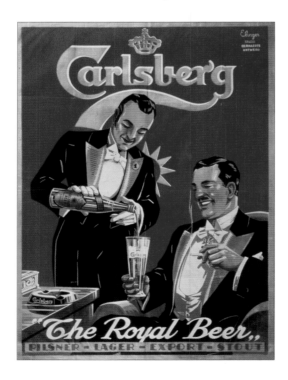

He began his career in his father's small brewery, producing beer in the middle of Copenhagen. The Danish capital was overpopulated and city hygiene was poor, often leading to spoiled beer. Jacobsen's desire to produce high-quality, consistent beer drove him to look outside the polluted capital.

A few miles outside the city's old ramparts, he found a location with lots of light, fresh air, clean water, and plenty of space. Here he founded Carlsberg. The company name combined the name of his five-year-old son, Carl, and the Danish word for hill *(berg)*.

Jacobsen had tasted imported German beer, and the idea of brewing Bavarian beer developed into a passion. He brought two liters of Bavarian beer yeast to Denmark and on November 10, 1847, he started the first Danish production of Bavarian-style beer at his new brewery.

The realization of the importance of science to beer production drove Jacobsen to establish the Carlsberg Laboratory, where skilled scientists could study the entire brewing process from its initial stages to the finished product. At the Carlsberg Laboratory, Emil Christian Hansen developed a method of propagating pure yeast to replace the wild yeast used at that time. The discovery, in 1883, meant that Carlsberg — and the entire brewing world — was able to produce beer more consistently, without the constant and unexplained failures in the brewing process that were common at that time. The yeast, known as *Saccharomyces carlsbergensis*, is still used for the brewing of pilsner and lager-style beers throughout the world.

Carlsberg has been an influential player in the international beer market for 125 years of its 150-year history. For decades, Carlsberg's quality products have been recognized and loved in faraway countries that bear little resemblance to Copenhagen.

In 1868, the first shipload of beer to Scotland started the Carlsberg export odyssey. The Scandinavian countries and the West Indies followed shortly after. Since then, Carlsberg has continued its global expansion, apart from the periods during the two world wars when exports stopped. In the aftermath of World War II, the internationalization of the company resumed, and Carlsberg was again exported to the remotest parts of the world.

In the past 25 years, Carlsberg has gone through a rapid globalization process and today is firmly anchored in around 140 markets and brewed in over 40 countries.

THE PRODUCT

Carlsberg Beer is the global premium lager in Carlsberg Breweries' portfolio, which includes hundreds of local and regional beer brands and soft drinks.

With its golden color and delicate smell of hops and malt, Carlsberg is the quintessential pilsner beer. Described as "the definitive beer" in consumer taste tests, Carlsberg is medium-bodied, dry, and well-proportioned with a characteristic hop bitterness that supports its fine structure. The beer's body, fine aroma, and pleasant hop bitterness make Carlsberg the perfect accompaniment for a meal or any occasion when good friends meet.

Each ingredient in a Carlsberg is carefully selected and must live up to a strict quality code. Specially chosen hops from unpollenated female hop flowers, malt from lightly roasted spring barley, and Carlsberg's famous yeast are brewed with pure water to create what is probably the best beer in the world.

RECENT DEVELOPMENTS
Carlsberg has recently developed a new brand positioning based on the results of consumer testing and research conducted over a one-year period. Focus groups showed that consumers overwhelmingly found Carlsberg to be a great-tasting beer, but the attributes they most identified with were "global" and "belonging." Those two qualities became the backbone for Carlsberg's brand positioning. The essence of the positioning, which best encapsulates the values and personality of Carlsberg, is "a drink with a world of friends."

More and more consumers around the world have a chance to enjoy a Carlsberg with friends as the brand is continually breaking into new markets and expanding its position in existing markets.

In June 2002, Carlsberg was launched in Russia, the fastest-growing beer market in the world. It is brewed and distributed under license by the Russian Brewery Baltika. Baltika, the largest brewer in Russia, has a market share of over 30 percent and is the only nationally distributed beer.

Carlsberg continues to grow in its largest market, the United Kingdom, and is strengthening its positions throughout Europe and the fast-growing markets of Asia and the Americas.

PROMOTION
Carlsberg has long been promoted as "Probably the best beer in the world." This classic example of Danish understatement has been the tagline of Carlsberg's "lorry campaign," which features the characteristic Carlsberg truck driving through exotic landscapes around the world. The campaign has run successfully for 16 years and has featured 50 motifs from 20 countries.

Carlsberg is an active sponsor of soccer, the world's most popular game. Carlsberg and soccer have been bringing together friends for decades, helping people forget their differences and giving them something to cheer about. When feuding brothers can agree on nothing else, they can always open a couple of cold Carlsbergs and talk about soccer.

The theme "Part of the Game" is used to reinforce the integrated role Carlsberg plays in the world's favorite sport. To further illustrate the relationship, the Parallel Game concept was developed, in which soccer situations are mirrored in beer-drinking environments.

The ties between Carlsberg and soccer stretch over four decades, with team sponsorships ranging from local clubs such as Copenhagen and Hibernian to international giants like Liverpool FC. On the global scene, Carlsberg has sponsored tournaments such as the 1990 World Cup, the 1996 and 2000 European Cups and Champions League in 1993 and 1994, the English FA Cup, UEFA Cup, and Super Cup. It sponsors the English and Irish national teams and will be the official sponsor of the 2004 and 2008 European Championships.

Carlsberg's soccer sponsorship is not only for the pros. Carlsberg also takes soccer directly to the fans by sponsoring the International Pub Cup, in which amateurs sponsored by local pubs and restaurants compete with other teams from around the world.

The finals are played in international stadiums like Wembley in England and Arnheim in Holland. In 2001, the underdogs from New York's Flynn's Inn took home the trophy. Another team from New York, Jameson's from the Upper East Side of Manhattan, made it to the finals in 2002.

Product placement also plays a strong role in Carlsberg's promotion strategy. In 2002, Carlsberg was proud to be part of the history-making action film *Spiderman*, which grossed an unprecedented $115 million on its opening weekend. Carlsberg has also had roles in *Insomnia*, *The Wedding Planner*, and *The Pledge*.

BRAND VALUES
All great beer brands offer good moments with friends, but Carlsberg makes its consumers feel part of a bigger world. Carlsberg takes pride in giving people everywhere a good reason to raise their glass, toast to friends old and new, and enjoy what is probably the best beer in the world.

THINGS YOU DIDN'T KNOW ABOUT CARLSBERG

○ The yeast developed by Carlsberg, *Saccharomyces carlsbergensis*, which revolutionized the brewing process, was given for free to the brewing industry by Carlsberg's founder J. C. Jacobsen.

○ Ninety percent of Carlsberg's sales are outside its home country of Denmark.

○ Carlsberg has been brewing on the same site since 1847 and has been exporting beer since 1868.

○ Carlsberg has produced special brews for royalty and VIPs such as Winston Churchill and Queen Elizabeth II.

○ Carlsberg's is the second-oldest logo still in use in the world.

○ A fjord on the eastern coast of Greenland and a submerged ridge in the Indian Ocean are named after Carlsberg, which sponsored the expeditions leading to their discovery.

THE MARKET

Arguably, there has been a market for air conditioning since the beginning of humankind. People languishing as the mercury rises. Their machines requiring controlled environments to maximize productivity. Add the torment of heat accompanied by high humidity, and you have a universal customer base, craving relief. But not until Willis Carrier created an "apparatus for treating air" for a Brooklyn printer in 1902 did an industry emerge to meet the market's needs.

A member of United Technologies Corporation, Carrier is the world leader in air conditioning, heating, and refrigeration systems. Its product line stretches from year-round home comfort systems to commercial and industrial climate-control systems to transport refrigeration systems. With markets in every corner of the world, Carrier is an integral part of our daily lives, providing comfortable living and controlled temperatures wherever people are living and wherever their machines are in use.

ACHIEVEMENTS

As Carrier celebrated 100 years of innovation in 2002, one realizes that Dr. Willis Carrier did much more than invent air conditioning. The summer blockbuster, the back-to-school sale, even the skyscraper all owe their debt to his inspired vision. Without air conditioning, who would pack a crowded theater in July? Who would endure a shopping spree carrying heavy bags and tired kids in the dog days of August? And who would build, let alone work in, a high-rise office building without a little A/C? Truly, Carrier's innovative approach has changed the way America lives, works, and plays.

Carrier also plays an important yet invisible role in preserving and protecting the treasures of the world for future generations. When air conditioning was needed to ensure Michelangelo's

timeless frescoes would survive the test of time, the Sistine Chapel called on Carrier. And when the National Geographic Society displayed its latest find, a 500-year-old Incan mummy frozen in the Peruvian Andes, the society could thank Carrier for controlling the climate in her custom-made 44-cubic-foot display case.

HISTORY

The year: 1902. The dilemma: The Sackett-Wilhelm printing plant in Brooklyn couldn't print a decent color image because changes in temperature and humidity kept altering paper dimensions and misaligning the colored inks. Enter Willis Carrier, who would invent the first modern mechanical air conditioner and become the father of air conditioning. Twelve years later, in 1914, Carrier took his modern marvel to the home and installed the first residential application of air conditioning in the Charles Gates mansion in Minneapolis.

Willis Carrier soon made his mark on other facets of everyday living. In 1924, J.L. Hudson's in Detroit prevented its customers from fainting in the heat of its basement bargain sales by becoming the first air-conditioned department store. In the summer of 1925, people came in droves to enjoy the latest motion pictures in the cool comfort of Carrier air conditioning in both Los Angeles' Grauman's Theater and New York's Rivoli Theater. That same year, thousands flocked to Madison Square Garden to take in the first professional hockey game to be played indoors. The rink was refrigerated by Carrier centrifugal chillers, and spectators were rewarded with a pregame glimpse of the inventor skating along the ice. The chambers of the U.S. House of Representatives and Senate were air conditioned by Carrier in 1928–29, so only filibustering lawmakers could be blamed for all the hot air.

Carrier also revolutionized transportation, beginning with the S.S. *Victoria* in 1930, the first vessel to provide air conditioning for passengers' comfort. In 1931, the "Martha Washington" railroad dining car became the first of its kind to offer conditioned comfort, also by Carrier. The first air-conditioned public bus was cooled by Carrier and hit the streets of San Antonio in 1946. And in 1949, the Boeing Stratocruiser flew farther, higher, faster, and with more passenger comfort (thanks to Carrier air conditioning) than any airliner in the world.

Fast forward to the 1990s, when environmental concerns took center stage. Carrier again led the way. With the 1994 proclamation of a worldwide CFC phase-out, a full ten-year warning in most markets, Carrier would become the first manufacturer to develop home comfort products using Puron® refrigerant, the chlorine-free replacement for R-22. As other manufacturers scrambled to switch over to chlorine-free refrigerants, Carrier meticulously built a full line of reliable Puron-based products to fulfill every possible application.

In 2000, ComfortChoice^SM, the first "Internet" thermostat, enabled utility providers to realize peak demand savings without compromising homeowners' comfort and controls. The 21st century has always held a promise of new discovery and innovation. And it's no wonder Carrier continues to lead the industry at this new dawn, utilizing technology that would even leave the great Dr. Carrier in awe.

THE PRODUCT
What began as an air conditioning company has developed into the world leader in year-round comfort. The most extensive product line in the industry boasts air handling units, compressors, condensers, unitary packaged and split system air conditioners, transport and commercial refrigeration equipment, room air conditioners, packaged terminal air conditioners, central station air conditioners, hermetic absorption and centrifugal water chillers, open-drive centrifugal chillers, hermetic screw chillers, reciprocating air and water cooled chillers, dehumidifiers, single packaged and split system heat pumps, electronic control systems, and air cleaners.

And the applications are just as numerous. Houses and hotels. Trucks and trains. Buses and ballrooms. Reactor cores and grocery stores. From the top of the world (skyscrapers) to the bottom of the ocean (nuclear submarines), Carrier products are there.

RECENT DEVELOPMENTS
Variable-speed technology and two-speed technology give homeowners the ability to control their home comfort more effectively and more cost-efficiently with multiple-staging and fan-speed options. The Thermidistat™ Control, introduced in the mid-1990s, controls both temperature and humidity automatically, adding to the increased efficiencies homeowners can realize.

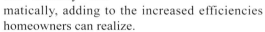
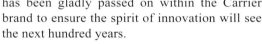

Homes are being built to tougher standards, and modern, airtight designs can create indoor air-quality issues, such as mold growth and stale air. Thankfully, Carrier is tackling those problems as well. A complete line of indoor air-quality products ensure that the air you breathe is clean and refreshing.

The greatest recent innovation, though, just might be the environmentally sound refrigerant, Puron. All over the world, governments are cracking down on environmental guidelines and regulations, and Carrier was the first to meet the needs of customers by staying ahead of the curve. How typically Carrier.

PROMOTION
Since the advent of modern air conditioning, Carrier has enjoyed a proud tradition of newsmaking promotions. The block-long lines that formed around the Rivoli Theater, where moviegoers flocked to enjoy Carrier comfort, were heavily promoted. Macy's department store even wrote a tongue-in-cheek newspaper ad that said it wouldn't blame shoppers for never wanting to leave the refreshingly cool conditions. Carrier's

unique igloo attraction at the 1939 World's Fair gave visitors a glimpse of how their futures and the future of air conditioning would commingle.

Today, the Carrier brand is recognized in 171 countries. An integrated advertising mix including television and radio, billboards, consumer and trade print, plus a comprehensive Web site, *carrier.com*, keeps the Carrier name in front of consumers. Partnership marketing gives independent businesses all over the world incentive to carry the Carrier name on their storefronts, vans, and uniforms. And the faithful fans of Syracuse University cheer on their Orangemen under the bright lights of the Carrier Dome. Of course, the equity built in the Carrier name and the innovative leadership that it stands for are the kind of advertising money just can't buy.

BRAND VALUES
When you invent an industry, you assume the moniker of Innovator. What you do thereafter determines whether you are entitled to keep that distinction. For over 100 years, Carrier has been the first name in air conditioning and has grown to include the whole scope of indoor comfort at home, at work, and everywhere in between. From 1902, when Willis Carrier produced one unit, to today when the company ships one unit every four seconds, Carrier has come a long way by any measure.

The genius of Willis Carrier gave birth to modern air conditioning and enabled incredible improvements to health care, manufacturing processes, research, building capacities, food preservation, art and historical conservation, general productivity, home comfort, and much more. He truly created a century of possibilities. A torch that has been gladly passed on within the Carrier brand to ensure the spirit of innovation will see the next hundred years.

THINGS YOU DIDN'T KNOW ABOUT CARRIER

○ Carrier products are designed in nearly 20 key engineering centers and manufactured in 108 plants spread across six continents.

○ Parent company United Technologies Corporation designs and manufactures high-technology products for the aerospace and building systems industries (NYSE: UTX).

○ In recognition for its overall contribution in World War II, Carrier Corporation was awarded the Army-Navy "E" six times, an honor attained by only 13 other companies.

○ At the end of the day, Carrier keeps more people comfortable as they sleep than any other brand.

○ In 1998, Willis Carrier was named one of *Time* magazine's "100 Most Influential People of the Century."

CATERPILLAR®

THE MARKET

Big. Strong. Yellow. You know one when you see one. Those giant, powerful machines that literally move mountains have become universal symbols of the heavy machinery industry. That's a brand with power.

But if you only see heavy machinery, you're not seeing the big Caterpillar picture. Through diversification, Caterpillar product lines include not only the heavy construction sector, but also road building, mining, quarry, forestry, and industrial waste handling. The company also makes compact construction equipment, diesel and natural gas engines, and industrial gas turbines, which satisfy an ever-growing need for power sources in the marketplace.

Caterpillar has built one of the industry's and the world's most efficient and responsive parts, service, and support organizations. It also develops and produces fluids for its machines, remanufactures used machines, and leads in the equipment rental business. Caterpillar offers varied financing options through its Financial Products Division. Moreover, Caterpillar Logistics Services, Inc. offers logistics management services worldwide, leveraging one of Caterpillar's internal strengths to serve external clients.

ACHIEVEMENTS

In 2001, Caterpillar — a Fortune 100 and Dow 30 company — stood atop its industry with worldwide revenues of more than $20 billion and an investment of nearly $700 million in research and development.

But the financial side doesn't paint the full picture. Caterpillar attributes much of its success to aligning itself with the work its customers do

rather than with the products they own — and to helping customers by solving problems, providing support, and offering financial and technical expertise. The company prides itself on its track record of keeping its customers up and running, maximizing their productivity, and reducing their cost of operation through a global dealer network that provides customer support, parts, and service in nearly 200 countries, literally overnight.

Among Caterpillar's other recent achievements:

- In the August 5, 2002, issue of *Business Week*, Caterpillar was ranked among the top 100 global brands. In order to qualify for this ranking, brands had to be global in nature, and the brand had to have a value in excess of $1 billion.
- Caterpillar is committed to the Six Sigma philosophy. Caterpillar has done something no other global company has been able to do: achieve greater benefits from Six Sigma in the first year than it spent. No other company has simultaneously launched across all its global divisions and been able to break even in year one.
- Caterpillar Inc. has been designated as one of "America's Healthiest Companies" by the Wellness Councils of America. The company

received the Gold-Level Workplace Award for the accomplishments of the Healthy Balance® program as the centerpiece of successful health promotion efforts.

- Caterpillar Inc. on-highway truck engines received the highest customer satisfaction rankings for the third year in a row from J.D. Power and Associates. According to the study, 50 percent of customers "definitely" would recommend Caterpillar engines, compared to 43 percent for the industry average.

HISTORY

Caterpillar leads its industry for good reason. It invented the industry in 1904 with the introduction of the first tracked machine that could lay down its own roadbed, allowing farmers to work in slippery fields without getting stuck up to their axles in mud. The product took hold, and Caterpillar endured.

The history of Caterpillar reads like a page out of the history of world events for the past 75 years. The company's machines have gone to war from World War II's battlefields in Europe and the Pacific Rim to the jungles of Vietnam to the Gulf War's blazing oil fields of Kuwait.

With their global presence, Caterpillar products are at work to make progress around the world possible. That work is most publicly visible in such high-profile projects as the Hong Kong airport, Egypt's massive efforts to green its vast deserts, and the building of the Three Gorges Dam in China. People also see Caterpillar at work helping to develop sustainable techniques in the tropical rainforests and bringing newfound prosperity and growth opportunities to communities as far flung as Piracicaba, Brazil, and Xuzhou, China. Caterpillar puts its strength behind this big world and helps to make it a better one.

THE PRODUCT

Caterpillar manufactures more than 300 different types of machines. The company also makes engines, power systems, and solar turbines, as well as providing parts, services, Power Electric Measurement (PEM) components, and work tools. Its equipment and other products are used worldwide across a range of industries as well as by government and military forces.

RECENT DEVELOPMENTS

People think of Caterpillar as a business-to-business company, not a consumer products one. That work-related connotation, however, has allowed Caterpillar to successfully extend its brand to other products, even into consumer markets. Because of the company's reputation for high-quality, durable products, its attributes carry over into other product lines. Perhaps the most successful extension of the Cat brand has been into the work boot market.

Caterpillar's licensing manager, Dan Hellige, notes that the extension into retail consumer markets has been slow and deliberate. "The team, first and foremost, has always had a goal of staying true to the Cat brand, only looking at extension opportunities that have a meaningful fit with Caterpillar. Caterpillar's licensed merchandise must have a connection back to Caterpillar; they must carry the brand's attributes such as being rugged, durable, and authentic; and they must be uniquely designed for Caterpillar. The licensed merchandise program is about creating a positive brand impact with both current and future decision makers. Caterpillar has the rugged construction work boots to appeal to our equipment customer and also a rugged casual line of footwear which introduces Caterpillar to a younger audience — those who will be the planners and influencers of tomorrow."

PROMOTION

The Peoria, Illinois–based corporation is Caterpillar Inc., but many simply refer to the company as Cat. Caterpillar has seen the value in flexing its brand, rather than trying to rigidly insist that only its corporate name be used.

As a result, both the Cat and Caterpillar names identify the company and its products and services. Having two equally established names was an important factor in the redesign of the company's logo in 1989. As a result, Caterpillar has two design marks, one incorporating the longer version of the name and one using the shorter version. While both are used to mark Caterpillar products, the flexibility of having a shorter version enables representation in a larger, more visible size. Therefore, the Cat brand usually takes the more dominant position in product promotion and identification.

BRAND VALUES

Caterpillar has a highly developed sense of what the company is and what it stands for. When the company reorganized in the early 1990s, a founding principle was to make sure the corporate image

was well defined and consistently communicated. Caterpillar works hard to instill a common understanding of its strategy and objectives not only to employees, but throughout its worldwide dealer network and its allied organizations.

The message comes through loud and clear in the company's statement of its attributes: Down-to-Earth, Straightforward, Gritty and Rugged. Enduring. Accessible. Honest. Responsive, Global, Serious, Thorough, and Industrious. Commanding. Highest Quality. Competitive. Industry Leader.

Bonnie Briggs, manager of Caterpillar's Brand Identity and Communication, travels the globe to spread the message of the importance of protecting and enhancing the brand's strength and value. She says, "Brands should stand for something. To be believed, they must be lived."

Caterpillar's more than 70,000 employees worldwide certainly understand what "living" Caterpillar means. Many often refer to themselves as having "yellow blood," a metaphor that sums up the pride they take in the company and their individual contributions to it.

In some cases, the strong work heritage associated with "yellow blood" has been passed from one generation to another. Kim Neible, manager of Caterpillar's Marketing & Brand Management Department, "grew up with Cat. Everyone in my family has worked for this company at one time or another. So, what Caterpillar represents and its

values are almost instinctive to me. The long-standing culture defined by its attributes is as prevalent within the organization as those yellow machines and engines in the factories. It sets Caterpillar's standards, drives its performance, and differentiates Cat from the rest of the industry."

Caterpillar has a strong commitment to meeting high ethical standards and has numerous measures in place to protect it. The company's Office of Business Practices and Code of Worldwide Business Conduct set a high standard for honesty and ethical behavior by every employee. In addition, the Caterpillar Board developed guidelines on corporate governance, which included the establishment of a fully independent board of directors, with the sole exception of its chairman, and a fully independent compensation committee. While not required by law, Caterpillar established share ownership guidelines in connection with stock option grants for corporate officers and directors over a decade ago. Shareholders have approved all of Caterpillar's equity-based compensation plans, and Caterpillar has never offered golden parachutes to any company officers.

THINGS YOU DIDN'T KNOW ABOUT. CATERPILLAR

- ❍ The Caterpillar family had reason to celebrate in 2002. NASCAR driver Ward Burton won the 44th Daytona 500 in Daytona Beach, Florida, in the Caterpillar-sponsored #22 Dodge.

- ❍ Caterpillar employees earned more than 2,800 patents in the past six years.

- ❍ The technology behind many Cat products is now available to outside companies through Caterpillar Technology Licensing.

- ❍ Caterpillar is developing ACERT ™ Technology for introduction in its truck engines in 2003. The technology is a "total" systems approach to emissions reductions. It relies on Caterpillar's leadership in four areas: combustion air technology, fuel injection systems, totally integrated and enhanced engine controls, and a simple, yet effective, after-treatment process.

- ❍ Caterpillar has again been selected as a component of the Dow Jones Sustainability World Indexes (DJSI). This selection recognizes Caterpillar's leadership in meeting DJSI's stringent economic, environmental, and social criteria.

- ❍ Caterpillar was named Company of the Year by the American Chamber of Commerce in Russia.

- ❍ The Cat Tough Loader from Power Wheels by Fisher Price was rated number three in the *Duracell Kids Choice Survey* and was featured on the *Today* show in November 2001.

THE MARKET

With the U.S. homeownership rate at record levels, more consumers are turning to the Internet to access information on buying or selling real estate. To serve this need, real estate professionals are integrating Web technology into their traditional sales offering to consumers: high levels of expertise and exemplary service.

Century 21 Real Estate Corporation, franchisor of the world's largest residential real estate sales organization and one of the most well-known brands, is doing just that. It has the largest broker network and greater global coverage than any organization of its kind. Simply put, CENTURY 21® is the most recognized name in real estate.*

ACHIEVEMENTS

Century 21 Real Estate Corporation has consistently increased its global presence and market share. Since its inception in 1971, the company has grown to 6,600 independently owned and operated franchised offices in more than 34 countries and territories.

The CENTURY 21 System also boasts the greatest level of brand recognition in the industry. A 2001 study conducted by research organization Millward Brown found that when asked to name a real estate company, 57 percent of consumers mentioned the CENTURY 21 System first, more often than any other real estate brand.

Century 21 Real Estate Corporation has also received accolades for its interactive marketing

efforts. In 2001, *Century21.com*, the CENTURY 21 System's Internet site, received three awards from the Web Marketing Association, including Outstanding Web Site and Standard of Excellence Awards, acknowledging *Century21.com* as one of the best in corporate Web design in terms of navigation, innovation, and usefulness.

The year 2001 also marked the redesign of Century 21 Real Estate Corporation's Intranet site, *21Online.com*. The site was redesigned to provide franchisees with news and information on a variety of CENTURY 21 programs and services. As a result, *21Online.com* earned a pair of 2002 APEX Awards of Excellence.

Century 21 Real Estate Corporation was also named to *Training* magazine's "2001 Training Top 100" list. This annual survey ranks the training and development programs of the nation's top companies, and recognized Century 21 Real Estate Corporation for its Internet-based CENTURY 21 Learning System®, a blended learning program that helps professionals hone their industry knowledge while earning credit toward professional designations and completing state-mandated post-license and continuing education requirements.

HISTORY

Century 21 Real Estate Corporation originated in 1971 in Orange County, California, created by real estate brokers Art Bartlett and Marsh Fisher. From the beginning, growth was rapid for the CENTURY 21 System. Within four years, combined sales of all CENTURY 21 companies topped $1 billion. In 1977, the company went public and began reacquiring the independently owned regions, which were originally sold as "master franchises."

Three years later, a merger between the company and TransWorld Corporation was approved, and in 1985 Metropolitan Life Insurance Company purchased the company that grew out of the 1980 merger. During the 1980s and early 1990s, Century 21 Real Estate Corporation became the first franchised real estate organization to create a quality service program and still systematically surveys buyers and sellers who use a CENTURY 21 broker or sales associate.

In 1995, Hospitality Franchise Systems, Inc. (HFS) acquired the corporation, and two years later HFS merged with CUC International to form Cendant Corporation (NYSE: CD). Century 21 Real Estate Corporation remains a subsidiary of Cendant Corporation today.

During its 30-year history, Century 21 Real Estate Corporation has developed a significant international presence, beginning in April 1975

There is a difference between a home and a home of distinction.

Century 21®
FINE HOMES
& ESTATES℠

Presenting CENTURY 21® *Fine Homes & Estates.*℠ An elite network of highly qualified professionals that understand the unique requirements of the discerning buyer and seller. So, while we can't promise an ornate column on the front lawn, you can expect CENTURY 21 *Fine Homes & Estates* sales professionals to deliver an exemplary level of expertise, service and results in over 30 countries. To locate a CENTURY 21 *Fine Homes & Estates* office near you, visit us at century21.com/luxuryhomes.

©2001 Century 21 Real Estate Corporation. ® & ℠ are licensed trademarks to Century 21 Real Estate Corporation. An Equal Opportunity Company. Equal Housing Opportunity. Each Office Independently Owned and Operated.

when Canada became the first international region. Global expansion in the succeeding years brought the company into 34 countries and territories, including the United Kingdom, Ireland, Mexico, Hong Kong, the Philippines, and Spain. Currently, over 50 percent of CENTURY 21® franchisees are located outside of the United States.

THE PRODUCT

As a franchise organization, Century 21 Real Estate Corporation provides its brokers and sales associates with the knowledge, skills, and tools they need to grow their businesses. The vision of Century 21 Real Estate Corporation is to provide its members with world-class marketing, technology, and franchise support programs.

For CENTURY 21 real estate professionals, the goal is to provide exemplary customer service, giving their clients "peace of mind" throughout their real estate transactions.

To meet the needs of different customers, Century 21 Real Estate Corporation has developed specialty programs. CENTURY 21 Fine Homes & Estates℠ markets high-end properties by providing specialized services and tools, while CENTURY 21 Recreational Properties® is dedicated to marketing vacation, summer, and second homes. To represent and assist both new home builders and new construction buyers, the company introduced the CENTURY 21 Builder Connections℠ program. Century 21 Real Estate Corporation also created CENTURY 21 MatureMoves℠ to meet the needs of America's senior population.

The CENTURY 21 System is not limited to residential sales. The CENTURY 21 Commercial Investment Network® was created to specialize in the sale and marketing of commercial and investment properties. In 2002, Century 21 Real Estate Corporation was included among the top 25 commercial brokerages, as reported by the *National Real Estate Investor*, with over $2.5 billion in commercial sales volume.

RECENT DEVELOPMENTS

Recent years have seen an increase of new initiatives within the CENTURY 21 System, designed to assist both consumers and real estate professionals.

To ensure that CENTURY 21 brokers and sales associates remain at the forefront of industry trends, Century 21 Real Estate Corporation developed one of the industry's premier learning programs, the CENTURY 21 Learning System® (CLS™). A Web-based, fully interactive educational system, CLS enables CENTURY 21 brokers and agents to engage in live educational sessions on industry and business-related topics from the convenience of their desktop as their own schedule allows. These frequent, accessible, and affordable learning opportunities ensure that CENTURY 21 professionals are equipped to meet the needs of homebuyers and sellers.

In 2002, Century 21 Real Estate Corporation unveiled the enhanced *Century21.com*. Its new,

fresh look and streamlined navigation mean a more robust, valuable experience for online customers. *Century21.com* is the most highly trafficked residential real estate sales organization Web site, with more than 1.6 million visitors each month.**

Century21.com offers a number of helpful features, including a quick and efficient way to sort and compare the properties listed on the site, a home planner that helps with move-in and home improvement projects, and online calculators and chats to help visitors make educated real estate financing decisions.

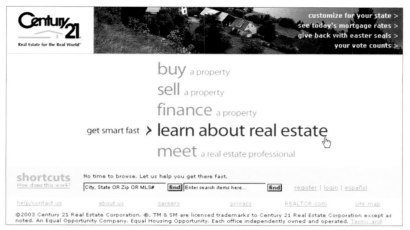

The relaunch of *Century21.com* also included the enhancement of *Century21Espanol.com*. This Spanish-language site features property, office, and agent searches and mortgage calculators, as well as the ability to search for offices with Spanish-speaking agents.

In 2002, Century 21 Real Estate Corporation increased its commitment to educating Hispanic Americans about the home buying and selling process by sponsoring a series of live Spanish-language radio programs on Radio Unica. These programs feature CENTURY 21 professionals providing real estate–related information and answering callers' questions. This program is part of the most comprehensive marketing effort in the real estate industry targeting Hispanic consumers.

PROMOTION

Century 21 Real Estate Corporation uses a unique combination of advertising and promotional programs to enhance its strong brand awareness.

In 1999, the CENTURY 21 System debuted its award-winning "Real Estate for the Real World®" advertising campaign. This campaign uses humor to show consumers that CENTURY 21 real estate professionals understand the anxieties associated with the home buying and selling experience, and are equipped to provide customers with a stress-free real estate experience.

That same year, Century 21 Real Estate Corporation partnered with Major League Baseball as the "Official Real Estate Organization of Major League Baseball." This alliance includes sponsorship of the CENTURY 21 Home Run Derby competition, the most-watched sporting event on ESPN after NFL football.

In association with Major League Baseball's Home Run Derby, Century 21 Real Estate Corporation sponsors the "CENTURY 21 Home Run Derby All-Star Sweepstakes," which gives consumers a chance to win a trip to All-Star Week and $250,000 toward a new home.

BRAND VALUES

Century 21 Real Estate Corporation is dedicated to providing its brokers and sales associates with the technology and marketing tools, as well as the franchise support services, they need to succeed.

The CENTURY 21 System is also committed to capitalizing on industry trends, including consolidation and expanded services, to deliver what clients and customers need while enhancing the company's leadership position.

Locally, all CENTURY 21 brokers and sales associates provide top-notch customer service by using their training, experience, and knowledge to reduce the anxiety often associated with the real estate transaction. While it may be the largest organization of its kind, the CENTURY 21 System also understands that each customer is unique and needs special attention and care.

*Source: 2001 Market Tracking Study. This survey included 1,900 telephone interviews (via computer-assisted program) with a national random sample of adults (ages 18–54) who have bought or sold a home within the past two years or plan to purchase or sell a home within the next two years. The continuous tracking survey was conducted between February 21 and March 5, 2000, and March 13 and October 15, 2002, by Millward Brown, a leading research agency. Statistical testing between reported numbers was performed at the 90 percent confidence level.

**As determined by Net Ratings.

THINGS YOU DIDN'T KNOW ABOUT CENTURY 21 REAL ESTATE CORP.

○ A longtime supporter of Easter Seals, in 2001, Century 21 Real Estate Corporation was named the all-time leading fund raiser for this nonprofit organization. The CENTURY 21 System donated more than $2.5 million to Easter Seals in 2001.

○ As part of the 2002 Major League Baseball All-Star Week in Milwaukee, Century 21 Real Estate Corporation hosted the first-ever CENTURY 21 Mascot Home Run Derby. "Junction Jack" of the Houston Astros took home first place in the fun-filled competition.

○ A video billboard of Century 21 Real Estate Corporation was featured in the 2002 Steven Spielberg film *Minority Report*, starring Tom Cruise.

○ Century 21 Real Estate Corporation was profiled on the Continental Airlines in-flight video program entitled "Luxury Quest — The Best of New Jersey," during the months of May and June 2002.

THE MARKET

Established in 1899, Chiquita helped create the banana category in North America. Since its introduction to the United States in the 19th century, the banana has become the country's most popular fruit. In fact, the banana is one of the most widely consumed foods in the United States, with 92 percent of all U.S. households purchasing bananas. Each year, the average person consumes almost 26 pounds of bananas; collectively, more than 7 billion pounds of bananas are purchased and eaten annually.

ACHIEVEMENTS

Chiquita was one of the first to recognize what an important role a brand could play in a commodity category, and the company has worked hard to cultivate a strong relationship with consumers. Chiquita is also one of the best-known brands in America. More than 90 percent of consumers know the Chiquita brand.[1] Today, Chiquita is the preferred banana brand among consumers[1] and the number-one-rated produce brand in overall quality.[2] Consumers love Chiquita, as do supermarket retailers. The strength of the brand results in greater sales for retailers who stock Chiquita.[3]

While Chiquita is well known as America's favorite banana brand, the company also pioneered many of the practices employed today in the growing, harvesting, handling, packaging, and ripening of bananas — and even operates its own fleet of shipping vessels. First launched in 1899, the ships — known as the "Great White Fleet" — were painted white to reflect the heat of the tropical sun and thus maintain the optimum temperature for bananas. Chiquita has since set many industry standards — including refrigerated shipping vessels, innovative packaging, and container ripening procedures. The company continues to combine state-of-the-art technical practices with careful handling in order to provide the best quality bananas possible.

Recognizing the need to protect the lands where its bananas are grown, Chiquita has led the industry in implementing environmentally responsible agricultural practices. In 2000 — after investing eight years of effort and more than $20 million in capital improvements — Chiquita became the first global banana brand to have 100% of company-owned banana farms receive certification from The Rainforest Alliance for meeting strict sustainable environmental and social performance standards. Each year, all Chiquita-owned farms — which total more than 28,000 hectares (69,000 acres) — are recertified by The Rainforest Alliance based on independent farm-by-farm audits of performance.

HISTORY

The history of Chiquita and the banana category dates back to the 1870s, when two industrious men saw an attractive business opportunity in the delicious yellow fruit. In 1870, Capt. Lorenzo Dow Baker purchased 160 bunches of bananas in Jamaica and sailed them to Jersey City, New Jersey. There, Baker sold the bananas for a profit, and in 1895, Baker established the Boston Fruit Company.

In 1871, Minor C. Keith traveled to Costa Rica, where he contracted to build a national railroad. In order to supply cargo and passengers for the railroad, he planted bananas alongside the tracks — to provide paying fares both inland and back to the sea. On March 30, 1899, Keith's railroad company merged with the Boston Fruit Company, forming the United Fruit Company. That merger marked the official creation of what is now known as Chiquita Brands International.

The history of the Chiquita brand begins in the 1940s. World War II brought the banana industry to a virtual standstill, as the British and American governments requisitioned company ships to aid in the war effort. In 1944, looking for new ways to invigorate the banana business, Chiquita introduced its now-famous Miss Chiquita character, along with a lively jingle. In 1963, the company added the Chiquita sticker to its fruit. Together, Miss Chiquita, the Chiquita jingle, and the Chiquita sticker became the most identifiable elements of the Chiquita brand. Familiar to generations of consumers, each brand icon has a history of its own.

Miss Chiquita. One of the most famous brand characters ever developed, Miss Chiquita debuted as an animated banana character in cinema advertising during the 1940s. Her famous Chiquita jingle educated Americans about the special ripening needs of bananas and informed consumers of the role of bananas in a healthy lifestyle.

Miss Chiquita has taken many forms over the years. Originally depicted as a "banana-lady," she evolved to human form in 1986. While her costume continues to adapt to the times, she has worn her distinctive fruit bowl hat from the beginning. Having celebrated her 50th birthday in 1994, Miss Chiquita continues to be one of America's best-loved characters.

The Chiquita Jingle. Fun, lively, and entertaining,

the Chiquita jingle introduced Miss Chiquita to the world with the lyric, "I'm Chiquita banana and I've come to say." Originally composed in 1944 by Len Mackenzie and Garth Montgomery, the jingle quickly took on a life of its own, becoming a part of American culture. At the height of its popularity in 1945, the jingle was airing 376 times a day on the radio, prompting *Time* magazine to publish this profile:

> *"Most spot commercials are either obnoxious or vapid. Chiquita Banana, sung to a catchy, Calypso-style tune, is so different that listeners actually like it. Last week, after more than eight months on the air, it had become the undisputed No. 1 song on the jingle-jangle hit parade. . . ."*

The Chiquita jingle lives on today in advertising and promotions — reminding a whole new generation of Americans that they can stay fit and healthy with the help of Chiquita bananas.

The Chiquita Sticker. Historically, bananas were shipped on the stem — making it impossible to affix labels. In 1963 — at a time when bananas were being shipped in cardboard boxes as individual bunches — Chiquita introduced its now-famous blue label. The Chiquita sticker has become an icon in American culture. Generations of imaginative children have amused themselves by affixing the Chiquita label to their foreheads, hands, and arms.

THE PRODUCT

Bananas are one of the most nutrient-dense foods found in nature. In fact, an average 100-gram banana is a good source of four important dietary nutrients: potassium, vitamin B6, vitamin C, and fiber.

But what makes Chiquita bananas so popular? First is a commitment that reaches around the world. From the banana farm to the supermarket

display, Chiquita is committed to delivering the highest quality bananas. When you see the Chiquita label, you know you're getting the freshest fruit, great taste, quality, and nutrition.

RECENT DEVELOPMENTS

Chiquita has leveraged its strong brand equity to introduce other Chiquita branded produce items. In recent years, Chiquita has introduced branded melons, grapes, peaches, plums, and pineapples — as well as fresh vegetables and other items. With this expansion came the need for a tagline that encompassed more than the well-known banana tagline ("Chiquita. Quite Possibly, The World's Perfect Food"). In 2002, the company introduced a new tagline — "Chiquita. Perfect For Life." — which speaks to the great taste, convenience, and nutrition of all Chiquita products.

Chiquita is committed to promoting healthy lifestyles as well as healthy products. Over the past decade, the company has introduced programs to educate children regarding the benefits of a healthy lifestyle and protecting the environment — through online efforts, in-school education programs, and educational promotional programs. The health benefits of Chiquita bananas were reinforced in 1997 when the American Heart Association certified the product as a heart-healthy food.

PROMOTION

Beginning with the introduction of Miss Chiquita, Chiquita has endeavored to develop innovative, entertaining, and effective methods of advertising and promotion. In fact, Chiquita was the first produce brand of *any* kind to advertise to consumers. The first Chiquita advertising took the form of 80-second cinema commercials that aired as animated shorts before movies in theaters.

Outside of advertising, Chiquita has developed high-impact retail promotions for its grocery partners. These promotions deliver millions of consumer impressions and generate great response. More important, these promotions deliver a significant sales increase for Chiquita retailers.

Other notable Chiquita programs have included sponsorship of the 1980 Winter Olympic Games in Lake Placid, New York; sponsorship of AYSO youth soccer in the early 1990s; sponsorship of the 2003–2004 men's and women's U.S. Soccer teams; participation in the American Heart Association's Heart Check program; and participation in The

Fool Father Time.

Day by day, whether you're twenty or several times that, your body loses essential vitamins B-6 and C, magnesium and valuable potassium. Eating one Chiquita® banana every day helps put them back. Which makes it a powerful ally against the ticking of the clock. Chiquita® Bananas. Quite Possibly, The World's Perfect Food."

Heart and Stroke Foundation of Canada's Health Check program.

BRAND VALUES

Fun, great taste, nutrition, and a healthy lifestyle are the hallmarks of the Chiquita brand. Having celebrated its 100th anniversary in 1999, Chiquita has been dedicated to helping consumers lead healthier, more enjoyable lives for more than a century.

1. *Harris International*, 2002
2. *Equitrend*, 2002
3. ems, 104 weeks ending 12/31/01

THINGS YOU DIDN'T KNOW ABOUT CHIQUITA

○ Bananas are not trees; they're really giant herbs, related to the orchid, lily, and palm family. The banana's massive leaves reach up to 30 feet (914 centimeters), making it the largest plant on earth without a woody stem.

○ Ancient Egyptian hieroglyphs depict people with bananas.

○ If all the bananas grown in the world were placed end-to-end, the banana chain would circle the earth 1,400 times.

○ When the Chiquita jingle was first performed at the offices of BBDO advertising, the singer rattled paper clips in a drinking cup to simulate maracas.

○ Among the famous celebrities to have performed the Chiquita jingle are Milton Berle and Bugs Bunny.

○ The original Miss Chiquita was illustrated by Dik Browne, who is also known for his famous "Hagar the Horrible" cartoon strip.

Club Med ♆

THE MARKET

In the early years, adventurous young people were Club Med's most enthusiastic members. And they still love Club Med. But today's typical Club Med vacationer is thirty-something; two out of three come as part of a family. Some villages offer a Mini Club Med program for children 4 to 11. Some also offer a Baby Club Med for infants and toddlers (from 4 months old) and a Petit Club Med for two- and three-year-olds. In addition, Club Med is reaching out to the growing number of lone travelers, single parents, and mature vacationers. Whatever their age, a very high proportion of Club members — about 70 percent — return year after year to soak up the sun, meet like-minded people, indulge in some golf, tennis, or water sports, whiz down the ski slopes, or try a new sport for the first time.

ACHIEVEMENTS

Half a century ago, Club Med invented the concept of the all-inclusive getaway. Now, Club Med is reinventing the concept, building a great future on a foundation of enduring values. As a first step, in 2003, Club Med launched "Total All-Inclusive"™ Vacations, introducing an open bar and snacking throughout the day and evening for one all-inclusive price. Over the next two years, every village will be repositioned. Family villages will offer every amenity that parents and kids need for the ultimate escape. At the adult villages, Club Med will redefine "sizzle."

Today, Club Med has more than 100 villages around the world, including 29 winter destinations, plus *Club Med 2*, which is the world's largest sailing

cruise ship. It sails the Mediterranean all summer and the Caribbean all winter.

Club Med has a total of 10 villages throughout the United States, Bahamas, Caribbean, and Mexico and three in Brazil. It would be hard to overstate the importance of the U.S. market today, or its potential for the future. After France — Club Med's historic home — the United States is the second biggest market, and thanks to a very aggressive marketing program, it may well become the number-one market within a few short years.

And Club Med feels completely at home in the United States. To the French recipe for gracious living, Club Med has added a measure of American vitality, a dash of Americans' love for action, and a little zest borrowed from Broadway and Hollywood. On the continental United States, Club Med has two unique villages — Sandpiper-Florida, a country club–like resort with 19 tennis courts and professional golf course on site, and Crested Butte, a one-of-a-kind ski-in/ski-out village in Colorado.

HISTORY

The year 2000 capped 50 years of Club Med history. The Club Med concept was born in 1950, when, during a camping trip with friends, Belgian sportsman Gerard Blitz recognized the need for a unique escape from the hardships of postwar Europe. He placed two small advertisements, announcing the first all-inclusive vacation on the exotic island of Majorca. The response was overwhelming — and Club Mediterranee was born. The very first village consisted of a number of army surplus tents in Alcudia, on the Balearic Island of Majorca. The first of Club Med's famous straw hut villages opened in 1952 on the island of Corfu, Greece. Five years later, Club Med opened its first ski village in Leysin, Switzerland, becoming one of the world's first ski tour operators.

THE PRODUCT

Club Med offers dream destinations — but is just as concerned about the dreams as the destinations. Club Med is the original, the largest, and the most comprehensive of the world's all-inclusive vacation organizations. One price covers round-trip airfare and transfers, world-class accommodations, endless gourmet buffets with complimentary beer, wine, and soft drinks with lunch and dinner. It also includes an array of sports and activities with daily lessons, Mini Club Med programs, and live entertainment. Winter sports vacations also include lift tickets and daily ski and snowboard lessons for the whole family.

Club Med has updated and improved its matchless array of more than 60 sports activities — everything from sailing and golf to inline skating and yoga. Levels of instruction range from beginner to advanced. Winter destinations offer many activities and excursions, including horse-drawn sleigh rides, dog sled tours, or snowmobile rides.

Of course, Club Med continues to offer more traditional activities, including golf and tennis. And when it's time to relax, there are fabulous meals and spectacular shows.

As the leisure industry grows in coming years, Club Med is poised to play a major role in shaping not only travelers' leisure activities, but also their way of thinking about leisure. Club Med's unique model makes it much more than just another tour operator or hotel organization.

To book a Club Med vacation, guests become Club Members or Gentils Membres (G.M.s), making Club Med the world's largest and most cosmopolitan Club in the world.

The founders invented the notion of the "Gentil Organizateur" (G.O.) — a term that translates roughly as friendly host. About 9,000 of Club Med's employees are G.O.s, and they are hosts, guides, friends, and coaches, combining a commitment to service with specialized skills and talents.

The Club Med brand now encompasses cosmetics and sportswear, and may expand to include insurance, television, a magazine, entertainment, music, sports.... The possibilities are endless.

RECENT DEVELOPMENTS

Club Med is the expert in all-inclusive vacations, with more than 100 villages in exotic locations in more than 40 countries worldwide, spanning the United States, the Caribbean, Latin America, Europe, and Asia. After 53 years of bar beads, books, and bracelets, Club Med will redefine itself with the launch of its Total All-Inclusive™ vacations for summer 2003, allowing guests to enjoy an all-day premium open bar, all-day meal service, and improved amenities (including newly added CD players in each room), in addition to more than 60 sports and leisure activities, endless gourmet buffets, and live nightly entertainment, for one all-inclusive price for three-, four-, or seven-night stays.

Building on its reputation as the leader in discovering pristine, exotic locations throughout the world, Club Med has opened Trancoso, its third village in Brazil. Trancoso resembles a traditional Brazilian fishing village. Its design is completely in harmony with the local architecture.

Marketing innovations allow Club Med to offer more customized solutions — with world-class comfort ratings plus upgraded amenities that help members find the village that best meets their needs and budgets. Villages are suitable for all lifestyles. Whether guests are single, married, or with children, everyone will find the right village so they vacation their way. More than $100 million has been invested in a state-of-the-art worldwide reservations system, allowing sales staff to respond more quickly to customers' requests. Club Med also developed a Travel Agent Web site to provide agents with trade news, collateral ordering system, and virtual tours; what's more, at the touch of a button, agents can create personalized promotional offers for their clients. Also available to Travel Agents is a "Custom Air Desk" that offers travel agents and customers air-inclusive packages to accommodate special requests and take advantage of low airfares.

Club Med has opened two Club Med Worlds, in Paris and Montreal. Staffed by G.O.s, Club Med World represents a whole new way to spend time right down the block — a place where members can chat, spend an hour, an afternoon or all evening long, enjoy a fabulous meal, and, while they're at it, climb a while or swing on a flying trapeze.

PROMOTION

Club Med is reaching new members with an integrated global communications strategy that focuses on "Total All-Inclusive" value, high-quality accommodations and freedom to do what you want when you want.

Of course, you can come to Club Med to just chill out. But those who want to play can take advantage of more than 60 sports, with different levels of instruction from beginners to advanced. Children (from 4 months to 13 years) can join in the fun in award-winning children's programs. A multitude of facilities and pros makes Club Med the world's largest Golf Club *and* Tennis Club. Special events scheduled for 2003 feature amateur tournaments (ski games, beach volleyball, water polo, football, sailing, kayaking, and other sports and games), as well as visits and demonstrations by pro teams (freediving, in-line skating, wakeboarding, and other sports). Mega-parties are part of the fun.

The Club Med brochure, *The Trident*, is available in 10 languages and has a huge print circulation as well as a strong Internet presence. Promotional efforts have been intensified by means of international partnerships in over 40 countries, such as those signed with Coca-Cola and COTY.

In addition, the Web site *www.clubmed.com* developed by Club Med Online is becoming a major international Internet player. The Web site now accounts for 8 percent of the company's individual revenues in France and 6.4 percent of individual revenues in the United States.

BRAND VALUES

A key to understanding Club Med's brand is realizing that the company is committed to redefining what it means to have or be a "brand." Club Med is not a destination — it is an identity. It is not a place people go to; it is something they become part of, and that becomes part of them. Club Med is an experience, a way of life, an attitude, an adventure. It is about being oneself and enjoying every experience to the fullest. These essential values define the Club Med brand.

Club Med is dedicated to constant improvement and innovation, building on its three strategic assets: its members, its G.O.s, and its brand. The goal is nothing less than total transformation, with a view toward achieving strong growth in all aspects of leisure, relaxation, sports, and vacation enjoyment.

THINGS YOU DIDN'T KNOW ABOUT CLUB MED

❍ Club Med incorporates the latest amenities in each of its superior rooms, from telephones to CD players, so that guests can find the comforts of a home during their vacation.

❍ Club Med is the only tourism group integrated under a single brand name worldwide.

❍ Each Club Med village is located on an average of 50 acres in exotic locations that embody the local country's culture, architecture, and people.

❍ Club Med Villages have tour desks where they offer a host of excursions to enhance vacation experiences by discovering local talent and treasures of that country.

❍ 53 Club Med villages offer children's programs.

❍ Club Med is truly multicultural. Its 9,000 G.O.s come from 80 countries and speak at least 40 different languages.

❍ Circus schools, complete with flying trapeze, are available to adults and children in over 20 villages worldwide.

❍ Club Med Decouverte (Discovery) now offers small-group, in-depth travel experiences — everything from week-long tours to short weekend getaways.

THE MARKET

Coca-Cola, the world's number-one brand, is a symbol of refreshment to people around the world. The familiar shape of the Coca-Cola contour bottle and the flowing script of its distinctive trademark are a familiar part of people's lives. In fact, nearly half a million times every minute of every day, someone chooses a Coca-Cola — classic, diet, or light, with vanilla, cherry, or lemon, with or without caffeine.

Soft drinks have been part of the American lifestyle for more than 100 years and continue to be America's favorite refreshment. In fact, one of every four beverages consumed in America today is a carbonated soft drink, and retail sales of soft drinks are $61 billion annually.

ACHIEVEMENTS

From its birthplace and headquarters in Atlanta, Georgia, The Coca-Cola Company now has operations in 200 countries. Coca-Cola, the company's flagship brand, has long been the number-one-selling soft-drink brand worldwide. People all over the globe enjoy Coca-Cola or one of the company's many other beverages. Today, the company is a total beverage company with product offerings that extend well beyond carbonated soft drinks to include juice drinks, sports and energy drinks, waters, tea, and more.

From the early days, Coca-Cola has been part of major events in North America and around the world. In World War II, the company assured that every member of the U.S. armed services was able to obtain a Coke for five cents regardless of the remoteness of duty station or cost to the company. To fulfill that pledge, the company assembled bottling plants in 64 locations in Europe, Africa, and the Pacific. The war effort extended the company's reach beyond North America, positioning the company for postwar worldwide growth.

Significant Coca-Cola milestones over the last 25 years include the opening of the Soviet Union as a market, re-entry of Coca-Cola products into China in 1979, and the launch of Coca-Cola into space aboard the Challenger space shuttle in 1985. Coca-Cola celebrated its centennial in 1986 and sponsored the 1996 Summer Olympic Games in Atlanta.

HISTORY

On May 8, 1886, pharmacist John Stith Pemberton made a caramel-colored syrup and offered it to the largest drugstore in Atlanta. But first-year sales averaged only nine a day, and Pemberton was never able to see his product's success. He died in 1888, the same year in which Atlanta businessman Asa G. Candler began to buy outstanding shares of Coca-Cola.

Within three years, Candler and his associates controlled the young company through a total investment of $2,300. The company registered the trademark "Coca-Cola" with the U.S. Patent Office in 1893 and has renewed it since. ("Coke" has been a trademark name since 1945.)

By 1895, the first syrup-manufacturing plants outside Atlanta had been opened in Dallas, Texas, Chicago, Illinois, and Los Angeles, California. Candler reported to shareholders that Coca-Cola was being sold "in every state and territory of the United States."

As fountain sales expanded, entrepreneurs sought additional sales by offering the drink in bottles. Large-scale bottling began when Benjamin F. Thomas and Joseph B. Whitehead of Chattanooga, Tennessee, secured from Asa Candler exclusive rights to bottle and sell Coca-Cola in nearly all of the country. They gave other individuals exclusive territories for community bottling operations. Those efforts laid the groundwork for what became a worldwide network of Coca-Cola bottling companies.

The company's response to the imitators who quickly arose included the adoption of one of the most famous product containers ever developed — the unique, contour Coca-Cola bottle. It was created in 1915 by the Root Glass Company of Indiana and approved as standard by the company's bottlers in the following year.

In 1919, a group of investors headed by Ernest Woodruff, an Atlanta banker, purchased The Coca-Cola Company from the Candler interests. Four years later, Robert W. Woodruff, Ernest's 33-year-old son, became president of the company and led it into a new era of domestic and global growth over the next six decades.

Since Woodruff's time, Coca-Cola has always placed high value on citizenship. Today, as part of the Coca-Cola Promise to "benefit and refresh everyone who is touched by our business," the company strives to refresh the marketplace, enrich the workplace, preserve the environment, and strengthen communities. Working through The Coca-Cola Foundation and other avenues, the company's lead philanthropic efforts are focused on education and youth achievement. The Coca-Cola Company's recent five-year, $1 billion commitment to diversity through a comprehensive empowerment and entrepreneurship program offers individuals and small businesses many opportunities as well.

THE PRODUCT

Life is a series of special moments, and each is an opportunity for Coca-Cola to add its bit of magic. From the look and feel of the bottle to the sound of effervescence, the tickle of fizz on the nose and tongue and, of course, the unique flavor, Coca-Cola is a sensory experience. But consumer emotions, memories, and values are even more powerful.

| 1894 | 1899-1902 | 1900-1916 | 1915 | 1923 | 1937 | 1957 | 1961 | 1975 |

The Coca-Cola Bottle

People love to speculate about the secret ingredient in Coke. One secret is indeed locked away in a secured vault. But another is readily available: the consistent quality of Coca-Cola products that are produced by Coca-Cola bottlers across North America. And that commitment to quality extends to the company's entire portfolio of brands, including Coca-Cola classic, diet Coke, Sprite, Fanta, Vanilla Coke, Cherry Coke, Barq's, Mello Yello, Dasani water, and a full line of Minute Maid sodas, juices, and juice drinks.

RECENT DEVELOPMENTS

The Coca-Cola Company continues to connect with people in exciting new ways, from the introduction of successful new products and packaging to a dynamic new visual identity.

Recent new product introductions offer consumers more ways to enjoy the taste of Coca-Cola. Vanilla Coke was one of the most successful soft-drink introductions in recent history while diet Vanilla Coke and diet Coke with lemon offer diet soda drinkers more flavor options. The Coca-Cola Company continues to lead in packaging innovation with the introduction of the longer, leaner Coca-Cola Fridge Pack 12-pack that fits easily in the refrigerator.

New graphics are part of what keeps the Coca-Cola brand relevant to today's consumers. The new visual identity introduced in 2003 offers a contemporary interpretation of traditional elements such as the Spencerian script, refreshing it with a lighter, more open look; a contemporary dynamic ribbon featuring multiple ribbons of white, silver, and yellow; and effervescing bubbles.

A broad overview of the history, growth, and contemporary activities of The Coca-Cola Company is available on the Internet at *www.cocacola.com*.

PROMOTION

Coca-Cola's promotional efforts began with an oilcloth "Drink Coca-Cola" sign on a drugstore awning. Asa Candler then put the newly trademarked name not only on syrup urns at soda fountains, but on novelty items such as fans, calendars, and clocks. Since those days, marketing and promotional efforts combined with a top-quality product have made the Coca-Cola trademark among the most admired and best-known in the world.

Today, the multi-dimensional "Coca-Cola … Real" marketing platform integrates advertising, music, promotions, and properties as well as the new packaging and graphics and reflects genuine, authentic moments in life and the natural role the brand plays in them.

Qualities such as genuine, authentic, and real are what people want today, and research shows that consumers identify these values more closely with Coca-Cola than any other brand. Authenticity, originality, and "real" refreshment — all a part of the heritage of Coca-Cola — are as relevant now as they were more than 100 years ago.

"Coca-Cola … Real" ads include appearances by R&B singer Mya and hip-hop artist Common; actors Penelope Cruz, Courteney Cox Arquette, and David Arquette; late night talk-show host Craig Kilborn; boxing great Muhammad Ali; world-class cyclist Lance Armstrong; and members of the Coca-Cola NASCAR Racing Family, including Winston Cup champion Tony Stewart.

The company also has extensive worldwide sports affiliations. As far back as 1903, its advertising featured famous major-league baseball players drinking Coca-Cola. One of the most notable and long-lasting sports affiliations is the company's 72-year association with the Olympic Games, including the successful 2002 Olympic Winter Games in Salt Lake City, Utah, and the 1996 Centennial Olympic Games held in the company's hometown, Atlanta.

The company has a long relationship with FIFA World Cup soccer, the Special Olympics, the Rugby World Cup, NASCAR®, the National Basketball Association, and the National Hockey League. A major multi-year agreement with the National Collegiate Athletic Association gives Coca-Cola marketing opportunities across 22 college sports and 87 annual college championships.

BRAND VALUES

The Coca-Cola brand stands for the most successful product in the history of commerce and for the people responsible for its unique appeal. Along with Coca-Cola, recognized as the world's best-known soft-drink brand, the company markets four of the world's top five soft-drink brands, including diet Coke, Fanta, and Sprite. Through more than a century of change and into a new era that promises even more change, Coca-Cola remains a timeless symbol of authentic, original, and "Real" refreshment.

THINGS YOU DIDN'T KNOW ABOUT COCA-COLA

◯ If all the Coca-Cola ever produced was in eight-ounce bottles on average-sized delivery trucks, it would take six years, four months, and seven days for those trucks to pass a given point driven bumper-to-bumper at 65 miles an hour. If those bottles were assembled, there would be more than 13 trillion of them. Stacked on an American football field, they would form a pile 346 miles high, 70 times the height of Mount Everest, the highest mountain in the world.

◯ The slogan, "Good To The Last Drop," long associated with a coffee brand, was actually used first by Coca-Cola in 1908.

◯ The Coca-Cola trademark is recognized in countries containing 98 percent of the world's population.

◯ The two countries in which per-person consumption of Coca-Cola is highest have little else in common, particularly climate. They are Iceland and Mexico.

THE MARKET

Since its inception in 1948, the cable industry has grown into a multibillion-dollar industry serving more than 69 percent of U.S. television households. Once considered an alternative television service for homes too far from broadcast towers, cable's broadband infrastructure provides an ideal pipeline for delivery of new and emerging technologies, including digital networks, video on demand, interactive television, high-speed Internet access, and phone service.

Comcast is primarily involved in the development, management, and operation of broadband cable networks and is also involved in

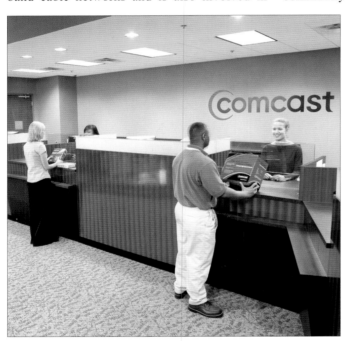

electronic retailing and programming content. Comcast, the nation's leading cable and broadband communications provider, serves more than 21 million cable customers in 41 states and has more than 6.3 million digital video customers, more than 3.3 million high-speed Internet customers, and more than 1.3 million phone customers. Comcast is also the majority owner of QVC, Comcast-Spectacor, Comcast Sportsnet, E! Entertainment Television, Style, The Golf Channel, Outdoor Life Network, and G4.

ACHIEVEMENTS

Comcast completed its acquisition of AT&T Broadband in November 2002 to become the market leader in eight of the top 10 U.S. markets. Comcast is the first national provider of cable

broadband products in the United States. Of the 98 million homes passed by cable in the United States, Comcast passes 38 million.

In addition to being a national market leader, Comcast is a local community leader. Comcast continues to adhere to its longstanding tradition of giving back to the communities it serves through community programs and partnerships such as Cable in the Classroom. Comcast Cares Day is the company's annual day of volunteer employee service. In 2002, approximately 8,000 employees, family members, and friends volunteered in 120 projects in 26 states.

Because of its strong commitment to community, Comcast was awarded the 2002 Multichannel News Innovator Award for community service as well as the Cable Television Public Affairs Association's Golden Beacon for the same year.

HISTORY

The history of Comcast is rooted in true entrepreneurial spirit. In 1963, Ralph J. Roberts purchased a 1,200-subscriber community antenna television system in Tupelo, Mississippi. From this small operation, which Roberts founded with Daniel Aaron and Julian Brodsky in the pioneering days of the cable industry, Comcast Corporation has become a leading provider of broadband cable services, electronic commerce, and original entertainment and sports programming.

In 1995, Comcast purchased a 57 percent stake in QVC and assumed management of the company. QVC, the world's leading electronic retailer, reaches more than 84 million homes in the United States and is forging a solid global presence, reaching more than 45 million households in the United Kingdom, Germany, and Japan. QVC continues to set the standard for innovation in electronic merchandising.

Today, Comcast is the leading U.S. cable operator and a Fortune 500 company.

THE PRODUCT

Digital Cable. Traditional cable television is a transmission of analog signals sent via coaxial cable. In recent years, technological developments have brought about digital cable television, which — thanks to digital compression technology — allows cable operators to offer anywhere from four to 12 digital video signals in the space that one analog signal would occupy. Comcast Digital Cable offers customers up to 270 channels, including dozens of commercial-free premium movie channels and pay-per-view channels with movies starting every half-hour. Comcast Digital Cable also features an interactive, on-screen program guide that lets viewers choose movies and shows by time, category, or channel, and a parental control feature to help prevent children from viewing inappropriate programs.

High-Speed Internet. By 2001, more than 9.2 million customers were enjoying real-time access to video, audio, and interactive game services thanks to the advantages of broadband cable. Comcast High-Speed Internet allows customers to connect to the Web via their cable line. The "always on" feature allows customers to turn on their computer and go online without the time-consuming and sometimes frustrating process of dialing into a server over a phone line. And since cable is ideal for quickly transmitting data, Comcast High-Speed Internet customers are able to surf the Web and download files up to 50 times faster than with a dial-up modem.

Telephony. Digital telephone service is provided via the same digital fiber-optic-based broadband platform that has made Comcast a new-technologies leader. Advanced fiber-optic technology assures a clear connection while providing the customer with a less expensive, high-quality alternative to traditional service.

RECENT DEVELOPMENTS
Recent technological developments have helped make Comcast a leading provider of emerging

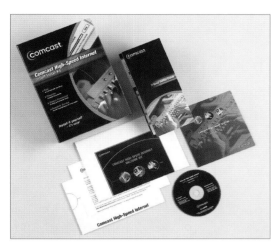

technology. With each of these developments, Comcast has been able to build on its existing broadband infrastructure to provide customers with additional products and services. One of the most exciting of these technologies is ON DEMAND, Comcast's video-on-demand (VOD) service, which offers digital cable customers the opportunity to choose from hundreds of video titles; start their selections at whatever time is convenient for them; and pause, rewind, or fast-forward the programs using their current digital cable set-top box and remote control.

Comcast has aggressively deployed ON DEMAND to more than 7 million homes. In most markets, the service consists primarily of hundreds of movie titles. In the Philadelphia, Pennsylvania, area, digital cable customers also can select content at no additional charge from leading cable and broadcast programmers — including A&E Television Networks, the Anime Network, Atom Television, Comcast SportsNet, Comedy Central, Court TV, C-SPAN, the Golf Channel, NBC, Outdoor Life Network, PRIMEDIA, and WISDOM Television. ON DEMAND from Comcast offers ultimate convenience and control to its customers by providing them with the power to rent a movie from their couch or watch the 6 o'clock news anytime after it first runs. While providing an additional

revenue stream from existing customers (there is a charge for each movie ordered), ON DEMAND also serves to add significant value.

Comcast is also leading the way in providing high-definition television. HDTV is a new standard of television featuring highly detailed picture quality, improved audio quality, and a wide-screen, theater-like display. HDTV picture quality is over five times the resolution of analog television. Comcast was one of the first cable companies to offer HDTV, deploying it on systems in the Philadelphia area in 2001. Comcast's HDTV service offers high-definition programming from major broadcast networks, as well as 24-hour HDTV channels from HBO and Showtime that are not available over the air. In addition, Comcast is working with cable and broadcast programmers to offer the most robust HDTV lineup possible.

PROMOTION
For 40 years, Comcast has been connecting customers to the news and entertainment that is important to them. In the first quarter of 2003, Comcast launched a campaign to introduce itself

to the new markets it's serving as a result of Comcast's acquisition of AT&T Broadband. This campaign, comprising television and print ads, features four-time Tour de France winner Lance Armstrong. Comcast's choice of Armstrong reflects the company's commitment to community, integrity, reliability, and success through hard work.

Despite its national presence, Comcast remains committed to its philosophy that running a cable system is very much a local business. The company utilizes a decentralized management structure, giving much authority and autonomy to the management

You could watch some football.

Or you could watch fear enter the eyes of a rookie quarterback as he hears the footsteps of a 320-pound madman.

HIGH-DEFINITION TV
NOW ON COMCAST DIGITAL CABLE

team in each division. Each of the company's local divisions is able to choose the best methods of promotion for their area. For example, one market may run a promotion featuring HBO's *The Sopranos*, while another may highlight NASCAR on TNT. The common thread in all of the company's communications is a focus on the power of connection and the convenience that broadband technology brings to life.

BRAND VALUES
Comcast is committed to being the company to look to first for the communications products and services that connect people to what's important in their lives. In every ad, every customer service script, and every direct-mail promotion, Comcast advances the idea that communications technology is a powerful instrument to connect its customers to news, family, community, entertainment, and education.

THINGS YOU DIDN'T KNOW ABOUT COMCAST

○ The name Comcast is an amalgam of the words "communications" and "broadcast."

○ Comcast is the majority owner of the NBA's Philadelphia 76ers and the NHL's Philadelphia Flyers. Comcast also owns the arena in which these teams play.

○ The company's 83-year-old founder, Ralph J. Roberts, still comes into the office four days a week.

○ The call letters QVC stand for "Quality," "Value," "Convenience."

○ In 1997, Microsoft invested $1 billion in Comcast.

THE MARKET

The U.S. dentifrice market is highly competitive, fueled by improved benefits and new product introductions. According to the latest available statistics, the dentifrice market accounts for nearly $2 billion in annual sales and is growing at an annual rate of 4 percent.

The market is segmented into base and premium, with base products offering cavity and tartar protection and premium products offering multiple benefits and whitening. The premium segment is driving category growth as consumers seek new and improved products.

ACHIEVEMENTS

Crest has been a leader in oral care innovations since its introduction in 1955 and has been the leading toothpaste brand in the United States over the past 45 years. It was the first dentifrice to be recognized by the American Dental Association and the first authorized to use the ADA name in advertising.

In 1976, the American Chemical Society recognized Crest with fluoride as one of the 100 greatest discoveries of the previous 100 years. Crest, in 1999, was the first whitening toothpaste to receive the ADA Seal of Acceptance for effectively whitening teeth by gently polishing away surface stains.

In December 2001, Crest Whitestrips was named one of the year's seven best new products in the *Good Housekeeping* Institute's annual Good Buy Awards. Crest Whitestrips also took home top honors in Cosmetic Executive Women's Best in Beauty Awards (the first time ever for an oral care product), and was voted one of the best new products by *Glamour* magazine's readers in 2002.

HISTORY

In 1928, natural fluoride in water was identified as a major factor in reducing tooth decay. The development of a fluoride toothpaste actually began in the early 1940s, when Procter & Gamble started a research program to find ingredients that would reduce tooth decay when added to a dentifrice. At that time, analysts estimated that Americans

developed more than 700 million cavities a year, making dental disease one of the most prevalent U.S. health problems.

In 1950, Procter & Gamble developed a joint research project team headed by Dr. Joseph Muhler at Indiana University. Dr. Muhler and his research team began the first clinical tests of the new toothpaste two years later, with startling results. One test among children ages 6 to 16 showed an average 49 percent reduction in cavities. Furthermore, the toothpaste also reduced tooth decay for adults to almost the same degree. In 1954, Procter & Gamble submitted the results of its extensive testing to the American Dental Association, which accepted the findings.

Test marketing of Crest with Fluoristan began in 1955. Though initial sales were disappointing, the company maintained confidence in the product, launching it nationally in January 1956. Still, consumers did not recognize Crest's unique advantage. Procter and Gamble needed a way to convince them that they were indeed benefiting from the product's decay-preventing quality. Since consumers could not see the benefit, they needed to hear it from a respected authority.

Crest's developers recognized early that the American Dental Association could grant such recognition. Beginning in 1954, P&G submitted to the ADA the results of the company's extensive clinical tests. The ADA, however, never before had recognized a toothpaste and had an attitude of suspicion toward dentifrice advertising. To its credit, the ADA maintained an open mind on the Crest presentation. As P&G's clinical evidence mounted, the ADA evaluated it carefully and asked for more data.

On August 1, 1960, the association reported, "Crest has been shown to be an effective anticaries (decay preventive) dentifrice that can be of significant value when used in a conscientiously applied program of oral hygiene and regular professional care."

The ADA did not merely recognize Crest's benefits. For the first time in ADA history, the

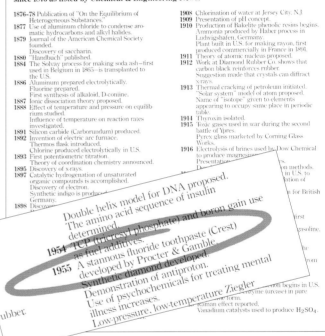

association granted the use of its name in consumer advertising for a commercial product. The response was electric. Within a year, Crest's sales nearly doubled. By 1962, they had nearly tripled, pushing Crest well ahead as the best-selling toothpaste in the United States.

THE PRODUCT

Crest's heritage is grounded in the dentifrice market, but the company has expanded into many other oral-care product lines. It now offers a broad range of products for dental needs and conducts the nation's best-known activities on behalf of good dental practices among children.

RECENT DEVELOPMENTS

The Crest brand has reached major milestones over the past two years that for the first time have made high-quality products and a beautiful, white smile affordable and accessible to everyone.

In May 2001, Crest Whitestrips was launched on store shelves nationwide. The tooth whitening system uses clear, flexible strips coated with an enamel-safe whitening agent — hydrogen peroxide, the same as dentists use. The strips are worn twice a day for 30 minutes at a time, for 14 days. At under $30 per box (which contains a two-week supply for the upper and lower teeth), having a noticeably whiter smile has never been easier.

In 2002, Crest launched the first major toothpaste made expressly for women. Crest Rejuvenating Effects is designed to help keep smiles looking and feeling younger longer through a combination of three properties to remineralize enamel, refresh gums and breath, and restore whiteness to the teeth. "Crest Rejuvenating Effects delivers the experience that women have come to expect from their beauty care products," says Diane Dietz, North American marketing director for Crest. "We've worked hard to push toothpaste to the next level — beauty — by listening to consumer insights on what women expect from a toothpaste. Everything about the product — presentation, packaging, aesthetics, and the sensory experience — evokes radiance and beauty."

Also in 2002, Crest Whitening Plus Scope became the only toothpaste to combine the whitening action of Crest with the freshening power of Scope for an all-in-one easy and convenient toothpaste.

Crest continued to expand its line of high-performance, battery-powered SpinBrushes in 2002 with the launch of Crest SpinBrush Pro, which brings consumers the technology, design, and cleaning power of more expensive brushes for a fraction of the price. The SpinBrush, says Michael Kehoe, P&G's vice president/general manager for global oral care, has "become the most popular power brush in America and is leading the conversion of

RIDGEWOOD DENTAL CLINIC
To the parents of: Johnny Potter
I have examined Johnny's teeth and find no new cavities.
NBM D.D.S.

"Look, Mom—no cavities!"

Crest Toothpaste with fluoride means far fewer cavities for every member of the family—including children of all ages.

Crest's fluoride is the same decay fighter that dentists apply directly on teeth. Ask your dentist about Crest.

Crest TOOTH PASTE fluoristan

manual brush users to powered brushes." The price of the Crest SpinBrush ranges from $4.99 to $6.99, which is affordable for most families.

Another landmark was the development of Crest Healthy Smiles 2010 (CHS 2010), a program created in May 2000 in response to a report by former U.S. Surgeon General David Satcher. The report stated that the country is suffering from an oral health epidemic — especially among children in low-income and minority communities.

With the goal of delivering dental health education, tools, and increased access to dental professionals to underserved children, CHS 2010 expects to reach at least 50 million children by 2010. Acting on the principle that oral health is integral to overall health, CHS 2010 has forged public/private partnerships with organizations including the Boys & Girls Clubs of America (B&GCA), the American Dental Association (ADA), the American Academy of Pediatric Dentists (AAPD), and leading members of the local dental communities to bring real change to the lives of underserved children.

CHS 2010 program initiatives provide substantive dental care and education to underserved communities with a variety of programs that include building dental clinics called Crest Smile Shoppes in nine cities, sponsorship of mobile dental van programs run by local dental schools, and treatment, screening, and education events year-round throughout the country.

CHS 2010 and B&GCA work closely to implement a curriculum program called the Cavity-Free Zone, which uses fun games and activities to teach club members about good oral health. All clubs are designated Cavity-Free Zones, a place where good oral health is a priority.

CHS 2010 reaches 90 percent of all first-grade classes in the United States through broad-based in-school oral health education programs.

PROMOTION

The advertising campaign that launched the Crest brand has become one of the most memorable in marketing history. In television commercials, smiling children proudly proclaimed, "Look, Mom — no cavities!" Along with the TV campaign, print ads illustrated by Norman Rockwell became classics.

In recent years, Crest has expanded its advertising efforts beyond the product to highlight the brand's commitment to promoting good oral health worldwide. This breakthrough equity campaign has showcased Crest's support of such key areas as dental education for children, geriatric dentistry, and professional dental education.

Both ethnic and interactive marketing have received increased attention in recent years. Crest has taken its marketing message to the growing Hispanic community, developing culturally relevant Spanish-language advertising that features as spokesperson Maite Delgardo, a popular Hispanic talk-show host.

The launch of Crest Rejuvenating Effects in October 2002 marks the first time Crest has used a major celebrity spokesperson to represent toothpaste in an advertising campaign. Multitalented actress and singer Vanessa Williams appeared in extensive TV and print ads, direct-to-consumer promotions, and in-store product displays.

You can't go too far to make a child smile.

Crest is going all the way to Zimbabwe. And Brazil. And India. And Vietnam. Since 1991, Crest has provided educational materials to Health Volunteers Overseas. It's helped bring oral health to countries where dental care is hard to find. As for the children of Chegutu village, the world is no wider than a smile.

Creating smiles every day. Crest

To bring its message of good oral health online, Crest developed the innovative Sparkle City Web site. Designed as an interactive teaching tool, Sparkle City supports the efforts of teachers, parents, and dental professionals to instill in children good dental habits that will last a lifetime.

BRAND VALUES

Crest is a brand that has continually pushed to improve oral health. Crest is among the most trusted household brands, a value reinforced by the continued recognition of its products by the American Dental Association.

Crest is committed to opening up the smiles of consumers around the world. Through innovative products and community outreach efforts, Crest is combining education with the proper tools to do the job for which Crest was created: improving the dental health of all its users.

THINGS YOU DIDN'T KNOW ABOUT CREST

○ The day after the American Dental Association gave its first-ever product endorsement to Crest on August 1, 1960, the volume of buy orders for Procter & Gamble stock was so great that trading was delayed for an hour and a half.

○ As one of the Procter & Gamble companies, Crest is part of a global organization that makes and markets health-care products in 140 countries with roughly $37 billion in annual worldwide sales.

○ Researchers tested more than 500 fluoride compounds before focusing on the two most promising — iridium and stannous fluoride — with the latter ultimately chosen.

○ The factors that led P&G to the development of Crest included awareness that children in several towns in the western part of the country were virtually cavity-free because of the natural presence of fluoride in their communities' drinking-water supplies.

CUNARD

The Most Famous Ocean Liners in the World℠

Queen Elizabeth 2

THE MARKET

Cunard Line is one of the world's most recognized brand names, with an illustrious history that dates back to 1840. Its flagship, *Queen Elizabeth 2*, is the epitome of luxury cruising with an atmosphere of refined elegance and impeccable service that hails from the Golden Age of transatlantic travel. *QE2*'s sister ship, *Caronia*, also delivers a classic cruise experience but on a smaller scale. In January 2004, *Queen Mary 2* will make her debut — the largest, longest, tallest, widest, and at $800 million, the most expensive cruise ship ever built.

With its worldwide itineraries and gracious lifestyle, Cunard caters to sophisticated, well-seasoned travelers who want to reclaim the legacy of Cunard White Star Service™ without sacrificing modern luxuries. With its longstanding British heritage and widely acclaimed enrichment programs, guests enjoy a cultured atmosphere on board.

ACHIEVEMENTS

Since 1840, Cunard has launched nearly 180 liners and achieved enough firsts and foremosts to be forever inscribed in the annals of transportation and travel history. Between 1840 and 1900, more than 18 million immigrants came to the United States, with Cunard playing a major role in

bridging the continents. During both world wars, Cunarders were the pride of the British Merchant Marine, serving as vital convoys in the transportation of troops to the war zones.

The first regular passenger sailing schedule between New York and Europe was put into effect by Cunard in 1847, and Cunarders have included some of the world's most celebrated and beloved liners. *Laconia* was the first ship to cruise around the world. *Servia* was the first ship to be lit with electricity. *Mauretania* held the Blue Riband for the fastest Atlantic crossing for 22 years. Then there were the most famous pair of liners ever: the *Queens Elizabeth* and *Mary*, floating palaces representing the quintessence of luxury travel.

Queen Elizabeth 2 was built to continue the tradition of these great monarchs. For over 30 years, *QE2* has maintained the legacy of her predecessors in providing a definitive annual World Cruise and the only scheduled transatlantic liner service. Widely known among royalty, rock stars, and the international jetset, *QE2* is indisputably the most famous ship in the world.

HISTORY

The British and North American Royal Mail Steam Packet Company was founded in 1839 by Samuel Cunard, principally to carry the Royal Mail. By 1907, the passenger trade had evolved into large, spacious vessels allowing for unheard-of comfort and conveniences at sea. In that year, Cunard reached a new height in excellence with the construction of *Lusitania* and *Mauretania*, magnificent "floating palaces" mimicking the architectural and decorative styles of great London hotels.

The company, which became known as Cunard Line, has had a "Queen" on the seven seas for more than 60 years. The glorious *Queen Mary* set sail in 1936 followed by *Queen Elizabeth* four years later. *Queen Elizabeth 2* was launched by Her Majesty the Queen in 1967, and the new *Queen Mary 2* will arrive in January 2004.

Cunard Line is a unit of Carnival Corporation (NYSE: CCL) and a member of the exclusive World's Leading Cruise Lines alliance, which also includes Carnival Cruise Lines, Seabourn Cruise Line, Holland America Line, Costa Cruises, and Windstar Cruises.

THE PRODUCT

QE2 and *Caronia* continue the tradition of elegance, grace, and luxury that made the Golden Era of ocean liners one of the most captivating in history. Superb British White Star Service™, gourmet cuisine, and sumptuous accommodations have secured Cunard's reputation worldwide. Candidates groomed in the top European restaurants and hotels are handpicked by Cunard and required to attend its elite White Star Academy before becoming full staff members.

Menus feature Continental cuisine, American favorites, traditional British dishes, and more eclectic offerings that combine seasonal and regional ingredients from different ports of call around the world. Cunard's culinary advisor, Daniel Boulud, one of the most famous chefs in the world, was recently engaged as a culinary consultant to build on the line's legendary reputation for excellence.

Cunard is also renowned for Illuminations[SM], a groundbreaking entertainment and enrichment program that includes a host of on-board guest lecturers and seminars, as well as computer, bridge, and dance instruction.

Queen Elizabeth 2. At a top speed of 32.5 knots, QE2 continues to be the fastest passenger vessel in the world today. She's the only ship offering regular six-day crossings between New York and Southampton, each featuring a theme from QE2's celebrated Spotlight Series[SM]. QE2's World Cruise is one of the great annual events, and she also offers cruises to New England and Canada, Norwegian fjords, the Mediterranean, and the Caribbean.

Cunard's 1,791-passenger monarch is a destination in her own right. Features such as a kennel, nursery with nannies, synagogue, florist, and even a museum-quality walking tour of ocean liner history create a virtual City at Sea[SM]. In addition to the lecture program, daytime activities include a golf driving range, movie screenings, a European-style spa and fitness center, and shopping at the only Harrods boutique afloat.

There are five sea-view dining rooms, including the Queens Grill, the highest-ranked restaurant at sea, along with a casual alternative venue. The dress code is mostly formal, an indulgence today where a dress code has all but disappeared on many other ships. West End–caliber performances

are held in the Grand Lounge showroom, while other diversions include a casino, disco in the Yacht Club, piano music in the Chart Room, karaoke in the Golden Lion Pub, and dancing in the Queens Room featuring the largest ballroom at sea.

Like the grand hotels of Europe, *Queen Elizabeth 2* has a wide range of accommodations, each paired with one of the elegant restaurants. A full complement of amenities includes 24-hour room service, nightly turn-down service, television, and direct-dial telephone.

Caronia. Caronia's graceful lines, expansive decks, and finishings of teak, mahogany, and brass combine the classic charm of a grand European hotel with the comforts of a modern luxury liner. The 668-passenger ship offers cruises to a variety of destinations including Western Europe, Norwegian fjords, the Mediterranean and Black Seas, the Caribbean, and South America.

All staterooms offer 24-hour room service, TV/VCR (satellite TV where available), direct-dial telephones, terry robes, hair dryer, nightly turn-down service, and daily newspaper. Over 85 percent of her accommodations are sea-view, some with private balconies, and her suites are among the most lavish afloat. The two-story Penthouse Grand Suites feature floor-to-ceiling windows and a private deck on both levels, Jacuzzi, sauna and exercise equipment, entertainment center with CD player, and a library of books and CDs.

Caronia features a single-seating main dining room as well as an alternative Italian bistro with both indoor and al fresco seating. Other amenities include lecture and enrichment programs, bridge and dance instruction, casino, computer learning center, deck sports, boutiques, European-style spa and sauna, full promenade and jogging track, golf driving range, gymnasium, indoor and outdoor pools, a library, and book shop.

RECENT DEVELOPMENTS

Queen Elizabeth 2 was recognized in 2001 as *Porthole* magazine's Reader's Choice Award for "Best World Cruise Itineraries," and one of the "Top 10 Large Cruise Lines" in the annual World's Best Awards from *Travel + Leisure*. Her 2002 awards include the top rating in the Large Ship category for her Grill restaurants from the *Berlitz Complete Guide to Cruising and Cruise Ships*, and the highest Six Black Star ranking from *Stern's Guide to the Cruise Vacation*.

In addition to the much-anticipated launch of *Queen Mary 2* in 2004, another unnamed new build has been scheduled for delivery in 2005.

PROMOTION

During the 1920s and 1930s, the heyday of transatlantic cruising, Cunard's motto, "Getting there is half the fun!" became a household phrase. Cunard's vessels represented the quintessence of luxury travel. Traveling Cunard was what one naturally chose on a voyage to Europe, and their renown attracted the great personalities of their time.

Today's QE2 has hosted more famous faces than any other ship in service, from screen stars like Meryl Streep and Elizabeth Taylor to royals and heads of state, including Margaret Thatcher, Nelson Mandela, Prince Charles, and even Her Majesty Queen Elizabeth II.

BRAND VALUES

Samuel Cunard's founding motto of "Speed, Comfort and Safety" demonstrated concern for the well-being of his passengers and crew. By the time of his death in 1878, his uncompromisingly high standards had made Cunard Britain's premier line. Throughout its 162-year history, Cunard's extraordinary liners have continued to validate the line's commitment to excellence and its tradition of style, comfort, and safety. The very name "Cunard" evokes an image of unabashed luxury and the Golden Age of transatlantic travel.

THINGS YOU DIDN'T KNOW ABOUT CUNARD

○ *Queen Mary* was the first vessel launched by a member of the Royal family.

○ *QE2* can travel in reverse at 19 knots, which is faster than many cruise ships go forward.

○ *QE2* is the only passenger vessel with a shipboard kennel so that passengers can bring along their dog, cat, or bird.

○ *QE2* uses approximately 1,900 lobster tails, 33 pounds of caviar, and 16,000 eggs on a six-night transatlantic crossing.

○ *QM2* will feature the first Canyon Ranch SpaClub, Planetarium, and Todd English restaurant.

THE MARKET

Pizza is a $30 billion-per-year industry, and approximately 3 billion pizzas are sold in the United States annually through 61,269 pizzerias. Each man, woman, and child in America eats an average of 46 slices of pizza a year, with pepperoni ranking as America's favorite topping. In 2001, Domino's Pizza sold 400 million pizzas worldwide.

Founded in 1960, Domino's is the recognized world leader in pizza delivery, operating a network of more than 7,100 company-owned and franchised stores in the United States and more than 50 international markets. In December 1998, investors, including funds managed by Bain Capital Inc., a leading private equity investment firm, together with management and others, acquired a 93 percent stake in the company. Currently, Domino's is the largest privately held restaurant chain in the world, and the eighth largest of all restaurant chains.

ACHIEVEMENTS

Ever wonder who invented 3-D car-top signs on taxis and driving school cars? Or why people *expect* food deliveries in *30 minutes or less?* Domino's Pizza, the pizza delivery experts, pioneered these and other revolutionary "firsts" in the pizza industry, while continuing to be the recognized world leader in pizza delivery. For example, did you know Domino's created the . . .

Domino's HeatWave® Bags — Introduced in 1998, these patented heating devices keep pizzas oven-hot during deliveries. The inner material of the bag is made of 3M™ Thinsulate insulation, which eliminates unwanted moisture and keeps pizzas hot and crisp.

Spoodle — This saucing tool combines the best features of a spoon and a ladle, cutting down the time spent saucing a pizza. The Spoodle was introduced at the 1985 World's Fastest Pizza Maker competition by the winner, Jeff Goddard.

Corrugated Pizza Box — This design keeps moisture from weakening the box, while preventing cheese from sticking to the top during delivery.

Unique Franchising System — Domino's "cornerstone" eligibility requirement to apply for a Domino's franchise is to have successfully managed a Domino's Pizza store for at least 12 months. Of course, no one could hope to manage any business without learning the basics. This system, which keeps the best managers in the company and gives all store employees an incentive to excel, has proven successful over the last 42 years.

HISTORY

What began as one man's dream has evolved into a company at the top of a competitive and thriving industry. The Domino's Pizza story is about teamwork, integrity, hard work, and having fun. It's about ambition, drive, and determination to do it better than anyone else!

Like most corporate success stories, Domino's started out small — with just one store in 1960 on a

college campus in Ypsilanti, Michigan. Once the business model was proven successful, Domino's began delivering to a massive pizza-craving population of thousands of college students living on campuses across the country.

In 1978, the 200th Domino's store opened, and things really began to cook. By 1983, 1,000 Domino's stores were in operation, including the opening of the first international store in Winnipeg, Canada. Because of its relentless expansion, Domino's was recognized in 1985 as the fastest-growing foodservice chain in history, with 951 units opened in one 12-month period! By 1989, Domino's had opened its 5,000th store and in 2001 Domino's clipped the ribbon on its 7,000th store worldwide, in Brooklyn, New York. Today, there are more than 7,100 stores — including more than 2,300 outside the United States.

THE PRODUCT

It all began with a simple concept: hot, fresh pizza and a cola delivered to your door.

After sticking to its "pizza and cola" only concept for 30 years, Domino's unveiled Pan Pizza in 1989, making it the company's first new product

since its original menu was established. Domino's began offering its customers new products at a dizzying pace in the early 1990s. Continuing its tradition of innovation in the marketplace, Domino's rolled out its highly successful Thin Crust Pizza (created by the team of franchisees in St. Louis, Missouri), bread sticks (the company's first non-pizza menu item), and Buffalo Wings, a side dish whose success shocked even the company and proved to be a great add-on to any size order.

In 1995, Domino's launched its Ultimate Deep Dish Pizza (which replaced Pan Pizza) and in 1996 rolled out flavored crusts, for limited-time promotions.

To launch the New Year in 2001, Domino's delivered its first-ever dessert to its customers' doors: Domino's Cinna Stix®, freshly baked bread sticks covered in cinnamon and sugar, with creamy icing for dipping.

In the fall of 2002, Domino's became the first national chain to roll out top-quality delivered chicken with Domino's Pizza Buffalo Chicken Kickers, tender cuts of all-white chicken breast with a kick of Buffalo-style flavor baked through and through.

RECENT DEVELOPMENTS

In February 2002, Domino's Pizza acquired 82 franchised stores in the Phoenix, Arizona market, making it the largest store acquisition in the company's history.

Domino's International division recently established Domino's first regional resource center with a majority-stake purchase of the franchise in the Netherlands, setting the stage for expansion on the European continent.

In Mexico, Domino's Pizza is now bigger than McDonald's® and Burger King® combined and is the largest quick-serve restaurant chain in the country!

Domino's Pizza began a long-term national partnership with the Make-A-Wish Foundation in 2001. Through this alliance, Domino's is dedicated to delivering wishes to children with life-threatening illnesses and assisting the foundation with its benevolent volunteer efforts through heightened awareness and direct contributions.

PROMOTION

Domino's recent ad campaign, *"Get the Door. It's Domino's,"* was launched in 2001 to focus on Domino's expertise and core premise: delivery. The message is simple. Domino's Pizza

consistently brings a hassle-free, convenient meal solution to your door.

"Get the Door. It's Domino's." ads have run on television, radio, and in print and feature a doorbell as the icon representing delivery. The ads are snapshots into everyday life — a family watching TV together, a young man staring into his refrigerator waiting for something appetizing to pop out at him, a frisky dog running to the door when he hears the doorbell ring — all ending with a Domino's delivery person seen in the reflection of the doorbell. The campaign has even extended to Domino's website, *www.dominos.com*, which features Domino's commercials' signature doorbell sound effect.

BRAND VALUES

For more than four decades, Domino's has delivered pizza and innovation to homes around the world. By promoting Domino's core pizza products as part of a family-friendly meal, Domino's has continued to deliver on the brand promise of being the in-home pizza meal experts.

For all products, Domino's Total Satisfaction guarantee states Domino's commitment to making "Perfect 10" pizzas: "If for any reason you are dissatisfied with your Domino's Pizza dining experience, we will re-make your pizza or refund your money."

Because of Domino's focus on taking great care of its customers and setting high standards of quality and consistency, Domino's Pizza has improved in all categories of the annual American Customer Satisfaction Index (ACSI). The ACSI, conducted by the University of Michigan Business School and the National Quality Research Center, surveys American consumers on a variety of topics related to their experiences with quick-service restaurant chains. After ranking sixth in 1999 and 2000, Domino's moved up to second place in 2002. Its overall score improved 9 percent and showed the greatest year-over-year improvement of all Quick Service Restaurant chains studied. That improvement level also ranks as the single best improvement since the survey began in 1994.

Behind the company's success is an exceptional team of pizza makers, delivery persons, store managers, franchisees, and many others — all working together with one vision: to be the best

pizza delivery company in the world. By utilizing the company's guiding principles — *demanding integrity, putting people first, taking great care of customers, making "Perfect 10" pizzas every day, operating with smart hustle and positive energy* — Domino's 140,000 team members around the globe are accomplishing amazing results.

THINGS YOU DIDN'T KNOW ABOUT DOMINO'S PIZZA

- ◯ In 2001, Domino's Pizza used 26.5 million pounds of pepperoni.

- ◯ Domino's Pizza uses a lot of cheese. In fact, Domino's uses more than 152 million pounds of cheese a year. That is 75,000 cows producing 6 to 8 gallons of milk every day of the year.

- ◯ Domino's World's Fastest Pizza Maker makes 14 pizzas in 2 minutes and 35 seconds.

- ◯ Domino's drivers cover 9 million miles each week in the United States alone. *(That's 37.5 round trips to the moon every week!)*

- ◯ Super Bowl Sunday ranks among the top five days for pizza deliveries annually, up there with Thanksgiving Eve, New Year's Day, New Year's Eve and Halloween.

- ◯ Ever wonder about what the three dots stand for in the Domino's Pizza logo? They represent the first three Domino's Pizza stores. The plan was to add a dot for every new store. However, with Domino's current store count over 7,100, that would have been quite impossible to continue.

- ◯ Because of the volume of people residing in high-rise buildings in Hong Kong, delivery times are influenced by traffic conditions on elevators! It often takes drivers longer to travel vertically than horizontally, as access to elevators is congested during "high peak" hours.

- ◯ When the first Domino's store opened in Japan in 1985, the Japanese had no word for pepperoni. Now pepperoni is one of the most embraced toppings in Japan, and the word has entered the Japanese language.

THE MARKET

Americans first fell in love with *French's*® mustard during the summer of 1904, when the zippy yellow sauce became forever "linked" with that brand-new American classic, the hot dog. The two met in St. Louis at the World's Fair. Today, *French's* mustard is still America's number-one branded mustard, and over the years, *French's* has grown to accommodate the needs and tastes of American consumers through brand development, product line expansion, and staying relevant with changing consumer preferences.

America's major condiment category — defined as mustard, mayonnaise, and ketchup — has grown into a $1.5 billion business. AC Nielsen reports that the mustard category has reached $307 million in 2002.

In an industry where hundreds of national and local companies compete to own a place on America's tables, *French's* has been — and remains — the number-one mustard, with over a 30 percent dollar share. Condiment companies come and go at a brisk pace in this industry, but *French's* mustard has been satisfying American taste buds for nearly 100 years and continues to drive the mustard category growth with sales outpacing all other yellow mustard brands.

ACHIEVEMENTS

With its line of delicious mustards that now share the famous red pennant logo, *French's* sells five times more mustard than any other nationally advertised brand. As America's leading mustard, *French's* knows American tastes. To continue to satisfy consumers' needs, *French's* now offers a family of flavors that reflect American's growing appeal for a variety of mustards. *Classic Yellow*, Napa Valley style Dijon, Sweet Onion, zesty Deli, and Sweet and Tangy Honey mustards are all part of the *French's* line of mustard products.

Over the years, *French's* mustard has aligned itself with many distinguished organizations and institutions from Little League to the Major League Baseball Players Association to NASCAR and USA Baseball. Today *French's* is proud to be the official mustard of the New York Yankees and New York's Madison Square Garden. Additionally,

French's sponsors the Mount Horeb Mustard Museum and the Napa Valley Mustard Festival.

As an active community leader, *French's* has supported Habitat for Humanity, the American Diabetes Association walks, the New York Artists and Writers charity softball game, and numerous children's museums across the country.

HISTORY

The *French's* name has stood as a symbol of excellence in food development since 1880 when Robert Timothy French established a spice company in New York City. But it was the founder's

sons, George and Francis, who provided both the drive and vision that propelled the firm into the forefront of America's flavor market.

By 1904, Francis French realized that mustard as a condiment was all but ignored by the public. "I want a new kind of pure prepared mustard," he told his older brother George, the president of the R. T. French Company. "One that is mild and has a true mustard flavor, and yet is light and creamy

in consistency and color. There is no condiment like I have in mind on the market, and I'm sure that such a mustard, even if it costs ten dollars a gallon, would have a ready and wide sale. It must be mild, for I believe that these hot mustards are used sparingly not because they are hot, but because people do not like them."

As the story goes, *French's* Cream Salad mustard was launched in 1904 at the St. Louis World's Fair with the hot dog, and both were an instant success. During this time, *French's* Cream Salad Brand was literally selling itself as brand awareness grew exclusively through word-of mouth. In 1915, the *French's* pennant became the brand's official logo, symbolizing *French's* affiliation with baseball and American celebration.

In 1926, the business was sold for $3.8 million to J & J Colman of the United Kingdom, a major mustard manufacturer. In 1938, Reckitt & Colman was formed through the merger of J & J Colman with Reckitt & Sons, a maker of starch and flour, founded in 1840.

Under the Reckitt & Colman name, *French's* continued to grow the mustard category through an ongoing commitment to innovation and new product development. The squeeze bottle was introduced in 1974. Soon after, specialty flavors were introduced: Sweet Onion in 1971, Horseradish in 1973, Deli in 1982, Dijon in 1983, and Sweet & Tangy Honey in 1998. In 2000, Reckitt & Colman merged with Benckiser to form Reckitt Benckiser. In 2001, *French's* continued its commitment to innovation and launched Sweet Onion in a 12-ounce squeeze bottle in the U.S. market to rave reviews in the media and from consumers.

THE PRODUCT

French's delivers the smooth body and full flavor Americans have grown to love. *French's* uses only No. 1 grade mustard seed in its mustards, harvested at just the right moment when the seed is fully developed. Only the highest-quality vinegar, spices, garlic, paprika, and proprietary flavor give *French's* its unique and consistent flavor every time you buy it.

RECENT DEVELOPMENTS

Great brands need to continually evolve and innovate to retain relevance and maintain their leadership position. *French's* recently announced new changes in its mustard line that will again redefine the mustard category.

With approximately 90 percent brand awareness, the *French's* pennant and familiar yellow bottle define what people see on their family's table today. So when considering changes, *French's* looked to their consumers to build the foundation for identifying improvements. From consumer insights and research, *French's* concluded that a package, dispenser, and graphic redesign was in order. As a part of the redesign process, *French's* talked to hundreds of consumers for insight.

The outcome of this research project is a sleek, new easy-to-squeeze bottle, with an innovative "stay clean" cap that makes dispensing mustard a snap. The stay-clean cap has a special vacuum seal that draws the unused mustard back into the bottle so there's less crusty mess.

Results found a four-to-one preference for the new easy-to-squeeze bottle and stay-clean cap versus the old barrel shape and twist cap.

French's mustard also carries a brand-new label prominently displaying the well-known *French's* pennant, making it more recognizable, bigger, and bolder. Each flavor label has a different eye-catching image that clearly defines the flavor profile.

PROMOTION

One of the most famous and popular promotional programs initiated from *French's* mustard in 1999 was the "Smile! You've got *French's*!" advertising campaign. Initially a television and print campaign

that featured images of smiling hot dogs, hamburgers, and sandwiches, the elements of this campaign were soon tied into a national public relations and promotional program — which included a contest that encouraged kids to play with their food, make a Funny Food Face, and win great prizes.

Thousands of entries were received each year for the Make a Funny Food Face contest. Prizes have included trips to New York City, the Napa Valley Mustard Festival, Universal Studios Orlando, and more.

The most recent advertising campaign began with a TV spot called "Talking Dog," which introduces the revolutionary new stay-clean cap and no-mess packaging. The commercial and print ads also introduced the slogan "Nothing Cuts the Mustard Like *French's*™." While capturing the brand's essence of superior taste, the commercials tell fun, relevant, and engaging stories about how far people are willing to go for the great taste of *French's* mustard. The creative approach and slogan in the ads are all designed to communicate *French's* leadership position as simply the best-tasting mustard you can buy.

BRAND VALUES

French's mustard has illustrated the importance of working hand in hand with their consumers to define the best solutions and future for their products. As an American icon, the makers of *French's* mustard take pride in being the undisputed leader in mustard — a true classic and an American icon. *French's* represents family, American tradition, and life's simple pleasures.

Double play.
French's® style.

The Official Mustard of the New York Yankees.

Nothing cuts the mustard like *French's*

THE MARKET

The snack food and wholesale bakery industry in the United States is a $90 billion business. Within this universe, the world of salty snacks represents $20 billion in sales. Of the salty snack world, the corn chip category accounts for approximately 4 percent of that consumption, which translated to nearly $700 million of retail corn chips sales in 2000. FRITOS® is far and away the largest player in the category, and the brand drives category growth. FRITOS® is the only national corn chip brand; with a 93 percent share of the market, as FRITOS® goes, so goes the category.

Corn chips provide consumers with a snacking alternative to the larger potato chip and tortilla chip categories. Frito-Lay sister products such as Lays®, Doritos®, and Tostitos® dominate the potato and tortilla chip categories.

ACHIEVEMENTS

In 1954, the brand celebrated its 25th anniversary by achieving $28 million in sales. Since then FRITOS® has grown into a global powerhouse brand with over $600 million in sales. FRITOS® is the fifth-largest brand in the Frito-Lay portfolio behind Lays, Doritos, Tostitos, and Ruffles®, but FRITOS® is arguably the brand with the most storied history because of its close ties to mainstream America. Year after year, FRITOS® continues to be one of the most recognizable of all consumer packaged-goods brands. When compared to other food brands, FRITOS® achieves high scores because of its product quality, differentiated nature, and reputation as a product that delivers exceptional value.

HISTORY

FRITOS® was the first brand of what is now an $11 billion food company, Frito-Lay, Inc. At the very depths of the Great Depression in 1932, a young Texan named C. E. Doolin launched a venture that resulted in the establishment of an entirely new and typically American industry. While operating a confectionery in San Antonio, Doolin first envisioned merchandising food products from display racks rather from the huge glass jars then utilized. At the same time, he discovered a product known as a corn

chip — with similar consistency to the present FRITOS®, but with the taste of a toasted tortilla. Doolin recognized this crudely packaged snack as a product that would lend itself to merchandising from the display racks he previously envisioned. For $100, Doolin acquired the recipe, the crude equipment for making the product, and the 19 retail accounts in the San Antonio area. Thus, the Frito Company was born.

Production soon moved from the family kitchen to production plants in Houston, Dallas, and Tulsa, and the company headquarters moved to Dallas. In 1945, the Frito Company granted to the H. W. Lay Company exclusive franchise rights to manufacture and to distribute FRITOS® Brand corn chips in the Southeast. The following chronology of events best reflects the evolution of the brand from its humble beginning to its present-day prosperity:

- In 1949, the words "FRITOS®, Golden Chips of Corn" were printed on bags of FRITOS®.
- In 1953, the Frito Kid was introduced, and three years later, he appeared on the *Today Show* with Dave Garroway. At the same time, the Frito Company became the first Texas company to advertise on the NBC Television network. The Frito Kid represented the brand until his retirement in 1967.
- In 1958, FRITOS® adopted a new theme, "Munch a Bunch! of FRITOS® Brand Corn Chips"; a year later, Vice President Richard Nixon took a bag of FRITOS® to Nikita Krushchev as a symbol of Americana.
- The year 1961 was a landmark for the Frito Company, when they merged with the H. W. Lay Company to form Frito-Lay, Inc.
- In 1971 W. C. FRITOS®, a caricature of the popular actor W. C. Fields, was introduced as the new mascot for the brand. At this point in its evolution, the FRITOS® brand eclipsed $200 million in sales and continued to build momentum through the 1980s.

THE PRODUCT

FRITOS® Brand Corn Chips are made with fresh, whole kernels of corn; this freshness helps create the hearty corn taste for which FRITOS® is famous. The corn arrives at the production facilities via railcar before being stored and dried to exact moisture requirements. Ultimately, the corn is cooked to soften the kernels before they are ground into a thick corn dough called "masa."

The masa is then put through an extruder that presses the dough at high pressure through narrow slits, creating ribbons of FRITOS® product. The ribbons are cut to the correct length to produce the classic FRITOS® shape. The strips of raw masa are then dropped directly into hot oil and fried at precise temperatures and duration. Once removed from the oil, the fried chips are allowed to cool before salt or one of nine other flavors is applied. The seasoned chips are quickly sealed into packages for shipment to stores nationwide.

A typical FRITOS® line produces over 1,000 pounds of FRITOS® every hour, or over 5 million pounds per year. Manufacturing plants are located throughout the country to minimize the time needed to bring the product to market. Over the course of a year, over 80 million pounds of oil and 170 million pounds of corn are used in the production of FRITOS® — enough corn to cover the turf of 1,000 football fields.

RECENT DEVELOPMENTS

The "Munch a Bunch! of FRITOS®" campaign was modified and re-introduced in 1991, and for the first time in 58 years, FRITOS® Brand Corn

Chips packaging was redesigned, with brighter colors and an updated logo. The year 1993 saw the launch of the "I Know What I Like and I Like FRITOS®" campaign, and a year later, FRITOS® Brand SCOOPS!® was introduced to the marketplace. SCOOPS! was created to meet consumer desire for a FRITOS® corn chip that was conducive to dipping. Since then, SCOOPS! has grown to a healthy $140 million business.

In 2000, FRITOS® adopted the tagline, "Nothing Satisfies Like FRITOS®," to communicate the hearty, filling, and satisfying nature that defines the product's attributes. Today, the FRITOS® Brand supports nine flavored products and three unflavored (Original, SCOOPS!, and King Size FRITOS® Brand Corn Chips). The Original FRITOS® Brand Corn Chip continues to be the volume leader and is responsible for nearly half of the brand's overall sales.

FRITOS® continually strives to innovate in meaningful ways. The brand's innovation comes from the desire to provide consumers with a consistent product that delivers uncompromising quality and value with each and every bag.

PROMOTION

One of the many strengths of the Frito-Lay Company and the FRITOS® Brand in particular has been the meaningful way in which advertising and merchandising have been married. The FRITOS® Brand engages consumers both in their homes and on their shopping trips through impactful advertising, promotion, and perhaps most importantly, its impressive shelf presence. Frito-Lay sells over 1.2 billion bags of FRITOS® in a typical year. This volume provides over a billion shelf impressions that serve as miniature billboards. In the complex and crowded snack food world, FRITOS® and the other Frito-Lay brands have an unequaled retail presence.

The FRITOS® Brand has utilized celebrity spokespeople throughout its history. From W. C. Fields to country singers Mark Chesnutt and Reba McEntire, the FRITOS® Brand has delivered a consistent product even though the faces have changed.

Today, the FRITOS® Brand is represented by NASCAR superstar Jeff Gordon and his #24 Racing Team. From 1998 to 2000, FRITOS® was an associate sponsor of Gordon's Busch Series PEPSI Racing Team. In 2001, FRITOS® and its sister company, PEPSI, became associate sponsors on Jeff Gordon's Winston Cup Racing Team. This valuable partnership allows the FRITOS® Brand to market its product to racing fans, who, as a group, are becoming an increasingly larger segment of mainstream America.

BRAND VALUES

Nothing but FRITOS® gives you the satisfaction you need when you're hungry. The classic corn taste and the hearty crunch fill you up and hold you over. Nothing Satisfies Like FRITOS®. The essence of the brand can be captured in one statement, "FRITOS® is the simple, hearty snack I can always count on to satisfy my hunger."

The brand identity is characterized as "classic, dependable, reliable, substantial, and satisfying." These unique product truths and values identify the brand. FRITOS® is truly a symbol of Americana and the American dream as illustrated by the Frito Company's roots in the Doolin family kitchen and its evolution as the number-one snack company in the world.

THINGS YOU DIDN'T KNOW ABOUT FRITOS®

- The Frito Company's Mexican restaurant, Casa de FRITOS®, opened in 1955 in Disneyland. The photo on the opposite page is of Frito Founder Elmer Doolin and Walt Disney with the Frito Kid.
- The first FRITOS® recipe book was printed in 1935.
- During its Silver Anniversary Year in 1957, FRITOS® sponsored the ABC Radio Network Program, *Don McNeill's Breakfast Club*.
- The popularity of FRITOS® is evident in its widespread availability: FRITOS® can be found just about everywhere, including 98 percent of the supermarkets and convenience stores in the United States.
- Over 250 million pounds of FRITOS® were produced in 2000 —about the weight of 100,000 automobiles.
- The "Family-Size" bag of FRITOS® in 1937 cost 15 cents in the supermarket.

Gateway™

THE MARKET

For more than a decade, the most recognizable manifestation of the Gateway brand was the company's ubiquitous black and white cow-spotted computer boxes. A frequent sight on both front porches and business loading docks, these boxes cemented Gateway into the public consciousness, and accelerated the company's rise to the top tier of the computer industry. These spotted boxes became such a potent corporate symbol that, in the latter half of the 1990s, Gateway incorporated a stylized version of the PC box into their company logo.

Times, however, change, and Gateway has wisely changed with them. Beginning in the late 1990s, Gateway had already broadened its focus beyond the PC with a variety of "Beyond the Box" offerings such as training and Internet service. With the saturation of the PC market following the Y2K ramp-up, and the overall decline of the global economy in the early 21st century, the need to decouple earnings from PC sales became critical to the company's future growth. The result was a radically different Gateway. Gone were the days when Gateway was simply a manufacturer and marketer of computers. On the consumer side, Gateway became an emerging force in the digital home entertainment market, stocking and/or selling digital photography systems, video cameras, MP3 players, and big-screen plasma televisions through its nationwide network of local Gateway® stores.

On the business and institutional side, Gateway complemented its PCs, notebooks, and servers with an increased emphasis on networking products and integration, eBusiness services, and other productivity-enhancing services and add-ons. By the end of 2002, Gateway had become a true digital solutions company with a new product line, a new outlook, a new logo, and an updated version of its famous cow-spotted boxes. Yet it still maintained the same "people focused" brand values that have become the hallmark of its business operations.

ACHIEVEMENTS

Perhaps Gateway's most important achievement is its ongoing ability to realign its product focus in response to changing market demands. Over the past 17 years, the company has evolved from a marketer of computer enhancements, to a top-tier PC manufacturer, to a provider of complete digital solutions. Along the way, Gateway has grown into a multibillion-dollar-a-year company, with stores located all across the United States. Although often regarded as a consumer company, Gateway has used its solutions-oriented approach to make significant gains in the competitive small and medium business market, to the point where business and institutional sales now account for nearly half of Gateway's total sales. In April 2002, *PC Magazine* recognized Gateway's growing prominence in this market with its Editor's Choice Award for Small Business Solutions.

Gateway's emerging role as a solutions provider was put to the ultimate test during the 2002 Olympic Winter Games. As the official computer hardware supplier to the Games, Gateway coordinated with software and communications vendors to integrate, deliver, and install over 5,400 fully customized Gateway® E-Series PCs, Gateway Profile® All-in-One computers, notebooks, and dual processor–ready servers to the Games. Due to the nature of the Games, Gateway systems were installed in some extraordinarily challenging operating environments. Yet the Gateway computers turned in a near flawless performance, earning words of high praise from the Salt Lake Olympic Committee, the press, and Gateway's technology partners.

HISTORY

Gateway was founded in September 1985 when friends Ted Waitt and Mike Hammond set up shop on the Waitt family cattle farm in Sioux City, Iowa. At that point, the PC world was in a state of transition. IBM PCs were emerging as the standard for both business and home, but there was still a large installed base of earlier technologies. When Computerland, one of the top PC retailers at the time, stopped selling parts and services for Texas Instrument (TI) PCs, Waitt and Hammond saw a potentially lucrative market niche. They seized the opportunity, and with a $10,000 loan from Waitt's grandmother, they began selling mail-order upgrades, parts, and software for TI computers. Waitt and Hammond ran the computer business from one of the farm buildings, taking and shipping orders in the day and often helping to unload cattle at night.

After just a little more than half a year of operations, they outgrew the farmhouse and moved to the historic Sioux City Livestock Exchange Building. By 1987, Gateway had recorded more than $1.5 million in sales and fully implemented the direct-sales-channel philosophy that still fuels its sales today. This direct-channel philosophy was a revolutionary approach at a time when most large PC manufacturers sold through resellers.

In 1988, Gateway ran its first national ad, and the company was rewarded with an 1,100 percent gain in year-over-year sales. Thanks to this explosive growth, Gateway once again outgrew its company headquarters, and in 1990 the company moved to the wide-open spaces of North Sioux City, South Dakota, where its cow-spotted buildings are still a local landmark.

Gateway became a publicly traded company in 1993 and cracked the Fortune 500. Soon after, it joined the elite ranks of multibillion-dollar computer companies. The first local Gateway store opened in 1996, laying the groundwork for the company's growth as a solutions provider, while its purchase of award-winning server manufacturer ALR in 1997 cemented its commitment to the business and institutional markets. Soon after, Gateway consolidated its corporate and business marketing operations in Southern California, although it still maintains extensive manufacturing, sales, and marketing facilities in South Dakota; several other sales, manufacturing, and support offices located throughout Kansas, Colorado, and Virginia; and hundreds of local Gateway stores from coast to coast.

THE PRODUCT

As would be expected, the Gateway product line of today is vastly different from the product line of 1985. TI computer parts and accessories have faded into the footnotes of history books, to be replaced by products as diverse as thin and light notebook computers and wide-screen plasma televisions. But one common thread has always run

Be Your Own DJ

College is all about freedom. You get to pick your own friends, your own food, your own music, maybe even a few classes here and there. Gateway digital music products give you the freedom you need to listen to the music you want to, when you want to. Download the latest promo tracks. Mix, match and burn CDs. Put it all on an MP3 player and turn off to class. Gateway has you covered with totally hot new PCs, notebooks, MP3 players, even training courses to help you put it all work together. And hey, you might even be able to use some of this stuff for school ;)

800-846-3000 | Click www.Gateway.com | Gateway

through the Gateway product line: Gateway sells solutions that allow customers to get more out of their technology investment and more out of life.

To do that, Gateway has become much more than a computer company. Certainly, PCs still account for a large part of the company's sales, but Gateway is also one of the nation's top training

vendors and a nationwide source for high-speed Internet access. Small businesses have come to rely on Gateway for its technology integration and support services, while consumers have discovered that their local Gateway stores are a great source for test driving and purchasing digital cameras, video cameras, MP3 players, widescreen plasma TVs, and a whole range of other digital accessories.

Nevertheless, Gateway still maintains a strong PC presence. In 2002, the entire product line underwent a complete redesign, resulting in some of the best-performing and best-looking PCs, notebooks, and servers around, as well as dozens of industry awards. The unique Gateway Profile 4, for instance, set new design standards and captured words of praise in venues as diverse as *C/Net* and *the Chicago Tribune*.

RECENT DEVELOPMENTS

In 2002, Gateway became a full-service electronics retailer, stocking an array of digital devices in its nationwide network of Gateway stores. Gateway also began offering high-speed, broadband Internet access through all of its stores, solidifying its position as a full-service digital technology provider. In recognition of its evolving business focus, Gateway launched a new logo and new branding campaign reflecting the company's added strengths.

PROMOTION

Gateway's first national magazine ad in 1988 featured the Waitt family cattle farm under the heading "Computers from Iowa?" The juxtaposition of Silicon Valley technology with heartland America contrasted greatly with the competitive ads of the day, and was credited with the sales explosion of 1988. Over the next few years, Gateway engaged in a number of unique — sometimes quirky — ads, often parodying movies and other popular social icons while poking fun at the computer establishment. Sales multiplied as the ads and Gateway's popular "You've got a friend in the

business."® tagline crept into the public consciousness.

But perhaps the most compelling promotional step ever taken by Gateway was the addition of cow spots to its shipping boxes in the early 1990s. The boxes became a conversation piece overnight, providing a constant reminder of the company's defining Midwestern roots and a bountiful source of free word-of-mouth advertising.

Gateway increased its visibility even further when it introduced its first national television spot in 1994. Starting in the late 1990s, the commercials were complemented with shrewd product placements of Gateway® PCs and Gateway-branded merchandise on popular shows such as *E.R.* Today, commercial television is an important element of Gateway's advertising strategies. Its newest spots echo the fun yet informative feel of the Web while still focusing on the benefits of technology on people's lives.

BRAND VALUES

From its earliest days, Gateway has positioned itself as a "people first" company — a direct extension of its Midwestern roots. Its mission is to empower people through the use of digital technology. This position has been a constant in Gateway's business efforts and is the very embodiment of the Gateway brand. It extends beyond Gateway's sales and marketing efforts and into local communities across the nation, where Gateway has donated thousands of PCs to Boys and Girls Clubs and other organizations as it works to make the digital revolution accessible to everyone.

THINGS YOU DIDN'T KNOW ABOUT GATEWAY

- During the 2002 Olympic Winter Games, Gateway employees traveled to Afghanistan to provide e-mail communications between the troops of Operation Enduring Freedom and the athletes in Salt Lake City, Utah. U.S. troops were also able to use the equipment to e-mail loved ones at home.

- The first digital signing of an official document by two world leaders occurred on a Gateway notebook PC, when U.S. President Bill Clinton and Ireland's Prime Minister Bertie Ahern signed an international electronic commerce agreement using a Gateway Solo® 3100 notebook PC.

- Working with Buena Vista University, Gateway helped to create one of the nation's first campus-wide wireless networks.

- Following the 2002 Olympic Winter Games, Gateway donated most of the more than 5,400 Gateway® PCs used for the Games to schools and charities across the United States.

THE MARKET

Born on the playing field in the late 1960s as part of a mission by scientists to help athletes prevent dehydration and perform at their best, Gatorade created the sports drink category. Today, more than 35 years later, Gatorade Thirst Quencher has become an American sports icon and a $2 billion-plus business. Gatorade is the unequivocal category leader with an 85 percent share of the market and availability in 47 countries around the world. Extensive ongoing research continues to prove that nothing rehydrates, replenishes, and refuels athletes better than Gatorade.

With a place on the sidelines, in the locker rooms, and on almost every field of play, Gatorade has become an essential part of the equipment of sports; many of the best athletes in the world at every level of competition drink Gatorade.

ACHIEVEMENTS

The success of the brand is a direct result of its functionality and commitment to being the optimal hydrator for athletes. In fact, more than thirty-five years of research now support the quality of the product. Established in 1988, the Gatorade Sports Science Institute (GSSI) has conducted and published research in leading scientific journals as well as educated sports health professionals and athletes on sports nutrition and exercise science. The information provided to athletes helps them understand how they can fuel themselves so they not only feel better but also perform better when training or competing. Located in Barrington, Illinois, GSSI also works with scientists from major universities around the world to further research and expand knowledge in exercise science and sports nutrition. In collaboration with these scientists, GSSI researchers produce educational materials for the continuing education of members of the sports science community. As the leading facility of its kind, GSSI has tested hundreds of athletes from around the world to show how nutrition and hydration affect athletic performance.

As the unparalleled leader in hydration, Gatorade has long been the preferred sports drink of most professional sports leagues and is a fixture on the sidelines of the National Football League (NFL), National Basketball Association (NBA), Major League Baseball (MLB), and U.S. Soccer Federation, among others.

The Gatorade Company has also developed formal relationships with many of the most prestigious sports health professional organizations, affiliations, and events in the world of sports.

HISTORY

The Gatorade name hails from the University of Florida football team, the Gators. Researchers at the university were looking for a way to help prevent the dehydration and cramping the team experienced because of their physical exertion in the heat. After analyzing players' sweat to see what they were losing, the scientists created a drink to help improve hydration, replace lost electrolytes, and provide much-needed energy to muscles.

In 1967, with the help of Gatorade, the Gators had become known as the "second-half team" by outplaying opponents during the second half of their games. Their ability to dominate in the third and fourth quarters led the Gators to win the Orange Bowl that year. When asked to comment on the game, the coach for the defeated Georgia Tech team, Ray Graves, was quoted in *Sports Illustrated* as saying, "We didn't have Gatorade. That made the difference."

In 1967, Stokely-Van Camp acquired the rights to produce and sell Gatorade. By the 1970s, Gatorade had become a staple on the sidelines in football, baseball, basketball, tennis, golf, track and field, and marathons, as well as stock-car racing.

The Quaker Oats Company acquired Stokely-Van Camp, including the Gatorade Thirst Quencher brand, in 1983. Four years later, the famous Gatorade "dunk" was born. The "dunk" became legendary when players Jim Burt and Harry Carson dumped Gatorade on Head Coach Bill Parcells during the Giants' 1987 Super Bowl–winning season.

Over the next decade, Gatorade expanded its brand presence across the globe by introducing the product in Australia, Mexico, Singapore, Brazil, China, Indonesia, Colombia, the Philippines, the Middle East, and South Africa.

In 2001, PepsiCo, Inc. acquired The Quaker Oats Company, including the Gatorade brand, creating a company sharply focused on convenient food and beverages. With pro-forma revenues

of about $25 billion, PepsiCo ranks as the world's fifth-largest food and beverage company.

THE PRODUCT

Gatorade Thirst Quencher is formulated to help rapidly replace the energy used, and the fluids and electrolytes lost, during physical activity.

The reason that Gatorade was created — to help athletes prevent dehydration and perform at their best — continues to be the brand's driving force. Gatorade is the most thoroughly researched sports beverage in the world, and ongoing research ensures that Gatorade continues to rehydrate, replenish, and refuel an athlete's body.

With its extensive study of hot and sweaty athletes, The Gatorade Company continues to innovate in the sports drink category with new products, packages, and flavors that help meet athletes' needs. In addition to the original Gatorade mainline flavors of Lemon-lime, Orange, and Fruit Punch, the brand has introduced specialized sublines — all with the same scientifically based formula as the original flavors — to appeal to a variety of taste preferences. In 1997, the brand launched Gatorade Frost, a lighter, crisper-tasting Gatorade, and in 1999 launched Gatorade Fierce, a more intensely flavored Gatorade. In 2001, the brand unveiled the Gatorade E.D.G.E. bottle (the *E*rgonomically *D*esigned *G*atorade *E*xperience) to provide a unique sport-bottle packaging that makes the product easier to drink when active.

The Gatorade product portfolio also includes the Gatorade Performance Series (GPS) developed specifically for college and professional athletes. In addition to Gatorade Thirst Quencher, the GPS includes Gatorade Energy Bar, Gatorade Energy Drink, and Gatorade Nutrition Shake to help meet the nutritional needs of athletes.

RECENT DEVELOPMENTS

In 2002, The Gatorade Company continued its long-standing tradition of bringing innovative products to the sports drink category with the introduction of several new offerings to meet the unique needs of its consumers. The Gatorade Company launched the Gatorade Ice subline as a

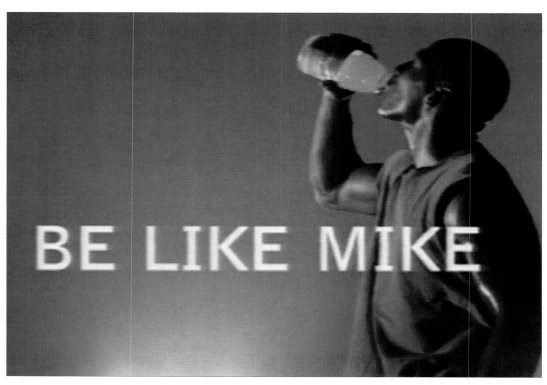

clear, crisp, clean-tasting Gatorade in three flavors: Orange, Lime, and Strawberry. A new Gatorade subline was also developed for Latino consumers, called Gatorade Xtremo, in flavors of Tropical, Citrico, and Mango. Gatorade All-Stars – a six-pack of Gatorade in smaller 12-ounce bottles that provide just the right size for tweens (ages 8–12) during casual play — was also introduced in 2002.

The Gatorade Company has leveraged its expertise in understanding the hydration needs of active people to introduce the first-ever fitness water. Introduced nationally in 2002, Propel Fitness Water is a lightly flavored, low-calorie water with vitamins, created for active people who typically drink plain water. Research shows that active people only replace about half the fluid they need to stay hydrated when they drink plain water during exercise. The light flavor in Propel helps people drink more so they can stay better hydrated and make the most of their workouts.

PROMOTION

Over the years, Gatorade has created several unforgettable advertising campaigns. With celebrated sports icons such as Michael Jordan, Derek Jeter, Vince Carter, and Mia Hamm, Gatorade continues to produce iconic campaigns that take their place among American pop culture.

In the 1980s, Gatorade appealed to Americans with its famous jingle, "Gatorade is thirst aid, for that deep-down body thirst." In the 1990s, Gatorade initiated its partnership with Michael Jordan and produced the memorable "Be Like Mike" commercials. Later in the 1990s, Gatorade introduced the popular "Is It In You? " series featuring athletes producing colored sweat in

green, blue, and orange — colors associated with popular Gatorade flavors.

As the brand celebrated its 35th anniversary in 2002, Gatorade introduced a new ad called "Origins," chronicling the true story of the invention of Gatorade. The commercial included appearances by inventors Dr. Robert Cade and Dr. Dana Shires, and Chip Hinton, a former Gator linebacker and original Gatorade "guinea pig." The television spot tells the amazing story of how a research project on the fields of the University of Florida has evolved into one of the most trusted and highly recognized brand names of all time. As the commercial poignantly notes with its final tagline, the legend continues.

BRAND VALUES

The Gatorade Company's strength lies in its ongoing commitment to help athletes perform at their best. For more than 30 years, Gatorade products have dominated the sports beverage industry and today are considered to be a basic part of sports equipment by many health practitioners, coaches, athletic trainers, and athletes.

For Gatorade, "Is It In You?" is not just an advertising tag line. The question resonates at the heart of the ongoing growth and success of the Gatorade brand.

THINGS YOU DIDN'T KNOW ABOUT GATORADE

○ Lemon-lime was the first Gatorade flavor, and is still the most popular, followed by Orange and Fruit Punch.

○ In 2001, NFL teams drank more than 10,000 gallons of Gatorade.

○ In a recent survey, 2.1 percent of those polled believed Gatorade contains "alligator juice" as its secret ingredient.

GEICO DIRECT

THE MARKET

The GEICO family of companies operates primarily in the private-passenger auto insurance market. This highly fragmented industry is one of the most competitive arenas of American business, as companies go to extreme lengths to maintain market share. Despite this difficult business environment, GEICO has experienced unprecedented growth over the last few years, doubling in size since 1997 to become the fifth-largest automobile insurer in the country, with almost 5 million policies in force.

ACHIEVEMENTS

For more than 65 years, GEICO has remained loyal to its customers by keeping costs low and passing the savings on to policyholders through attractive rates. The company is the premier "direct" writer of insurance, selling directly to the consumer as opposed to using the more traditional network of local agents.

Over the years, the company has refined and improved upon the direct model approach, using direct mail and other marketing initiatives to attract customers to its toll-free number. Well ahead of the competition, the company in 1981 introduced 24-hour, 365-day telephone service for sales, service, and claims. GEICO was the first major carrier to offer this service to its customers and remains one of the few providing complete 24-hour service.

In 1995, GEICO started using the service mark "GEICO Direct" in all its marketing materials to highlight the key difference between GEICO and most other major insurance companies. The service mark is highly visible in the company's television and print campaigns. The introduction of the GEICO Direct name coincided with a significant increase in advertising expenditures, aimed at capturing a much larger share of the private-passenger auto insurance market. The increased marketing budget, coupled with the use of humor in the commercials (a rarity in the stodgy insurance industry), has made the GEICO Direct brand one of the most visible in the insurance industry. GEICO now places among the top three insurance companies in brand recall among consumers; it wasn't even in the top ten a decade ago.

HISTORY

GEICO founder Leo Goodwin joined the insurance industry in 1925 when he was offered a job with San Antonio–based United Services Automobile Association (USAA). Over the next nine years he learned the technical intricacies of the insurance business while rising steadily through the ranks to the position of general manager. Goodwin had progressed as high as he could go in the company because only a retired military officer was allowed to hold the top spot at USAA. So he took a leap of faith by leaving USAA to start his own insurance company during the height of the Great Depression.

Goodwin took a page out of the USAA book — which he himself helped create — by choosing a very select group of consumers for his customer base: federal employees and non-commissioned officers. But rather than offer dividends to customers for any favorable loss experience, as mutual companies do, Goodwin chose to sell policies at discounted rates and pass the savings directly along to customers right up front. He also marketed directly to his customer base, allowing him to charge lower premiums and still earn a profit. These same tenets make up the essentials of the GEICO business model that remains successful today.

By the end of World War II, GEICO sales soared to $1.6 million and then to $2.4 million the following year, due in large part to the growing number of cars in production and improvements in roads, availability of gasoline, and the overall improving economy. The decade ended on a high note in 1949 with GEICO creating a life insurance company and an auto finance company.

The next two decades were a period of enormous growth for the company, as policies in force passed 2 million. But the days of strong growth had a downside, as the company's loss reserves dwindled because of underwriting and investment losses. Chairman and CEO Jack Byrne arrived in 1976 to turn things around. He developed a recovery plan that included the strictest of cost controls and a complete reunderwriting of the company's entire book of business. The plan worked, quickly returning GEICO to profitability.

The late 1970s and early 1980s brought GEICO back to financial health, and the company embarked on a mission to build stronger internal operations to better service its customers. In 1994, GEICO launched its four-company strategy (see next page), now offering rate quotes and policies to people who did not meet GEICO's preferred-risk guidelines. The new inclusion of standard-

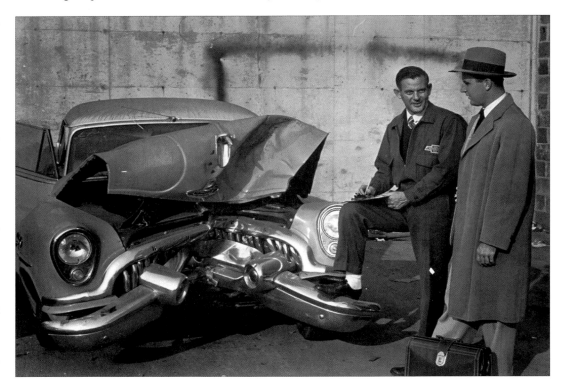

and nonstandard-risk business coincided with a large increase in advertising.

THE PRODUCT

The GEICO Companies offer lower-cost auto insurance coverage to consumers through a four-company strategy:

• Government Employees Insurance Company — preferred-risk coverage to military and government employees.

• GEICO General Insurance Company — preferred-risk coverage to nonmilitary and non-government customers.

• GEICO Indemnity Company — standard-risk business.

• GEICO Casualty Company — nonstandard-risk business.

The four companies operate collectively under the GEICO Direct service mark. GEICO sells its policies over the phone, on the Internet, and through a network of local offices located near major military installations throughout the country.

In addition to auto insurance, GEICO offers many other outstanding products, such as emergency road service coverage, mechanical breakdown insurance, motorcycle insurance, and umbrella liability policies. Auto coverage is also available in more than 200 countries overseas.

RECENT DEVELOPMENTS

The year 1996 was significant in GEICO's history as it became a wholly owned subsidiary of Berkshire Hathaway, Warren Buffett's investment organization. Buffett first purchased GEICO stock in 1951. His holdings grew in percentage terms due to GEICO's own corporate stock repurchases, until he owned more than half of all outstanding shares. In 1995, Buffett, through Berkshire Hathaway, made a bid to purchase the remaining shares of GEICO's outstanding stock. Shareholders responded favorably to the offer and GEICO became part of the Berkshire Hathaway family of companies.

GEICO's Web site, geico.com, which allows users to get a free rate quote and coverage information, also went online in 1996, and the company has continued to refine and enhance its Web site since then. Customers choosing to do business over the Internet can now complete many sales, service, and claims transactions online. The site is also available in Spanish, catering to GEICO's growing Hispanic customer base.

The Internet was an ideal fit for GEICO, which has more than six decades of dealing with customers using a direct model. The site continues to increase rapidly in popularity, and has already set weekly records for quotes and sales several times in 2002.

PROMOTION

Awareness of GEICO has soared in recent years, thanks to a large increase in television advertising. The company uses humor to differentiate the spots from the serious tone found in most insurance advertising. Ads such as a dog laughing at his owner's insurance bill and a claims spot showing a jogger colliding with a fake deer convey an upbeat tone for a product that many consumers view as a necessary evil. Of course, too, there's the GEICO Gecko, the company's hugely popular "spokescreature" that burst onto the scene in 1999 in a 15-second "press conference" spot that made him a star.

Since this first ad appeared, the Gecko has starred in numerous commercials, several direct mail campaigns, and outdoor advertising. The campaign has proven hugely successful, particularly among children. These youngsters may not be of driving age yet, but it's never too soon to familiarize them with the GEICO name or have them influence their parents' purchasing decisions.

BRAND VALUES

GEICO aims to be the insurance industry's low-cost operator, passing the savings on to customers in the form of lower premiums, but the GEICO brand stands for much more than low prices. The true value of GEICO auto insurance stems from the outstanding service GEICO provides to its customers.

As one of the first companies to offer 24-hour, 7-day-a-week, 365-day-a-year policy service via toll-free telephone numbers, GEICO pioneered in auto insurance what is today a service standard across industries. Now, with the easy-to-use Web

site geico.com, customers can access and update policy information on their own, anytime.

GEICO claim service also receives high marks from policyholders. In a recent GEICO survey, claim satisfaction levels reached an all-time high, as well over 90 percent of claimants surveyed rated GEICO service good or excellent.

The company-wide emphasis on providing excellent service is part of GEICO's roots. When a severe hailstorm hit Washington, D.C., in 1941, founder Leo Goodwin anticipated the huge call for windshield repairs. Practically before the last hailstone hit the ground, Goodwin had already arranged for several local glass repair shops to work 24 hours a day exclusively for GEICO. He even had truckloads of auto glass on hand in anticipation of the glass shortage that occurred after the storm. This swift response to an emergency set the GEICO standard for policyholder service that still holds firm today.

THINGS YOU DIDN'T KNOW ABOUT GEICO

○ GEICO stands for Government Employees Insurance Company. The company originally offered insurance only to government employees and noncommissioned officers because of their steady income and better-than-average driving records.

○ GEICO is the largest insurer of U.S. enlisted military personnel, with almost a 40 percent market share.

○ From one tiny corporate office in Washington, D.C., GEICO has grown into a nationwide network of regional offices located in eight states: California, Florida, Georgia, Hawaii, Iowa, Maryland, New York, and Virginia. GEICO serves policyholders in 48 states and the District of Columbia from these regional sites.

○ GEICO experimented with several different voices for the GEICO Gecko, including a Scottish brogue and a southern accent, before choosing a British accent. The proper English voice seemed the funniest coming from this little green creature. The voiceovers are actually recorded in Britain using a British actor.

GUARDSMARK®

THE MARKET

According to the FBI, crime is on the rise. In fact, the total number of crimes rose 2.1 percent last year, the first increase from year to year since 1991. Robberies rose 3.7 percent, while property crimes such as burglary, larceny, and arson rose 2.3 percent, to 10.4 million cases. The total value of stolen property reached $17.1 billion.

Reliable security has never been more important. But trying to find the right security firm can

be largely problematic, given that the market for security is heavily splintered, with over 13,000 "mom and pop" companies across the United States that operate with no clear standards. Foreign conglomerates have acquired many of the larger-sized security firms.

Guardsmark, one of the world's largest security services organizations, has consistently set the highest standards of professionalism in the security industry for 40 years. Under the same leadership since its inception, Guardsmark brings integrity and unmatched experience to the security market by establishing the most rigorous employment processes, providing above-market employee compensation and benefits, and strictly following a detailed ethics policy.

ACHIEVEMENTS

Guardsmark believes that reliable and effective security begins with a set of common standards and ethical practices. Guardsmark has become one of the most recognized names in private security, with 18,000 employees in more than 145 offices, serving clients in over 400 cities in North America by offering professional, well-trained security officers that abide by Guardsmark's strict ethical guidelines. Guardsmark's client relationships, some of which have lasted for decades, have turned Guardsmark into a half-billion-dollar company, with consistent double-digit annual revenue increases that are driven wholly by organic growth, not acquisitions or mergers.

Guardsmark has one of the lowest incident levels of any security organization, including the police and the FBI, by bringing a seriousness of purpose to management's approach to security. Guardsmark's rigorous selection and screening process, including extensive background checks and ongoing drug testing, isn't simply the toughest in private security — Guardsmark's employment standards exceed many police and government organizations. Only one in 50 applicants is chosen, and Guardsmark has one of the lowest employee turnover rates in the industry — less than 25 percent of estimated industry averages. Security officers at Guardsmark develop careers at the firm, not just transitional jobs.

Guardsmark has tackled the pitfalls that have plagued the security industry by following a detailed Code of Ethics, one that adheres to principled business conduct and an unparalleled commitment to offering the best security — regardless of profit motivation. That's why Guardsmark withdrew from airport security in 1988, believing that the airlines were not committed to supporting true security for their industry. As a result of the company's dedication to ethics, Guardsmark is a recipient of the American Business Ethics Award and the 2002 Corporate Citizenship Award from the Committee for Economic Development. Guardsmark's ethics program has also been featured in several books, including *Ethics Matters* and *Eighty Exemplary Ethics Statements.*

Guardsmark is the only security services firm to receive at its U.S. home office and several branch offices ISO 9001 registration — a top registration program in American business that recognizes select firms who have adhered to a superior-quality control system with a detailed and effective workflow. In his bestseller *Liberation Management,* management expert Tom Peters praised Guardsmark as the "Tiffany's of the security business." *The New York Times, The Washington Post,* and *Time* magazine among many others have described Guardsmark as the best national firm in the business.

HISTORY

Following the end of World War II, demand for proprietary security services began to grow, particularly in the aerospace and defense industries. At that time, security meant employing a static "night watchman" — an often-unskilled person who simply provided "presence" and qualified companies for discounted insurance rates. The typical security guard was passive, untrained, and — in many cases — unnecessarily armed.

In the early 1960s, a young Ira Lipman witnessed firsthand the need for high-quality security service while selling the investigative services of his father, Mark Lipman. At the age of 21, Ira Lipman created the concept of Guardsmark: a name that combined the nature of the business (protection services) with "mark," which not only honored his father but also carried the connotation of quality and excellence.

In July 1963, Mr. Lipman turned his dream of a professional security service company based on quality and ethics into a reality. Ira Lipman started Guardsmark with limited assets — a small amount of borrowed money, his entrepreneurial energy and vision — but it was enough to launch one of the great success stories in American business.

THE PRODUCT

Guardsmark creates and implements custom-tailored security programs for clients in a wide range of industries and settings, from corporate headquarters and high-technology facilities to manufacturing plants, research and development centers, office buildings, hospitals, campuses, museums, and foundations. These sophisticated plans address a multitude of needs, from access

control and perimeter security to terrorism and workplace violence prevention — all with the overall goal of ensuring employee safety and business continuity.

Guardsmark's security officers are the best in the industry because Guardsmark has set the highest standards in screening, hiring, training, and compensation. Guardsmark's selection process includes an extensive background investigation that includes a 40-page application, personal interviews, a criminal records check, numerous references, and investigations into military service, driving records, and educational attainment. All Guardsmark employees are initially tested for twice the number of illegal drugs as government employees and are subject to ongoing random drug testing.

In addition to an initial, industry-leading training process that includes specialized classroom sessions, Guardsmark training includes documented monthly learning and development lessons, and access to Guardsmark's vast library of CD-ROMs

that address topics such as diversity, workplace violence, letter bombs, and biological and chemical warfare. Guardsmark's emphasis on education doesn't end with security; employees are also offered a tuition assistance program. Guardsmark has been named the best-educated workforce in the field by a major trade journal.

Guardsmark clients gain access to a wide range of expertise, from proprietary conversion specialists to former counterterrorism agents. Guardsmark's service offerings include:
- The Worldwide Executive Protection Division, which designs and provides protective services for executives, their homes, their families, and the human assets of their companies. The division offers comprehensive service in the workplace, in transit and at executive residences, giving guidance in handling daily routines, direct threat situations, and special events.
- The Technical Services Division, which surveys client security needs, performing risk assessments and threat analyses. Guardsmark experts recommend and implement an innovative plan for enhancing security, giving the organization a comprehensive strategy to guide their overall protection program.
  - The Mark Lipman Division, which provides highly regarded backgrounding services. In addition, skilled professionals investigate employee theft, fraud, workers' compensation abuse, and drugs in the workplace.

RECENT DEVELOPMENTS

The company's historic dedication to meeting needs of customers and prospective clients served well in the wake of the terrorist attacks on September 11, 2001. Guardsmark initiated an emergency nationwide action plan, meeting all demands for additional security coverage and disseminating information it had published on terrorism. A new Guardsmark CD-ROM, which addressed biological and chemical warfare and had been in production for several months prior to the September 11 assaults, was effectively used by Guardsmark clients around the nation.

Guardsmark remains on the cutting edge of security-related innovations and developments that pertain to antiterrorism procedures and computer security, among other areas. That's why Guardsmark's senior management includes dozens of retired top officials from the FBI, with experience in security countermeasures, counterterrorism, and military operations.

PROMOTION

Guardsmark is committed to dispelling the myth of security as a "commodity." Guardsmark continually seeks value for the customer that saves reputation, prevents loss of life, and provides crisis management. As one example, a Midwestern company facing a crisis at a major facility turned to Guardsmark, and in short order, Guardsmark produced 150 managers, security officers, and former police officers.

The Lipman Report®, a management-level newsletter, has provided cutting-edge intelligence since November 1977. Each edition addresses a

specific security threat, including terrorism, workplace violence, computer security, crime trends, and drugs in the workplace. The newest volume, published in 2002, features newsletters on theft, fraud, and embezzlement.

Guardsmark also stands out with high-quality, informative advertisements in major national publications that reflect an uncompromising focus on ethical standards and seriousness of purpose. But the company firmly believes that it's one thing to say the right things about security; it's another to implement them. Guardsmark has built solid relationships with its clients that have lasted for decades by developing meaningful security solutions that work, not by creating effective advertising.

BRAND VALUES

Guardsmark's motto — "Truth, Courage and Judgement" — is the cornerstone of the company's value system. Guardsmark has maintained a steadfast commitment to quality and principle that's evident in the faces of Guardsmark security officers and corporate management.

Guardsmark has been a pioneer in employing and promoting team members from diverse backgrounds. The company and its founder share a documented history of taking courageous stands on championing human rights and encouraging diversity. Above all else, Guardsmark is relentlessly focused on developing dedicated, highly trained, and highly motivated security professionals.

THINGS YOU DIDN'T KNOW ABOUT GUARDSMARK

- ○ Guardsmark is the largest employer of former FBI agents in the world.

- ○ Guardsmark's intensive 40-page application for employment asks the applicant to provide a detailed life history since the age of five.

- ○ As a high school senior in Little Rock, Arkansas, CEO Ira Lipman publicly denounced segregation at Central High School, which became integrated with the addition of the "Little Rock Nine."

- ○ *The New York Times* editorially praised Guardsmark for reducing the number of unnecessarily armed security officers, an action that cost the company a significant amount of business at the time.

THE MARKET

Denim wear has evolved drastically in past years from its origin as basic work attire to a highly fashionable and profitable business that is now a $10 billion industry in the United States. From high-end haute couture designers to mass-market retailers, everyone in the fashion industry wants a piece of this lucrative business. In the prevailing denim war, GUESS? has come out on top with innovative designs, original washes, and stylish trends.

ACHIEVEMENTS

GUESS? has grown from a small California jeans company in 1981 into GUESS?, Inc., a global lifestyle brand. While jeans form the foundation of the company's history and success, GUESS? designs, markets, and distributes full collections of women's, men's, and children's apparel, as well as accessories. GUESS? became a public company in August 1996, and three of the Marciano brothers still head up the company. GUESS? has successfully granted licenses for the manufacture and distribution of many of its product categories. Additionally, GUESS? has licensees and distributors worldwide.

The GUESS? retail environment encompasses freestanding stores and in-store shops in some of the world's most prestigious malls and department stores. The GUESS? wholesale business is represented in approximately 1,900 department store

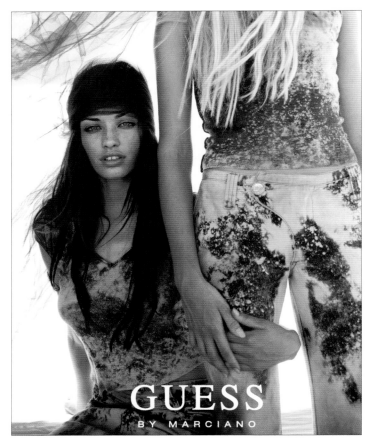

GUESS
BY MARCIANO

GUESS
BY MARCIANO

and specialty store locations. Approximately 1,135 in-store GUESS? shops are available to young men and women throughout the United States. Domestically, GUESS? has approximately 200 retail stores, including outlet stores and GUESS? Kids stores.

Through licensee and distributor arrangements and its store network, the company has attained a worldwide presence with over 400 stores in 42 countries now featuring the GUESS? brand. GUESS? derives its net revenue from the sale of GUESS? men's and women's apparel and licensed products through its network of retail and factory outlets primarily in the United States and Canada; their on-line store, *www.guess.com*; worldwide sale to wholesale customers and distributors; and net royalties from worldwide licensing activities.

Reaching out to the community is an essential aspect of the GUESS? mission. The GUESS? Foundation was established in 1994 as an extension of the company's view of the need for philanthropy and its sense of corporate responsibility. The scope of the nonprofit organizations it supports grows each year. The foundation devotes careful attention to requests for financial assistance and is a benefactor to organizations that work in many areas, including improving public

education, assisting the homeless, and preserving and protecting the environment. The GUESS? Foundation has supported cancer and AIDS research and treatment, disaster relief, and many other causes. GUESS? Community Outreach donates time, money, food, and GUESS? merchandise to help organizations that reach the needy in many communities.

Paul Marciano is a true visionary who has shaped the direction and look of GUESS? advertising from its inception. Recognized by its industry peers, GUESS? advertising has won every prestigious design award including the coveted CLIO Award, the Belding Award, the One Show, the London National Advertising Award, the P.I.A. Award, the Mobius Award, and the Benny Award, among many others. The Metropolitan Museum of Art selected the GUESS? Press Book and Nashville catalogue for the museum's Permanent Library Collection.

HISTORY

In the early 1980s, fashion jeans had little direction. People felt denim was dated, and jeans were not considered a fashion statement. Combining a love of the American West with a European sensibility, the Marciano brothers, creators of GUESS? Inc., would change that perception forever. Raised in Marseilles, France — a region that cultivated a passionate understanding of French design and the essence of style — the Marcianos' designs were timeless, sensuous, strong, and chic. The GUESS? approach was fresh and set the standard for the future of denim.

Initially, retailers greeted GUESS? with skepticism. Buyers weren't interested in denim, but the brothers' infallible instincts and persistence prevailed. Their three-zip stone-washed Marilyn jean was sexy, with a unique style and attitude. Bloomingdale's finally agreed to sell two dozen pairs of the three-zip Marilyn jean as a favor to the Marciano brothers. The entire stock sold out within hours, and the rest of the GUESS? history reflects an exciting synergy of product and image.

GUESS? quickly infiltrated popular culture and became a late-twentieth-century icon. GUESS? created groundbreaking advertising campaigns featuring sultry models previously unknown in the industry and turned them overnight into superstars. Models such as Claudia Schiffer, Carrè Otis, Laetitia Casta, Eva Herzigova, and Naomi Campbell launched their careers in the original

GUESS? campaigns. Directed by the keen eye of Paul Marciano and shot by then unfamiliar photographers such as Wayne Maser, Ellen Von Unwerth, Neil Kirk, and Raphael Mazzucco, the GUESS? brand was brought to life from the deserts of the American West, to the beaches of Rio and in the streets of Paris.

With striking images and fresh new product, the brand began gaining momentum and nationwide recognition. In the 1980s, GUESS? product expanded beyond jeans to include Baby GUESS?, GUESS? Watches, GUESS? Footwear, GUESS? Eyewear and GUESS? Parfum. In the 1990s, rapid international expansion brought the GUESS? American tradition to Europe, Asia, South America, Africa, Australia, and the Middle East. The second decade of GUESS? also brought the introduction of GUESS? Collection, GUESS? Handbags, Activewear, Jewelry, Swimwear, Golf, Home, Innerwear, Leather, Athletic, Belts, Neckwear, and Men's Classics. In the mid-'90s, GUESS? became a public company and launched its first Web site, *www.guess.com.* Prior to the new millennium, *www.guess.com* became an E-commerce site, and the GUESS? family continued to grow in 2000 with the launch of *GUESSKids.com* and *babyGUESS.com.*

THE PRODUCT

GUESS?' spirited philosophy is conveyed through its design sensibility. GUESS? style celebrates the human form, demonstrated not only by the truly spectacular faces who grace GUESS? signature photos, but more importantly by the very real customers who are the true inspiration. With a touch of international flair, the all-American style of GUESS? has always been original. GUESS? fashions feature great attention to detail and a European passion for cut and

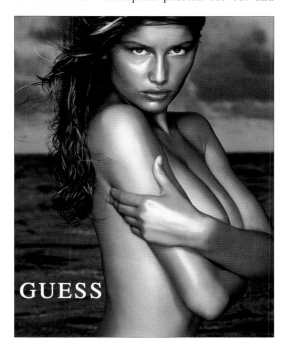

fit. Quality and attitude set GUESS? apart, running the gamut from casual hip to downtown chic. The look of GUESS? is classic yet stylish and modern in every sense. The GUESS? customer has developed his or her own personal fashion identity, finding a balance between the fantasy of fashion and the reality of life. Known for quality, trend setting, and marketing creativity, the company designs and markets a leading lifestyle

collection of casual apparel and accessories for men, women, children, and babies. GUESS? licensed products now include footwear, eyewear, belts, jewelry, leather, swimwear, watches, and handbags.

RECENT DEVELOPMENTS

Two decades after the birth of the first GUESS? jean, the Marciano brothers — Maurice, Paul, and Armand — continue to guide the company. Co-Chairman and Co–Chief Executive Officer Maurice Marciano has overseen the company's design direction and led its unwavering and extraordinary expansion since 1982. Co-Chairman and Co–Chief Executive Officer Paul Marciano is credited with the vision behind the GUESS? image and is responsible for creating some of the most innovative images in advertising; he also oversees licensing, e-commerce, and the retail business. Senior Executive Vice President Armand Marciano directs processing, factory stores, and customer relations for GUESS?.

Moving into the 21st century, GUESS? continues to challenge its already high standards to remain a driving force in the world of fashion. With revenues of $678 million in 2001, GUESS? sells clothing and accessories to enhance the casual lifestyle of people with a flair for individualism. In the fall of 2000, GUESS?, Inc., introduced G Brand, a complete line of superior men's and women's jeanswear. Using the highest quality ring-spun denim imported from Italy and European designs, this line stands alone in a saturated industry. G Brand can be purchased in select GUESS? retail stores or at *www.guess.com.*

PROMOTION

The image of the GUESS? model has become a pop culture icon in fashion advertising. Accessible yet mysterious, the GUESS? Girl is portrayed as confident, spirited, and sensuous. The captivating images enable the viewer to act as voyeur, glimpsing what is simultaneously public and private. The GUESS? image is defined by its simplicity, proving that great design and creativity need not be overly complex. GUESS? images have been showcased in international print campaigns in virtually all major magazines, on television, billboards, bus shelters, and telephone kiosks throughout the world.

BRAND VALUES

GUESS?, Inc., is one of the most recognized and influential brand names in the fashion world today. The label stands for quality and an innovative, distinctive product design that consistently satisfies its customers. For two decades, GUESS? has been on the cutting edge of fashion and style with industry-leading designs and unparalleled creativity in its advertising and marketing. GUESS? incorporates a timeless quality into every product it creates for men, women, and children, as well as home. As it expands to fulfill every aspect of its customers' lifestyles, the company remains true to its original inspiration.

THINGS YOU DIDN'T KNOW ABOUT GUESS

- ❍ The numbers inside the triangle logo represent the suite numbers of the first GUESS? offices.
- ❍ The name GUESS? was inspired by a billboard spotted by Georges Marciano that read, "Guess what's in a Big Mac?"
- ❍ Approximately 30 people are involved in producing one pair of GUESS? jeans.
- ❍ GUESS? advertising campaigns have jump-started 85 percent of their models to become household names.
- ❍ The Metropolitan Museum of Art features GUESS? advertisements as part of its permanent library collection.
- ❍ Juliette Lewis, Drew Barrymore, Mila Kunis, and Tom Skerritt were all GUESS? models.

THE MARKET

Look into any closet or drawer in America. Chances are that you'll find something with the *Hanes* label. Since producing its first union suit in 1901, *Hanes* has grown from a basic line of men's underwear to the leader in men's, women's, and children's clothing, including socks, shoes, underwear, and casual apparel. Today, *Hanes* is the number-one brand of apparel in America.

Established as a quality brand that meant both comfort and value, the *Hanes* brand heritage drove its growth from a regional brand to the powerhouse it is today. As the retail landscape evolved over the decades, *Hanes* evolved to meet the changing needs of consumers. Initially sold through distributors to department stores nationwide, *Hanes* is now the number-one brand at large mass retailers, who since the early 1990s sell more basic apparel — underwear, socks, and casual clothing — than any other retail channel. Today, more than 40 percent of all apparel sold in the United States is purchased at mass retailers.

ACHIEVEMENTS

Across every segment, from casual apparel and underwear to intimate apparel and socks, *Hanes* and *Hanes Her Way* lead almost every consumer survey in brand recognition and reputation. Every year, retailers from across the country recognize *Hanes* and *Hanes Her Way* for their contributions to the business landscape through Vendor of the Year and Vendor of the Quarter awards. Virtually every year since it has been given, *Hanes* and *Hanes Her Way* also have won the prestigious SPARC Award (Supplier Performance Award by Retail Category), a national program organized by *DSN Retailing Today* magazine.

Hanes and *Hanes Her Way* have been consistently rated the number-one men's and women's apparel brand in a biennial survey by *DSN Retailing Today* magazine. *Hanes Her Way* also has been recognized for many years in a biennial survey conducted by Fairchild Publications on brand awareness called the Fairchild 100. In the most recent survey, *Hanes Her Way* ranked fourth among all women's fashion brands. But perhaps the most meaningful tribute to the brand were the results of a recent survey by NPD Group Inc., rating *Hanes/Hanes Her Way* as the most comfortable and best-fitting brand in America.

HISTORY

In 1901, Pleasant (P. H.) Hanes formed the P. H. Hanes Knitting Company to produce underwear for men. As an extension of the one-piece wool underwear that was the standard, Hanes introduced two-piece underwear, a radical departure from the traditional style for that time. The same year, brother J. Wesley Hanes formed the Shamrock Mills Company to produce men's hosiery. By 1920, both companies had expanded and refocused — P. H. Hanes into undershirts, briefs, sleepwear, and knitted shorts, and Hanes Hosiery, as it was renamed, into the new market of women's hosiery.

Even through the struggles of the Great Depression, both the Hanes Knitting Company and Hanes Hosiery grew into strong and prosperous companies. In the 1940s, both companies participated and contributed greatly to the WWII effort, supplying underwear for servicemen and shutting down hosiery production to supply the military with nylon. In 1965, the two Hanes companies merged to form Hanes Corporation, the first time two companies with the same name merged.

In 1979, after several more years of strong growth, the hosiery and knit products businesses were once again separated when Hanes Corporation was acquired by Sara Lee Corporation, then known as Consolidated Foods Corporation. The hosiery business and the knit products business, both strong branded businesses, took on two visibly different brand identities from this point on, and the portfolio of *Hanes* knit products like underwear, socks, and T-shirts began to emerge.

In 1986, *Hanes* introduced the *Hanes Her Way* brand for women and girls, launching with women's panties, expanding into other intimate apparel, and later adding casualwear and socks. The *Hanes Her Way* identity was closely tied to its successful *Hanes* heritage through advertising and packaging.

THE PRODUCT

Hanes has an extensive line of product for the whole family including:

- Underwear
- Intimate Apparel
- Casualwear
- Socks

String Bikini | Quilt Squares Print

Hanes Her Way · Hanes comfort. It's a beautiful thing.™

• Babywear
• Sleepwear
• Casual Shoes
• Sheets and Towels

RECENT DEVELOPMENTS

With the turn of the new millennium, *Hanes* and *Hanes Her Way* have evolved as leaders in clothing for the entire family that is comfortable, stylish, and innovative. Products like underwear and T-shirts that originated in knit cotton fabrications have been updated with the latest in textile technology, including stretch fabrications and microfibers. *Hanes* has parlayed these advances into a steady stream of breakthrough products, including the new *Hanes* Tagless T-shirts, Stay-Clean® shoes, Body Creations™ intimate apparel, and ComfortSoft® jersey and fleece collections.

With *Hanes* and *Hanes Her Way*, comfort has never felt so good or looked so stylish.

PROMOTION

During the past 20 years, *Hanes* has created some of the most memorable commercials of our time. From the 1980s, consumers remember with fondness the *Hanes* advertising campaigns featuring the hard-nosed Inspector 12 with her trademark, "They don't say *Hanes* until I say they say *Hanes*." During those same years, *Hanes* also created the After the Game series, featuring athletes such as Boomer Esiason, Lyle Alzado, Steve Largent, and Mike Ditka, while *Hanes Her Way* brought forward a more feminine side with commercials featuring Carol Alt and Phylicia Rashad. Heading into the 1990s, *Hanes* introduced new commercials featuring sports greats Joe Montana and Michael Jordan as well as a new campaign, "Just Wait'll We Get Our *Hanes* on You," which ran for eight years.

In 1999, *Hanes* introduced an overarching campaign for all of the *Hanes* products called "Be You." The campaign featured everyday people as well as celebrities in a variety of playful vignettes emphasizing the importance of being comfortable and being ourselves. Energizing music by Perry Como, Muddy Waters, and Cheryl Lynn set an upbeat tone for a very contemporary campaign.

Throughout the 1990s and into the new millennium, *Hanes* created numerous commercials with Michael Jordan featuring the newest collections of men's underwear from briefs to boxers and, more recently, boxer briefs. In 2002, one of the newest *Hanes* commercials — featuring Michael Jordan in a locker room pulling out the latest styles of *Hanes* boxers and boxer briefs from his gym bag — was rated one of the 10 best commercials of the year.

To introduce the new *Hanes* Tagless T-shirt in the fall of 2002, *Hanes* "retired the tag" in parties across the country with celebrities such as Dick Clark, Mr. T, Yogi Berra, and Alex Rodriguez, and unveiled its first billboard in New York's famed Times Square. *Hanes* also introduced the tagless T-shirt with advertising in which Michael Jordan urged men across the country to "go tagless." A second tagless T-shirt commercial featuring Michael Jordan and

martial arts actor Jackie Chan debuted during Super Bowl XXXVII.

Starting in 2002, *Hanes* introduced a new creative campaign with the theme "*Hanes* comfort. It's a beautiful thing." This campaign celebrates

the comfortable style of *Hanes* with real, engaging people in simple, fun scenes that are easy to relate to. The campaign is set to uplifting music with lyrics stating that *Hanes* is "a beautiful thing."

BRAND VALUES

Today more than ever, the core values of *Hanes* — comfort, quality, and value — are resonating with consumers who describe the brand as "for everyone," "stylish," "real," and "honest."

THINGS YOU DIDN'T KNOW ABOUT HANES

❍ *Hanes* celebrated the making of its one billionth *Hanes Beefy T* in 2001.

❍ If all the boxes of underwear *Hanes* ships in one year were put on a football field (to cover the entire field), the boxes would be as high as a 20-story building.

❍ There is approximately 3 ½ miles of yarn in a *Hanes* T-shirt.

❍ *Hanes* sells enough Women's casualwear shirts in one year that — when folded and stacked — would be as tall as 96 Empire State Buildings.

Honeywell

THE MARKET

Honeywell offers technologies and solutions in four main business sectors: aerospace, automation and control solutions, specialty materials, and transportation and power systems.

ACHIEVEMENTS

Sales in 2002 for Honeywell's four business sectors totaled $22 billion. The list of Honeywell's customers reads like a Who's Who of global business leaders: Airbus, Alcoa, BASF, Boeing, Chevron-Texaco, Cisco, DaimlerChrysler, DuPont, General Motors, Procter & Gamble, Sun Microsystems, and Wal-Mart are just a few of the companies that depend on the expertise of Honeywell's employees and the quality of its systems, services, and products for their success.

Over the years, Honeywell and its predecessors and affiliates have been at the forefront of technology in a wide variety of areas — everything from cockpits, clocks, kilns, and chemicals to space exploration, sensors, and advanced circuits. Honeywell is one of the 30 companies included in the Dow Jones Industrial Average, a reflection of the significant contribution that Honeywell makes to the world's economic landscape.

HISTORY

Today's Honeywell emerged in fall 1999 from the merger of two global leaders, AlliedSignal and Honeywell Inc., but the company's history goes back more than a century.

The Honeywell Connection — Honeywell's heritage dates to 1885, when Albert Butz patented the furnace regulator and alarm. In 1886, he formed the Butz Thermo-Electric Regulator Company in Minneapolis, Minnesota, and the company introduced the "damper flapper," a device that automatically controlled the dampers on a coal-fire stove. The device was the first in a long line of complex closed-loop sensor and control systems that fueled Honeywell's growth for generations.

In 1904, Mark Honeywell, a young engineer in Wabash, Indiana, was perfecting a heat generator as part of his plumbing and heating business. In 1906, he formed the Honeywell Heating Specialty Company, specializing in hot water heat generators. Minneapolis Heat Regulator and Honeywell Heating Specialty merged in 1927 to form Minneapolis-Honeywell Regulator Company, with W. R. Sweatt as chairman and Mark Honeywell as president.

In 1957, Minneapolis-Honeywell Regulator Company purchased a fire detection and alarm firm, the first of many acquisitions that would build its security business into a global leader today.

In 1986, the company significantly enhanced its position in the aerospace industry with the purchase of Sperry Aerospace, making Honeywell the world's leading integrator of avionics systems.

The AlliedSignal Connection — AlliedSignal is the second major component of today's Honeywell.

During World War I, the United States faced critical shortages of products such as dyes and drugs. In response to this situation, *Washington Post* publisher Eugene Meyer and scientist William Nichols formed the Allied Chemical & Dye Corporation in 1920, which unified five American chemical companies. In 1928, Allied opened a synthetic ammonia plant and soon became the world's leading producer of that chemical.

In 1958, the company was renamed Allied Chemical Corp. and moved its headquarters from Times Square in New York City to Morristown, New Jersey.

In 1981, under its new name, Allied Corporation purchased the Bendix Corporation, an aerospace and automotive company.

In 1985, Allied merged with the Signal Companies, which operated in the aerospace, automotive, and engineered-materials industries. Signal was originally a California-based oil company that later merged with the Garrett Corporation, a Los Angeles–based aerospace company.

In mid-1991, a new Allied-Signal CEO, Lawrence A. Bossidy, was hired from General Electric. Bossidy and a revamped management team began a comprehensive transformation of Allied-Signal. The name was changed to AlliedSignal in 1993 to reinforce the one-company image and to continue to drive the integration to its businesses.

The new Honeywell embodies the best of its AlliedSignal and Honeywell heritages. In 2002, David M. Cote was named to succeed Bossidy as chairman and CEO. Under Cote's leadership the company focuses on five key initiatives: Growth, Productivity, Cash, People, and the Enablers — DigitalWorks and Six Sigma. Central to the company's growth initiative is to do for its customers every day an absolutely superb job in quality, delivery, value, and technology.

THE PRODUCT

To understand the scope of Honeywell's operations, consider some of the products and services that Honeywell offers:

Aerospace: Honeywell is the world's premier supplier of aircraft engines and systems, avionics and other products and services for airliners, regional and business aircraft, military aircraft, and spacecraft. Its aerospace products include engines, auxiliary power units, flight control systems, environmental control systems, spare parts, and support and services for space and communications facilities.

Automation and Control Solutions: Honeywell's Automation and Control Solutions is a global leader in providing product and service solutions to create efficient, safe, and comfortable environments, and to help business and industry improve productivity and profitability. Its products range from heating, ventilation, humidification and air-conditioning equipment controls, and security and fire alarm systems, to automation systems and sensors, switches, and control products for industrial applications.

Specialty Materials: Honeywell's Specialty Materials division is a world leader in high-performance specialty materials, such as nylon, polyester, polyethylene, fluorocarbons, and specialty chemicals. Honeywell is one of the top-five providers of materials and solutions to the electronics industry.

Transportation and Power Systems: Honeywell is the world's leading innovator of automotive turbochargers, and is also the producer of some of the best-known consumer automotive product brands, such as Prestone® antifreeze/coolant, Autolite® platinum spark plugs, Holt Lloyd's Teflon®, Simoniz® premium car care products, and FRAM® automotive filters.

RECENT DEVELOPMENTS
In a company like Honeywell, product innovation is not just a slogan. It's the way the company looks at its mission; staying on top of the customers' needs is the pathway to success.

• Honeywell's Primus Epic® integrated avionics system will now display Jeppesen® navigation data, including electronic aeronautical charts, obstacle data, geopolitical boundaries, and airport information. With Primus Epic's Interactive Navigation (INAV), pilots will be able to view aircraft position, terrain, weather, and traffic on a moving map display in the cockpit. The first implementations of Primus Epic with INAV will debut in the PlaneView™ cockpit in the Gulfstream G500 and the EASy cockpit in the Dassault Falcon 900EX.
• Honeywell's Field Automation Service Technology (FAST) initiative equipped 1,400 North American building systems service technicians

with handheld computers to automate dispatching and record-keeping, with a view toward improving service across the United States.
• Japan's Institute of Space and Astronautical Science chose Honeywell to provide wheel assemblies to stabilize, position, and control its Solar-B exploratory spacecraft.
• Honeywell's Spectra® composite material was selected by C&D Aerospace, TIMCO, and AIM Aviation, Inc. as the primary ballistic protection material for new fortified doors for aircraft

cockpits. Spectra® fiber is one of the world's strongest and lightest synthetic fibers, being pound-for-pound 10 times stronger than steel.
• Sales of Honeywell's Garrett turbochargers are growing 65 percent in Asia as car and truck manufacturers rely on the technology for its ability to enhance fuel economy without sacrificing performance.
• Honeywell's global home-automation capabilities allow homeowners to manage indoor climate controls, fire and security systems, Web cameras, lights, and appliances from home or remotely.

PROMOTION
Consumers around the world can literally wrap their hand around the most recognizable of Honeywell's products: the T-86, the Honeywell Round™ thermostat. This simple and elegant control device is found in more homes than any other thermostat in the world. Continuously produced since 1953, the Round continues to symbolize the modern home and serves as an icon for one of the world's most respected companies.

BRAND VALUES
In a world that's becoming more complicated and uncertain all the time, Honeywell is meeting challenges. Supplying superior products is important — and Honeywell does it well. But what Honeywell does best is solve customers' problems.

Great customer relationships drive performance and create growth opportunities — and Honeywell's are improving all the time. Honeywell's leading technologies, problem-solving expertise, and performance zeal continue to build bonds with consumers as well as the best companies in every industry Honeywell serves.

When it comes to productivity, Honeywell is a one-of-a-kind double play. For years, customers have turned to Honeywell for technology solutions that make their companies more effective, efficient, and profitable. But that's only half the story. Inside Honeywell, Six Sigma is more than a company priority; it's a way of life. The Honeywell repair and overhaul facility in Singapore uses

Lean Manufacturing techniques to increase efficiency and customer satisfaction. Holt-Lloyd employees in Europe reduced inventory by $2 million with improved forecasting processes. The Software Solutions Lab in Bangalore earned the Software Engineering Institute's highest capability rating — Level 5 — and India's Rajiv Gandhi quality prize. In 2000, Honeywell also won Australia's top business excellence award, which has standards so high that no one else has earned it in almost a decade.

Honeywell's people are the company's greatest differentiator. Performance really matters here; all employees have tough goals and are held accountable to them.

In the end, it's all about performance. Honeywell has worked hard to build a culture that emphasizes results and gives its people the skills, resources, and motivation to focus on what's important: satisfying customers, meeting or exceeding commitments, and driving innovation and productivity across the company.

THE MARKET

Despite the fact that it is a mature industry, floor care sales continue to grow, nearing about $5 billion annually. This figure is especially impressive in light of the fact that about 98 percent of American households already own at least one full-size vacuum.

Where is this growth coming from? For starters, many homeowners are choosing to have a variety of floor care products in the home. More homeowners are buying floor care products designed for specific tasks, like wet carpet extraction or hard-floor cleaning.

Further, the floor care market is no longer a replacement market. Rather, it is driven by a continuous, ever-quickening flow of products with new features that add convenience to life or meet consumers' desire for something new. Advertising helps drive this behavior.

Another reason for the industry's growth is the ever-increasing range of distribution channels. The Hoover Company sells its products through mass merchandisers, department stores, catalog showrooms, appliance stores, do-it-yourself stores, and vacuum cleaner specialty shops, to name a few. It sells through its own network of company-owned service centers and retail outlets. Television home-shopping networks and Hoover's Web site, *www.hoover.com*, are other avenues of opportunity.

ACHIEVEMENTS

Today, Hoover is the market leader in floor care in North America. The company takes great pride in its commitment to innovation, quality, and customer service, striving to give customers not just what they want, but far more than they expect. These efforts have not gone unrecognized. The company has received the prestigious SPARC Award (Supplier Performance Awards by Retail Category) in the floor care category for eight years straight, and in 2001, Hoover won the SPARC Hard Line Vendor of the Year. These awards, resulting from polls of retail executives, are based on product innovation, quality control, advertising support, and on-time delivery.

In recent years, Hoover has received vendor-of-the-year awards from Sears, Target, Wal-Mart, and other retailers. The Hoover® WindTunnel™ upright was the first vacuum cleaner to win *Good*

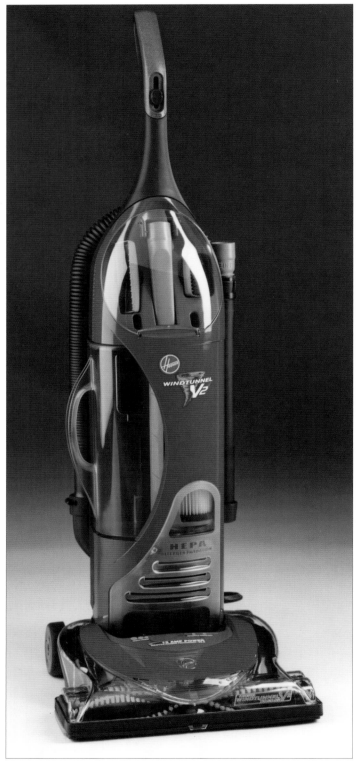

Housekeeping magazine's Good Buy Award. The annual award, given to fewer than a dozen manufacturers, recognizes products that provide "exceptional performance and ingenious problem-solving features."

Hoover is also among a small number of businesses that have won the Ohio Governor's Award

for Outstanding Achievement in recognition of efforts made to develop and maintain environmentally safe manufacturing practices.

In the community, Hoover is well-known for its civic leadership and social responsibility.

HISTORY

Innovation has been the hallmark of The Hoover Company since 1908, the year it was founded in North Canton, Ohio. The company's first product — the Model O upright — would become the first commercially successful portable electric vacuum cleaner.

The product was born from need. James Murray Spangler, a department store janitor, had difficulty sweeping the floor because dust aggravated his asthma. An inventive man who held patents on farming implements, he created a contraption from a tin soap box, sewing machine motor, broom handle, and pillow case. The device managed to pick up dirt, channeling it into the pillow case and away from the air he breathed.

Spangler received a patent for his "suction sweeper," but did not have the funds to market it. He contacted William Henry Hoover, a family acquaintance and a leather-goods entrepreneur, who saw the potential of the machine. Hoover bought the patent, retained Spangler as factory superintendent, and built a company that would become the leader in floor care and a name recognized around the world.

Even early on, The Hoover Company was a leader in its industry with a series of developments in-house, including the spiral beater bar for deep-down cleaning, the vacuum cleaner headlight, and the disposable paper bag. Later, the company developed the side-mounted hose configuration and a transmission that allows uprights to be self-propelled.

THE PRODUCT

Hoover offers an array of floor care products at a range of price points to accommodate the budgets and the diverse cleaning needs of every consumer. These products include uprights, canisters, extractors, hard-floor cleaners, stick cleaners, hand-held cleaners, central vacuum systems, and commercial products.

A far cry from their bulky predecessors, today's Hoover cleaners are lightweight but sturdy, thanks to durable plastic casings. They are energy efficient and have convenience features that save time and effort.

Most importantly, Hoover products are built for superior cleaning effectiveness. Market research continues to show that what consumers want foremost in a vacuum cleaner is a product that gets the dirt out of their carpet.

That research drove Hoover to develop Wind-Tunnel technology for its uprights in the late 1990s. Dirt is channeled into a dual-duct arrangement in the nozzle that prevents dirt from being scattered back onto the carpet. This technology, which Hoover has patented, improves cleaning effectiveness, which is the ability to get dirt out of carpet.

The company develops its products by blending technology with intense consumer research to

create breakthrough offerings, providing superior features that offer the ultimate in consumer satisfaction. Hoover wows the consumer by coming to market with innovations even before the consumer realizes the need for them. Here are just two examples:

- The Floor MATE™ hard-floor cleaner is a vacuum, a floor washer, and a floor dryer — all in a single, lightweight appliance. It cleans a variety of floors, including stone, vinyl, ceramic, laminates, linoleum, and sealed hardwoods.

  The Floor MATE hard-floor cleaner has two tanks, one for clean water, one for dirty. This design ensures that only clean water (mixed with cleaning solution) is used on the floor. Compare that to the mop-and-bucket, in which the mop is rinsed in increasingly dirty water.
- The Embedded Dirt FINDER™ feature, found on many Hoover uprights, uses red and green lights to indicate the amount of dirt being picked up. A red light tells the user that more vacuuming is needed in a certain area. A green light means the cleaner is no longer picking up dirt and that the user can move on to another area.

RECENT DEVELOPMENTS

Hoover engineers continue to develop new technologies. For instance, Hoover recently introduced a line of Dual V™ WindTunnel uprights and SteamVac™ deep cleaners with a split-nozzle design. This design creates two air paths in the nozzle, effectively spreading out the airflow for more focused cleaning, edge to edge.

The WindTunnel upright with this dual-duct design also has two agitators that counter-rotate. This action spreads the carpet fibers, exposing deep-down dirt to the full suction power of the upright.

Many SteamVac extractors have five or six round SpinScrub™ brushes under the nozzle. The brushes, which interlock, work together to clean all sides of the carpet fibers.

Hoover also offers a SteamVac model with an Auto Rinse™ feature that rinses the carpet at the same time it is cleaned. The model also has the dual-duct nozzle design and heated cleaning.

PROMOTION

William Henry Hoover realized as early as 1908 that advertising was necessary to tell the country about his suction sweeper, so he placed his first national advertising in the *Saturday Evening Post*. The promotion offered a free, 10-day cleaner trial at home and generated hundreds of inquiries.

Today, Hoover invests millions of dollars annually in memorable television and print advertising, seeking to capture the attention of potential customers and to build its brand.

The company's advertising explains how Hoover technology can help simplify cleaning. The ads often show how the technology enables Hoover products to clean better. Less time is spent cleaning, which leaves more time for leisure. The company's slogan — Time For Hoover™ — underscores this approach.

Other Hoover promotional efforts include in-store merchandising and promotions, trade-show participation, editorial placements, TV and radio endorsements, and its Web site, *www.hoover.com*.

BRAND VALUES

Hoover is the North American market leader in floor care, with 95 years of equity behind a brand name that is the best known in the industry. The

Hoover brand is an American icon and a household word. Further proof of that came when *BrandMarketing* magazine included Hoover in its listing titled "One Hundred Brands That Changed America."

Both the Hoover name and its widely recognized red-and-white circular emblem represent trust, longevity, quality, reliability, and innovation. For generations of consumers whose loyalty is legendary, Hoover has been considered a helper in the home, its products akin to trustworthy family members.

THINGS YOU DIDN'T KNOW ABOUT HOOVER

- ❍ The first Hoover vacuum cleaner weighed 40 pounds.
- ❍ The boyhood home of Hoover Company founder William Henry Hoover flourishes today as the Hoover Historical Center. This museum houses an intriguing collection of pre-electric carpet cleaners, milestone Hoover models, company memorabilia, and Victorian-period furnishings, and is open to the public free of charge.
- ❍ During World War II, Hoover ceased production of vacuum cleaners and aided the war effort by manufacturing helmet liners, parachutes for fragmentation bombs, and the proximity fuze for missiles. As a result, the company and its employees earned many government honors.
- ❍ Hoover tests products from a consumer's point of view in its Human Engineering Lab, a room inside its headquarters building that duplicates in-home conditions.

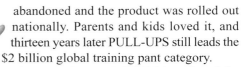

THE MARKET

Today and every day, about 11,000 babies are born in the United States alone. Before they're an hour old, almost all of them will be wearing their first piece of clothing — a disposable diaper. And every day, another 11,000 toddlers will begin toilet training, most with the help of disposable training pants.

Over the course of a year, there are 4.1 million brand-new potential consumers for HUGGIES® products, just in the United States. Worldwide, families use over 72 *billion* disposable diapers a year, and nearly one-third of them are branded HUGGIES. It's a "growth" market in every way: Estimates are that globally, disposable diapers account for probably less than 30 percent of all changes, which leaves a lot of growing room as incomes and hygiene standards rise around the world.

ACHIEVEMENTS

HUGGIES® diapers were first introduced by Kimberly-Clark in 1978, and they've been reinvented every year since. Refastenable diapers, breathable diapers, and stretchy diapers are all HUGGIES firsts. At the controls of the HUGGIES innovation engine are everyday consumers. The art of understanding and anticipating consumer needs — sometimes before customers do themselves — has led not only to product advances but the creation of whole new categories, businesses that didn't exist before.

In 1989, HUGGIES created the disposable training pant category. Unlike diapers, which parents fold on around their children, PULL-UPS® training pants are more like real underwear that toddlers can pull on and off all by themselves. When Kimberly-Clark launched PULL-UPS in a test market, demand was so great that the test was abandoned and the product was rolled out nationally. Parents and kids loved it, and thirteen years later PULL-UPS still leads the $2 billion global training pant category.

Five years later, HUGGIES introduced the first super-premium diaper. While most diapers felt paper-y or plastic-y, new HUGGIES® Supreme diapers felt like cloth. Instead of tape closures, they had fasteners from Velcro USA that made it easy for parents to check and adjust the diapers at will. Then as now, HUGGIES® Supreme diapers are the "Ultimate in Care®" and well worth a premium price to many moms. "A few cents more per diaper?" says one consumer. "That's meaningless when you're talking about making my baby more comfortable!"

In 1994, HUGGIES created the youth pant category by taking on a new — and often taboo — subject: bedwetting. Some 5 to 7 million American children wet the bed at night, but no garment was available on the market to spare them from the wet sheets and embarrassment they faced. The creation of GOODNITES® absorbent underpants became a cause inside Kimberly-Clark. This is another new market that K-C has led from wire to wire, but the GOODNITES team

will tell you that the rewards go deeper than market share numbers.

In 1998, HUGGIES invented the swim pant category. Almost as trim as bathing suits, HUGGIES® LITTLE SWIMMERS® disposable swimpants provide diaper protection for infants during water play. But unlike diapers, they don't swell up or come apart in the water. LITTLE SWIMMERS lead their market and are now sold in 55 countries around the world.

At the core (literally) of many of these advances is a new class of materials pioneered by Kimberly-Clark. Nonwoven fabrics combine the softness and the stretch of cloth with other almost magical properties. Some let air through, but not liquids. Others allow liquids to travel in only one direction: away from a baby's skin. In a diaper, the fabric is impermeable to leaks but allows air to circulate, helping keep a baby's skin drier and healthier.

In 1998, these new, "smart" fabrics propelled HUGGIES to leadership in still another category — baby wipes. For reasons that are not hard to understand, disposable wipes have largely replaced

washcloths for clean-ups during diaper changes. Parents prefer HUGGIES® Baby Wipes because they are thicker and more durable than other brands. Of the 30 *billion* baby wipes Americans will use this year, nearly one out of every three will be made by Kimberly-Clark.

HISTORY

Kimberly-Clark was born in 1872 as a paper company in Wisconsin's Fox River Valley, which many still call the "Paper Valley." Entering its second century, the company made a momentous decision. Rather than slugging it out with competitors in commodity paper businesses, K-C elected to focus on higher-margin consumer products.

Kimberly-Clark's first entry into the disposable diaper market created by Procter & Gamble's Pampers® brand was a major advance, but not for long. K-C's superior new entry was quickly surpassed by competitors, and ultimately withdrawn. The KIMBIES® diaper saga became a lesson learned: performance is everything in consumer markets, and it had better improve. Or else.

In 1978, Kimberly-Clark tried again with HUGGIES® diapers — baby-shaped diapers with elastic at the legs to help stop leaks, just like the rubber pants so many consumers used over cloth diapers at the time. Consumers flocked to HUGGIES, and this time Kimberly-Clark followed up with improvement after improvement. In 1985, HUGGIES took leadership of the category for the first time, and has been the number-one selling diaper in America since 1993.

Looking back, KIMBIES® diapers may have been the best thing that ever happened to Kimberly-Clark as a consumer product company. Today, HUGGIES introduces a demonstrably better product every year, and the imperative to innovate extends far beyond the HUGGIES® diaper franchise. It's no accident that Kimberly-Clark offers consumers the number-one or number-two brand in 80 countries.

THE PRODUCT

HUGGIES® Ultratrim, introduced in 1992, is the brand's most popular diaper and a great example of the continuous innovation that keeps HUGGIES on top of so many market segments. HUGGIES Ultratrim began with a technological breakthrough: a way to make diapers radically less bulky with zero sacrifice in protection. Most of us don't usually think of diapers as high-tech

products, but that's what the HUGGIES Ultratrim diaper is. The materials and processes that go into it are guarded by *hundreds* of separate patents. The result is a product costing about a quarter that gets better every year. Last year's model reduced leaks by over 25 percent. A HUGGIES Ultratrim diaper can easily absorb three wettings while keeping a baby's skin almost completely dry — with little chance of any leakage.

RECENT DEVELOPMENTS

One of HUGGIES greatest success stories is on the Internet, where *Parentstages.com* aggregates the Web's most useful child-rearing information. Developed in partnership with online leaders like Yahoo! and iVillage, this award-winning site saves today's busy parents time by providing an objective, one-step information resource, organized by their child's stage of development. *Parentstages.com* is now Kimberly-Clark's most-visited Web site.

Meanwhile, the HUGGIES innovation engine keeps turning. Consumers who've tested the improved HUGGIES® Supreme are already buzzing about the first diaper with all-over stretch. It fits better — from waist to legs — and keeps its fit, no matter what a busy baby may be up to.

PROMOTION

Any survey of the world's best-loved advertising puts HUGGIES high on the list, partly because the brand's messages reflect an insight into the consumer that has proved to be universal. HUGGIES advertising and promotion activity on five continents reflects how most moms see their own babies. HUGGIES "Happy Babies" live in what one mom calls the "photo moments" when a baby is the star of his or her own life. This "Happy Babies" insight lives in all the brand's interactions with consumers, including television commercials, print ads, retail promotions, and on the Internet. It's no coincidence that Disney characters have appeared on HUGGIES for years.

A fully integrated brand message, delivered in one of the world's most enduring marketing campaigns, is one of the reasons market research firm ACNielsen recently ranked HUGGIES®

diapers (and KLEENEX® Brand Tissue, another Kimberly-Clark brand) among only 43 truly global, billion-dollar brands.

BRAND VALUES

HUGGIES has a special relationship with parents, and not simply because diapers do an important job. HUGGIES reminds us of what we love about our babies and what we hope to be as parents.

HUGGIES babies are Happy, with a capital H. They are brave and smart and independent. Their job is making the world their own, and that's how most of us hope our children will grow up. As one HUGGIES mom says, "I want him to run out in the rain, to get dirty, and touch leaves across his face."

Who wouldn't want to be a HUGGIES Happy Baby!

THINGS YOU DIDN'T KNOW ABOUT HUGGIES

❍ Members of the HUGGIES extended family of brands are number one in diapers, training pants, youth pants, swimpants, and baby wipes.

❍ Over 30 million HUGGIES® Baby Wipes are used every day in the United States.

❍ The first babies to use HUGGIES® diapers will celebrate their 25th birthdays in 2003.

Hush Puppies®

THE MARKET

The shoes on your feet are a big business in the United States. Americans bought over 1.3 billion pairs of footwear in the twelve-month period ending May 2002, spending almost $41 billion, according to NPD ShoeBiz, the footwear marketing intelligence service. Casual shoes and sandals represent over 68 percent of all footwear sold.

Casual is booming, and that's really no surprise. Since the mid-1990s, America has been the center of a worldwide casual boom. Khaki trousers and comfortable knit shirts have replaced more tailored European fashions. Businesses established "Casual Friday" dress codes that soon extended to the rest of the week. "Uniform" business attire has given way to a relaxed, more individual style of dress. And Hush Puppies — the footwear brand that "invented casual" — has kept pace with relevant product styling that supports its brand values of Relaxed, Confident, Youthful, and Modern.

ACHIEVEMENTS

Since its introduction in 1958, Hush Puppies has become the world's best-loved shoe brand. Sold in 96 countries around the world, Hush Puppies enjoys a brand recognition of over 90 percent in the United States and nearly that high in most countries in which the brand is sold. Somewhere in the world, a pair of Hush Puppies is sold every two seconds throughout every day!

HISTORY

The history of Wolverine World Wide, the parent company of Hush Puppies, dates back to 1888, when a leather-tanning operation began on the Rogue River in Rockford, a small community north of Grand Rapids, Michigan. By 1904, the first shoe factory was open, making ladies' dress boots and men's rugged work boots for farmers.

In the early 1950s, the U.S. government approached Wolverine and asked them to devise an effective way to tan and use pigskin leather. Pigskin is one of the world's most durable leathers, but tanning it was not economical. Wolverine's chairman, Victor Krause, took a leave of absence to work on the project and invented the process used around the world to this day.

Mr. Krause realized he needed a venue to showcase the now abundant supply of this new leather.

He looked at the country and saw the postwar boom. Servicemen returning from the war were building homes and starting families. The original baby boom was under way. Families were leaving cities and expanding into newly created suburbs, to homes on lots with lawns and driveways.

But what would this new generation of Americans wear on their feet? At the time, there

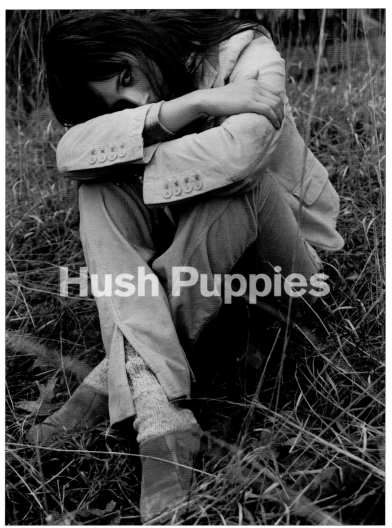

were no true "casual" shoes. Men wore wingtips to work and once they were old, bought a new pair for work and used the old pair to mow the lawn. Women wore heels or canvas sneakers. Mr. Krause believed that this new consumer was ready for a new type of footwear. He took his new pigskin — naturally durable, treated in the tanning process to be water and stain resistant — and attached it to a lightweight crepe sole. The world's first "casual shoes" were born!

The history of the Hush Puppies name is also a slice of Americana. Jim Muir, the company's first sales manager, was traveling in Tennessee

with this new-yet-unnamed line of men's and women's comfortable suede casual shoes. He stopped at a friend's house for a fried catfish dinner. His friend served hush puppies — fried cornmeal dough balls — with the catfish. When he asked where they got their name, he was told that farmers "use them to quiet their barking dogs." Jim laughed because in the 1950s "barking dogs" was an expression for tired, sore feet.

The result? Jim had an interesting idea . . . and that very day the comfortable shoes that soothe aching feet became "Hush Puppies." The Hush Puppies brand and famous Basset Hound logo soon became a part of American folklore.

That original Hush Puppies' style has been an example of classic, American style for over 40 years. *Footwear News*, a trade magazine, named it one of the best-selling shoe styles of all time. In 1996, the Council of Fashion Designers in America gave Hush Puppies their "Best Accessory" award, which put the brand in the company of such fashion icons as Ralph Lauren, Calvin Klein, and Tom Ford from Gucci. In 1997, Hush Puppies was named "Brand of the Year" by *Footwear News*.

THE PRODUCT

Today, Hush Puppies offers a lot more than the original suede shoe that made them famous. Hush Puppies produces complete collections of contemporary casual footwear for men and women. There are styles appropriate for work, for play, for all aspects of today's busy lives.

Hush Puppies also markets a full collection of children's footwear with dress and play styles for boys and girls. You can also find the Hush Puppies brand name on your favorite accessories from handbags to watches, eyewear, socks, and even plush toys.

While styles may change, one thing remains the same with today's Hush Puppies: their comfort. Hush Puppies have long been known as "the world's most comfortable shoes," and designers and technicians continually work to ensure comfort is a top priority. Wolverine World Wide has received over 120 proprietary design patents over the course of its history.

Hush Puppies

RECENT DEVELOPMENTS

Today, Hush Puppies offers a wide range of comfort technologies, from "ZeroG" — lightweight footwear built to athletic specifications — to "HPO2 Flex," a unique cushioning system designed to give incredible flexibility.

In fall 2001, Hush Puppies introduced its new Float FX cushioning — a nitrogen oxide–filled heel bubble, ABS stabilizer, and nonliquid forefoot gel pad to customize the entire walking motion from heel-strike through toe-off.

Hush Puppies also introduced its HP360 Collection, which is designed for active men and women seeking a simple yet contemporary look for "wherever the day takes you." This collection captured the attention of both the retailer and the consumer, and as a result, has been expanded each season since its introduction.

PROMOTION

The Hush Puppies Basset Hound remains one of the world's great icons. It is as well known as "the Hush Puppies dog" as it is by its breed. Basset hounds were first introduced in many countries around the world with the introduction of the Hush Puppies shoe brand.

The Hush Puppies brand was one of the first nationally advertised shoe brands, appearing on the *Tonight Show* with Johnny Carson and the *Today* show with Hugh Downs. There have been many memorable Hush Puppies moments in advertising — from shoes that "make the sidewalk softer" in the 1960s to "We Invented Casual" in the 1990s. In 1988 Hush Puppies won the prestigious Gold Lion at the Cannes Festival for a television commercial showing the Basset Hound on a subway grate with its ears flapping in the air as a train passed below. The ad was later named one of the top 100 television commercials of all time by *Entertainment Weekly* magazine.

Today, the Hush Puppies spirit is reflected in its contemporary imagery, which positions the brand as relaxed, modern, and confident. The image conveys that Hush Puppies understands fashion and has the right shoes for today's ready-to-wear.

BRAND VALUES

Hush Puppies was built on the foundation of innovation, its reputation for comfort, and a style distinctly its own. The brand is authentic, as it invented the first casual shoe. It is established as one of the most recognizable names in footwear throughout the world. And while the roots of the Hush Puppies brand are firmly planted in the relaxed and casual lifestyle that is embraced today, the shoes express a fresh new style, which is youthful and modern. All of these attributes make Hush Puppies very relevant to fashion today.

THINGS YOU DIDN'T KNOW ABOUT HUSH PUPPIES

○ Nearly 40,000 pairs of Hush Puppies shoes are sold every day around the world.

○ In 1959, just one year after being introduced in the United States, Hush Puppies began its globalization with its entrance into the Canadian marketplace.

○ Many celebrities have worn Hush Puppies, including Tom Hanks, Sharon Stone, Nicolas Cage, and Susan Sarandon.

○ Hush Puppies shoes have been featured in many major movies, including a recent appearance in *Austin Powers in Goldmember*.

○ The actress Rene Russo appeared in a Hush Puppies catalog in the 1970s, early in her modeling career.

THE MARKET

In 1997, IBM coined the term "e-business" to convey the various ways that the Internet would transform business and society. Even in the early stages, IBM believed that the Web would dramatically affect lives, in commerce certainly, but also in government, healthcare, and education, among many other areas.

Today, e-business is a widely adopted industry and business term. According to International Data Corporation, e-business has helped fuel worldwide information technology (IT) spending to $800 billion annually. e-business has also propelled IBM into the IT leadership role once more.

But that's not all. Over the last few years, e-business has changed the way the Web is used — from the early stage of access to information to access to transactions, and now to e-business on demand, IBM's current strategic focus.

"On demand" means that if a company has, end-to-end, integrated processes internally as well as externally with key partners, suppliers, and customers, that company can respond flexibly and quickly to any customer demand, market opportunity, or external threat.

e-business on demand enables leaders to see and manage their company as an integrated whole, and to create a dynamic, constantly adjusting enterprise.

ACHIEVEMENTS

IBM Research, the largest private research organization in the world, is credited with many scientific breakthroughs that have advanced today's IT industry. Last year alone, IBM earned 3,411 new patents, more than the other 12 largest U.S. IT companies combined.

IBM's most significant contributions have historically been in applying technology to improve how businesses operate and how people live. Today, IBM continues that legacy by helping customers find the most current and advantageous ways to use Internet technologies for business advantage.

As a corporate leader, IBM has extended the role of employer, enriching lives of employees through a well-developed corporate culture and extensive employee benefits. IBM was one of the first companies to provide group life insurance,

survivor benefits, and paid vacations to employees; recently, partner benefits were added. The company also frequently tops lists recognizing the best places for minorities, women, and working mothers to work.

HISTORY

IBM's origins can be traced to 1896, when Herman Hollerith formed the Tabulating Machine Company.

This firm merged in 1911 with two other firms to form the Computing-Tabulating-Recording Company, or C-T-R, which manufactured products including time recorders, tabulators, and punch cards.

In 1914, rapidly growing C-T-R turned to Thomas J. Watson, the former number-two executive at the National Cash Register Company, to be its general manager. Watson, who would become president and chairman of the board, instilled more effective business tactics and fervent company pride and loyalty in every worker. Watson also stressed the importance of the customer, a lasting IBM tenet.

To reflect C-T-R's growing worldwide presence and focus on tabulators, its name was changed to International Business Machines, or IBM, in 1924. In what was called "the biggest accounting operation of all time," IBM fulfilled a government contract during the Great Depression and performed so well that other U.S. government orders quickly followed.

By the 1950s, IBM had developed powerful computers that could handle business applications such as billing and inventory control. In 1959, IBM unveiled the 7090, which used transistors

rather than vacuum tubes. The computer could perform 229,000 calculations per second and would be used to run American Airlines' SABRE reservation system.

This period of rapid technological change also featured a new generation of IBM leadership. In 1952, Thomas Watson passed the title of president on to his son, Thomas Watson Jr., who foresaw the role computers would play in business and pushed IBM to meet the challenge.

IBM in 1964 introduced the System/360 mainframe, the first large "family" of computers to use interchangeable software and peripheral equipment, a move that transformed IBM into an industrial giant that posted 1972 revenues of more than $9 billion. The number of employees rose to over 260,000.

A new era of computing began in 1981 with the birth of the IBM Personal Computer, or PC. The IBM PC put the most desirable features of a computer into one small machine. In 1985, IBM introduced networking technology that permitted computer users to exchange information and share printers and files. These advances laid the foundation for today's network-based computing, but threw IBM into turmoil.

PC and networking technology unleashed the client/server revolution in the 1990s — a development that emphasized personal productivity — and the desktop moved business-purchasing decisions to departments and individuals. IBM's traditional customer relationships had not been formed at this organizational level, and by the early 1990s, IBM had fallen on hard times.

The arrival of Louis V. Gerstner Jr. in April 1993 began a turnaround that would restore IBM to its position as one of the greatest brands in the world. Despite pressures to break the corporation into many companies, Gerstner kept it as one entity, recognizing that in an increasingly global world, IBM's key strength was its ability to provide integrated solutions around the globe.

The growth of the Internet once again put IBM at the center of dramatic change, but this time the company was better prepared to meet the challenge with its combined strengths in services, products, and technologies.

In the fall of 1995, Gerstner articulated IBM's new vision: that network computing would drive the next phase of industry growth and would be the company's overarching strategy. Two years later, IBM was the first to articulate the remarkable potential of the Internet, the ultimate network, with the phrase "e-business."

Now, a 21st-century IBM is still building e-businesses and driving to the next stage of evolution: e-business on demand, the way to help companies operate at the speed of the market and in step with constituents' needs.

Under the new leadership of Sam Palmisano, previously president and chief operating officer, the company is well positioned for growth. Since becoming CEO, Palmisano has led a number of major initiatives designed to augment the company's services and maintain industry leadership.

THE PRODUCT

IBM invents technology, then applies it to solve customers' problems, in small, mid-size, and large enterprises. The company has a heritage of consistently large investments in research and development.

IBM's technological innovations have enabled unparalleled end-to-end solutions that address the totality of customers' business needs, providing for today and preparing for the future. These solutions are designed to make doing business easier.

Once upon a time,

there was a company in desperate danger of getting left behind. Their customers were demanding more personal service, more customization, more value. More, more, more. Instantly. *On demand.* But the company was inflexible. *Stuck.* They couldn't respond quickly. Things were dire.

SO THEY BOUGHT A TIME MACHINE. *THAT'S RIGHT, A TIME MACHINE.*

Flick a switch, they could go forward in time – and understand what their customers were going to need before they actually needed it. Touch a button, they could go back and undo investments in proprietary technology – stuff that slowed them down. Then, they could respond *like that.* They could catch up. It was exciting. *They were jazzed.* There was only one problem: the time machine was a dud. It didn't work.

And that's when they called IBM.

In 2002, IBM acquired PriceWaterhouseCoopers Consulting, which strengthened the company. PWC was rated number one by *Consulting Monitor* for "understanding client's industry," creating synergy with IBM, which itself garnered IDC's number-one ranking for a Business and IT Strategy Consultant. Together, the companies have formed the world's largest on-demand consultancy.

RECENT DEVELOPMENTS

Anticipating that the pace of data volumes and transaction flow will keep quickening, and that information systems will continue growing in complexity, IBM is working towards autonomic computing. Just as human systems allow functions such as breathing and heart rates to occur without our controlling them, autonomic computing systems will be self-managing without our intervention. The systems will be more reliable, self-protecting, and even self-healing, so enterprises can focus on more creative areas, such as new uses for the systems.

In its labs, IBM is studying the "e-workplace." e-workplaces will address a changing workforce with radically different expectations, a changing marketplace with no time for bureaucracy or time-zone disruption. Along the way, the traditional office will become obsolete.

For many of tomorrow's most massive computing challenges, IBM scientists expect to see 10 times the energy efficiency at the same costs. "Cellular architectures" of thousands, or perhaps millions, of simpler microprocessors that will work in parallel on discrete areas of a problem will make this achievement possible. When the aggregations of these power-efficient chips combine their resources over virtualized computing networks, supercomputing could come within an individual's reach — not just for enterprises anymore.

IBM has a vision of an interconnected, shared computing infrastructure through which people will be able to access the world's computational resources. This emerging global infrastructure will act as one big computer. How? Through technology called "grid" computing, where millions of computers are interwoven into a gigantic grid that people will use like a utility, as is currently done with electricity.

PROMOTION

IBM maintains a broad range of traditional advertising, sponsorship, and marketing activities.

In the spring of 1998, the company launched the e-business campaign, one of the highest profile and most successful ever for IBM. The e-business campaign, still running today, embodies a strategy for the entire company to speak with one voice. Moreover, the ads continue to explain new ways of using the Web, such as e-business on demand, and they've helped make IBM one of the companies most identified with the Internet.

Extending IBM's embrace of e-business has been its trend-setting online advertising strategy. One of the first to recognize the advertising opportunities that the Internet presents, the company sponsored the HotWired Web site as early as 1994. Since then, IBM has leveraged its Internet site as online "investments" with Web events such as coverage of the famous chess match featuring the company's supercomputer Deep Blue, the first computer to defeat a sitting world champion. IBM also capitalizes on its e-business expertise through Web sites created in support of marketing sponsorships of events such as the Wimbledon and U.S. Open tennis championships.

BRAND VALUES

Over the years, IBM has acquired deep operational and industry experience, know-how, and expertise. With a long, continuing history of providing quality, reliable products that customers can trust – and that deliver value for the money — integrity, honesty, and truthfulness have always distinguished IBM.

One of the company's greatest strengths is its people. IBM seeks, hires, and inspires the best global talent, providing a work environment that fosters creativity and recognizes vision.

THINGS YOU DIDN'T KNOW ABOUT IBM

○ IBM research has produced five Nobel prizes, four U.S. National Medals of Technology, and three National Medals of Science.

○ IBM is known for its deep science and engineering research, with investment of more than $5 billion annually. The results? In each of the last nine years, IBM was awarded more patents than any other company in the world.

○ IBM has long benefited from collaborations with some of the world's greatest leaders in design, architecture, and art. Graphic designer Paul Rand created the classic blue-bar logo as well as much of the IBM design aesthetic. Charles Eames developed a variety of IBM World's Fair, Museum, and Film exhibitions, and world-renowned architects such as Mies van der Rohe, Eero Saarinen, and I. M. Pei designed various IBM work sites.

○ In 2002, IBM ranked first among *Business Ethics* magazine's 100 Best Corporate Citizens. *Fortune* placed IBM at the top of the 10 Most Admired Computer Companies.

Document Efficiency
At Work.^{SM}

THE MARKET

Document management is a rapidly changing and dynamic industry. It is no longer a market simply defined by hard copy documents. Today's technologies provide new ways for people to communicate and exchange information in the office environment.

Within this changing environment, IKON is uniquely positioned to meet the changing needs of its customers. IKON offers customers a range of equipment and services that is simply unsurpassed, from solutions for offices of all sizes, to those for high-volume print and data centers, to a complete set of outsourcing offerings.

IKON is meeting demand for today's color and digital office equipment with exceptionally strong choices from leading manufacturers such as Canon, Ricoh, and Hewlett-Packard, and offering very competitive solutions for high-volume production needs. Furthermore, the company offers the technology and expertise — in software, networking, and document systems analysis — to deliver customized solutions that meet customers' enterprise-wide document needs by streamlining workflow and enhancing efficiency.

The strength of IKON's portfolio is a direct result of its business model: IKON is a distributor, not a manufacturer. By aligning itself with the best vendors in the industry, IKON offers the best technologies to its customers. With this strategy, the result is a custom solution based on the right combination of hardware, software, and services.

ACHIEVEMENTS

During the late 1990s, IKON was acquiring numerous local office products dealers in major

markets throughout North America and Europe. Each of the over 450 acquisitions completed had a different name and its own established brand recognition within its local market. The name IKON Office Solutions was established in 1997, and the company began to transition each local dealer to the IKON brand in each market. The changeover from numerous disparate brands in splintered markets to one single brand name with an international presence was no small task. Today, IKON has established itself as the largest independent distributor of document management products and services in the United States with approximately 600 locations worldwide including Canada, Europe, and Mexico.

HISTORY

IKON Office Solutions was founded in 1965 as Alco Standard Corporation. Alco Standard was a holding company made up of several diversified manufacturing and distribution companies. Throughout the 1960s and 1970s, the company carried numerous product lines within a variety of industries. In 1983, the Alco Office Products division, an office equipment distributor, began to acquire local office products dealers throughout North America and Europe and became one of the more profitable divisions within Alco Standard. By the late 1990s, two divisions remained: Alco Office Products and Unisource Worldwide, a paper and related products distributor.

In 1997, company shareholders approved a spin-off whereby Unisource emerged as a separate company. At this time, Alco Standard changed its name to IKON Office Solutions to reflect the new technology evolving within the industry as well a "total solutions" approach for new services IKON was now offering in addition to traditional office equipment.

Today, IKON is committed to delivering flexible and customized solutions and services that enable customers to fully utilize digital technology in order to improve document workflow with increased cost efficiency.

THE PRODUCT

IKON provides a range of products and services to meet document workflow needs in the office — copying and printing in black-and-white or color, digital workflow and electronic document

distribution, as well as job management tools and application support.

One of the most important segments of the product portfolio is the array of devices and software systems that IKON offers to connect, manage, and optimize printers and copiers. These products are of tremendous value to customers as tools to increase productivity and efficiency, maximizing their investment in equipment. To IKON, they also serve as key differentiators in the marketplace, enabling the copier/printer devices to act as portals into all aspects of the document life cycle — from document capture to distribution, output, storage, and retrieval.

To deliver these solutions, IKON specialists start with a thorough analysis of customer needs that might include an assessment of current printing and workflow. Then, the company's Professional Services team uses their expertise to implement and support a customized solution based on best-in-class technology. This approach could include software solutions that enable scanning and document distribution and management from a digital copier/printer. Or it could include a differentiated print management system designed to manage printing to multiple devices, provide job tracking and accounting, offer specialized color controls, or support key applications like variable data printing or forms management. In fact, IKON offers a range of solutions as broad and varied as the needs of its customers.

Document outsourcing represents an area of particular promise for IKON since it happens to be both a sector of growth within the industry and also one of IKON's greatest points of strength. IKON's success in outsourcing is based on a range of offerings that can meet nearly any client need, including services provided on-site, off-site, and in custom combinations of the two. On-site, IKON offers flexible and scalable facilities management services, including management of copy/print centers and mailrooms, as well as fleet management services for approximately 1,300 customers in industries ranging from health care, legal services, manufacturing, education, and communications. Off-site, IKON offers comprehensive print services through our network of regional digital print production centers. And through Digital Express®, IKON's Web-based document management service, IKON helps its customers manage frequently printed materials.

IKON is also a leader in providing copy/print and document management services to one of the most document-intensive industries: the legal community. Our extensive network of legal document production centers offers quick and accurate document reproduction services to law firms and corporate legal departments, as well as IKON Scan-to-file Services[SM] and legal document coding.

RECENT DEVELOPMENTS

IKON is proud of the unique position it holds within the industry. IKON is equally proud to receive recognition from outside sources that cite the company's people and organization for successful approaches to solving customer challenges and offering the best customized solution to fit their needs.

For example, IOS Capital, LLC, a wholly owned subsidiary of IKON, was recently named to Standard & Poor's Select Servicer List. IOS Capital provides lease financing to customers and is one of the largest captive finance companies in North America. Reflective of the company's well-established track record for servicing office equipment leases, IOS Capital is the first equipment leasing company to be named to the Select Servicer List. IKON's customers benefit from the convenience of a single-source provider for all of their document-related needs as well as from a variety of financing options offered through IOS Capital.

PROMOTION

IKON's top-notch sales team — made up of 5,000 highly trained professionals — uses a consultative approach with customers in order to fully understand their challenges and business goals, and then applies IKON's expertise to recommend best-in-class technology effectively to drive efficiency and boost productivity. With IKON's approach to selling, it's no surprise that IKON was recently named by *Selling Power* magazine as one of the "25 Best Service Companies to Sell For" and one of the "50 Best Companies to Sell For Overall." In the comprehensive analysis, *Selling Power* ranked companies based on data in the areas of compensation, training, and career mobility.

BRAND VALUES

IKON Office Solutions *(www.ikon.com)* is a leading provider of products and services that help businesses manage document workflow and increase efficiency. In today's tough economic climate, IKON Office Solutions is committed to bringing customers improvements in their document workflow and increased efficiency as well as helping them to leverage their technology investments. IKON is a company that has an array of products and services that is simply unsurpassed in the industry. Backed by highly trained and skilled professionals who have a single-minded focus on meeting customer needs, IKON is a name that customers can rely on to help them succeed in a competitive world.

THINGS YOU DIDN'T KNOW ABOUT IKON OFFICE SOLUTIONS

○ IKON is the largest independent distributor of Canon and Ricoh copiers in the United States.

○ At *IKONSupplies.com*, customers can purchase supplies for their businesses, up to 30,000 items from paper to toner.

○ IKON's technicians undergo, on average, more than 100 hours of product, connectivity and systems training each year.

ITT Industries
Engineered for life

THE MARKET

In a movie theater, if you're noticing the film's score, the music isn't doing its job. ITT Industries realizes that technology works the same way. The best technology is invisible to its users; if it's working perfectly, every time, you never notice it.

Each day, millions of people use an ITT Industries product without ever knowing it. The company's products are embedded in the world's infrastructure, making it possible for people from China to Chicago to turn on their kitchen faucet; place a call on a wireless phone; travel by air, rail, or automobile; or walk the streets safely without thinking twice about it.

How ingrained is ITT Industries in our everyday lives? Every time somebody talks to you about tomorrow's weather, they're using weather service predictions made possible by satellites utilizing ITT's data-gathering imagers and sounders.

ITT Industries' transparency is a function of its products. Sometimes the products are hidden from view, like the tiny electronic connectors found in one out of every three mobile phones in the world today or the highly advanced sensors inside GPS satellites that can pinpoint your location to within three feet from 11,000 miles away in space. At other times, the ITT Industries name takes a backseat to its better-known product brand names, like Flygt, Goulds Pumps, Bell & Gossett, KONI, and Cannon.

The need for clean water is increasing at an alarming rate, and experts say that by 2025 we'll need up to three times the amount of fresh water that is currently available. ITT Industries' markets

will grow as the world's population grows. Consumers around the world are already purchasing nearly 500 million mobile handheld devices each year, and projections call for that figure to grow steadily during the next decade. As the world reacts to increasing threats from global terrorism, demand for defense related products and services could increase as well.

ACHIEVEMENTS

ITT Industries is the largest pump manufacturer in the world, having grabbed the top spot in 1997 with the acquisition of Goulds Pumps. Today, if you're moving fresh water or treating wastewater, chances are you're probably using ITT Industries technology.

When it comes to the phone of the future — portable, palm-sized, and Internet-connected — all five leading mobile phone handset manufacturers use ITT Industries, Cannon connectors, switches, and keypads.

The company's KONI brand shocks are installed on the world's fastest trains and were on board the French TVG train that set the world speed record of 320 miles per hour.

In the Defense Electronics area, ITT Industries is the world's leading producer of frequency-hopping combat net radio systems, which allow seamless communications between aircraft, vehicles, and soldiers as part of the U.S. Army's Tactical Internet. The military, municipal police, and Coast Guard use ITT's Night Vision equipment.

Among the awards that ITT Industries has won in recent years are the Engineering Excellence award from the Institute of Chemical Engineers for PumpSmart™ Control Solutions, which provides internal logic for pumping systems, and the Innovation Award from the National Marine Manufacturers Association for Jabsco's silent-running, energy-efficient Sensor Max™ Pump. The U.S. Air Force cited the Avionics Division's AN/ALQ-172 as the "most successful electronic countermeasures system" in its inventory.

HISTORY

The achievements of ITT Industries and the companies it has acquired span more than 150 years — from pioneering the world's first all-metal pump in 1848 to developing high-tech radar systems

that the U.S. Armed Forces will still be using 40 years from now.

As a corporate entity, ITT has existed for just over 80 years. ITT began in 1921 as International Telephone & Telegraph, primarily involved in telephone switching equipment and telecommunications. Through the 1970s, the company diversified through acquisition — buying companies on all continents, with products ranging from food to oil wells to manufactured homes.

In 1980, the company's name was officially changed to ITT Corporation. ITT stayed on a continuous course of restructuring and divestiture/acquisition to more clearly organize in terms of product and to increase shareholder value.

ITT Corporation split into three separate companies in 1995, and in December of that year, ITT

Industries, the legal successor to the original ITT, began trading independently on the New York Stock Exchange.

Through a series of strategic acquisitions and divestitures, ITT Industries has grown into a diversified global company with 25 business units, 38,000 employees, and approximately $5 billion in annual sales. Louis J. Giuliano now serves as the company's chairman, president, and chief executive officer.

THE PRODUCT

Considering the types of products that ITT Industries manufactures, it's hard to imagine an aspect of life where an ITT product doesn't play a vital role. The company manufactures products in four main business segments: Fluid Technology, Defense Electronics & Services, Electronic Components, and Motion & Flow Control.

In the Fluid Technology area, ITT produces pumps and systems for every application from fire fighting to irrigation to wastewater treatment. More than 2 million Flygt pumps have been installed since 1947, and its new non-clogging N-pump further reinforces Flygt's leadership position in the wastewater market. When Mother Nature turns nasty, Goulds Pumps provide drought protection for farmers and flood protection for homeowners. Chemical companies turn to anti-corrosive pumps made by its Richter unit to move harsh fluids, and pharmaceutical firms depend on Pure-Flo's hygienic valves to keep out contamination.

In Defense Electronics & Services, ITT Industries companies develop airborne electronic warfare systems, traffic control radars, night vision equipment, and space-based remote sensing technologies. True to its roots, ITT even works in communications and voice technologies. The services side of this business is growing rapidly, with ITT Industries engineers, scientists, and personnel staffing critical military outposts and monitoring space traffic from inside the U.S. military's Cheyenne Mountain complex.

Under the ITT Industries, Cannon brand, the company's Electronic Components business has worked with the world's leading telecommunications companies to help create technology that improves the way mobile phones and computer modems communicate. ITT's components are also the backbone of today's smart buildings, and every Boeing 777 aircraft includes over 100 switches, connectors, cable assemblies, valves, actuators, and other ITT parts.

The products from ITT Industries' Motion & Flow Control business are meeting many important needs. Automobile enthusiasts encounter ITT products in shock absorbers, automotive fluid handling systems, and other components. Weekend boaters count on systems, pumps, and accessories made by the company's Rule and Jabsco businesses for smooth sailing. And all around the world, whirlpools and soda dispensers use ITT's pumps and controls.

RECENT DEVELOPMENTS

ITT Industries has as its focal point a vision of becoming a premier multi-industry company in

In China, 8% of the world's water has to serve 22% of the world's people. ITT Industries helps make that easier to live with.

FLUID TECHNOLOGY · Flygt · Goulds Pumps · Sanitaire
DEFENSE ELECTRONICS AND SERVICES
ELECTRONIC COMPONENTS
MOTION AND FLOW CONTROL

ITT Industries
Engineered for life
www.itt.com

every sense of the word. To achieve premier status, it has embraced three key corporate strategies for leadership, growth, and operational excellence.

As part of its growth strategy, ITT Industries has made several adjacent acquisitions intended to strengthen or further its core market capabilities and global presence. The company's organic growth strategy is built around new product development, increasing its global presence, and serving new markets.

Leadership is also a key strategy. The company recently created a new position, chief learning officer, to speed the deployment of its Leadership Training effort. Through a Leadership Academy, the company will develop future leaders to serve as mentors, role models, coaches, and facilitators. These future leaders will serve to motivate and inspire their team to take their businesses to greater heights.

ITT Industries' operational excellence strategy centers around Value-Based Six Sigma, its overarching strategy for continuous improvement. Thousands of employees are being trained as Champions, Black Belts, and Green Belts, and all are focused on improving customer responsiveness and taking waste out of ITT's processes. Now, with its Value-Based Product Development effort, the company is teaching itself to more closely listen to the customer's voice in improving its product development process.

PROMOTION

Frankly, with a company like ITT Industries, promotion and advertising are not as easy as they might be for a corporation with the newest game system or sporty SUV. ITT can't simply buy up all the advertising time on *Friends* to hawk its rapidly evolving Monolithic Microwave Integrated Circuit–based active array radar technology.

The solution: Promote ITT's engineering excellence and showcase its ability to provide solutions to customers' everyday problems.

ITT Industries' advertising reflects the belief that it's not about the technology; it's about life.

To get this point across, the company isn't afraid to take a humorous approach to the simple fact that its end users will likely never understand what it does. ITT's first television ad campaign featured fish, crabs, whales, and frogs singing Handel's "Hallelujah Chorus" in celebration of the company's clean-water products.

The most recent ad campaign placed spots in print media such as the *Wall Street Journal*, *New York Times*, *Barron's*, *Institutional Investor*, and *Financial Times* and business- and news-based television programming. The company also sponsored *Water: The Drop of Life*, a PBS documentary on the global water crisis and its solutions.

ITT's product brands advertise heavily in their respective industry trade journals. While the corporate ITT ads focus on the company's overall strengths, the product brands' ads showcase their products' strengths. Taken together, customers, prospects, and investors hear a powerful message.

BRAND VALUES

ITT Industries is a multibillion-dollar, multi-industry company with a single focus: developing advanced technologies and highly engineered products that meet the most basic human needs. ITT Industries is "Engineered for life."

THINGS YOU DIDN'T KNOW ABOUT ITT

○ ITT Industries employees are located in 50 countries around the world and all 50 states in the United States. The states with the most ITT Industries employees are California, New York, Indiana, Virginia, and New Jersey. The countries with the most ITT Industries employees are the United States, China, Germany, Italy, and Sweden.

○ As an indicator of ITT's international scope, the company's employee newsletter is available in English, French, German, Italian, Spanish, and Chinese.

○ An ITT heating system warms the Statue of Liberty, its connectors provide power to the International Space Station, and its fire pumps protect the world's tallest building, the Petronas Towers in Kuala Lumpur, Malaysia.

○ In 2001, ITT took over space launch operations at both Vandenberg Air Force Base in California and Cape Canaveral Air Station in Florida, the first time one company has been awarded both contracts.

○ Philo T. Farnsworth, the inventor of the television, worked for a company that belonged to ITT. His technology was the basis for sensors developed by ITT for today's weather satellites.

JOCKEY

THE MARKET

The men's underwear and women's intimate apparel categories are multibillion-dollar retail businesses. Status designers, mainstream brands, and store labels all compete for a share of this lucrative business. The demand for comfortable, high-quality fashionable undergarments continues to grow each year. In recent years, "unmentionables" have generated widespread interest from the fashion and mainstream press. Underwear has evolved from basic white product, still the number-one seller, to a category featuring the latest in fabrics and styling innovation.

ACHIEVEMENTS

The Jockey brand is a remarkable success story. In its history, the company has not just influenced the underwear market but actually created parts of it and shaped other parts as well. The entire underwear industry literally changed its underwear to keep up with revolutionary Jockey inventions, including the brief, the bikini brief, the torso mannequin, transparent underwear packaging, and the underwear fashion show.

Unlike many other firms in the apparel industry, Jockey has not gone public, merged with other firms, or diversified into unrelated areas.

Today, Jockey is the number-one-selling brand of men's underwear and women's panties in department stores in the United States. The brand has over 95 percent consumer awareness and is one of the top apparel brands in the United States. Internationally the brand is sold in over 120 countries.

HISTORY

In 1876, Samuel T. Cooper's dedication to serving and helping others gave birth to the company now internationally recognized as Jockey International. Cooper, a retired minister with no textile experience whatsoever, was concerned about lumberjacks in the American Midwest whom he had learned were suffering from blisters and infections caused by their poor quality hosiery. Their socks, crudely shaped and made mostly from shoddy wool, wore prematurely and erratically.

When Cooper could not buy better socks for the lumberjacks anywhere in the region, he turned

a livery stable into a tiny sock factory, S. T. Cooper and Sons. While others were primarily in business to make money, Samuel Thrall Cooper and his sons were in business to serve others first, which would in turn earn them the right to make a profit.

For the Jockey brand, it all started in 1934, when a senior vice president at Coopers, Arthur Kneibler, happened to see a postcard from the French Riviera which showed a man wearing a swimsuit that ran just from the waist to the upper thigh. He was immediately inspired with an idea for a men's undergarment that would provide the same support as an athletic supporter, known colloquially as a "jock strap."

In subsequent strategy sessions, it was decided that the new garment would need a clever name that would somehow connote this function, yet would be discrete enough for sensitive lady shoppers. After much brainstorming, the

only name that appeared on everyone's list was JOCKEY, and the more they thought about it, the more they liked it. The JOCKEY brief was born.

The brief's public debut was as unusual as the garment itself. On January 19, 1935, Chicago's Marshall Field & Co. set up a department store window display to introduce the strange new JOCKEY underwear. But when the city was hit with one of the worst blizzards of the year, the store's management was afraid that the brief would be an absurd contrast to the biting winds, freezing temperatures, and drifting snow. It was decided that the window display would be pulled and the promotion canceled. However, the display men were delayed, and the window remained as it was. The entire stock of JOCKEY briefs was sold out before noon, in the midst of the snowstorm, economic hardships of the year notwithstanding.

That same year, Kneibler refined his invention further by developing the Y-FRONT opening, so named for the design of fabric panels, which offered consumers a buttonless fly.

In 1959, the company created a briefer brief that was to cause almost as much of a sensation as the original Jockey brief did in 1935 — bikini underwear, marketed under the trademark SKANTS. Although profitable in 1959, consumer demand for SKANTS bikinis exploded in the 1970s.

The company became so famous internationally for the Jockey brand and its attendant innovations that in 1972 the company was christened Jockey International, Inc. In 1978, Donna Wolf Steigerwaldt assumed the chairmanship. Under Mrs. Steigerwaldt's leadership, the company made a bold venture into a new frontier: women's intimate apparel. Perhaps the most lucrative move since the creation of the brief, the company developed a ladies' counterpart to what had been known only as a men's brand for nearly half a century. The company introduced

THE
NEXT BEST
THING
TO
<NAKED

⊕ THE NO PANTY LINE PROMISE® COLLECTION

Throughout its history, Jockey had featured a number of "Real People" promoting the brand. In the 1930s and 1940s, sports celebrities such as Babe Ruth, Tommie Armour, and Sammy Baugh endorsed Jockey underwear.

Jockey was the first to advertise underwear on television on NBC's *Home Show*, with Hugh Downs and Arlene Francis. In the 1970s, football stars Paul Hornung and Bart Starr were featured in television spots. In the 1980s, Hall of Fame pitcher Jim Palmer and Bart Conner, the two-time Olympic Gold Medalist in gymnastics, were spokesmen. In 1992, Nadia Comanici, the 1976 Olympics "Perfect 10," became the spokesperson for Jockey's women's products.

As the 21st century dawned, Jockey's marketing efforts returned to its "Real People" roots, promoting everyday comfort for everyday people. This approach recognized that consumers felt comfortable with the brand on an emotional level, identifying with a brand that identified with them — their lifestyles and their attitudes. Comfortable underwear was just the beginning.

JOCKEY FOR HER panties and tops in 1982, meeting with immediate success; sales surpassed even the most optimistic expectations.

THE PRODUCT

Jockey products are designed with a commitment to comfort, fashion, quality, and innovation. Jockey markets and distributes underwear and underwear-related products through department stores, chains, and specialty stores.

Jockey markets underwear for men, women, boys, and girls. For men, Jockey produces a full range of classic cotton underwear and fashion underwear in a variety of styles and fabrics. For women, Jockey makes panties in a variety of styles, patterns, and fabrics including cotton and microfiber.

Jockey has entered a number of underwear-related categories through licensing agreements, including activewear, thermalwear, sleepwear, hosiery, socks, and clothing for infants and toddlers.

RECENT DEVELOPMENTS

Jockey has continued to lead the market, offering innovative products to meet consumers' needs. In 1999, by popular demand, Jockey introduced its first constructed-bra line, delivering the same comfort, quality, and fashion that made Jockey panties a huge success. In September 2000, *www.jockey.com* was launched to provide consumers with the opportunity to shop 24/7 for Jockey underwear. The following year, the company revolutionized the industry once again, with its Jockey No Panty Line Promise collection. A breakthrough in underwear technology, the product was the right thing at just the right time. The No Panty Line Promise collection prevents panty lines just as fashions are becoming more form-fitting — and more prone to the panty-line problem.

PROMOTION

Jockey has always been an innovator in underwear advertising. Jockey advertising has always reflected the values of comfort, performance, fun, and quality. In a revolutionary move for its time, Jockey commissioned the *Saturday Evening Post*'s legendary artist J. C. Leyendecker to produce a series of color illustrations of underwear, which would be used in the company's advertising program. The first ad appeared in the *Saturday Evening Post* in 1911.

Rubber has gone to war but ...
YOU *STILL* GET THE
Same SUPPORT
Same COMFORT
Same Y-FRONT CONSTRUCTION
IN THE NEW WAR MODEL
Jockey
UNDERWEAR
WITH ADJUSTABLE WAISTBAND
ORIGINATED AND MANUFACTURED BY *Coopers*

BRAND VALUES

To millions in the United States, Jockey stands for comfort, quality, and value. Jockey's leadership in basic and fashion underwear has firmly established it as the classic American underwear brand.

The Jockey brand enjoys an international reputation for providing comfortable and high-quality undergarments. The Jockey brand positioning is comfort. Jockey brand products provide both physical comfort through a great-fitting product and emotional comfort through a relaxed and enjoyable wearing experience. The core values of the brand include youthfulness, fun, quality, value, confidence, and innovation.

THINGS YOU DIDN'T KNOW ABOUT JOCKEY

- ❍ Jockey created the world's first brief. Jockey developed this new-fangled underwear in 1934 with the assistance of a urologist to provide men with "masculine support."

- ❍ Jockey was the first to sell underwear in cellophane. Prior to 1937, underwear was sold in boxes like shoes for fear that seeing underwear in public would offend people.

- ❍ Jockey was at war with Hitler before the rest of the world. Jockey launched the world's first underwear fashion show featuring a "cellophane wedding" in 1937 (see photo). But after Hitler saw it in *Life* magazine, he denounced it in speeches as "immoral."

- ❍ Jockey designed underwear for the moon. In 1963, Jockey created special long underwear for the space program, complete with elastic straps to keep sleeves down in zero gravity.

Kellogg's ®

THE MARKET

Grain-based products are at the heart of a healthy American diet. The U.S. Department of Agriculture's food pyramid recommends six to eleven servings a day of products made from grain.

As Americans build grain-based foods into their diets, ready-to-eat cereal plays a most important role. The average U.S. resident consumes nearly 11 pounds of ready-to-eat cereal each year, providing both the goodness of grain and the added value of vitamin fortification.

Kellogg Company, the world's leading producer of cereal, manufactures cereal products and a wide range of other convenient, nutritious grain and vegetable-based products, including toaster pastries, cereal bars, frozen waffles, cookies, crackers, and veggie foods.

Even as Kellogg's® great-tasting convenience foods respond to the growing number of consumers who eat "on the run," the company also serves the approximately 70 percent of children and adults who continue to eat breakfast at home.

ACHIEVEMENTS

Headquartered in Battle Creek, Michigan, Kellogg Company has a record of nearly 100 years of excellence and a reputation for products that provide value and contribute to a healthy diet.

With projected annual sales of around $8 billion, Kellogg Company brands include *Kellogg's, Keebler, Pop-Tarts, Eggo, Cheez-It, Nutri-Grain, Rice Krispies, Murray, Austin, Morningstar Farms, Famous Amos, Carr's, Plantation, Ready Crust,* and *Kashi.* Kellogg icons such as *Tony the Tiger* and *Snap! Crackle! Pop!* are among the most recognized characters in advertising.

Over the years, Kellogg's products have won professional as well as consumer acclaim. For example, in 1999, *Kellogg's Raisin Bran Crunch* cereal became the only U.S. cereal ever to win advertising's prestigious Gold Lion Award.

Kellogg Company has compiled a long record of food industry leadership and global business growth. Kellogg products are manufactured in 19 countries and marketed in more than 160 countries around the world.

Kellogg Company also has a substantial record of social and environmental responsibility. In addition, Kellogg Company's largest share owner, the W. K. Kellogg Foundation, is one of the world's leading philanthropic organizations.

Always committed to environmental stewardship, Kellogg Company is proud of its nearly century-long record of being one of the world's largest users of recycled paperboard. In fact, the very first cartons that came off the Kellogg production line in 1906 were made of recycled fibers.

HISTORY

Kellogg Company's worldwide leadership in its industry stems from the invention of flaked cereal — by accident — at the Battle Creek Sanitarium. The "San" was an internationally famous Seventh Day Adventist hospital and health spa. Its elite patients were offered a regimen of exercise and fresh air, plus a strict diet that prohibited caffeine, alcohol, tobacco, and meat.

Sanitarium Superintendent Dr. John Harvey Kellogg and Will Keith (W. K.) Kellogg, his younger brother and business manager, experimented to find good-tasting substitutes for the hard and tasteless bread on the San's menu. Wheat was cooked, forced through granola rollers, then rolled into long sheets of dough. One day, after cooking the wheat, the two men were called away. Although the wheat was rather stale when they returned, the brothers decided to see what would happen when the tempered grain was forced through the rollers.

Instead of the usual long sheets of dough, each wheat berry was flattened into a small, thin flake. When baked, the flakes tasted crisp and light. The San's patients loved the new food.

Seeing the commercial opportunity of ready-to-eat cereal, W. K. Kellogg left the San in 1906 and formed the Battle Creek Toasted Corn Flake Company, later renamed Kellogg Company.

Mr. Kellogg boldly advertised his new product. He spent much of his working capital to buy a full-page ad in the July 1906 issue of *The Ladies Home Journal.* The results astonished him. Sales burgeoned from 33 cases to 2,900 cases per day. With more widespread ads and promotions to tell the public about "The Original and Best" Kellogg's Corn Flakes, the small company's annual sales surpassed 1 million cases by 1909.

W. K. Kellogg quickly expanded into international markets. He also expanded his product line, introducing Bran Flakes (1923), All-Bran (1916), Rice Krispies (1928), Kellogg's Frosted Flakes (1952), and Special K (1955) cereals. Pop-Tarts toaster pastries, launched in 1964, became an American institution of its own and, not surprisingly, the company's top-selling convenience food.

Kellogg Company also led the way in communicating good health. In the 1930s, Kellogg Company became one of the first companies to print nutrition messages and recipes on cereal package side and back panels.

In the second half of the 20th century, Kellogg Company's commitment to nutrition evolved into active support of scientific studies that have underscored the value of grain-based foods in a healthy diet.

In the 1990s, even as worldwide consumption of cereal continued to increase, Kellogg Company built an increasingly strong convenience-foods portfolio that now — after its recent acquisition of Keebler Foods — accounts for 43 percent of the company's global sales.

THE PRODUCT

Kellogg's products are a perfect fit for a healthy lifestyle. Many are low in fat and often help provide the dietary fiber that is lacking in the diets of many Americans. They also provide nutrition, great taste, and convenience.

The appeal of Kellogg's products also encourages consumers to eat what nutritionists agree is the most important meal of the day: breakfast. Research shows that people who eat breakfast tend to have less anxiety and improved memory. Children who go to school without breakfast have more trouble concentrating, and their schoolwork can suffer as a result. Regular breakfast eaters have better diets and generally enjoy better overall health than breakfast skippers.

Kellogg's products also have a long-standing reputation for consistently delivering the highest level of quality to consumers around the world.

RECENT DEVELOPMENTS

With its world-class research and development resources at W. K. Kellogg Institute for Food and Nutrition Research, Kellogg Company continues to be a global leader in food innovation. Just a sampling of Kellogg Company's recent innovations includes:

- Kellogg developed a high-potential natural and frozen foods division that includes the acquisitions of Worthington Foods Inc. in 1999 and Kashi Co. in 2000.
- In 2001, Kellogg put the power of red into breakfast with the introduction of Kellogg's® Special K® with Red Berries cereal. This unique cereal combines sweet and crunchy flakes with delicious slices of real strawberries.

- Kellogg acquired Keebler Foods Company in March 2001, the second-leading cookie and cracker manufacturer in the United States. A multiyear global relationship formed between Kellogg and Disney in 2002, and several new cereal and snack food products have been introduced to the market as a result.
- In 2002, Kellogg celebrated the 50th birthday of *Tony The Tiger™*. Ten outstanding children were awarded $10,000 scholarships, a trip to New York City, and the opportunity to appear on boxes of *Kellogg's Frosted Flakes®* cereal with *Tony The Tiger™*.
- Today, Kellogg produces more than 40 different cereals on six continents. The company markets its products worldwide and employs over 15,600 people in its worldwide organization.

PROMOTION

W. K. Kellogg was a master of creative advertising and promotion.

In the company's early years, "Give the Grocer a Wink" won shoppers free samples of Kellogg's Toasted Corn Flakes. *The Funny Jungleland Moving Pictures* book in 1910 became the first of thousands of premiums offered to consumers who bought Kellogg's cereal. From the world's largest electric sign at Times Square in New York City to small grocery store windows, the Kellogg name, written in W. K. Kellogg's distinctive script — *Kellogg's* — reminded the public that "None Genuine Without This Signature."

Kellogg Company's marketing leadership continued through the decades as consumers sent their box tops to Battle Creek for Kellogg premiums, and as Kellogg became a leader in creative radio and television advertising. Kellogg sponsored early family shows on TV, including *Superman* and *Wild Bill Hickock*.

The tradition of marketing leadership continues today as Kellogg has launched the cereal industry's first frequent-flyer promotion, with American AAdvantage Miles, as well as promotions based on popular Disney and Cartoon Network characters. Kellogg also leverages sponsorships such as

NASCAR, the Olympics, and the Susan G. Komen Breast Cancer Foundation Race for the Cure to bring value-added promotions to its consumers.

BRAND VALUES

Nearly a century after Kellogg Company was founded, Kellogg remains one of the best-known and most popular brand names in America and all around the world.

Kellogg's brands enjoy tremendous consumer loyalty. For example, more than 40 percent of the millions of Americans who eat Kellogg's Frosted Flakes have been doing so for more than 20 years, and it remains America's favorite cereal.

Kellogg Company's commitment is to continue to build its brands and to deliver superior value to consumers in the new century.

Consistent with the words of founder W. K. Kellogg, "We are a company of dedicated people making quality products for a healthier world."

More information about the company's products, vision, marketing, and mission is available at Kellogg's Web site, *www.kelloggs.com*, and Keebler's Web site, *www.keebler.com*.

THINGS YOU DIDN'T KNOW ABOUT KELLOGG

○ *Kellogg's Pop-Tarts* toaster pastries are incredibly popular with American consumers. If all the Pop-Tarts produced each year were laid end-to-end, they would circle the earth more than six times.

○ With powerful brands such as *Kellogg's Raisin Bran* and *Kellogg's Raisin Bran Crunch* cereals, Kellogg Company is the largest purchaser of raisins in the United States — about 60 million pounds each year.

○ *Tony the Tiger* is as well liked by young American children as Mickey Mouse.

○ The Kellogg product providing the most dietary fiber is *Kellogg's All-Bran with Extra Fiber* cereal, which provides 13 grams of fiber per serving, which is about half the daily amount of fiber recommended for adults.

○ Twenty percent of *Kellogg's Rice Krispies* cereal is used to make marshmallow squares at home.

KeyBank

Achieve anything.

THE MARKET

Twenty-first-century Americans — individuals and families, small businesses and international corporations — rely on financial institutions for an ever-widening variety of money-management products and services to help them achieve their financial goals. The solution is Key. Key transforms money, expertise, and opportunity into comprehensive financial solutions that help its clients achieve those goals. Key is dedicated to building enduring relationships with its clients, relationships that will enable Key to deliver on its brand promise: *Achieve anything.*

ACHIEVEMENTS

Cleveland-based KeyCorp is one of the nation's largest and most respected bank-based financial services companies, with assets of approximately $85 billion. Among its achievements, Key is

- Ranked number 257 on the Fortune 500, *Fortune* magazine's flagship list, based on total revenues (April 2002). In its 500 ranking, *Forbes* magazine places Key at number 177.
- Rated Outstanding in the past five consecutive exams by the Office of the Comptroller of the Currency for compliance with the Community Reinvestment Act.
- Key was ranked number 1 in corporate governance standards among large banks by Prudential Financial.

HISTORY

Key's roots date back to 1849, when the Society for Savings of Cleveland, Ohio, was incorporated; and to 1825, when the Commercial Bank of Albany, N.Y., was founded.

Key has grown to become one of the nation's largest bank-based financial institutions. Key companies provide investment management, asset management, retail and commercial banking, retirement, consumer finance, and investment banking

products and services to individuals and companies throughout the United States and, for certain businesses, internationally.

Key operates 910 full-service KeyCenters in 24 geographical districts across 12 states (45 states total are served by all of Key-related businesses). Nearly 21,000 Key employees serve more than 3.8 million households and commercial clients through KeyCenters and offices, a network of 2,200 ATMs, telephone banking centers at 1-800-KEY2YOU® (1-800-539-2968) and at *Key.com*®, which provides account access, online banking and investing, and financial products 24 hours a day, seven days a week.

THE PRODUCT

Key delivers its full range of financial products and services through experienced Relationship Managers who understand each client's financial goals, and through specialized resources that can help turn those goals into financial achievements.

Key Consumer Banking. Through 24 geographic districts across the United States, Key's community-focused retail bank serves consumers with a client-centric relationship sales and service philosophy. In the consumer banking field, Key is the first to operate as a single, nationwide retail bank; KeyBank National Association offers a wide array of financial solutions to meet each client's needs. Key is also the nation's 10th-largest home equity lender and the seventh-largest education lender. Moreover, Key Recreation Lending is one of the largest lenders for marine and recreational vehicles in the United States.

- *Key Small Business* continues to lead the way for small business owners with a powerful combination of products and value-added services, ranging from retirement benefits, to equipment purchasing and leasing, to cash management and investments. Small businesses can apply for loans and leases by calling 1-888-KEY4BIZ®, visiting a KeyCenter, or going online to *www.Key.com/smallbiz*.

Bumping up against capacity?

The Solution is Key.

Reaching capacity or outgrowing capital structure can make you feel like a fish out of water. Tap into the insight and capabilities vital to your expansion and get solutions appropriate to your situation with KeyBank and our more than 100 investment banking team members at McDonald Investments. With our full range of financing options, from traditional bank debt to equity capital, you're sure to find us to be a perfect fit. Now more than ever, the solution is Key.

KeyBank

For more information, call 1-800-KEY6070, or visit Key.com.
Achieve anything.

McDonald Investments Inc. member NASD/NYSE/SIPC.
©2002 KeyCorp. The Solution is Key is a registered service mark of KeyCorp.

- *Key Electronic Services.* Key Electronic Services meets the needs of global electronic audiences through exceptional products and services: online banking, *Key.com*, Key Bill Pay, merchant services, payroll processing, debit cards, credit cards, and Key's automated teller network, which with 2,200 ATMs is the nation's 10th largest. Key has approximately 400,000 small business and consumer online banking clients. Key is the sixth-largest MasterCard® Master Money debit card issuer, and Gomez Internet Quality Management has ranked *Key.com* among the top-10 online banks.

Key Corporate Finance. Key provides specialized financing to meet the needs of a broad range of businesses, with specialized products and teams of experts dedicated to specific client segments. For example, chosen by the United States Postal Service to provide depository/cash management services in all or part of 14 states, including several outside of Key's traditional market areas, Key now processes more than $6.7 billion in transactions for the USPS annually.

- *Key Commercial Real Estate,* the nation's fifth-largest commercial real estate lender, provides construction loans, interim loans and equity, as well as long-term commercial mortgages

nationwide for virtually all property types. Its 450 professionals finance nearly $6 billion in commercial real estate annually through 25 offices in major U.S. markets.

- *Key Equipment Finance*, the nation's sixth-largest bank-affiliated equipment leasing organization, manages an equipment portfolio of more than $7 billion. For everything from small businesses to multinational corporations, Key provides customized financing solutions for capital equipment acquisitions.

- *Key's Global Treasury Management Group* pairs experienced cash management and international partners with the resources, the state-of-the-art technology, and the wide array of products and services companies need to maintain close control of cash functions.

- Over the last 60 years, *Key's Media and Telecommunications Finance* group has committed $20 billion in capital to media and communications-related businesses.

Key Capital Partners. Key Capital Partners provides asset management, investment banking, capital markets, insurance, financial planning, and brokerage expertise to clients to allow them to adapt to ever-changing financial markets.

- *Capital Markets* professionals offer investment banking, capital raising, hedging strategies, trading, and financial strategies to public and privately held companies, institutions, and government organizations. This unit is the third largest mergers and acquisitions advisor to the U.S. banking and thrift industries (transaction volume).

- *McDonald Financial Group* professionals offer comprehensive financial planning and asset management services to affluent individuals and families. MFG provides banking, real estate, financial, and retirement planning; brokerage; trust; portfolio management; insurance advice and services; and charitable giving counsel. MFG is the nation's 21st-largest wealth manager (private bank assets under management).

- *Victory Capital Management* professionals manage or advise investment portfolios, on a national basis, for corporations, labor unions, not-for-profit organizations, governments, and individuals — in separate accounts, commingled funds, and the Victory family of 27 mutual funds. Victory Capital Management is the 12th-largest investment manager affiliated with a U.S. bank (assets under management).

Technology. Key's technology is at the forefront of its financial services. Its technology delivers banking services to all Key clients through its linked network of KeyCenters, ATMs, telephones, and PCs. Key was the first nationwide bank to link branch, ATM, telephone, and PC/Internet transactions for instantaneous account information. Key averages approximately 14.5 million electronic transactions per month (through ATM, telephone, and PC/Internet channels).

Customer Service. Key received more than 7 million customer calls last year, and has dedicated teams to answer clients' questions 24 hours a day, 7 days a week, 365 days a year — including specialized teams in such areas as corporate

banking, Key PrivateBank, retail banking, and online banking.

RECENT DEVELOPMENTS
In 2002, Key continued to pursue its policy of strategic expansion in specific geographic and business markets with the acquisition of Denver-based Union Bankshares, Ltd., and the mortgage loan and real estate business of Hartford, Connecticut–based Conning Asset Management.

Union, through its principal subsidiary Union Bank & Trust, operated seven banking offices in the Denver area. This acquisition significantly enhances Key's presence in Denver and surrounding Colorado communities, where it already operates 44 offices.

Key Commercial Mortgage, the permanent lending unit of Key Commercial Real Estate, expanded its product set with the acquisition of Conning's mortgage loan and real estate division. This acquisition provides the ability to originate and service loans on behalf of life insurance companies and pension fund clients.

Key's recent marketing efforts have featured a new emphasis on market segmentation. This approach differentiates the Key brand by focusing on the unique financial needs of consumer and business clients at specific life stages, emphasizing the important service a Key Relationship Manager provides in analyzing and determining solutions to meet those needs. Key's tagline sums up the benefit the company provides to clients: *The Solution is Key*.

PROMOTION
More than 1,700 Key bankers — senior executives, Relationship Managers, and product specialists — took Key's new brand message, The Solution is Key, across America in October 2002 in a series of one-day marketing blitzes that reached more than 10,000 clients and thousands of additional prospects.

The effort helped clients identify financial services needs and solutions in Key's market areas in Vermont, New York, Ohio, Indiana, Michigan, Washington, Oregon, Colorado, Utah, and Idaho. In addition to face-to-face client meetings, Key executives addressed high-profile business groups, discussing trends in financial services technology. In two cross-country examples, Patrick J. Swanick, president of Key's Retail Bank, spoke before the Greater Seattle Chamber of Commerce and at the Hudson Valley (New York) Technology Development Center.

As Americans entered the 2002 holiday season, Key provided a convenient solution to the

problems of "what to give" and "how to carry travel money safely" with its new Key Possibilities prepaid gift card. The Key Possibilities card, which can be used anywhere MasterCard® is accepted worldwide, is a secure alternative to cash and has wider acceptance than travelers' checks. Available in denominations from $25 to

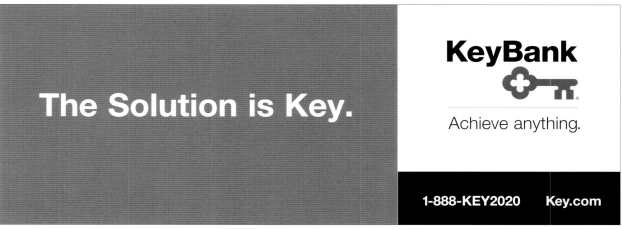

1-888-KEY2020   Key.com

$2,500, the Key Possibilities card can be used to purchase anything from lunch to airline tickets, or to get cash from an ATM. The Key Possibilities card is the perfect way to provide college students with the "cash" they need while they're away at school.

BRAND VALUES
A company as complex as Key serves a tremendous range of client groups, ranging from financially savvy investors and highly sophisticated business leaders to senior citizens on fixed incomes and small children opening their first bank accounts. All communications work to ensure that each client remembers one thing when facing a financial need at any life stage: The Solution is Key.

Key's objective is to create a genuine, enduring relationship with each client — a relationship dedicated to achieving that client's unique financial goals. Its brand positioning statement reflects those values by defining its audience, what Key is, what it does, and how it does it:

> *Key's trusted advisors deliver solutions that make it easier to achieve your financial goals.*

This in-depth positioning statement of Key's values is captured simply and directly in the brand promise that concludes every item of communication it issues:

Achieve anything.

LENNOX®

THE MARKET

Lennox Industries is a worldwide leader in home comfort. The company markets its air conditioning, heating, and indoor air quality products through a network of more than 7,000 dealers worldwide.

ACHIEVEMENTS

A passion for new ideas. That's what Dave Lennox had when he built the first riveted steel furnace, working in what one observer described as "an overgrown blacksmith shop" in Marshalltown, Iowa, in 1895. Far more durable than the cast-iron furnaces common at that time, the Lennox furnace set new standards for indoor comfort and safety for the industry.

In 1935, Lennox pioneered the introduction of a forced-air furnace for residential heating, drastically improving heating efficiencies and comfort. The Lennox Stowaway gas furnace, developed in the late 1930s, was the first home furnace designed for attic or crawlspace installation, the perfect solution for heating homes with no basements.

More product innovations came in the 1960s with the Duracurve, a new heat exchanger that reduced noise problems common in furnaces of the time. The first packaged multi-zone units for commercial heating and cooling were built by Lennox in 1965, ushering in a new era of efficiency and comfort for schools, churches, and office buildings.

In the 1970s and 1980s, the company led the industry into the high-efficiency heating and cooling markets. Lennox increased air conditioning efficiency with the development of the two-speed hermetic compressor in 1973, and with the first high-efficiency gas furnace in 1982.

In 1994, the company became the first major manufacturer to produce a combination high-efficiency residential space/water heating system.

Important product innovations in commercial air conditioning were introduced in the 1990s. Lennox' factory configure-to-order system for commercial air conditioning began in 1995, with the introduction of the L Series® commercial line.

In 2002, the company introduced its Dave Lennox Signature® Collection of top-of-the-line home comfort equipment, utilizing its own Silent-Comfort® technology that has allowed it to produce the quietest air conditioners and furnaces on the market today. The company also introduced its new PureAir™ air purification system, an appliance that cleans the air in a home better than any other system on the market, according to independent test results.

HISTORY

Sweating for long hours in his "overgrown blacksmith shop" in Marshalltown, Iowa, Dave Lennox began building the first Lennox furnace. Lennox, son of an expert railroad mechanic, used his own mechanical genius to design and build the first riveted steel furnace in 1895, thus revolutionizing the home heating business. The riveted steel furnace was a vast improvement over the cast-iron furnaces then available.

Lennox started the Lennox Machine Company when he first came to Marshalltown in 1888. He got his start as a manufacturer of architectural materials, boilers, engines, and farm implements.

The superiority of Lennox' redesigned furnace was obvious, and Lennox furnaces quickly became popular. But by 1904, Lennox was tired of the furnace business. An interested group of local businessmen bought the furnace business from him for $54,789.14. During their first year of ownership, the Lennox Furnace Company sold 600 furnaces. One of the primary new owners was David Windsor (D. W.) Norris, who later purchased the remaining company stock.

Long after Dave Lennox sold the company to the D. W. Norris family, that same passion for innovative new product and growth strategies continued. D. W. Norris tapped into that same spirit of innovation in the way he marketed Lennox furnaces, choosing to sell directly to the installing contractor using a one-step distribution strategy.

By the 1920s, Lennox was expanding beyond its Iowa roots into other parts of the United States. By the end of the 1930s, because of innovations made in its product line during that decade, Lennox was the world's largest manufacturer of forced warm-air heating systems. While special government orders kept Lennox from making furnaces during most of World War II, the company retooled its factories and prospered through defense work.

By the early 1950s, Lennox had established operations across the United States and Canada,

and in 1955 its name was changed to Lennox Industries Inc. In 1952, Lennox moved into the cooling business, despite skepticism from many industry experts, and developed the first residential central air conditioning system. The company scored an overnight success.

In 1960, Lennox' first international division was formed, expanding its growth into England, Holland, and Germany. The company continued to grow in the 1970s. Dave Lennox would hardly recognize his overgrown blacksmith shop today, but he would recognize the same dedication to new ideas and industry leadership. It's a tradition of innovation that began in the horse-and-buggy days — and is just as vital in the 21st century.

THE PRODUCT

Lennox' century-old commitment to quality products and services continues as it implements sophisticated, lean manufacturing processes at many of its facilities, resulting in better products for its customers, built faster.

Lennox is developing highly sophisticated e-commerce systems that make it easier and faster for customers to communicate and do business with the company. The company is constantly exploring new ways to enhance its products and services by listening to customers, refining processes to improve quality and efficiency, and evaluating emerging technologies.

Originally led by Dave Lennox, Lennox has carefully expanded its product line to include many models of air conditioners, heat pumps, boilers, hearth products, and furnaces, as well as products to improve indoor air quality. At the same time, it has ensured that each product represents the traditional Lennox standards of reliability and trust.

RECENT DEVELOPMENTS

Dave Lennox' emphasis on practical innovation lives on in Lennox' commitment to expanding its fast-growing e-commerce systems with input

from customers. The emphasis on innovation is also evident in the recent development of Web-based controls for residential and commercial comfort systems.

To meet consumers' growing demand for quieter heating and cooling equipment, Lennox recently introduced the quietest furnace and central air conditioner on the market, based on independent laboratory testing. Innovative new technology developed by Lennox is making it possible for the company to introduce home cooling systems as much as 16 times quieter than current products on the market, as well as home heating systems up to 84 percent quieter than current systems. Several key engineering developments — part of Lennox' SilentComfort® technology — made critical advances in sound reduction a practical reality.

In 2002, the company also introduced its new PureAir™ air purification system, an appliance that cleans the air in a home better than any other system on the market, according to independent test results.

PROMOTION

Lennox has had some of the most memorable advertising campaigns in the heating, ventilation, and air conditioning industry. In the 1970s, the "Dave Lennox" character evolved quickly into a widely used company spokesperson. "Dave Lennox," wearing his overalls and cap, represents Lennox' tradition and innovation. The phrase "Atta boy, Dave," used in television and print ads, became popular. As the highly successful campaign continued,

"Dave Lennox" began to work with Lennox dealers in their local advertising markets. Thirty years later, the popular icon makes personal appearances at various industry events and is featured in Lennox advertising.

BRAND VALUES

Both Dave Lennox and D. W. Norris defined the basic values that helped Lennox grow from an overgrown blacksmith shop in a small Iowa town to a global leader in the climate control industry. Even in today's far more complex business environment, Lennox still finds success and growth opportunities in following and expanding on those same values. After growing in the midst of many difficult domestic and global challenges over more than a century, Lennox is firmly committed to maximizing its performance in the public sector.

THINGS YOU DIDN'T KNOW ABOUT LENNOX

○ Lennox managed to survive during the Great Depression partly by securing government contracts, including heating the barracks of workers in the Civilian Conservation Corps.

○ The Lennox Equator was the first commercially produced furnace to utilize a blower, a major development in the industry.

○ In 1943, Lennox contributed to building submarine-hunting destroyer escorts for the U.S. Navy.

○ In the 1950s, Lennox manufactured a number of innovative products, including the Prairie Schooner, a popular way to spot heat garages and building construction sites, and the Holiday House, an aluminum structure used as a garage or a screened-in entertainment center. Other Lennox innovations were the crop drier; the tobacco drier, which was later used to provide warehouse heating to keep stored canned goods from freezing; and the Kittytrack™ lawn tractor, which featured tracks instead of wheels.

THE MARKET

Chocolate continues to be America's favorite flavor when it comes to confectionery products. Americans ranked eighth worldwide in the consumption of chocolate, with England having the highest rate of consumption. In a recent poll, 52 percent of American men and women voted for chocolate as their favorite flavor in confectionery products and desserts. Within that group, 65 percent chose milk chocolate and 27 percent voted for dark chocolate. The remaining 8 percent did not have a preference.

Chocolate sales have been increasing during the past year, possibly due to the news of antioxidants found in chocolate and the health benefits provided by its consumption. Halloween is the number-one candy-consuming holiday in the United States, followed by Christmas, Easter, and Valentine's Day. Retail candy sales in America were an estimated $24 billion last year. Retail chocolate sales alone were worth $13.1 billion (sources: National Confectionery Association, U.S. Department of Commerce).

ACHIEVEMENTS

Today, the M&M'S® Brand is sold in over 100 countries and is the largest, most popular confectionery brand in the world. In North America, M&M'S Candies are the number-one brand and is 50 percent larger than the number-two brand. Over the last 20 years, sales have grown by more than 1,000 percent, rocketing the brand to approximately $2 billion in retail sales, while growing at twice the rate of the category and achieving nearly double-digit compound growth since 1995. M&M'S has maintained its leadership in the category by its commitment to making its essence of colorful chocolate fun, fresh, and relevant to its millions of loyal and new consumers.

In 1941, the M&M'S Brand transformed chocolate from a dark or light brown product into a colorful, bite-sized chocolate treat. Even today, more than 60 years since its launch, no one has been able to

encroach upon this truly unique product platform or positioning. In fact, the unrivaled format of M&M'S has enabled the brand to become the mainstay of the confectionery category, continually driving growth for over 50 years. In a time of the five-cent candy bar, M&M'S led the trend from impulse candy buying to in-home future consumption. The brand also led the way into mass merchandising in the 1960s and more recently into online ordering. Whether driven by being the first confectionery product to advertise on TV in 1954, or the brand's constant commitment to innovative promotions like the 1995 "Color Vote," or its imaginative novelty packaging, M&M'S has clearly set the industry standard. In short, an innovative product format, coupled with a steadfast positioning, elevated M&M'S to the position of confectionery leader. Today, the M&M'S Brand has established itself as an American icon brand.

HISTORY

Following the path of nearly every other great American dream, M&M'S Chocolate Candies came about as an idea garnered from a faraway land, gaining great popularity and finding success across the world and even in space. As the story goes, Forrest Mars Sr. visited Spain during the Spanish Civil War and encountered soldiers who were eating pellets of chocolate in a hard, sugary coating. The coating kept the chocolate from melting. Inspired by the idea, Mr. Mars brought his dream back to America, went back to his kitchen, and invented the recipe for M&M'S Plain Chocolate Candies.

Originally sold to the public in 1941, M&M'S Plain Chocolate Candies earned a solid reputation from American GIs serving in World War II who first enjoyed the candies in their food rations. Chocolate candy that could survive in hot weather was unheard of during that time. The colorful candy shell on the M&M'S candies solved that problem, and, after its introduction in 1941, Americans could enjoy chocolate in the form of brown, yellow, orange, red, green, and violet M&M'S Plain Chocolate Candies all year.

During the 1950s, M&M'S Chocolate Candies were quickly becoming a staple in the American household. Advertising helped increase the popularity of these irresistible candies, using the famous

slogan, "The Milk Chocolate Melts in Your Mouth — Not in Your Hand."

Since their creation, M&M'S had served America's military, so it was only natural that the candies were officially made part of the American space program as well. They became part of the first space shuttle astronauts' food supply in 1984. In 1984, M&M'S made their first trip into space on the shuttle and have been a part of shuttle missions ever since. Aside from venturing into space, M&M'S Chocolate Candies also began venturing out of the United States and began to be sold internationally. Also in the 1980s, M&M'S made an appearance at the Olympic Games, as the "Official Snack Food" of the 1984 Games in Los Angeles.

As the 20th century came to an end, the M&M'S Brand Characters proclaimed themselves the "Official Candy of the New Millennium."

THE PRODUCT

M&M'S Chocolate Candies are a unique blend of the highest-quality milk chocolate with a strong taste that is not too sweet and not satiating. Individual candies are covered with a thin, crisp, colorful sugar shell that imparts the unique M&M'S texture. The shell colors are bright, shiny, and lustrous. The milk chocolate inside and the crisp outside sugar shells provide all the taste — the color has no taste.

M&M'S are made in nine varieties: Milk Chocolate Candies (the original M&M'S), Peanut Chocolate Candies, Peanut Butter Chocolate Candies, Almond Chocolate Candies, Crispy Chocolate Candies, Mint Chocolate Candies, MINIs Milk Chocolate Candies, Milk Chocolate and Semi-Sweet Chocolate Mini Baking Bits, and COLORWORKS Chocolate Candies.

M&M'S COLORWORKS are a collection of 21 vibrant-colored Milk Chocolate Candies that can be selected in any combination to create personal color choices. They can be used in a colorful blend to add innovative touches to parties, conferences, events, and as gifts.

RECENT DEVELOPMENTS

Over the years, the M&M'S Brand and the M&M'S Brand Characters have evolved into true American icons. They were "C" rations in World War II (MREs today) and since 1984, space food for U.S. astronauts, which earned them a permanent display at the Smithsonian Institute. They are popular costumes for Halloween, and in recent years the "M" Characters have participated in the Macy's Thanksgiving Day Parade. In Las Vegas, "M&M'S WORLD" occupies a 28,000-square-foot "retail-tainment" store on the Strip. In fact, M&M'S is so much a part of the lives of Americans that during the brand's 1995 "Color Vote," over 10 million consumers voted for the new color of M&M'S Chocolate Candies.

To young and old alike, the brand is a special part of our everyday lives, either as a delicious

snack or as a tool to teach children counting and colors. The consumers' relationship with the brand is further manifested through the immense popularity of the M&M'S Spokescandies. After 37 years, they are more popular than ever, allowing the brand to successfully expand into the world of licensed merchandise. Simply, while many mature brands begin to lose relevance, the M&M'S Brand has proven its appeal to be evergreen.

PROMOTION

Historically, the M&M'S Brand has had one of the most memorable taglines: "The Milk Chocolate Melts in Your Mouth — Not in Your Hand." Along with that slogan, M&M'S promotion has been distinguished by the presence of the brand's famed Spokescandies. In 1995, along with the legendary "Color Vote" promotion when Blue joined the characters Red and Yellow in life, the Spokescandies transformed from cartoon characters to real-time animation, bringing characters to a more celebrity-like status.

In 1996, *USA Today* rated the advertising campaign featuring the characters number-one among more than 60 campaigns. The characters' popularity with consumers reached new heights, surpassing that of Mickey Mouse and Bart Simpson, according to Marketing Evaluation, Inc.

That same year, the characters went "Virtual Hollywood" on the Internet with the opening of the M&M'S Studios (*www.mms.com*). Visitors to the site find themselves within the star-studded,

glamorous world of the M&M'S Brand Spokescandies. The site employs Shockwave and RealAudio technology for the characters' lifelike animation and sound.

Not only were the characters having fun on the Internet, they were speeding around the NASCAR Winston Cup Series as the title sponsor of the #36 M&M'S racing team. Ernie Irvan drove the car in the early years followed by Ken Schrader after Irvan's retirement. For 2003, Elliott Sadler will share the track with the famous M&M'S Spokescandies in the new #38 car.

A highlight of 1997 was the debut of Green, who was not only the first female among the characters, but was also a talented author. She starred in a number of popular commercials and "toured" the country promoting her biography, *I Melt for No One*.

In 2000, a major event changed the ever-famed M&M'S Plain Chocolate Candies. M&M/MARS decided that the candies were just too good to be called "Plain," and their name was changed to M&M'S Milk Chocolate Candies.

In 2002, the world was asked to choose the next color of M&M'S in the Global Color Vote™. More than 200 countries participated in the selection of purple as the newest color to join the bag for a limited-time promotion.

BRAND VALUES

The M&M'S Brand has represented superior quality and enjoyment to customers since Mr. Mars developed the brand in 1940. The appeal of M&M'S Chocolate Candies is universal, crossing age, gender, and national boundaries, bringing colorful chocolate fun to everyone.

McDonald's

THE MARKET

Dining out has always been a popular social activity. These days, eating away from home is a part of everyday life that many people take for granted. However, meals in restaurants were once only an occasional indulgence enjoyed by a privileged few. The popular food service revolution of the last 50 years changed all that. Today, dining out is a social activity enjoyed every day throughout the world by people of all ages and backgrounds. In fact, 16 percent of all meals in the United States are eaten away from home. For McDonald's, this little bit of sociology translates into 22 million customers every day across the nation.

ACHIEVEMENTS

McDonald's has become the world's most extensive retail organization, generating some $40 billion in annual sales from more than 30,000 restaurants worldwide. Its market share in the United States is more than its next two competitors combined. Internationally, McDonald's represents 50 percent of all globally branded outlets and captures more than two-thirds of those sales.

HISTORY

The McDonald's story began 48 years ago in San Bernardino, California. Ray Kroc was a salesman supplying milkshake multi-mixers to a drive-in restaurant run by two brothers, Dick and Mac

McDonald. Kroc, calculating from his own figures that the restaurant must be selling over 2,000 milkshakes a month, was intrigued to know more

about the secret behind the success of the brothers' thriving business. He visited the restaurant, which promised its customers "Speedee Service" and watched in awe as restaurant staff filled orders for 15-cent hamburgers with fries and shakes every 15 seconds. Kroc saw the massive potential and decided to become involved. The McDonald's brothers accepted Kroc's offer to become their national franchising agent. On April 15, 1955, he opened his first McDonald's restaurant in Des Plaines, Illinois, a suburb just north of Chicago.

Rapid growth followed. McDonald's served more than 100 million hamburgers within its first three years, and the 100th McDonald's restaurant opened in 1959. In 1961, Kroc paid $2.7 million to buy out the McDonald's brothers' interest, and in 1963 the billionth McDonald's hamburger was served live on prime-time TV.

The brand proved equally popular outside the United States. McDonald's quickly established successful international markets in Canada, Japan, Australia, and Germany. Today, more than 1.5 million people work for McDonald's around the globe. What started as an American phenomenon has become a truly international brand.

THE PRODUCT

From its early roots as a small, family-run hamburger restaurant, McDonald's has evolved into a multibillion-dollar quick-service restaurant industry. While hamburgers and fries remain the mainstay of McDonald's business, an instinctive ability to anticipate and fulfill real consumer needs has been central to McDonald's success. A prime example of this approach is the Filet-O-Fish sandwich, which was conceived by Lou Groen, a Cincinnati-based franchisee in a predominantly Catholic area. Groen noticed that his business was negatively impacted on Fridays, which was then a day of abstention from meat for many Catholics. He developed a fish-based product to meet the needs of the local community. The Filet-O-Fish sandwich was launched in 1963 and went on to become a popular menu item in many of McDonald's international markets.

Another franchisee — Jim Deligatti from Pittsburgh — was responsible in 1968 for the creation of McDonald's most successful menu item ever, the Big Mac sandwich. Nine years later, Herb Peterson, another franchisee, was the driving force behind the development of the Egg McMuffin for McDonald's

breakfast menu — a move that would change the breakfast habits of millions of Americans.

RECENT DEVELOPMENTS

McDonald's published its first-ever Global Social Responsibility Report in 2002, detailing its commitment to doing what is right, to being a good neighbor and partner in every community it

serves, and to conducting its business with the environment in mind.

McDonald's history of giving back to local communities represents a longstanding commitment, and the report demonstrates that this legacy is alive and well even in a changing world. Being a global brand brings global responsibilities with it, and the report not only details McDonald's accomplishments to date, but also sets an aggressive agenda of social responsibility to strive for in the future.

More details about McDonald's social responsibility efforts are available by visiting the company's Web site at *www.mcdonalds.com/corporate/social/*.

PROMOTION
Needless to say, McDonald's promotional skills are virtually second-to-none. From the global presence of the Golden Arches to the fact that their spokesman, Ronald McDonald, speaks 25 languages, McDonald's devotion to promotion is legendary.

But what can happen when a company like McDonald's turns up the promotional heat on an issue of global concern? The answer is: Great Things.

On November 20, 2002, a visit to McDonald's brought extra value to the lives of millions of children in need around the world. On that day, participating McDonald's restaurants in more than 100 countries united for a history-making fundraising initiative called World Children's Day, benefiting Ronald McDonald House Charities (RMHC) and important local children's causes. In the United States, McDonald's donated $1 from the sale of every Big Mac, Egg McMuffin, Happy Meal, and Mighty Kids Meal to RMHC. Money collected internationally went to children's causes of local interest.

While specific fund-raising programs varied by country, McDonald's restaurants shared a single goal: to join with customers in a global effort that would make a difference for children in their communities and around the world.

World Children's Day activities took place in, among other places, New Zealand, Hong Kong, Russia, Jordan, Egypt, Germany, France, Mexico, and Western Samoa. Of course, McDonald's restaurants in cities across the United States held their own activities as well, with nationally known celebrities participating in Chicago, New York, and Los Angeles.

"With the help of many generous people around the world, World Children's Day was the most expansive single-day fundraising event in McDonald's history, probably any company's history," said Ken Barun, RMHC president and CEO.

Ronald McDonald House Charities, a nonprofit, 501(c)3 organization, creates, finds, and supports programs that directly improve the health and well-being of children through its network of 174 local Chapters currently serving in 44 countries. Named one of America's Top 100 Charities by *Worth* magazine in 2001 and 2002, the charity makes grants to not-for-profit organizations and provides support to Ronald McDonald Houses and Ronald McDonald Care Mobiles worldwide. To date, Ronald McDonald House Charities' national body and global network of local Chapters have awarded more than $340 million in grants to children's programs.

BRAND VALUES
Founder Ray Kroc developed his brand vision for McDonald's around a simple but effective consumer-driven premise of quality, service, cleanliness, and value. Kroc's winning formula was quickly shortened to QSC&V — an acronym that would become and remain an enduring cornerstone of the brand.

If QSC&V is the cornerstone of the McDonald's brand, then trust is its bedrock. To its customers, McDonald's is a brand that can be trusted to place the customer at the center of its world and to know the right thing to do.

The key to McDonald's success has been its capacity to touch universal consumer needs with such consistency that the essence of the brand has somehow always been relevant to the local culture,

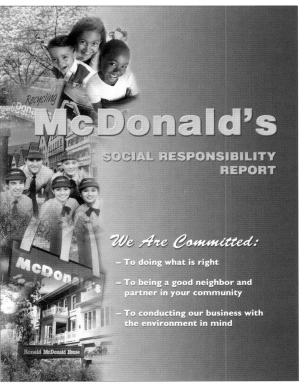

no matter how different that culture might be from McDonald's origins. With one of the most powerful brands in the business, McDonald's appears set to enjoy healthy growth long into the future.

THINGS YOU DIDN'T KNOW ABOUT McDONALD'S

○ McDonald's partners with the Red Cross to help communities when natural disasters and other events prompt a need for assistance. For example, the company provided more than 750,000 free meals around the clock in New York City, at the Pentagon, and in Pennsylvania after the terrorist attacks of September 11, 2001. The company believes that's what neighbors do in times of need.

○ The company's promotional efforts also support many youth activities. Last year, for instance, McDonald's not only celebrated the 25th staging of its All-American High School Basketball Game in New York, but also inaugurated its first annual game featuring the top high school girls in the nation.

THE
COMPANY

THE MARKET

The United States is home to over 134 million dogs and cats. Six out of 10 households in the United States own a pet, and 90 percent of those pets are dogs or cats. Since 1990, the cat population has risen 25 percent. The average cat owner has 2.1 cats, and cat ownership is expected to increase 6 percent between 2000 and 2005, keeping pace with U.S. household growth. Lifestyle and demographic shifts favor pets such as cats, because of both their ease of care and busier consumer lifestyles.

Research shows that pet owners are in stores more often and spend more money per trip than do non–pet owners. Expenditures for pet care are growing at more than 7 percent each year. In terms of total grocery/mass dollar sales, the pet aisle ranks number three in the store.

Cat owners themselves are a special breed. An oft-heard homily is that "For cat owners who think they own their cats, in a cat's mind, the reverse is quite true." Whether a family lives with one of the ubiquitous American Shorthairs or a more exotic Abyssinian, people view their cats as part of the family — unique individuals to be nurtured and appreciated as much as any family member. Meow Mix is a perfect fit for this type of cat family.

ACHIEVEMENTS

Meow Mix is the number-one brand of dry cat food in the United States, which is no small feat. With the battle for grocery-store shelf space

always intense, and when so many companies offer seemingly endless varieties of their product, Meow Mix makes cat owners this simple offer: Buy this product and you can be assured that your cat is eating a tasty blend of food that will keep him or her healthy at all stages of life.

The Meow Mix brand has developed significant equity with its signature yellow packaging and tagline, "Tastes so good cats ask for it by name!"

The Meow Mix jingle has been an integral part of all marketing efforts since its introduction in 1974.

HISTORY

Ralston Purina first introduced Meow Mix in 1974. Nestlé later purchased Ralston Purina but needed to divest its Meow Mix and Alley Cat brands based on FTC concerns, at which point in time The Meow Mix Company was formed. The Meow Mix Company is now a privately held and completely cat-focused company based in Secaucus, New Jersey.

THE PRODUCT

The Meow Mix Company offers customers two brands of cat food: Meow Mix and Alley Cat.

Meow Mix is a 100 percent nutritionally complete and tasty diet for cats in all life stages. Two delicious flavors are available for cats to enjoy: Original and Seafood Middles. Original Meow Mix is a tantalizing mixture of flavors and shapes (chicken, turkey, salmon, and oceanfish). Meow Mix Seafood Middles offer scrumptious mackerel and tuna flavors with crunchy, seafood-flavored middles.

Pleasing to the cats are the tempting taste and variety of the Meow Mix blends. Of greater importance to cat owners are the healthful aspects of Meow Mix. The brand offers complete and balanced nutrition for cats, coming packed with wholesome grains, proteins, and other high-quality ingredients. Meow Mix gives cats everything they need for strong bones, healthy teeth, shiny coat, and lots of energy.

Alley Cat is America's number-one selling value brand of cat food. Alley Cat provides 100 percent complete and balanced nutrition at a great price and is available in two delicious flavors that cats love: poultry and seafood, and oceanfish and tuna. And just because Alley Cat is a value-focused brand doesn't mean that cat owners are holding back on providing their cats the nutrition they need. Alley Cat is enriched with essential vitamins to keep cats healthy, while the cats enjoy the great taste and fun shapes. The crunchy morsels of Alley Cat also ensure healthy teeth.

RECENT DEVELOPMENTS

The Meow Mix Company remains focused on building the brand's equity while raising brand awareness to all-new levels. During 2002, the company brought back its 1974 commercial by refreshing the way that the jingle has been used over the past 30 years.

Meow Mix is also making available a full new line of toys and accessories designed to entertain and stimulate cats and to allow owners to spend more quality time with them. Such items include the Meow Dangler, the Meow Puff Ball, the Meow Mouth Treater, and accessories including food and water bowls, pet blankets, and pet pillows.

On September 16, 2002, The Meow Mix Company opened its wholly owned plant in Decatur, Alabama. The new plant will be the only pet food plant in the United States that is 100 percent dedicated to producing dry cat food, affirming the company's commitment to make the best cat food in America.

PROMOTION

With a cultural icon like the Meow Mix jingle, the challenge becomes keeping such a creative concept top of mind while not wearing it out in the minds of consumers, or in Meow Mix's case, purchasers. To that end, Meow Mix is constantly developing different ways to enhance and freshen the jingle. One way the company accomplished this feat in 2002 was to add VH-1-style "pop-ups" to its commercials. The jingle's presence in *Austin Powers* certainly didn't hurt either. In September 2002, Meow Mix introduced its new "Catchy Tune" commercial.

Meow TV — a new creative element in the Meow Mix mix — is the first television programming created for cats and their owners. The purpose of this ongoing show will be not only to raise brand awareness for cat food purchasers, but also to offer entertainment for the cats

themselves, with squirrels, birds, bouncing balls, and other cat-pleasing visuals dancing across the screen.

And, Meow TV isn't the only form of entertainment that Meow Mix has to offer. Don't be surprised if you see an 18-foot-long calico cat heading your way. That's just one of the company's famous Meow Mix Mobiles making its way across the country to further entertain and educate consumers. The Meow Mix Mobile Tour is scheduled to cross the United States throughout 2003, inviting cat owners to sing the Meow Mix jingle when they see the vehicle. Meow Mix is also using the Mobile Tour to build relationships with retailers.

Meowmix.com is a Web site with the theme of "Keeping Cats Happy" and offers a fun place for cat owners to show off their cats and find product information. On the Web site, cats and their owners can find fun and games, product news, sweepstakes, loyalty programs, and photo contests.

BRAND VALUES

From advertising to sales, the central focus of the Meow Mix Company is keeping cats happy. What else is there to say?

THINGS YOU DIDN'T KNOW ABOUT MEOW MIX

○ The Meow Mix Mobile is an 18-foot-long calico cat licking its chops, weighing 9,850 pounds and with a motorized tongue that does 20 whisker-to-whisker licks per minute.

○ On *meowmix.com*, visitors can vote for their favorite photo of a cat owner with a bag of Meow Mix. At press time, posted pictures included Meow Mix at the Eiffel Tower and the Gateway Arch, and a smiling couple holding a bag of Meow Mix and magnum of champagne. The person who submitted the favored photo in the contest won $500 and a year's supply of Meow Mix.

○ Studies have shown that Meow Mix tastes better to cats than other cat food brands.

○ Among cat owners in the United States, Meow Mix has a 93 percent brand awareness, the highest of any dry cat food brand.

○ Meow Mix has some unique customer testimonials in its files: According to one Meow Mix fan, not only do his four cats love Meow Mix, but his pit bull loves it, too. Meow Mix also has received reports from happy turkey and iguana owners who say that their animals enjoy a Meow Mix meal.

THE MARKET

In recent years, a great deal of growth has occurred in the plumbing industry as manufacturers create new products that make consumers want to change their faucets, showers, and bath accessories. New styles, functions, and innovations are leading consumers to replace faucets not because they have worn out, but because something new on the market will make their lives easier and their homes more comfortable and stylish.

ACHIEVEMENTS

Moen Incorporated is the number-one faucet brand in North America. The company conducts extensive research to identify consumers' needs and develops products to meet those needs. Moen understands that design is a critical element in the home, so everything about Moen's collection of premium bath and kitchen faucets combines distinctive style and function with durable craftsmanship and innovation.

Industry observers have taken note of Moen's style and innovation. In 2001 alone, *Professional Builder* magazine cited Moen as the Faucet Brand Used Most by Builders and the Most Preferred Brand of Kitchen and Bath Faucets. *Kitchen & Bath Design News* gave Moen an Industry Leadership Award recognizing Moen's importance in the plumbing industry.

Such recognition continually sets Moen apart from other companies in the building and home improvement marketplace.

HISTORY

In 1937, Al Moen changed the course of plumbing history — literally by accident. One day, while trying to wash his hands with a conventional, two-handle faucet, he scalded them under the hot water. This incident led him to invent the world's first single-handle mixing faucet.

Though many plumbing equipment manufacturers appeared uninterested in his invention, Al Moen convinced Ravenna Metal Products of Seattle to produce his design. Soon afterward, the first single-handle mixing faucet was sold in San Francisco, retailing for approximately $12. Production at that time was about 5,000 faucets a year. With its growing popularity, the single-handle faucet caught the attention of Standard Screw of Chicago, which was looking for a new major product line and purchased Ravenna Metal Products.

The rest of the story is plumbing history, with continual improvement to the single-handle faucet, as well as the introduction of many other new plumbing products. Along the way, numerous plumbing industry firsts came from Moen, including the replaceable cartridge, the push-button tub/shower diverter, swivel spray, the pressure-balancing shower valve, and LifeShine® non-tarnish finish.

THE PRODUCT

Moen offers a complete line of residential and commercial faucets and showering products in a wide assortment of styles and finishes. The company also manufactures kitchen sinks, bathroom accessories, and plumbing repair parts. All faucet products contain Moen's one-piece, washerless cartridge design that features fewer parts than competitive faucets, which means that fewer things can go wrong.

Much different from the look of Al Moen's first model in 1937, today's faucets and showering products go beyond functionality to be truly distinctive design elements for the home.

Research revealed that as rooms become more open and the focus on design shifts to entertaining in the home, integrating fixtures into an overall design is key. To address this concept, Moen products provide complete coordination of faucets and sinks in the kitchen and bar. A wide range of faucet styles and finishes allows consumers to coordinate their faucets with their décor, including the popular Monticello® style that

even comes in a dramatic high-arc Cathedral™ design. The company also offers MoenStone® Granite sinks as well as stainless steel sinks in a range of bowl shapes and sizes.

In addition to design and integration, research indicated that consumers want more functionality from their faucets. Moen responded with innovations

such as pullout faucets in the kitchen that make it easier to clean the sink or fill large cooking pots. Each Moen pullout faucet brings its own unique design, from the traditional look of Colonnade™ to the modern look of Salora™ or extensa™.

In the bathroom, Moen takes a suite approach where faucets, showering products, and accessories provide a complementary look throughout the entire room with customized designs and finishes. In this category, Moen offers three popular collections: Asceri®, Monticello®, and Villeta™.

In the shower category, Moen functionality is demonstrated with valves that offer customized shower options and protection against scalding. Moen's Posi-Temp®, Moentrol®, and ExactTemp® shower valves allow consumers to find the shower that best meets their needs. In particular, the ExactTemp valve is one of the industry's first to combine precision thermostatic control with pressure balancing. This feature allows consumers to dial up and maintain a consistent shower temperature day after day.

Moen's research in the shower indicated that consumers want luxury bath options, which led to its creation of the vertical spa experience. This customizable showering system offers the choice of valving, body sprays, showerheads, hand showers, and tub spouts. Unlike other systems on the market, Moen's vertical spa features standard half-inch piping, so the system still fits most existing common household plumbing.

Durability in the plumbing category is a major concern for homeowners. In the past, chrome was the only finish that could truly be called long-lasting, but Moen's introduction of the LifeShine finish allowed a host of other finish options to also resist tarnishing, flaking, and corrosion. The LifeShine titanium-strengthened PVD finish has

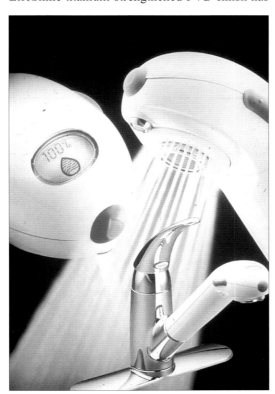

been extended to such popular finishes as Satine™, Classic Gold, copper, brushed stainless, polished brass, nickel, and others.

Moen's product innovations even extend to a new product category — water filtration. In recent years, consumers have become greatly concerned with the quality of their drinking water. Moen

responded with the first filtering faucet, the PureTouch®, to provide better-tasting water with reduced lead, chlorine, and harmful cysts. The PureTouch line has been expanded to include pullout and fixed-spout faucets and the new PureTouch AquaSuite™ filtered water dispenser, which provides an under-counter filter with a designer spout that installs next to the existing faucet in the kitchen or the bath.

RECENT DEVELOPMENTS

With each product launch, research continues to drive the innovations at Moen. For instance, recent showering research indicated that consumers want the ability to easily adjust a shower stream to fit their moods and preferences.

The end result is Moen's Revolution™ massaging showerhead. The Revolution showerhead takes ordinary water, spins each drop, and then twirls the entire stream, creating the ultimate showering experience. The patented FreedomDial™ allows for continuous adjustability of the stream — from a deep, therapeutic massage to a rainlike shower.

Another new introduction, the M•Pact™ valve system, makes Moen the only major plumbing manufacturer to offer the ability to upgrade the plumbing in the entire bathroom without going under the sink or behind the shower wall. Each faucet trim piece in the M•Pact system fits on a common valve underbody. When customers want a new look, they simply unscrew the handles and spout, lift them off, and replace them with a new style. Replacing the shower trim is accomplished in the same easy manner.

Moen's new Asceri Accents, built on the M•Pact system, further expand the Asceri line by offering dramatic handle and spout insert designs, giving consumers another way to express their design creativity in the bath.

PROMOTION

Not only is Moen the number-one brand of faucets sold in North America, Moen also ranks first in consumer unaided awareness and intent to purchase. A combination of national television and magazine advertising targeted to the home enthusiast and do-it-yourselfer supports and promotes this strong image. Moen also provides informative product packaging and point-of-sale displays as well as an aggressive public relations campaign to keep its products and the brand foremost in the minds of consumers.

In addition, Moen's award-winning Web site, www.moen.com, provides consumers with helpful product information, a virtual design center, a virtual showering experience, and a convenient local retailer/wholesaler locator.

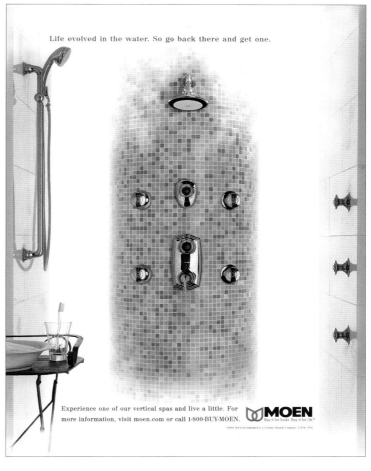

Life evolved in the water. So go back there and get one.

Experience one of our vertical spas and live a little. For more information, visit moen.com or call 1-800-BUY-MOEN.

MOEN Buy it for looks. Buy it for life®

BRAND VALUES

"Buy it for looks…buy it for life" says it all. Moen's tagline is the epitome of what consumers want — and expect — when they choose faucets, sinks, showering products, and bath accessories. People know that Moen is synonymous with great-looking and long-lasting plumbing products. Moen's lifetime warranty guarantees that the company will replace any part for the life of the product.

THINGS YOU DIDN'T KNOW ABOUT MOEN

○ Before he retired in January 1982, Al Moen had acquired more than 75 patents, some of them in fields totally unrelated to plumbing.

○ The Moen single-handle faucet was chosen by the world's leading designers as one of the 100 best-designed mass-produced products, ranking above Henry Ford's Model T and Ben Franklin's stove.

○ Al Moen only wanted the title "Inventor" on his business cards.

○ In 1950, Moen gained national recognition by supplying single-handle faucets for the first prefabricated kitchens.

○ Moen's LifeShine PVD non-tarnish finish set the industry standard when introduced and today offers one of the largest choices of finish options.

○ Moen's M-Pact valve system was one of the first in the industry to offer the ability to change out the trim from above the sink and in front of the shower wall.

NYSE
New York Stock Exchange®

THE MARKET

When you think of Wall Street, the U.S. markets, global capitalism, or the center of the financial world, what's the most likely icon to pop into your mind? If you're like most investors, the answer is the New York Stock Exchange, as well as its majestic facade. The NYSE's imposing neoclassical building at the corner of Wall and Broad Streets in downtown Manhattan has been a renowned symbol of world finance since the beginning of the 20th century.

With some 2,800 listed companies valued at nearly $15 trillion globally — more than 470 of which are from outside the United States — the NYSE is world's largest equities market. The quality of the Exchange marketplace is reflected in the superior, world-class brands it trades every day, including General Electric, Bayer, McDonald's, Polo Ralph Lauren, Nokia, Kraft, Coca-Cola, Kodak, Sears, Sony, Nike, American Express, and Harley-Davidson. Listed companies range from large "blue-chip" corporations to many smaller and mid-sized companies.

No other market provides today's public companies with the most liquid, efficient, and equitable marketplace for the trading of their shares. Tremendous advances in technology enable the NYSE to smoothly trade an average of 1.45 billion shares each day.

Shareholders are confident in knowing that they own shares of the world's best companies and, when buying and selling shares, that their orders are being handled in the most efficient and fairest way possible. That's because as a self-regulatory organization, the Exchange oversees each and every trade. With more than one-third of its workforce dedicated to market oversight, the Exchange goes to all lengths to make sure investors are protected.

ACHIEVEMENTS

The Exchange recognizes that such investor confidence and broad participation have driven the market's growth, creating a nation of shareowners unlike any other. When that confidence was shaken recently, the NYSE was one of the first to respond to the demands for meaningful reform. The Exchange formed the NYSE Corporate Accountability and Listing Standards Committee in February 2002. Four months later — following an extensive information-gathering process involving investors, issuers, and many other Exchange constituents — the Committee proposed new standards and changes in corporate governance and listed-company practices. In August 2002, the Exchange approved many of the proposed initiatives, which it hopes will strengthen accountability and transparency among issuers and markets. The NYSE remains committed to taking steps necessary to further strengthen investor trust.

In fact, public confidence in markets is a critical component of the NYSE brand. As a private

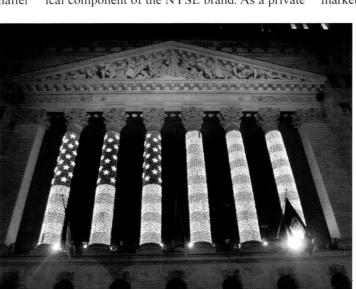

institution with a public purpose, the NYSE makes every effort to safeguard and protect investors, regardless of the size of their portfolios. The Exchange has played a pivotal role in shaping corporate governance and accountability for more than 150 years. And the NYSE continues to take very seriously its duty to educate investors and issuers, understand their needs and concerns, and to foster a dialogue on the issues affecting them and their ability to make sound investment decisions. In the days following the events of September 11, it became all too clear the significant role that markets play in building public confidence. Never was there a more critical time for the U.S. markets to open smoothly than that following Monday morning, when all eyes were focused on 11 Wall Street for leadership in moving forward in the face of tragedy.

HISTORY

For the past 210 years, the NYSE has been building upon its reputation as the world's leading equities marketplace. Since its inception in 1792 under a buttonwood tree, the NYSE has also stood as one of the world's best brands and leading financial institutions. As business and commerce evolved on a global scale, so too has the Exchange, ever expanding its role at the center of global business. Over the years, the NYSE has changed to support capital markets, and has continued to evolve to meet the needs of issuers and investors alike.

Today, the NYSE is viewed as one of the most prestigious organizations in the world economy. Perhaps no single entity represents the global economy better than the NYSE. Thanks in part to its stringent listing standards, a New York Stock Exchange listing has achieved status as a globally recognized signal of strength and leadership. And because the

Exchange is home to the world's greatest enterprises, the NYSE brand, in turn, is built on the strength of its companies.

THE PRODUCT

The strength of the NYSE brand is also built upon its commitment to technology and innovation. The Exchange's $2.5 billion investment in technology over the past 10 years has meant rapid and continuous improvements in trading systems and capacity, unrivaled reliability, and continued deployment of new market-information products and order-execution services. As the world's most technologically advanced marketplace, the NYSE delivers unmatched liquidity and depth, the opportunity for price improvement, and the option of high-speed, automatic executions. Through Network NYSE™, investors can choose from a variety of information products and execution services.

One of the most recent development is NYSE OpenBook™, which allows market professionals to see the full range of buy and sell orders on the NYSE limit-order books, bringing greater transparency to the NYSE marketplace and providing investors with instant access to point-of-sale information. Another important component of the Network NYSE suite is MarkeTrac™, a data-rich online tool that allows investors to manage and monitor their portfolios. It offers a 3-D, virtual representation of the trading floor with news, activity map, and historical price charts; customizable portfolio and index tracking; and detailed quote views and performance graphs.

RECENT DEVELOPMENTS

To help investors better gauge the performance of its companies and the quality market that the NYSE delivers, the Exchange launched several new indexes whose components are strictly listed companies. They include the NYSE U.S. 100 Index™, the NYSE International 100 Index℠, the NYSE

World Leaders Index℠, and the NYSE TMT Index℠. These indexes are expected to become the basis for tradable products such as exchange-traded funds (ETFs). The Exchange began trading ETFs in December 2000 with its first listing of an ETF product (ticker symbol: IOO), which is based on the NYSE-sponsored S&P Global 100 index. The NYSE continues to grow its ETF business by listing and trading more and more of these investing products as they grow in popularity.

PROMOTION

The Exchange continues to position itself at the center of global business, as the world's first truly global marketplace, and as the most open and

visible entity for communicating with investors and issuers. One of its most visible expressions is its logo, which was recently modified to incorporate the NYSE's strongest brand attributes. Launched in 2000, the new, contemporary logo, in keeping with the Exchange's business model, adopted a "portal," reflective of market transparency, openness to change, and access and connectivity for all market constituents. The Exchange's first logo, in place from the 1860s through 1900, featured an elaborate coat of arms fashioned out of the intertwined letters N, Y, S, and E.

While the logo has evolved over time to reflect the evolution of the Exchange itself, the tag line that accompanies the logo, "The world puts its stock in us.™" has been in place for more than a decade. As one of the great thematic lines of all time, research shows how it reflects and supports the confidence and trust investors and companies alike place in the New York Stock Exchange.

Advertising is another way the Exchange reinforces and strengthens its brand. The NYSE's recent campaigns not only showcase the companies that make up its brand, but serve to educate the investing public and help bridge the gap between Wall Street and Main Street.

Helping to close that gap has been the media presence at the NYSE. The Exchange is the center of financial and business news. With more than 20 domestic and international network broadcast bureaus on site and live programming from the trading floor every day, more people have access to the financial markets than ever. The opening and closing bells have become the most-watched daily events in the world. Millions of global viewers each day tune in to see business leaders, government officials, world leaders, and celebrities open and close the trading day.

BRAND VALUES

As the Exchange continues to develop and launch new and exciting products, study after study consistently shows how the NYSE is ultimately a mark of excellence, a symbol of success, and a sign of global leadership. The NYSE is frequently called "the place for tomorrow's business leaders," "truly innovative," and "progressive," and is associated with "integrity" and "long-term stability." Companies that list on the New York Stock Exchange are considered "very established, well respected and important," "stable," "credible" and "global"; are looked upon as "solid companies with strong financial positions"; and are viewed as having "investors that are treated fairly."

Because of this reputation, many companies use the NYSE-listed emblem, which marries a company's trading symbol or logo with the NYSE brand, to elevate public awareness of their status as a listed company. Analogous to the *Good*

Housekeeping seal of approval, as studies reveal, the emblem is often used in corporate marketing materials, on product packaging, in annual reports and other financial documents, in print advertising, on corporate Web sites, and on business cards and stationery.

Working to build brand awareness for all its listed companies, the NYSE provides multiple visibility opportunities. Many companies have partnered with the Exchange to reach their most important audiences by using the NYSE facilities at 11 Wall Street in New York City to host street events, press conferences, employee-relations programs, analyst and board meetings, product launches, and branding campaigns. Listed companies are also featured on *nyse.com*, which receives millions of hits each day, and in the pages of *The Exchange* monthly newsletter and bimonthly *nyse magazine*. One of the Exchange's newest outlets for its listed-company leaders is NYSE 4 on the Floor℠, an exclusive Webcast interview program featuring the foremost decision-makers, executives, and leaders of our time, which can be viewed at *nyse.com*.

THINGS YOU DIDN'T KNOW ABOUT THE NEW YORK STOCK EXCHANGE

○ The NYSE has invested more than $2.5 billion in technology over the past 10 years.

○ Nearly $44 billion worth of stocks change hands on the Exchange each day.

○ The global market capitalization of the NYSE's 2,800 listed companies from 52 countries is nearly $15 trillion.

○ Ninety-three percent of all orders are delivered to the trading floor electronically.

○ The NYSE's optical cable network stretches for 250 miles.

○ The NYSE has about 365 member firms, which employ 100,000 registered workers.

○ The NYSE was the first equities market to fully convert and to trade in decimals.

○ In 1996, the NYSE was the first equities market to adopt wireless handheld trading.

OSHKOSH® EST. 1895

THE MARKET

Few brands represent the quintessential American spirit as purely as OshKosh B'Gosh. Founded in 1895 in Oshkosh, Wisconsin, this small-town manufacturer of adult work wear has transformed itself into a leading brand of children's products that are sold in more than 50 countries.

In an ever-changing competitive environment, OshKosh has stood the test of time by creating stylish, contemporary products that continue to meet the highest standards of quality, durability, and comfort. Although the company is careful not to lose sight of the future, the brand also hearkens back to a traditional, simpler way of life. Families today more than ever are seeking that type of approach in a fast-paced world.

ACHIEVEMENTS

Since its humble beginnings over 100 years ago, OshKosh B'Gosh has become America's favorite children's wear brand. Today, three out of four moms nationwide rank OshKosh before all other major children's brands, including Old Navy and GapKids, according to the *2002 EquiTrend Survey* of all major children's wear brands. That same study also concludes that moms believe OshKosh B'Gosh is the highest-quality apparel brand, ranking it above other famous brands like Levi's children's clothing. OshKosh B'Gosh also outperforms the apparel category as a whole in the category of online customer satisfaction, according to *BizRate.com*, a leading customer satisfaction monitoring Web site.

HISTORY

The OshKosh story begins with the dream, but not the one you might imagine. Four partners — Frank E. Grove, J. Howard Jenkins, James Clark, and George M. Jones — founded the Grove Manufacturing Company in 1895 as a maker of sturdy bib overalls for farmers, railroad men, and industrial workers. One year later, Jenkins and Clark took over sole ownership of the renamed Oshkosh Manufacturing Company, determined to become the best available work wear brand.

Hailed by retailers and customers as being "tough as a mule's hide," the overalls quickly generated a reputation for quality, leading the company to prosper and expand distribution throughout the Midwest. By 1910, the company began making a pint-size version of the men's overalls as a novelty item for proud parents.

In 1911, a dapper apparel salesman named William Pollack became the company's general manager, changing the name yet again to the Oshkosh Overall Company. More significantly, Pollack created the OshKosh B'Gosh brand name for its adult and children's overalls. As its garment line grew beyond overalls to include pants, shirts, and jackets, so did the company, employing almost 300 people by the early 1920s.

In the following decade, new leadership emerged from an unexpected place. Earl Wyman, a former insurance specialist and newcomer to the apparel industry, saw a unique business opportunity with OshKosh B'Gosh. In 1934, Wyman purchased interest in the company and began to successfully manage growth, always looking at ways to further increase product awareness and distribution. Seeing the potential power of the brand, Wyman spearheaded the change of the company's official name to OshKosh B'Gosh in 1937. This name, this brand, and a growing staff of 450 would eventually lead to the company's international success.

Family ties steered Wyman's son-in-law Charles "Fritz" Hyde into the business. Learning from the ground up, Hyde demonstrated a natural talent and staunch work ethic that led him to become CEO of the company in 1963.

Under Hyde's leadership, the company enjoyed continued success throughout the years, generating growth leading to sales of $26 million by 1975. Not until 1978, however — when a local mail-order firm featured a pair of children's bib overalls in its national catalog — did sales of the item really take off. Prompted by the strong response, OshKosh B'Gosh expanded distribution into specialty and department stores, and gradually broadened its children's wear line to include a diverse range of styles, colors, and fabrics.

Today, OshKosh B'Gosh, Inc. is a $463 million premier marketer of children's apparel and accessories. While proud of its substantial growth, the publicly held company still operates under family leadership and never forgets the core values of quality and durability that have always served as its foundation. Led by CEO Doug Hyde, who succeeded his father Fritz in 1992, OshKosh B'Gosh continues to earn its reputation as America's Family Brand.

THE PRODUCT

While the classic bib overall will always be the cornerstone product for OshKosh B'Gosh, today the company represents so much more. From its adorable layette for newborns to "cool" and colorful styles for older kids in the Genuine Girl and Genuine Blues lines, OshKosh has created a global brand for children ages newborn through 10. Though the classic hickory stripe overall remains a favorite, contemporary pants, dresses, outerwear, and swimwear provide a multitude of children's fashion options.

Beyond apparel and accessories, the company has also developed quality licensing extensions into a wide variety of children's products, including strollers, car seats, footwear, toys, and bedding. Today, you can find OshKosh B'Gosh just about everywhere as the brand continues to expand its international presence in 50 countries. With a click of the mouse, OshKosh fans can purchase a wide array of products online at *www.oshkoshbgosh.com*, or they can visit leading department and specialty stores as well as over 150 OshKosh company-owned stores located in outlet malls across the United States.

RECENT DEVELOPMENTS

At the root of OshKosh's success is its constant drive to energize and diversify its products. In 2002, the company underscored its commitment to delivering exciting and fashion-relevant products with the launch of a design team and studio based in the heart of New York's stylish Soho district. The team's mission is to provide new trend insights and explore brand extensions that will create high-quality, authentic, and trend-right products, staying true to the OshKosh heritage.

OshKosh B'Gosh also works hard to ensure that its product is available wherever moms shop. With this in mind, the company has solidified relationships with a variety of family-oriented value retailers including Kohl's Department Stores and plans to introduce a sub-brand at Target stores in the near future.

PROMOTION

Even in its early days as a work wear manufacturer, the company recognized the appeal of featuring an overall-clad dad and son together with the advertising slogan, "Work Clothes for Dad, Play Clothes for Sonny." Only in the late 1970s, when parents and grandparents emerged as the major consumer base for the children's overalls, did the company make adorable kids the centerpiece of its marketing efforts.

Today, OshKosh B'Gosh marketing continues to provide a strong reflection of its heritage in America's heartland. As America's Family Brand, OshKosh wants its loyal customers to know about the continued emphasis on quality, durability, and style on which the brand has built its reputation.

Everywhere you look, you'll continue to see those fresh faces of OshKosh kids, from the covers of national magazines to billboards in Times Square. OshKosh styles are spotlighted on young celebrities in popular TV shows such as *Friends* and *Everybody Loves Raymond* and feature films such as *Lassie* and *Jerry McGuire*. Even Great Britain's royal family couldn't resist the all-American charm of OshKosh overalls, which were seen on Princes William and Harry as children.

BRAND VALUES

Since OshKosh B'Gosh was founded, many men and women have contributed their talents to make the company the industry leader that it is today. The creativity and determination of its employees have shaped its

character for over a century and helped it to achieve its vision of becoming the dominant global marketer of branded products for children ages newborn to 10. Although many things have changed at OshKosh throughout the years, its commitment to quality, innovation, and value remain strong. That guarantees that OshKosh B'Gosh will always be "America's Family Brand."

EquiTrend Survey, May 2002; *Bizrate.com*, November 2002.

THINGS YOU DIDN'T KNOW ABOUT OSHKOSH B'GOSH

❍ While on a buying trip to New York in 1911, the company's general manager William Pollack attended a vaudeville show and heard the phrase "oshkosh, b'gosh" in a skit. By fall of that year, the company adopted OshKosh B'Gosh as its garment brand name, replacing the J&C (Jenkins & Clark) label named for the company's founders.

❍ The company's original mascot was Uncle Sam, who spent more than 50 years promoting the OshKosh B'Gosh clothing brand.

❍ The oldest pair of OshKosh B'Gosh bib overalls, discovered during the company's 1995 centennial, is owned by a Sarasota, Florida, family. The 98-year-old pair of overalls was made by an uncle who was a tailor with the company in the late 1890s.

❍ One of the largest bib overalls that the company ever manufactured was for an elephant "cast member" of the Cabrini Circus, who gracefully modeled them in the film *Big-Top Pee Wee*.

❍ Although OshKosh B'Gosh manufactures over 48 million units of children's clothing per year, the company still sells over 1.5 million of its famous basic bib overalls annually.

❍ Time required to make a pair of OshKosh B'Gosh children's bib overalls: 16.55 minutes.

Panasonic ideas for life

THE MARKET

For over forty years the Panasonic brand has been on the global stage as one of the world's largest and most diverse technology brands, offering a vast range of products from the world's smallest semiconductors to the most advanced, networked systems for the home, office, and industry. Serving nearly every major market, and touching nearly every aspect of consumers' lives, the Matsushita Electric family of companies, best known worldwide as Panasonic, is poised to become the critical brand for the 21st century.

ACHIEVEMENTS

From the introduction of the Panasonic transistor radio in 1960 to the digitally networked systems of the new century, Panasonic has been at the forefront of technological innovation. Today, Panasonic is a world leader in digital technology, with enviable distinctions in audio/video products and systems, as well as optical disk, storage, and networking technologies.

As a leading U.S. manufacturer of digital TVs and systems, the world's first digital TVs and set-top boxes — as well as the first high-definition television (HDTV) tuner decoders — were from Panasonic. Today, Panasonic engineers push the technological envelope, creating flat panel plasma and rear projection TVs with exceptional resolution, multi-task functionality, and ultra-slim, ergonomic design. Behind the scenes, Panasonic also produces optical disk products and systems that have revolutionized professional recording technology. Panasonic's DVC Pro High Definition (HD) camcorders are the platinum standard for the television, sports, news, and entertainment industries. Not surprisingly, Panasonic has won 15 Emmy Awards for its achievements in the broadcast and film industry. But Panasonic's optical disk innovations aren't just for news and entertainment. They include breakthrough medical cameras so small they can fit on the tip of an endoscope, and security cameras that are so advanced they capture fast-moving images in the dark.

Seizing the digital moment, the Panasonic brand also leads the way in digital and networking storage technology. Panasonic was first with DVD recorder/players and currently has a 50 percent market share. The company was also first with portable DVD players, DVD audio systems, and DVD-ROM and DVD-RAM drives. At the forefront of automotive electronics, the Panasonic rear-seat DVD audio system is found in many of today's most prestigious cars and SUVs. A prime mover in networking storage technology, Panasonic's Secure Digital (SD) Memory Card, developed in con-

junction with SanDisk and Toshiba, allows for secure Internet downloads and optimized data storage and security. About the size of a postage stamp, the new 1GB card can hold up to 16 hours of CD-quality music. Panasonic is also the market leader for in-flight entertainment systems that provide an array of audio and video content as well as Internet connectivity. Designed with future technologies in mind, these near-limitless systems will soon rival most office environments.

HISTORY

Panasonic was the vision of Konosuke Matsushita, chairman of Japan's Matsushita Electric Industrial Co., Ltd., who saw the vast potential of the U.S. market. Begun in 1959 as a sales company with a three-person staff, its U.S. operations went on to become a leading sales and manufacturing company with 25,000 employees, over 1,500 products, and 150 business locations throughout North America.

With a keen eye on the U.S. audio electronics market of 1960, corporate executives were quick to adopt the brand name Panasonic, meaning "wide-ranging sound." Soon, Americans were twisting to Chubby Checker on Panasonic

transistor radios, and watching their favorite TV programs on Panasonic's popular black-and-white TVs. If Panasonic rocked in the 1960s, it rolled through the 1970s, developing an impressive line of entertainment, home, office, and automotive electronics. Every day, Americans woke up to Panasonic's digital clock radios, used Panasonic pocket calculators, and cooked entire meals in Panasonic microwave ovens. The Panasonic brand would continue to grow, and in 1975, the company opened its expansive Secaucus, New Jersey, headquarters.

Panasonic would come of age in the 1980s with the introduction of the "talking" chip, as well as CD players, camcorders, VCRs, and sophisticated broadcast systems, thus establishing itself as a key player in the consumer entertainment and broadcast industry. As Panasonic entered its fourth decade in the United States, new strategies emerged to usher in the digital revolution. Key strategic alliances were formed, and R&D facilities were expanded to a network of 15 domestic research and development groups. By the end of the 1990s, Panasonic would become one of America's most successful brands and an established global leader in digital and networking products.

Empowered by the legacy of founder Konosuke Matsushita "to enhance the lives of all people," Panasonic would also point the way in educational and environmental initiatives. Founded in 1984, the multimillion-dollar Panasonic Foundation works with local school districts by providing valuable assistance for educational reform. Since 1989, Panasonic's Kid Witness News™ program has helped children in over 200 schools across the country with its hands-on video education program. Pioneering the development of energy-saving technologies, Panasonic has also earned the U.S. government's coveted Energy Star Home Electronics Partner of the Year Award, and currently produces over 425 Energy Star–labeled products, more than any other manufacturer.

THE PRODUCT

Panasonic is a developer and manufacturer of digital products and systems for nearly every customer market. Restructured in 2001 to serve these varied markets more efficiently, Panasonic's businesses are now organized into three key areas serving the consumer, systems, and industrial sectors.

Panasonic's Consumer Sector is home to many of Panasonic's flagship categories, including consumer entertainment products, cameras, telecommunications, and home and personal care appliances. Leading the way are Panasonic's vast range of cutting-edge DVD products, hard disk recorders, plasma TVs, and SD products. Designed for modern lifestyles, Panasonic's new flat panel plasma displays provide crystal clear reception, and are thin enough that they can be hung on a wall. Harnessing the power of the Internet, Panasonic has developed SD memory cards, SD audio products, as well as Web-connectable wireless phones, and digital cameras and camcorders that connect to personal computers. In personal care and home appliances, Panasonic is partnering with market leaders in hair care products such as Pantene to promote their new ionic hairdryers. Panasonic also makes the "world's fastest shavers," state-of-the-art complexion care, robotic pets, and ultra-pampering electronic loungers.

Functioning as a "one-stop shop," the Systems Sector coordinates product selection and purchasing to help build cost-efficient technology infrastructures for large organizations and institutions. A key systems provider to leading stadiums and sports organizations, Panasonic has brought the Olympic Games to billions of viewers worldwide since 1984, and recently outfitted San Francisco's Pacific Bell Park with a state-of-the-art giant Astrovision™ screen. Panasonic also provides CCTV security systems and television and entertainment systems for luxury stadium suites, and has even pioneered a revolutionary digital-based coaching system. In the area of security, Panasonic has employed the latest security technology for the Vatican, as well as several U.S. government buildings, leading hotels, and Las Vegas casinos. Panasonic also provides state-of-the-art products for the office such as the Workio® copier. This modular document imaging system can copy, fax, scan, and e-mail data with the touch of a button. In the field of medicine, Panasonic paves the way for medical advances with sophisticated optical systems that are critical to today's breakthrough, non-invasive procedures.

In the Industrial Sector, Panasonic companies provide many of the components and parts for several of today's brand-name computers, cameras, and audio/video products. Panasonic also provides crucial micro-components, such as the new multifunctional LSI semi-conductors that allow manufacturers to literally shrink the total size of their product, while adding phenomenal multi-task efficiency.

RECENT DEVELOPMENTS

From streamlining business operations to creating advanced networking products to forging critical business alliances, Panasonic is positioning itself as a leading brand for customers worldwide.

Panasonic has recently developed a new brand identity: "Panasonic ideas for life." This new initiative is now being reflected in the company's advertising and marketing efforts. By presenting a consistent theme and graphic style in all communications, this approach further defines and extends

Panasonic's brand image with maximum impact while supporting sales and business goals.

Turning the digital dream house of tomorrow into tangible reality, Panasonic is currently developing home networking applications that are part of a broadband gateway system that links household appliances and utilities to the Internet, including a Web-based home-care solution system that connects homebound patients with their doctors, and Bluetooth-supported wireless communications equipment.

The Panasonic SD memory card has also been employed in several hot new products marketed under the name of e-wear®. Panasonic's line of SD audio players are so slim and wearable that they have become fashion essentials for a whole new

generation. The SD Memory Card can be used to hold a wide variety of data from PowerPoint presentations to music, video, and JPEG images. In partnership with AT&T, Panasonic debuted two multi-network cellular phones and has a third under development with Internet capability and a digital camera. In a licensing agreement with Iridian Technologies, Inc., Panasonic developed and manufactured Authenticam®, a security identification device using the fastest, most accurate, scalable, and stable biometric technology in the world. As the Internet gives rise to a new world economy, the Panasonic Internet Incubator will also continue to seek out and nurture lasting relationships with today's most innovative e-businesses and entrepreneurs. One such example is The Panasonic Digital Concepts Center in Silicon Valley teaming with the Women's Technology Cluster in San Francisco, California.

PROMOTION

In keeping with the founding philosophy of Konosuke Matsushita — who believed that true success begins with an idea that adds real value to people's lives — the new branding initiative of Panasonic "ideas for life" has transformed Panasonic's brand and is reflected in all its advertising and marketing efforts.

Once the new brand message was established, a core identity was developed and transformed the company in all its communications. New advertising campaigns in print and other media were created to reinforce this message. Advertisements can be seen across the United States in key markets, from the Lincoln Tunnel to LAX, floating on the Hudson River, and in major newspapers like *The Wall Street Journal*, *The New York Times*, and

USA Today. Panasonic marketing strategy has truly re-invented the company.

Understanding the customer is key to successful marketing. The Hispanic market is one of the fastest-growing segments of the population, and Panasonic recognized the need to communicate "ideas for life" into this ever-expanding market. Through commercials and print advertising, Panasonic demonstrates how "ideas for life" are in harmony with Hispanic life.

As Panasonic continues to create breakthrough technologies and products that genuinely enrich customers' lives and add value to business, the company can now directly communicate the message of "ideas for life" to all audiences.

Supporting Panasonic's advertising is a wide artillery of other marketing tools, including Shadow Traffic radio, which reaches listeners daily in key markets nationwide, major sporting events and awards programs throughout the year, and powerful corporate sponsorships such as the Olympic Games.

Along with exciting on-line Web services, vivid signage in major stadiums and arenas across the nation, and of course, the signature NBC Astrovision™ screen by Panasonic in Times Square — a three-story-tall icon that has become virtually synonymous with New Year's Eve in America — Panasonic comes forward as a leader in this new age of communication. Marketing efforts ensure that Panasonic emerges from the intensely competitive fray as the brand to know and to trust.

BRAND VALUES

From its introduction, Panasonic upholds the philosophy of Konosuke Matsushita to put the "Customer First." Understood in its most profound sense, Panasonic's is a lifetime partnership with every customer; from idea generation to customer care to the continued development of newer, more innovative products. That approach has led to products of uncompromising quality, value, and service that define the Panasonic brand. The final, underlying objective is "to enhance and improve the lives of all people."

THINGS YOU DIDN'T KNOW ABOUT PANASONIC

❍ Grand Central Station in New York City shows off its refurbished beauty by illuminating it with Panasonic lighting.

❍ Beginning in 1999, the U.S. Environmental Protection Agency has named Panasonic "Partner of the Year" for four consecutive years in recognition of the company's development of over 425 energy-saving products.

❍ The Panasonic Digital Concepts Center in Silicon Valley nurtures new companies and has teamed up with the Women's Technology Cluster.

❍ Panasonic's rugged Toughbook™ PC is popular with U.S. government agencies to provide mobility combined with wireless capabilities.

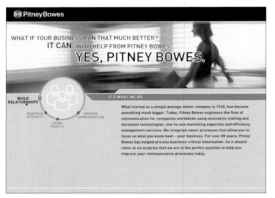

Pitney Bowes

Engineering the flow of communication™

THE MARKET

The physical or digital documents and mail that flow throughout the work world are primarily mission-critical business communications that help sustain our economy. These communications take many forms — billing statements, e-mails with attached reports, faxed contracts, and medical records updated with test results, to name a few. They may flow exclusively through electronic channels, travel more traditionally via the physical mail system, or both. Some communications are designed to be shared; others are confidential.

No matter what form communications take, both senders and receivers want them to be accurate, timely, and secure. The demand for business information and the need for businesses to communicate and build relationships with their customers have never been greater. Pitney Bowes has the technology and services that enable accurate, timely, and secure communications that build internal efficiency and customer loyalty for businesses of all sizes.

For more than 80 years, Pitney Bowes has earned a reputation as a global leader in the mail and document management industry with a full range of innovative products and services that help its customers cut costs, streamline operations, uncover revenue opportunities, and add maximum value to their mail and document processes.

ACHIEVEMENTS

The strengths behind Pitney Bowes work-enhancing products and services are technology and people. Proprietary state-of-the-art encryption technology and other patented processes enable Pitney Bowes to offer safe, secure Internet-based money transactions and information transmissions. Credited with more than 3,400 patents worldwide, Pitney Bowes remains among the top 200 firms receiving U.S. patents each year.

The company has received numerous customer service, preferred supplier, and design awards as well as recognition for best practices related to diversity and the environment. In 2002,

Business Ethics magazine named Pitney Bowes one of the "100 Best Corporate Citizens" for the third year in a row.

Today, more than 35,000 employees support Pitney Bowes mail and document solutions for more than 2 million customers in more than 120 countries around the world.

HISTORY

Founded in 1920 by the remarkable Arthur Pitney and Walter Bowes, Pitney Bowes opened for business with a seemingly simple, yet significant invention: the world's first U.S. Postal Department-approved postage meter.

A tradition of innovation enabled the company to continually optimize its offerings to make mailing faster, easier, more cost-effective, and safer, providing both small- and large-sized business customers all over the world with highly advanced mailing systems that offer postal discounts as well as the ability to track and trace, all without a trip to the post office.

The company entered the new millennium as a leading mail and document solutions provider, making history with attention to the customer, excellence in product and service design and development, and quick recognition of and response to changing market needs.

Key developments in the Pitney Bowes success story include:
- April 23, 1920 — The Universal Stamping Machine Company and American Postage Company merged to form the Pitney Bowes Postage Meter Company.
- 1922–23 — The government collected $4,339,070 in postage from the first commercial installations of 400 meters, and Pitney Bowes products began to be sold outside the United States.
- 1930s — Pitney Bowes expanded meter use by meeting the cost-saving needs of many Depression-era businesses.
- 1940 — Company income topped $4 million with the new "R" line meters capable of printing variable amounts of postage and employees numbered 1,243.
- The War Years — Pitney Bowes received four Army-Navy "E" awards for war production excellence for 28 different products.
- 1950s and '60s — The demand for meters grew rapidly, particularly the "DM" desk

model C. New products included folders, Ticko-meters, and an electric mail opener.
- 1970s and '80s — Pitney Bowes had nearly 800,000 postage meters producing more than $1 billion revenue and introduced electronic POSTAGE BY PHONE® technology, full lines of facsimile, copier/printers, and other computerized document and mail inserters, folders, and related products. The U.S. Postal Service collected $8 billion through postage meter resettings, representing 49 percent of their total postage revenue. Pitney Bowes Management Services was created to provide mailroom management and other outsourcing services.
- 1990s — Pitney Bowes introduced solutions that manage the secure production, routing, multi-channel delivery, and tracking of documents and Intellilink™ technology, the next generation of advanced mailing systems that capture important customer data. Pitney Bowes celebrated its millionth customer of POSTAGE BY PHONE® technology.
- 2000 — New products and services included electronic statement presentment and bill payment, and software-based tools that track and manage documents and package flow.
- 2001 — During the anthrax threats that followed the terrorist attacks of September 11, Pitney Bowes shared its expertise through a mail security campaign to address the immediate needs of customers and the public. The company divested its copier and fax business to focus on its core strengths in mailing and document management.
- 2002 — Pitney Bowes launched Intellilink™ technology globally. Pitney Bowes continued to expand its capability in the mailstream and increase its presence worldwide with strategic acquisitions, signaling an exciting new beginning for the company.

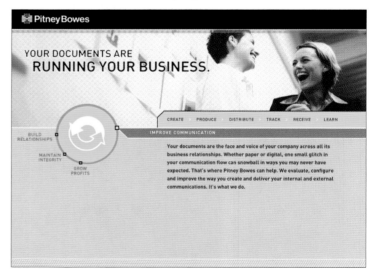

THE PRODUCT

Mailing Systems Equipment. The Intellilink™ technology-based series of mailing systems offers the highest quality mail processing with data-capture capability and track and trace features at speeds to suit customer requirements. For lower-volume customers in the small business and home business sector, the PersonalPost™ meter is an economical choice.

Mid- to large-sized businesses can enhance their mailing operations with additional mailing system components that print personalized documents and matching envelopes, add preprinted sheets, accumulate and fold this material, add a business reply card, insert the completed mail piece, and seal the envelope. Pitney Bowes has solutions for physical billing that are equally effective. At the same time, Pitney Bowes equipment can significantly cut the time and labor involved in collating, folding, and inserting mail pieces. Pitney Bowes POSTAGE BY PHONE® system processes billions of dollars in postal funds with remote meter resetting capability, enabling customer efficiencies and convenience.

Pitney Bowes also offers equipment for high-volume document producers and mailers who require collating multiple pages of statements, folding and inserting them into envelopes, adding advertisements or other enclosures, addressing the envelopes and sorting them for processing, in conjunction with meters that weigh and affix postage. The new line of inserters achieves unparalleled high speeds.

Software Products. Pitney Bowes delivers advanced solutions for both physical and digital document processing, from creation through delivery and receipt. Pitney Bowes research has led to the development of software programs that can, for example, correct addresses and show comparative carrier rates for shipping packages, make post-processing changes and enhancements to documents before they reach print operations, and provide multi-channel delivery and electronic bill presentment and payment options.

Pitney Bowes has solutions for ordering and online fulfillment logistics that provide advanced multi-carrier shipping and transportation management that integrate data throughout the supply chain and expedite the receipt of accountable mail and packages. Also, shipping management software enables businesses to optimize small-package carrier selection, track delivery status, audit carrier performance and security, and keep every shipment "in sight" throughout the delivery process. Integrated software solutions help customers monitor processes and manage their decisions. Pitney Bowes database and marketing software programs work together to help small and large businesses do personalized marketing.

Outsourcing and Professional Services. Pitney Bowes provides outsourcing services that allow customers to focus on their core business by staffing and running other companies' mailrooms and managing their records and document centers for them, including applicant screening, education and training of staff. Pitney Bowes handles the full array of customers' document management needs and can create, produce, and distribute reports at the customer's site or at an offsite loca-

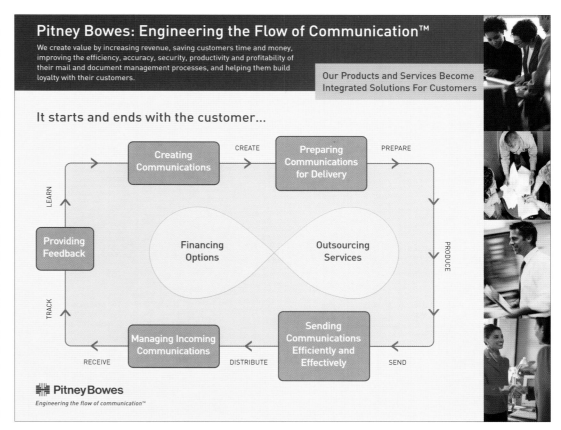

tion and provide business process backup for disaster recovery to enable continuation of business during an emergency.

Pitney Bowes also shares its expertise with customers in mail and document process redesign and improvement. Pitney Bowes research helps customers achieve the highest level of security through patented technology and first class services.

Financial Services. Finally, Pitney Bowes offers a variety of financing options that help customers manage cash flow, costs, and productivity and acquire essential business tools and resources — such as supplies, postage, equipment, and services — more affordably. Customers can take advantage of credit accounts that enable fast, reliable, high-value Internet transactions, postage credit lines and general credit and payment management services, equipment leasing, and small business lending and credit services.

PROMOTION

Pitney Bowes launched a major advertising campaign in 2003 to create awareness of its integrated mail and document solutions among organizations of all sizes from large enterprises to mid-sized companies to the small/home office. Pitney Bowes has a new tagline — *Engineering the flow of communication™* — that demonstrates its capability to improve the critical flow of business information by increasing the efficiency and improving the effectiveness of customer response.

RECENT DEVELOPMENTS

An aggressive acquisition strategy has furthered the company's global reach in Europe and the United Kingdom, Africa, the Middle East, Latin America, Canada, and the Asia-Pacific region. Ongoing technological development enables Pitney Bowes to penetrate adjacent industries that provide growth outside the company's core business areas. With state-of-the-art Intellilink™ technology, Pitney Bowes set new industry standards for mailing systems during its 2002 worldwide launch.

BRAND VALUES

Pitney Bowes has a heritage and values that are founded in its innovative spirit and commitment to provide its customers with real-world solutions that drive the critical business flow of communication. Throughout its history, the company has built a strong leadership position by anticipating, recognizing, and preparing for its customers' changing needs. In the global market where businesses now compete, companies turn to Pitney Bowes for its market leadership, expert solutions and services, and consistent commitment to the success of its customers.

THINGS YOU DIDN'T KNOW ABOUT PITNEY BOWES

❍ The U.S. Postal Service receives more than $15 billion each year — 61 percent of its annual metered postage revenue — from 1.4 million Pitney Bowes mailing systems.

❍ Pitney Bowes products enable the processing, folding, and inserting of 100 million pages of financial credit card statements each month

❍ Pitney Bowes manages facilities that produce 1.7 million copies each hour. That's more than 28,000 every minute.

❍ More than 6.25 million pieces of mail per day are processed by Pitney Bowes.

❍ Pitney Bowes Financial Services' Purchase Power® — a revolving line of credit — helps more than 300,000 companies finance postage costs.

❍ Pitney Bowes invests in programs that support literacy, education, and diversity as well as employee giving and volunteering efforts in communities worldwide.

Polaroid

THE MARKET

Nothing captures the moment like pictures. Whether it's recording priceless family activities or documenting work, photography has truly become an essential part of life. And nothing could be more captivating or magical than witnessing those pictures develop before your very eyes. Polaroid instant cameras and film make this magic possible. For more than 50 years, Polaroid has continued to expand its line of products and engage people in a way that only instant photography can.

Developed in the late 1940s by scientist and inventor Dr. Edwin Land, the Polaroid one-step photographic process and cameras were a breakthrough in technology that was quite literally ahead of its time. Since then, Polaroid has built upon its original concepts to create a full line of smarter, faster, easy-to-use instant photographic products, in all formats, that elevate the picture-taking experience to new heights. Polaroid understands that people will always be keenly interested in capturing memories on instant film. Consumers will always celebrate holidays, professionals will always need to document their work, and artists will always look for new forms of expression. So, as long as people continue to take pictures, Polaroid will be there to make it possible.

ACHIEVEMENTS

As the originator of self-developing film, Polaroid is the worldwide leader in instant imaging. Since its invention, Polaroid instant photography has provided photographers with new mediums to explore, whether for personal, professional, scientific, artistic, or proofing purposes. From everyday moms and dads taking photos of their child's first smile, to renowned artists such as Ansel Adams, Andy Warhol, David Hockney, and Annie Liebowitz creating one-of-a-kind works of art, Polaroid has played an important role in capturing memorable images.

Through innovative products such as the One-Step instant camera, Polaroid has appealed to people who believe there is no substitute for seeing their pictures instantly. The introduction of the Spectra instant camera has continued Polaroid Corporation's commitment to technological improvements and larger format films. With each new camera, Polaroid has advanced instant photography by providing consumers with an easier-to-use product and a higher-quality instant image. The release of the best-selling i-Zone Instant Pocket camera became the first camera specifically designed for the teen generation. The phenomenal popularity of this fun, hip camera and film has proven that instant photography and the Polaroid brand appeal to a wide range of audiences.

In fact, Polaroid has a long history of working with dedicated professional photographers who utilize Polaroid materials in the creation of great imagery. Polaroid instant prints are in the permanent collections of museums around the world including The New York Metropolitan Museum of Art, The Museum of Modern Art in New York, the Victoria and Albert Museum in London, and the Centre Georges Pompidou in Paris.

Having pioneered many professional cameras and film, Polaroid is responsible for creating the world's largest instant camera, the one-of-a-kind 40x80 camera. The 40x80 is capable of producing prints measuring 44 inches wide and up to 100 inches long, and was used by photographer Joe McNally to document the tragic events surrounding September 11 for a photo expose entitled "Faces of Ground Zero." Polaroid also created the 20x24 large-format camera, which stands five feet tall and weighs 235 pounds. This unique camera was developed to accurately reproduce works of art, especially paintings and tapestries, but was also intended as a creative tool to make original photographs. These remarkable cameras are just part of the Polaroid commitment to expanding the personal and commercial bounds of instant photography.

Polaroid instant cameras have been the first choice of professionals in many fields. The Macro 5 SLR camera, a fully automatic, portable camera with five built-in close-up lenses, was designed specifically for medical documentation, manufacturing, and law enforcement. The Polaroid line of film-based instant identification systems are utilized worldwide to meet customers' high-level security needs.

While Polaroid has made numerous achievements in the world of instant photography, they have also made several important contributions to child safety and education. To increase national awareness of missing and exploited children, Polaroid and the National Center for Missing & Exploited Children created "Project KidCare," a child photo identification and safety education program. As part of this commitment, Polaroid has raised more than $1.3 million in donations to date. Polaroid has placed its trusted name behind this campaign in hopes of educating parents and protecting their kids.

Polaroid also has been instrumental in the fight against sexual assault and domestic violence, working closely with police departments and medical and nursing personnel, as well as prosecutors across the country. Polaroid has been a leader in developing imaging protocols that bring healthcare professionals together with law enforcement agencies and city prosecutors to support prevention and prosecution of domestic violence cases.

HISTORY

In 1944, Dr. Edwin Land, the founder of Polaroid Corporation, was inspired to create the instant camera and film as a response to his young daughter's curiosity over why she could not see the picture he had just taken. Dr. Land first demonstrated instant film at the Optical Society of America meeting in New York City in 1947. The Model 95 Land Camera and Type 40 sepia-toned instant roll film went on sale for $89.50 at Boston's Jordan Marsh department store in 1948. Dr. Land hired Ansel Adams as a consultant the following year, as sales of the Polaroid Land Camera exceeded $5 million in its first full year on the market.

During the 1960s and throughout the 1970s, Polaroid continued to bring innovations to instant photography, from the first camera with automatic exposure, to professional models with macro- and microphotographic capabilities for use in research labs, hospitals, universities, and industry.

Over the years, Polaroid has carried on its proud tradition of pioneering innovations in instant photography, and continues to be a permanent fixture in people's lives.

THE PRODUCT

As the leader in instant photography, Polaroid has created the most recognized instant cameras and film for use by the general consumer. Through constant advances, Polaroid is able to offer a full line of consumer instant products that range from self-adhesive i-Zone mini-photos to floppy disk–sized Spectra pictures.

Professional photographers have also come to rely on the Polaroid family of products. Whether for final art or reliable proofs, Polaroid offers professionals a variety of quality film and media for any application.

And through the advent of branded instant film, Polaroid has provided numerous large corporations — such as Unilever, Miller Brewing, Procter & Gamble, Oscar Meyer, The Jelly Belly Candy Company, and PBS — with a unique opportunity to enhance their own brand awareness. Pre-exposed film allows clients to place their logo, artwork, or any custom message directly within the instant film image area, so each photo develops displaying their message or logo on it. Pre-Printed Border Film comes with a company's name or special message pre-printed directly on the border surrounding the image.

RECENT DEVELOPMENTS

Since the earliest days of Dr. Land's remarkable invention, innovation has been at the heart of everything Polaroid does. In recent years, Polaroid has captured the imagination and excitement of a whole new generation with the i-Zone Instant Pocket camera, currently the world's number-one selling camera among teens. Adding to the photo-taking experience, Polaroid introduced i-Zone Fortune Film, a new instant film that reveals fortunes, messages, or jokes on every picture when pulled from

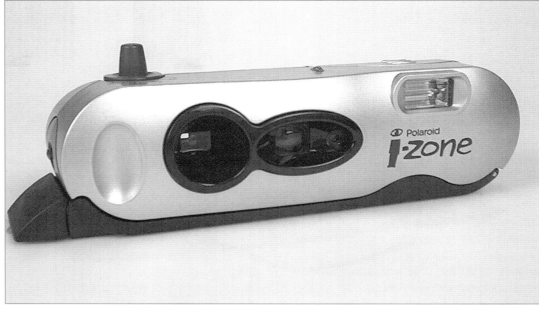

the camera. As the picture develops, the mysterious phrase fades away.

Looking toward the future, Polaroid is applying its advanced technology expertise to deliver Instant Digital Printing. This new technology is intended for a variety of applications from digital camera photo prints to retail advertising displays, and will be capable of producing high-quality, digital prints with features and speeds never before seen or imagined. Instant Digital Printing promises to completely revolutionize digital printing forever.

PROMOTION

From its inception, Polaroid has understood the importance of advertising and public relations in its pursuit of widespread brand recognition. National television advertising has helped to deeply ingrain the Polaroid name in the minds of the American public. One of the more memorable campaigns paired Mariette Hartley and James Garner, who charmed consumers with their wit and chemistry for more than half a decade. In the new millennium, Polaroid has found tremendous success with its new tag line: "Click Instantly." The latest ad campaign, entitled "Let Me In," has had significant impact on brand perceptions, nearly doubling the recall average, and expanding the product appeal well beyond the traditional core audience.

Polaroid Corporation's award-winning public relations efforts have been equally successful in keeping the Polaroid brand top-of-mind with consumers. Seeking to reach a larger teen audience, Polaroid sponsored singing sensation Britney Spears' North American concert tour. This event was the perfect opportunity to promote the youth-oriented, ultra-hip i-Zone Instant Pocket Camera to Spears' teen audience and further solidify Polaroid's connection to Generation Y.

BRAND VALUES

For consumers and professionals alike, the name Polaroid stands for instant photography. Polaroid has always recognized that its brand value rests on two essential concepts: quick and simple. Developing products that are meaningful to the customer, and putting forth innovations that address the needs and demands of the mass-market consumer and professional have been the hallmarks of Polaroid's unique vision.

Because instant photography has the power to entertain, teach, amaze, inspire, document, catalogue, record history, evoke emotions, and preserve memories, the medium's importance cannot be overstated. On those occasions when you want to capture the moment and be able to enjoy it instantly, then there's simply no substitute for Polaroid.

"Polaroid," "i-Zone," "Polaroid Macro," "OneStep," and "Spectra" are trademarks of Polaroid Corporation, U.S.A.

THINGS YOU DIDN'T KNOW ABOUT POLAROID

○ Polaroid 3-D glasses were used to view the first 3-D stereoscopic movie, *Bwana Devil*.

○ In 1965, Polaroid sponsored a new public television show, *The French Chef*, hosted by Julia Childs.

○ Polaroid produced goggles and vectrograph 3-D pictures for use in aerial reconnaissance surveys in World War II.

○ The billionth pack of instant film was produced in 1991.

○ Nearly 15 Polaroid pictures were taken every second in 2001.

○ The Polaroid i-Zone camera has become the number-one selling camera in the United States.

○ Polaroid creator Edwin Land served as a member of President Kennedy's Foreign Intelligence Advisory Board.

○ More than 300 million instant sticky pictures have been snapped during the i-Zone brand's brief three-year history.

○ In the United States, a Polaroid instant camera has been standard equipment for more than one out of three law enforcement officers.

ROADWAY® *Express*

THE MARKET

The motor carrier industry moves more than 75 percent of the nation's economic product and employs more than 7 million people. Total industry revenue approaches $30 billion.

Roadway Express, Inc. is a leader in the less-than-truckload (LTL) segment of the trucking industry. LTL carriers pick up shipments from multiple customers, sort them by destination, and load them onto trailers for transport to terminals within their distribution networks for delivery.

Roadway specializes in two-day and beyond deliveries throughout North America. The carrier transports industrial, commercial, and retail goods in the two- to five-day regional and long-haul markets. Seamless freight services are provided between all 50 states, Canada, Mexico, and Puerto Rico, with import and export services for 140 countries. Under the Roadway umbrella are subsidiaries Reimer Express Lines Ltd., providing domestic and cross-border Canadian freight services; Roadway Express S.A. de C.V., offering domestic and cross-border services for Mexican markets; and Roadway Reverse Logistics, Inc., a provider of returns management solutions.

ACHIEVEMENTS

For a customer-centric company like Roadway, recognition from customers is the highest level of achievement. For the 13th consecutive year, Roadway was honored as the 2002 LTL nationwide carrier of the year by the National Small Shipments Traffic Conference. Roadway was also recognized as one of the top carriers for 2002 in *Logistics Management* magazine's annual Quest for Quality survey — the 18th consecutive year Roadway has received this honor. More than

3,000 readers responded to the Quest for Quality survey, which is the largest customer satisfaction study in the transportation/logistics field. In addition, Roadway received the Military Traffic Management Command Quality Award and the United States Postal Service Quality Supplier Award in 2001, and also receives numerous awards for superior service from customers in the private sector every year.

Roadway is recognized as an industry leader in information technology as well. For the third consecutive year, *ComputerWorld* magazine named Roadway among the 100 best places to work in information technology in 2002. For demonstrating integrated technologies and procedures to improve products, services, and relationships with partners and customers, *CIO* magazine ranked Roadway among the top 100 companies in information technology in 2002. For the third straight year, *InformationWeek* magazine in 2002 named Roadway as one of the 500 most innovative users of information technology.

Treating the nation's highways as a public trust that must be shared responsibly, safety is at the forefront of Roadway operations. This concern includes programs for the benefit of Roadway's employees and the motoring public. Roadway has also implemented innovative programs to conserve resources. The company's proactive efforts include employee training, recycling, fuel-efficient engines, and use of alternative fuels and advanced leak detection devices on underground storage tanks.

Roadway employees are among the safest in the industry. Over 18 percent of Roadway's active drivers have logged more than 1 million consecutive miles without a preventable accident. The average motorist would take 83 years to drive 1 million miles safely.

HISTORY

Roadway dates back to 1930 when Akron was on its way to becoming a major center for tire production. Former high school teacher Carroll Roush noticed the lack of a transportation service to bring tires to assembly plants in other cities. To fill that void, he established a new company, which moved its first shipment — a load of tires — from Akron to St. Louis, on February 22, 1930. A month later, Carroll's older brother Galen, an attorney, joined the company. By the end of the year, the brothers were working with a crew of 10 owner-operators servicing Chicago, Detroit, and Kansas City.

The brothers soon incorporated, and their company became Roadway Express, Inc. Within months, the fledgling company opened terminals in Atlanta, Baltimore, Birmingham, Charlotte, Chicago, Indianapolis, Knoxville, Memphis, Nashville, New York, and Philadelphia.

In 1945, the company began using its own trucks instead of owner-operators. By 1956, the company had fully converted to a fleet of modern, reliable, company-owned and -operated vehicles.

That same year Carroll Roush opted to sell his shares in the company, and Roadway became a publicly traded company.

Early on, the company emphasized information technology as a tool for improving operational efficiencies and providing value-added services to customers. In 1982, Roadway introduced QUIKTRAK®, a computerized shipment-tracking system. In 1983, Roadway launched E•Z RATE®, the industry's first simplified ZIP code–based shipment rating system.

Throughout the 1990s, Roadway continued to invest in technology to give customers better service and real-time shipment information. Roadway's time-critical transportation product, which was introduced in the mid-1990s, relies on information technologies to meet precise pickup and delivery requirements. Customers order pickups, track shipments, obtain delivery receipts, and conduct other shipping transactions through *my.roadway.com*, a secure Web site featuring a personalized browser interface launched in 1999.

As shippers continued to speed their supply chains, Roadway reduced transit times, expanded time-definite services, and improved Web-based offerings. In 2000, Roadway became the first national LTL carrier to have its freight network and management systems certified to the ISO international quality standards for shipping goods from pickup to delivery.

In 2001, Roadway Corporation was formed. Roadway Corporation, also located in Akron, is a holding company dedicated to pursuing acquisition, merger, partnership, and other opportunities related to Roadway's core competencies in transportation and related e-business solutions. Roadway Express became a subsidiary of Roadway Corporation.

THE PRODUCT
Over 70 years ago, Roadway cofounder Galen Roush understood that Roadway had only one product to sell: service. From the first deliveries in 1930, he realized that carriers that kept their commitments could attract and keep customers.

Today, Roadway is as keenly focused on service as ever. With a continental presence and broad service offerings, Roadway is a single source for freight transportation for businesses across North America. Manufacturers, retailers, and wholesalers depend on Roadway for timely and efficient freight transportation services.

Along with vast geographic coverage, businesses often require the highest levels of reliability and speed. Roadway's Time-Critical Services combine speed of transit with precise shipment pickup and delivery times throughout North America. Delivery is 100 percent guaranteed. Rounding out Roadway's full-service capabilities are freight services for truckload shipments, tradeshow exhibits, cold-sensitive products, product returns, international freight services, and door-to-door heavyweight air freight.

Operating alongside Roadway's vast physical network is an advanced information network that supports freight operations and provides real-time shipment information to customers through a variety of channels, including the Internet.

RECENT DEVELOPMENTS
Driven by the ever-changing demands of its customers' supply chains, Roadway continues to refine its network and operations. Faster transit times, expanded regional service, and delivery quality improvements were all achieved in 2002. Roadway is the first LTL carrier to implement a system that combines cellular and satellite technologies for gathering and transmitting data along pickup and delivery routes. This two-way messaging and vehicle-tracking system features in-cab computers that capture shipment data at pickup. Roadway is also adapting to the challenges of today's market environment through a progressive approach to organizational development. Cooperative programs designed to develop leadership skills among all employees at all levels of operations are improving performance.

PROMOTION
Roadway's promotion strategy is built around employees who deliver exceptional customer service. Knowledgeable freight transportation professionals, supported by advanced information technologies, are based at Roadway facilities throughout North America. By demonstrating Roadway's core values of engagement, pride, innovation, and customer focus, employees work to meet customer needs. External advertising in industry trade magazines and an award-winning Web site emphasize the focus on service, and the Roadway name in large logotype on the side of trailers reinforces brand awareness.

BRAND VALUES
Roadway's core competencies are a group of skills, systems, and operations that establish capabilities and credibility for customers. These competencies are the foundation for achieving goals, a platform for the commitments made to customers, and the basis of Roadway's reputation.

This reputation, as externally measured in research efforts like *The Wall Street Journal Corporate Perceptions Industry Report*, is a key indicator of employees' success in building relationships with customers and delivering Roadway's service promise consistently. *The Wall Street Journal Corporate Perceptions Industry Report* is issued annually and charts the relative reputations of 838 major companies in 60 industry classifications.

This report shows Roadway scoring first for Total Familiarity (for the fifth straight year), first in Quality of Management (up from second in 2001), first in Reputation of Company (up from second in 2001), and second in Investment Potential (up from sixth in 2001).

THINGS YOU DIDN'T KNOW ABOUT ROADWAY EXPRESS

○ Four Roadway trailers share the No-Zone safety message about truck blind spots with motorists in a public safety campaign sponsored by the U.S. Department of Transportation.

○ Free transportation is provided for Christina's Smile, a charitable dental clinic that travels in two 48-foot trailers with the PGA/Senior PGA Tour. The program provides hundreds of disadvantaged children with free quality dental care each year.

○ Roadway and the U.S. Department of Labor's Job Corps program partnered to develop a tractor-trailer driver training program. Job Corps recognized our commitment to this school-to-work program for economically disadvantaged youth with its Alpha Award in 2001.

THE
ROYAL DOULTON
COMPANY

THE MARKET

Pottery and ceramics are a strong indicator of the art and lifestyle of a given age. Indeed archaeologists rely on pottery fragments to establish the level of sophistication of past civilizations.

Today, consumers are more demanding and discerning than ever before. The rise in home entertainment has been matched by the introduction of contemporary, functional tableware. At the other end of the spectrum, the decrease in traditional family meals and rise in solo eating, TV dinners, and convenience foods have seen companies extend their casual tableware ranges.

When it comes to gifts, despite many alternatives, the ceramic form is sought after as offering true qualities of heritage, traditional craftsmanship, and real, long-lasting value. In fact, ceramic giftware has enjoyed considerable growth — gift-giving, home decoration, and investment being the main motivations.

The key markets worldwide for premium ceramic tableware and giftware are the United Kingdom and Continental Europe, North America,

include Minton, Royal Albert, and the core Royal Doulton brand.

With almost 200 years of heritage, Royal Doulton, the company, is a thriving global business, with around $280 million in annual sales, employing about 6,000 people across its U.K. production houses and numerous distribution operations worldwide. Approximately half of its sales are generated outside of the United Kingdom.

The company's Hotel and Airline Division is also the world's largest supplier of bone china to the international airlines industry. Indicative of its position, the division holds major contracts with British Airways, Emirates, and South African Airlines as well as other leading airlines. All three are noted for their high-quality in-flight

HISTORY

Royal Doulton has been producing ceramic items for almost 200 years. As far back as 1815, the company founder, John Doulton, began producing practical and decorative stoneware from a small pottery in Lambeth, south London, in the United Kingdom.

His son, Henry, built the business, relocating it 60 years later to Stoke-on-Trent in Staffordshire, England, known around the world as "The Potteries." By 1901, the quality of Doulton's tableware had caught the eye of King Edward VII, who permitted the company to prefix its name with "Royal," and the company was awarded the Royal Warrant.

The company expanded its production facilities and by the 1930s was involved in the manufacture of figurines and giftware.

Royal Doulton was awarded the Queen's Award for Technical Achievement in 1966, for its contribution to china manufacture — the first china manufacturer to be honored with this award.

During the 1960s and 1970s, Royal Doulton discarded its drainpipe production interests and acquired Minton, which had begun china production in 1793, and crystal manufacturer Webb Corbett. In 1972, Royal Doulton was bought by conglomerate Pearson and merged with Allied English Potteries, adding a number of key brands, including Royal Albert.

In 1993, Royal Doulton was demerged from its parent and became a public company listed on the London Stock Exchange.

THE PRODUCT

Each of Royal Doulton's principal brands — Royal Doulton, Minton, and Royal Albert — enjoys a long association of royal patronage, and holds at least one Royal Warrant. They are also trademark registered.

When drawing up new product design, Royal Doulton designers study the market, analyze consumer research, and often refer to their own archives for inspiration. The Royal Doulton Archives, located at the Sir Henry Doulton Gallery in Burslem, Stoke-on-Trent, house a variety of material dating from 1815 to the present. The Royal Doulton Pattern Books contain over 10,000 hand-painted watercolors, illustrating the talent of artists over the years. Apart from providing an

Asia Pacific, and Australasia. The global market overall is estimated to be worth more than $2.1 billion.

ACHIEVEMENTS

Royal Doulton plc is one of the world's leading manufacturers and distributors of premium ceramic tableware and giftware. Its illustrious brand names

service, and Royal Doulton — aware of the need for brand differentiation — prides itself on creating uniquely distinctive product offerings for each client.

In total, Royal Doulton produces around 30,000 different items across a broad range of product groups.

invaluable historical record of decorative ceramic styles — from the exquisitely gilded and delicately hand-painted cabinet and table-ware of the Victorian and Edwardian era to the bright, bold, angular design of 1930s Art Deco — this col-lection is inspirational for today's Design Studio.

As well as a wide range of tableware, Royal Doulton today lists among its prod-ucts an extensive giftware collection, which includes character jugs, china flowers, and an array of collectable figurines and sculptures. Some of the figurines are inspired by history and literature — such as the figures of Heathcliffe and Cathy from *Wuthering Heights* and Shakespeare's tragic lovers, Romeo and Juliet.

For junior members of the household, Royal Doulton produces nurseryware, although many of these product lines are of interest to adult collec-tors as well. The most popular collection is "Bunnykins," while "Brambly Hedge" giftware and the Disney collections such as "Winnie the Pooh" have also excited and sustained much interest.

Royal Albert, which traces its origins back to 1896, has become an internationally recognized brand, offering domestic tableware and gift items. Royal Albert's "Old Country Roses" is the world's best-selling bone china pattern, with over 150 million pieces having been sold since its introduction in 1962.

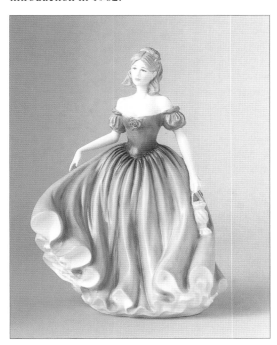

Equally famous, with an illustrious heritage dating back to 1793, is the Minton brand, cur-rently best known for its popular Haddon Hall pattern, a particular favorite of the Japanese mar-ket. Minton is also renowned for its intricate gold decoration, where one plate can cost $7,000. Many of these unique works of art are purchased as heirlooms.

Royal Doulton has a manufacturing capacity of around 500,000 pieces per week. Its tableware production factories are considered among the most advanced in the world — a tribute to the research and development department based in Stoke-on-Trent. The company is noted for its high standard of working practices and technology, which is heralded as among the most developed and pro-fessional in the entire international china industry.

With a corporate goal of generating 50 per-cent of its sales outside of the United Kingdom, an extensive distribution chain is required to over-see global sales and marketing. The company cur-rently operates in over 80 different markets with its own distribution companies in key markets — in New Jersey in the United States, and in Canada, Australia, and Japan.

RECENT DEVELOPMENTS

Royal Doulton is in an important period of change in its history, currently implementing a brand master-vision as a first step in repositioning the company's brands. Clarity for the position of the Royal Doulton and Royal Albert brands within the tableware and collectables marketplace has been key to the review.

The company has segmented the Royal Doulton brand into five categories — Classics, Archives, FUSiON, Studio and Café — and iden-tities have been created for each, together with a new Royal Doulton brand logo. New global mer-chandising systems, in-store environments, point-of-sale, and trade and exhibition design have all been identified as key to the repositioning.

Of course, despite significant changes in direction, Royal Doulton has continued to do what it does best: produce top-quality chinaware col-lections. The new ranges of casual diningware are stylish, functional, and user friendly, suited to all modern appliances.

The Licensing Division, created in the mid-1990s to propel the Royal Doulton brand into new product sectors, has achieved considerable suc-cess, not least the launch of "Doulton" luxury perfume, created by Patricia Bilodeau, senior per-fumer at Dragoco.

Other categories inspired by the company's rich heritage and design include an extensive collection of decorative fabrics and furniture sold in the United States as well as teas, textiles, and ties in Japan. In the United Kingdom, licensed products include kitchen textiles, Flemish tapes-tries and throws, stationery, children/baby gifts, and accessories.

PROMOTION

Central to Royal Doulton's promotional and mar-keting activity has been the repositioning of the brand. The introduction of everything from new logos to in-store point-of-sale and branded fix-tures has demanded that the focus of activity be centered on the communication and effective introduction of the recent significant changes.

To fulfill its goal of increasing its global pres-ence, Royal Doulton is focusing on offering greater consumer relevance through a diversity of products and an extension of its product in con-temporary creations.

At the grass roots, Royal Doulton continues to employ a variety of traditional promotional tech-niques ranging from trade fairs, in-store promotions, and selected magazine and press advertising, backed by strong, effective public relations campaigns.

Added to this approach, the visitor center at the main Royal Doulton factory, in Stoke-on-Trent, is very popular. Open seven days a week, the produc-tion facility features the world's largest public dis-play of Royal Doulton figures, numbering over 1,500. Visitors can tour the factory during the week, although bookings have to be made in advance.

BRAND VALUES

Around the globe, Royal Doulton is valued for its sense of heritage and Englishness. As one of the oldest and best-recognized chinaware brands in the world, Royal Doulton has earned itself a rep-utation for excellence, quality, and distinctiveness of design — values that the company intends to build on to take the brand forward through the new millennium.

Prized by collectors the world over, Royal Doulton has an international reach extending far beyond its English roots and product. To sustain its position, Royal Doulton's emphasis for future brand growth centers on its ability to focus on people, to understand its consumer base fully, and then to produce products that suit individual tastes and needs.

THINGS YOU DIDN'T KNOW ABOUT ROYAL DOULTON

❏ The largest and most expensive figure that Royal Doulton makes takes more than 160 hours to hand paint and costs in excess of $20,000.

❏ Royal Doulton was the first china to enter space. China plates were carried on the inau-gural flight of the space shuttle *Discovery* in 1984.

❏ Royal Doulton ceramics are included in a time capsule inside the base of Cleopatra's Needle on the Thames Embankment in London.

THE MARKET

The automotive industry is more dynamic now than it's ever been, and every brand has to be smarter, more inventive, and more responsive in order to attract new customers and maintain existing ones. As always, the ultimate goal is to create the most appealing combination of customer service, product performance, features, value, and styling. In order to meet the needs of an ever more diverse customer base and fulfill these goals, Saturn has been aggressively expanding its portfolio. In just the past two years, the brand has developed two entirely new model lines and extensively redesigned a third.

ACHIEVEMENTS

Saturn has always been focused on providing top-notch service, so

it's safe to say that the brand's greatest achievement is its staunchly loyal customer base. Whether developing a new product feature or an entirely new model line, Saturn always starts with the same objective: Put people first.

The Saturn experience begins the moment a guest enters a Saturn retail facility. The environment is designed to be welcoming, and some have amenities like a fireplace or even an Internet workstation, so guests can be productive while waiting for their paperwork or for their vehicle to be serviced. Every Saturn retailer understands that buying a new car is a big decision, so they take

the time to guide you through the process by explaining every step of the transaction. Ultimately, the retailers genuinely feel that buying a Saturn is a smart decision, and they want customers to feel that way, too.

That same respect and honesty extends to the owning experience as well. Saturn has always been dedicated to forming long-term relationships with consumers, and Saturn owners are as valued as much as potential customers. Each Saturn retailer has his or her own way of showing customer appreciation. One might wash every vehicle that comes in for service; another might leave a thank-you card on the dashboard. While these courtesies are certainly part of Saturn's approach to earning sales, they are also a true reflection of the retailers' respect for customers.

In fact, Saturn's customer-centric principles are designed into every vehicle Saturn builds. The brand doesn't develop technology for technology's sake. Instead, product features are designed using a process that first identifies customer needs, and then engineers solutions to fulfill them. For instance, Saturn's polymer panels help keep vehicles looking new, resale value high, and time spent in the body shop to a minimum. Saturn's spaceframe technology, which is usually found in more expensive luxury cars, was designed to provide a superior level of safety.

The fact that customers appreciate Saturn's way of doing business is apparent from the numerous customer satisfaction awards that Saturn has received over the years. Saturn has ranked first in

the J.D. Power and Associates Sales Satisfaction Studies[SM] three years in a row. In 2002, Saturn was also ranked the #1 Nameplate in Customer Satisfaction with Retailer Service in the J.D. Power and Associates Customer Service Study[SM].*

HISTORY

In the 1980s, General Motors led the evolution in the automotive industry through its efforts to redefine the consumer's retail experience. A group of GM dealers and Saturn leaders was convened to research and study what consumers valued, both in a vehicle and customer service. The results of that study effort helped GM launch Saturn with both an innovative, customer-centric product and a unique sales environment. Recent studies have shown that 79 percent of Saturn owners would have otherwise purchased an import car, so Saturn clearly has been successful in appealing to a valuable market niche.

THE PRODUCT

Putting people first has always been an integral part of the Saturn design philosophy. Smart solutions take precedence over quick fixes, and user-friendly technology trumps high-tech gimmickry. The Saturn approach often requires engineers and designers to throw away old formulas and take a fresh look at customers' lifestyles, and then develop new products and unexpected features that truly meet customers' needs.

Saturn's three-door coupe is a good illustration of the combination of insight and innovation.

Well aware that two-door coupes have a limited functionality, Saturn designers, engineers, and even retailers brainstormed ways of increasing functionality without sacrificing safety or the coupe's sporty styling. When the idea of adding a rear access door was proposed, it was a clear "a-ha!" moment for the entire group, and the world's first three-door coupe went into production in 1999. The 2003 ION quad coupe builds on the solution: by adding a fourth door, the back seat is accessible from both the driver and passenger sides. The ION sedan also includes inventive features like raised theater seating, which gives back-seat passengers a better view.

Another example of Saturn's people-centric approach is the VUE's real-world functionality. Customers had been telling Saturn they wanted an SUV that drove like a car, but had the ruggedness and cargo space of a larger vehicle. Engineers and designers working on the project spent many hours observing exactly how people interact with their cars, how they load and unload cargo, and what aspects frustrated them. The Saturn team was able to incorporate their findings into the VUE, with features like a low, easy-to-load liftgate; a fold-flat front passenger seat that accommodates longer loads; and a foldaway cargo organizer for groceries, sporting equipment, and other miscellaneous items.

RECENT DEVELOPMENTS

Saturn is continuing to expand its portfolio. For the 2003 model year, the brand unveiled the new-from-the-ground-up ION. Available in both a sedan and a quad coupe, the ION was developed specifically to target the youth market. The midsize L-Series sedan and wagon underwent a dramatic redesign in

2003 with additional refinements that appeal to customers looking for a luxurious car at a reasonable price. And the VUE, which was introduced in 2001, continues to attract consumers to the compact sport utility vehicle segment.

Maintaining a dialogue with customers is critical in terms of developing new lifestyle-specific packages and customization options. The Active Expression VUE is one example of this type of offering. The package combines an exclusive exterior color with elements specifically designed for a more outdoorsy lifestyle: roof rack cross bars, front grille guard, side step bars, and interior neoprene seat covers. The ION sedan and quad coupe, meanwhile, offer roof rails and interior trim kits that can be customized with a variety of patterns, an industry first.

Another important facet of Saturn's growth is its concept vehicle program, which not only allows designers to explore new technologies and market segments, but also provides an opportunity for Saturn to shift people's perceptions about the brand. A sleek, modern roadster called the SKY, one product of Saturn's concept vehicle program, can currently be seen on the auto show circuit.

PROMOTION

Saturn's first advertising agency, Hal Riney & Partners, developed the brand's original tagline, "A different kind of company. A different kind of car." Communicating the idea that the company and the car are inexorably intertwined was the key to Saturn's early success. Advertising focused on the folksy charm inherent in personal stories told by Saturn's employees and customers. The theme was clear: Saturn was a brand you could believe in, a

brand you could trust. Collectively, the work balanced poignancy with humor and lofty goals with commonsense objectives.

In early 2002, Saturn moved its account to Goodby, Silverstein & Partners. Since then, the advertising has helped to evolve the brand to make it more modern and relevant, and to give a greater emphasis to Saturn vehicles. To that end, the tagline has become, "It's different in a Saturn." Humor remains an important component of the work, along with a sense of authenticity and the overarching theme of putting people first. The message was strikingly illustrated in the agency's first brand TV spot for Saturn. Rather than standard car shots, the commercial presents images of drivers without their cars — the idea being that Saturn designs vehicles specifically for the people who will one day drive them.

BRAND VALUES

Numerous case studies have been written about Saturn, mainly because of the success the brand has had in building customer loyalty by incorporating its values into everything it does. Those values are inherently human: smart, honest, friendly, intelligent, and creative. In addition to the role that those values play in developing products and maintaining a high level of customer service, they also play a role in how the company interacts with the community. Each year, for instance, Saturn retailers partner with the National Association of Letter Carriers to organize America's largest one-day food drive. Last year, more than 60 million pounds of food were collected and distributed. Similarly, Saturn and the UAW team up each year to sponsor Donor Day, which is America's largest one-day drive for blood, marrow, organ, and tissue donations. In addition, Saturn has dedicated itself to developing more and more environmentally friendly manufacturing processes.

*J.D. Power and Associates 2000–2002 Sales Satisfaction Study℠. 2002 Study based on 39,315 consumer responses. J.D. Power and Associates 2002 Customer Service Satisfaction Study℠. Study based on 49,830 consumer responses. *www.jdpower.com*.

THINGS YOU DIDN'T KNOW ABOUT SATURN

❍ The company was named by chief designer Phil Garcia after the Saturn rockets that carried American astronauts to the moon during the space race in the 1960s.

❍ The first Saturn ever — a metallic red four-door sedan — rolled off the production line in Spring Hill, Tennessee, at exactly 10:57 a.m. on July 30, 1989.

THE MARKET

Just 10 years ago, if you had heard of someone "logging on," you might have thought they were involved in a lumberjack competition. Now more than half of the U.S. population is online. That's about 150 million Americans. And it's not just chit-chat and checking out ball scores; Internet usage is expected to fuel an estimated 40 percent of the world's gross national product.

That blinding advancement in technology has come thanks in large measure to a dynamic telecommunications industry — one fueled by extraordinary competition and one constantly reinventing itself.

In the midst of this revolution, SBC Communications Inc. and its family of companies (SBC) has transformed itself from the smallest of the "Baby Bells" into one of the world's largest and most technologically advanced companies in the telecommunications market. As America's preeminent provider of DSL Internet service and one of the nation's leading Internet service providers (ISPs), SBC is now shaping the future of the industry with its state-of-the-art broadband infrastructure.

ACHIEVEMENTS

Talk about your ringing endorsements. For six straight years, SBC has been named the World's Most Admired telecommunications company in *Fortune* magazine's annual report card. In fact, SBC ranked first in its industry in all nine categories of corporate reputation: quality of management, quality of products, innovation, long-term investment value, financial soundness, employee talent, social responsibility, globalness, and use of corporate assets.

What's more, when *CIO* magazine went searching for 100 companies that were achieving "customer service nirvana," SBC was on its list — joining an elite group identified as having mastered the customer connection.

Among its accomplishments, SBC played a pioneering role at two critical stages of Internet development — making contributions that helped spur the Net's rapid growth and commercialization. First, SBC companies contributed to the

development and deployment of "packet technologies" that laid the foundation for the Internet. Then, in 1994, SBC companies were awarded two of the original four Internet Access Points (NAPs) granted by the National Science Foundation. The creation of the NAPs, which became operational in 1995, signified a fundamental change in the architecture of the modern public Internet. It was now accessible, reliable, and scalable — not to mention fun.

The next wave has already begun. SBC is the nation's leading provider of DSL broadband Internet access, with more than 2 million customers. Through a $6 billion network transformation, SBC plans to bring high-speed DSL Internet access to as many Americans as possible by the end of 2003.

A recent report showed that widespread use of high-speed Internet services could contribute as much as $500 billion annually to the U.S. economy — with consumers benefiting from online home shopping, entertainment, health services, and reduced commuting.

HISTORY

Reliable . . . trusted . . . committed . . . all of these words are grounded in SBC's rich heritage, which spans some 100 years. The company is a familiar name and a recognized business leader, innovator, and community neighbor. Alexander Graham Bell is the patriarch of the SBC family tree. The company's ancestry goes back to the Bell Telephone Co., one of the companies founded between 1877 and 1880 to leverage Mr. Bell's patent rights — and the only one to remain in business when those patents expired during the 1890s. SBC's predecessor company was Southwestern Bell, which was formed in 1917.

The breakup of the Bell System came in 1984, making possible the formation of SBC as a separate company, independent of AT&T and the other regional Bell companies. Divestiture in 1984 forever altered the telecom landscape and allowed SBC to expand its presence beyond its traditional five-state territory of Texas, Missouri, Kansas, Oklahoma, and Arkansas.

SBC's 1987 eye-catching purchase of Metromedia's wireless telephone properties made it the first Bell operating company to buy wireless operations outside its traditional territory — laying the groundwork for SBC's growth into one of the leading wireless communications providers in the United States.

When the Federal Telecommunications Act of 1996 was signed into law, SBC was the first to outline a strategy for becoming an integrated, national competitor. In 1997, SBC completed the first merger of two major telecommunications companies when it acquired Pacific Telesis Group. In 1998, SBC acquired Southern New England Telephone in Connecticut and in 1999 took another major step with its landmark merger with Ameritech Corporation — thus becoming the first major telecom company to aggressively expand competition for services to businesses and residential customers on a nationwide scale.

THE PRODUCT

The need for speed has never been greater. SBC has responded with laserlike focus, expanding its fiber-rich broadband network to more and more neighborhoods and businesses nationwide. The company already provides DSL Internet access to more than 28 million customer locations, with plans to reach millions more by the end of 2003.

Speed is only part of the equation. SBC is creating the content-rich, broadband-enabled applications that will travel over its next-generation network to provide products and services that will forever change the way people live and work — delivering the full promise of the Internet: conveniences such as distance learning, videos on demand, home security, online games, and much more.

SBC has become a communications powerhouse, offering local and long distance service, voice and data services, wireless services, e-business services, network integration, Web site and application hosting, messaging, and directory advertising. SBC also owns 60 percent of Cingular, the second-largest wireless company in the United States and a leader in providing wireless data services.

The second-largest local service provider in the United States, SBC's service area spans approximately one-third of the U.S. population and is home to nearly half of the Fortune 500

company headquarters, and it continues to grow. SBC meets its customers' data and voice communications needs through nearly 58 million access lines nationwide.

RECENT DEVELOPMENTS

In mid-2002, SBC and Yahoo! launched a landmark strategic alliance to provide broadband access to millions of consumers — two great brands pairing the strengths of the number-one global Internet destination with one of the largest Internet service providers to offer a cobranded, premium DSL Internet and dial-up service.

But don't blink. SBC is widely deploying optical technologies throughout its metropolitan networks. These networks use Dense Wave Division Multiplexing (DWDM), channeling data over multiple colors of light to deliver nearly limitless bandwidth — up to 160 Gigabits per second on a fiber pair.

SBC has also entered the long-distance business with force, capturing nearly 6 million access lines in less than three years and becoming the first of the original Bell operating companies to begin selling

long-distance solutions in its original region, which includes Texas, Arkansas, Oklahoma, Kansas, and Missouri. Today, SBC Long Distance service is also available in Connecticut and California as well as 30 markets outside its traditional service area. The company seized the next logical step — entry into the national data and IP services market, an estimated $30 billion market to which SBC previously had little access because of regulatory restrictions. By mid-2003, SBC will complete its data and IP backbone networks, enabling the company to serve customers in the nation's 50 largest markets. SBC also is enhancing its portfolio of business offerings to deliver managed service options, which enable customers to take advantage of the cost savings and efficiencies of outsourcing their communications network design, delivery, and ongoing management.

PROMOTION

Already sporting an excellent reputation, SBC recently set out to raise the profile of its brand. Through an aggressive advertising campaign and a newly branded visual mark, SBC has streamlined its family of brands, moving to a single national brand and taking full advantage of its value. Building upon the strengths of SBC's traditional regional brands — Southwestern Bell, Ameritech, Pacific Bell, Nevada Bell, and SNET — the move provides a more unified presence and helps customers recognize SBC as a national data communications provider and industry leader.

The message: SBC is a reliable, dynamic, forward-thinking, data-driven, customer-oriented company. The new brand represents the best of what SBC has to offer:
- Strong telecommunications heritage
- Commitment to delivering innovative, quality products and services
- Commitment to supporting communities
- A company built for the 21st century
- A best-in-class workforce
- National presence

BRAND VALUES

The SBC brand represents trust, reliability, character, and strength, grounded in more than 100 years of unwavering commitment — to its employees, customers, and communities.

SBC has a long tradition of providing reliable, high-quality products and services, and meeting customers' communications needs. In fact, SBC's network is reliable 99.999 percent of the time — a track record unsurpassed in the industry.

In today's ever-changing technology environment, the SBC brand also stands for responsibility. SBC's advancements in communications technology have always been in step with its commitment to enhancing the quality of life in the communities it serves, through generous corporate giving and active involvement. As a community partner, SBC is committed to supporting projects that, through technology, improve education, economic development, and the quality of life — building stronger communities nationwide.

THINGS YOU DIDN'T KNOW ABOUT SBC

○ SBC recently received the Ron Brown Award for Corporate Leadership, the only presidential award given to recognize outstanding corporate citizenship. The award recognized SBC's leadership in supporting community development through its supplier diversity program.

○ Since 2000, SBC also has been recognized as one of America's Top 10 Companies for Minorities by *Fortune*, as one of America's Top 25 Companies for Executive Women by *Working Women*, as America's Top Company for Latinas by *Latina Style*, and as Corporation of the Year by the American Society on Aging.

○ SBC's Pioneers, the country's largest company-sponsored volunteer organization — comprising 215,000 active employees and retirees — contributed 7.6 million hours of community service in 2002, or more than $100 million worth of sweat equity toward building stronger communities.

○ Through corporate and SBC Foundation giving, SBC contributes millions annually to communities nationwide and is consistently ranked among the nation's top-five corporate foundations.

○ SBC contributed $10 million to establish the creation of The Women's Museum: An Institute for the Future, the nation's first comprehensive museum dedicated to chronicling the accomplishments of women. This corporate gift was the single largest ever made to a women's organization in the United States.

○ SBC has deployed more than 2 million miles of fiber optic strand across its 13-state region, enough to circle the earth at the equator more than 85 times if each strand were placed end to end.

THE MARKET

At home or away, few products are considered more indispensable than toilet paper. Annual global sales exceed $19 billion. While this statistic isn't likely to come up in daily conversation, the fact remains: Everybody needs toilet paper.

Everyone seems to have an opinion about it, too. Four attributes — softness, strength, absorbency, and value — lie at the core of this ongoing debate. Some other concerns are aesthetic qualities, such as tissue color and designer patterns. Whether the paper should unroll from above or beneath is an issue that may never be resolved.

Paper towels and paper napkins are other important segments in the steadily growing tissue product market. In these categories, consumer preferences are strongly influenced by product aesthetics in addition to basic qualities of physical performance.

ACHIEVEMENTS

The SCOTT® brand is a leader in the paper products industry with a heritage of innovation. Scott was the first company to market rolls of tissue specifically for use as toilet paper. By 1939, SCOTT was the largest-selling brand in the United States.

In 1907, Scott also introduced the first paper towel in America. Originally sold only to commercial customers, this breakthrough product invention was easily dispensed and disposable while providing an economical and sanitary option to cloth-roll towels in high-traffic restrooms. Scott also was the first to introduce paper towels to the consumer market. SCOTTOWELS®, rolled out in 1931, were the first paper towels sold in grocery stores. This product was a winner for consumers looking for a convenient, hygienic solution to kitchen tasks.

Scott introduced the first paper napkin as well. The company was the first to introduce pastel-colored tissue products in all three categories, and later the first to introduce designer prints on SCOTT Towels. Among its many packaging "firsts," Scott introduced the largest paper towel roll — the Mega Roll — in 1991. In 2001, *Good Housekeeping* rated SCOTT Towels a "Best Buy."

HISTORY

In the late 19th century, the public's desire for better hygiene coincided with improvements in residential and commercial indoor plumbing —

The epitome of common sense.

Softest Ever!

Scott Tissue

1000 Sheets

UNSCENTED BATHROOM TISSUE

1000 sheets that last and last. Plus being our softest ever. And not to get too highfalutin, but we think you'll find that adds up to an uncommon value as well.

Common Sense on a Roll.

a convenience we take for granted today. Brothers E. Irvin and Clarence Scott founded Scott Paper Company Limited in Philadelphia in 1879. Scott became the first company to market rolls of tissue specifically for use as toilet paper rather than its previous use as a medical item.

Developing the emerging category wasn't easy. The market was limited and the subject was unmentionable in the Victorian 1890s. Consumers wouldn't discuss it, merchants wouldn't display it, and publications wouldn't advertise it. To overcome this resistance, the Scotts devised an interesting strategy. They gave their merchant customers (primarily druggists and variety stores) a proprietary interest in selling toilet tissue by customizing the product to each customer's specifications for the size and form of the package, the weight of the tissue, and the name and design that appeared on the wrapper. Under this private-label arrangement (then known as "ghost manufacturing"), the Scotts purchased large "parent" rolls of paper and converted them into the various small rolls and packages of toilet tissue.

The strategy worked. Business grew steadily each year as toilet tissue became an essential

item in homes and workplaces. The company expanded, and with the added capacity Scott was producing private-label brands for more than 2,000 customers.

Around 1896, the company began to phase out the private-label business and concentrate on the manufacture of its own distinctive brands. By 1911, SCOTT-branded products accounted for nearly 80 percent of SCOTT Tissue's annual sales.

In 1907, a Philadelphia schoolteacher blamed a mild epidemic of colds on the fact that all of her students used the same cloth towel, which she believed was the source of infection. She cut heavy paper into squares and gave them to the children for individual use. Her idea sparked a new idea for the Scott Paper Company: the paper towel. Called SANI-TOWELS originally, the product was manufactured from thick, heavy rolls of creped tissue that were made into smaller rolls of towels and perforated into individual sheets. As other uses emerged, the product was renamed SCOTTISSUE TOWELS. One of its popular slogans was "For use once by one user." The product line was also expanded to include SCOTT paper napkins.

When Scott celebrated its 75th anniversary in 1954, its sales of $228 million represented 750 percent growth in the decade following

Today, millions of women are finding kitchen work easier... cleaner with ScotTowels

ScotTowels FOR KITCHEN USE

NO WONDER WOMEN WANTED MORE SCOTTOWELS THAN WE COULD MAKE

World War II. Five products — bathroom tissue, paper towels, paper napkins, facial tissue, and wax paper — accounted for most of the sales. Four of the five products were unknown when the company was founded, and the fifth — bathroom tissue — was considered a luxury item at the time of Scott's inception.

Significant activity occurred outside of Scott's core businesses over the next two decades — from feminine napkins and air conditioner filters to BABYSCOTT disposable diapers and leisure furniture. Scott continued to be a leader in a variety of product categories, but the company fell on hard times in the early 1990s. The result was a harsh wave of restructuring that left Scott lean and ready to become part of Kimberly-Clark Corporation.

THE PRODUCT

As cofounder Irvin Scott once stated, "Quality cannot be acquired by good intentions alone, but must actually be built into the products." For more than a century, the SCOTT® brand has stood for quality products at a fair price. Generations of smart shoppers trust the quality and value of SCOTT® products. When customers purchase the SCOTT brand, whether it's bathroom tissue, paper towels, or family napkins, they know they've made the common sense choice.

SCOTT® bathroom tissue is famous for its common sense value. With 1,000 sheets per roll and surprisingly good softness, it's no wonder that SCOTT Tissue is the only brand so many parents choose for their families. SCOTT Tissue is also safe for sewer and septic systems. In fact, it's safe for RVs and boats as well. Made from 100 percent virgin fiber, SCOTT Tissue is available in white or solid colors: pink, blue, and beige.

Made from 100 percent virgin fiber, SCOTT® Towels are available in one-, three-, six-, eight-, and 12-roll packages, with 64 sheets per roll. The SCOTT Mega roll has 96 sheets per roll. SCOTT Towels also offers Choose-A-Size rolls that enable consumers to dispense the appropriate size towel for each job.

SCOTT® Napkins are available in an attractive array of contemporary colors and designer prints with kitchen, contemporary, and floral themes, in 120-, 250-, 400-, and 600-count packages.

RECENT DEVELOPMENTS

Announced on July 17, 1995, the merger of Kimberly-Clark and Scott Paper was completed December 12 of the same year, following overwhelming approval by shareholders of both companies.

After the merger, Kimberly-Clark continued to build quality into SCOTT® products. In 1999, SCOTT® bathroom tissue was improved to become the softest SCOTT Tissue ever. Still 1,000 sheets per roll, the improvement further elevated the value delivered by the brand, reinforcing its consumer appeal.

In 2001, SCOTT® Towels introduced a revolutionary product feature: Fast-absorbing wide ridges. These ridges have a unique channeling action, so they absorb like no other towel. This physical product distinction, along with Scott's enduring reputation for honest and practical value, has the product well positioned for the 21st century.

PROMOTION

With the 1927 hiring of a new advertising company, J. Walter Thompson of New York, Scott became aggressive in communicating its benefits relative to competitive products. Other products were inferior — filled with pieces of wood and other rough material. Ads also cited the health advantages of using SCOTT® products and warned consumers of contracting "Toilet Tissue Illnesses." Statements from doctors were used to support Scott's views. Statements such as a child saying, "They have a pretty house, Mother, but their bathroom paper hurts," caused a storm of complaints from competitors. A new policy was more positive, and subsequent advertising stressed SCOTT® quality.

Today, "Common Sense on a Roll™" is the slogan brandished by national television and print campaigns promoting SCOTT® brand products. The theme captures a philosophy that has driven SCOTT® quality, value, and advertising for over a century: Caring for family and the pride that can only be known by making a sensible choice.

BRAND VALUES

All SCOTT® branded products share a genuine commitment to practical quality and good value that our consumers appreciate. What's more, because each SCOTT® product has a unique balance of quality, quantity, and price, SCOTT® customers don't sacrifice their families' comfort — or their pocketbooks.

Portions of this article were taken from *Shared Values: A History of Kimberly-Clark* by Robert Spector (Greenwich Publishing, 1997).

THINGS YOU DIDN'T KNOW ABOUT SCOTT

○ In 1913, SCOTTISSUE with 1000 sheets per roll was introduced at a cost of 10 cents per roll and was considered a medical item. Print ads were used to increase awareness and address embarrassment.

○ Over 1 billion rolls of SCOTT bathroom tissue are produced annually. Unrolled, they would circle the earth over 2,900 times.

THE MARKET

The Scotts Company is the world's leading supplier of consumer products for lawn and garden care, with a full range of products for professional horticulture as well. The company owns what are by far the industry's most recognized brands. In the United States, consumer awareness of the company's Scotts, Miracle-Gro, and Ortho brands outscores the nearest competitors in their categories by several times, as does awareness of the consumer Roundup brand, which is owned by Monsanto and marketed exclusively by Scotts worldwide.

ACHIEVEMENTS

Since its founding in 1868, The Scotts Company has nurtured a reputation for quality — and for helping consumers and professionals obtain the best possible results. Studies show that consumers acknowledge the company's commitment: In a survey of discount store shoppers, Scotts and Miracle-Gro brands were rated as the top two preferred lawn and garden brands.

Scotts research has resulted in innovations such as the first lawn spreader, the first selective

control for broadleaf weeds in lawns, the first crabgrass preventer, the first patented Kentucky bluegrass, and many more.

HISTORY

The company known today as The Scotts Company began as O.M. Scott and Sons. Orlando McLean Scott managed a seed elevator in Marysville, Ohio, and in 1868 he purchased a hardware store and seed business. After the turn of the century, the company began to focus on grass seed and sold 5,000 pounds of Kentucky bluegrass seed to a New York real estate firm that was building one of the nation's first golf courses. Within five years, one of every five golf courses in America was being seeded with Scotts grass seed.

In 1928, Scotts created a product that would begin an entirely new industry in the United States. Until that year, people who wanted to improve their lawns used farm fertilizers. Then Scotts discovered a readily available nutrient source with a high concentration of nitrogen. Turf Builder fertilizer was born, and in 2003 this product celebrates its 75th anniversary.

Miracle-Gro was founded by Horace Hagedorn and Otto Stern in 1951. Horace realized a greater opportunity existed in marketing a consumable product — rather than just selling plants and trees. They began shipping a small packet of water-soluble fertilizer with each plant. Customers soon asked for more plant food. That same year, a full-page Miracle-Gro ad in a New York City newspaper produced $22,000 in cash orders, and the company was on its way to success. Today's awareness tests show an astounding 99 percent of gardeners recognize the Miracle-Gro brand. In 1999, Scotts entered the control industry through agreements with the Monsanto Company for exclusive agency and marketing rights in the United States, Canada, the United Kingdom, France, Germany, and Australia to Monsanto's consumer Roundup herbicide products — and for the purchase of the Ortho and related lawn and garden business. The Ortho business group was established and moved to Marysville.

More consumers use Roundup than all other weed control products combined. Roundup quickly eliminates virtually every weed — more than 125 varieties in gardens and yards.

THE PRODUCT

Miracle-Gro and the powerful advertising behind it have played a major role in the growth of the entire lawn and garden industry. Before the introduction of Miracle-Gro, gardeners had to buy large bags of agricultural fertilizers for their plants and shrubs without knowing how much to use.

But then came Miracle-Gro, a water-soluble plant food that was easy to use and which guaranteed results. Suddenly, growing beautiful plants and flowers was easy.

Scotts makes control of bugs and weeds in lawns and gardens a simple matter of product selection. Ortho's popular "B-Gon" is the perfect name for a product, instantly telling the consumer exactly what it does. If you have weeds in your yard, use Weed-B-Gon. If bugs are the problem, there's Bug-B-Gon.

RECENT DEVELOPMENTS

In 1998, Scotts began research in the field of biotechnology, which could lead to commercial development of genetically transformed turf-grasses, flowers, and woody ornamentals.

Scotts introduced in the year 2000 Miracle-Gro Garden Soils — a pre-mixed, rich organic product made of manure, sphagnum, and peat-moss. The mixture quickly became a hit and one of Scotts' most successful product launches. In 2002, Scotts introduced yet another new product, Miracle-Gro Select Plants.

Scotts is also branching out into other territories by introducing Scotts LawnService. Roughly 15 percent of homeowners use professional lawn care services. Scotts has staked out the premium end of this market, leveraging brand power with Scotts LawnService and Miracle-Gro Tree & Shrub Service. In 2002, Scotts LawnService had entered nearly half of the top 100 markets for do-it-for-me lawn care.

PROMOTION

Mention brands like Scotts Turf Builder or Miracle-Gro and many people think of the extensive advertising Scotts uses to support them.

Investing money in advertising has been a major factor in the success of our brands. But the company brings much more than advertising to the equation.

A product has to deliver results. Scotts, with its "strong roots" beginning with the industry's largest research and development organization and the most advanced production technology, makes sure its products deliver these results. The scale of the company's operations and its use of patented technologies in key areas not only enable Scotts to deliver superior results, but create important competitive advantages in the marketplace.

In 1972, Scotts introduced the toll-free Consumer Helpline to provide homeowners with a reliable source for helpful lawn care advice. The service is so popular that Scotts lawn and garden consultants now receive nearly 1 million calls per year.

To further help gardeners figure out just what those weeds and bugs in their gardens are and how to control them, the Ortho group publishes a Problem Solver book. The book is now available online at the Scotts Web site.

That Web site, *www.scotts.com*, generates more that 3 million visits each year and provides one of the Internet's largest libraries of lawn and garden content. A recent survey of Scotts' Internet visitors found that 70 percent have bookmarked the site, indicating that they find it helpful and plan to return to it.

BRAND VALUES

The Scotts Company's goal is to plant, protect, and nurture. The company is working to secure its leadership position by continuing to produce quality, environmentally sound products that meet consumers' needs.

The Scotts Company believes in the importance of community involvement —supporting community initiatives by participating and giving back. The Scotts Company's corporate caring program is called Give Back to Grow and focuses on causes such as feeding the hungry, taking abandoned lots and turning them into flower gardens, introducing children to the wonder of gardening, and encouraging teenagers to consider a career in agriculture or horticulture.

The company's constant mission is to strengthen its position as the world's foremost marketer of branded products and services for the lawn and garden, while meeting challenging profit and return-on-investment goals. More information on The Scotts Company is available at the Scotts Web site: *www.scotts.com*.

THINGS YOU DIDN'T KNOW ABOUT SCOTTS

○ In one year alone, Scotts sold more than 6 billion pounds of potting and planting soils, barks and mulches, and other organic products throughout North America. That's 50 million wheelbarrow loads — enough to fill the Rose Bowl 20 times.

○ A beautifully landscaped lawn can add up to 15 percent to a home's value.

○ The front lawns of just eight average houses have the cooling effect of 70 tons of air conditioning; the average home central air unit has only about a three- to four-ton capacity.

THE MARKET

Mattresses are big business in the United States. Consumers will spend $4 billion on bedding this year. Yet some people still see their mattress as a commodity and make purchasing decisions accordingly. Unfortunately, they often pay for it with poor sleep. Simmons has always seen the mattress differently: as a way to help people sleep better. This point of view reflects a unique, company-wide passion that's also right on the money, especially when considering the facts about sleep.

A recent survey shows that one out of four adults categorize their sleep as fair or poor. Over one half of them consider themselves sleep deprived. The effect of inadequate sleep is real. The National Sleep Foundation found that inadequate sleep can lead to health problems and impaired performance at work, increasing the risk of injury and on-the-job mistakes. Statistically, the average amount of sleep per night dropped 20 percent during the 20th century.

In a recent sleep poll, Americans agreed that the sleep surface is very important to a deep/restful sleep. They also recognized that a better quality mattress can provide a better night's sleep.

By constantly innovating and producing mattresses that are not only comfortable, durable, and aesthetically pleasing, but also are designed and built to promote sounder sleep routines and better overall sleep, Simmons is responding to America's call.

ACHIEVEMENTS

Simmons, one of the world's largest brand names in bedding, is represented in over 100 countries.

Changing people's lives around the world through better sleep is quite an achievement in itself, but Simmons is not one to rest on its laurels. The company is also committed to revolutionizing its own industry and has become a leader in the home furnishings field.

Through industry-leading research and development, innovative consumer-driven products, memorable advertising, dynamic retail programs, progressive employee relations, and its imaginative Web site, Simmons continues on its course of cutting-edge leadership on many fronts.

One of the best physical examples of the company's drive to be the best is the Simmons

Institute for Technology and Education (SITE). Completed in 1995, the 38,000-square-foot facility houses Research and Product Development, Manufacturing Services, Quality Assurance, Transportation, and Distribution. SITE is the seedbed for the kind of groundbreaking technology for which Simmons has become recognized.

Another place in which Simmons' achievements are now archived is the Smithsonian National Museum of American History in Washington, D.C. The Simmons entry encompasses everything from manufacturing innovations (including many patents and trademarks) and a case study in marketing to the classic growth of a family business.

HISTORY

The history of Simmons Company is one of continuous innovation spanning more than 130 years. The Simmons story began in 1870 when Zalmon Simmons bought a cheese-box factory in Kenosha, Wisconsin. He also owned a country store where one day, as payment for a bad debt, he accepted a patent for a woven bedspring. Simmons assigned a local inventor to the project and in 1876 they manufactured the first mass-produced woven wire mattress.

This idea was definitely ahead of its time. While the bed was becoming a fixture in American bedrooms, the mattress was still a rarity. As the 1920s began, most Americans still slept on lumpy pads stuffed with cotton or hair. This habit continued until 1925 when Simmons Company came up with the Beautyrest® Pocketed Coil® spring mattress and changed the history of sleep forever.

As the decades passed, Simmons continued to make bedding history by catering to changing lifestyles. In 1930, they introduced the studio couch and 10 years later the innovative Hide-A-Bed®. The first electric blanket (1946) was another Simmons invention. In 1958, Simmons became the first mattress company to offer both king and queen sizes. As Americans became more stressed and grew physically larger, Simmons saw to these needs with solution after solution. BackCare® was introduced in 1995. The non-flip mattress (a maintenance-free design that has radically changed the way bedding is made) debuted in 2000. And the Olympic® Queen, with its imaginatively designed space so a queen sleeps more like a king-sized mattress, came a year later.

Today, the company remains on a historic mission: to provide quality sleep and better overall health for the changing needs of society.

THE PRODUCT

Uniquely designed consumer-driven products with tangible built-in benefits set Simmons apart.

Simmons® Beautyrest®, the company's flagship brand for over 75 years, has been proven to provide better sleep for people who share a bed. How? Beautyrest® Pocketed Coil® Springs are designed to reduce motion transfer across the

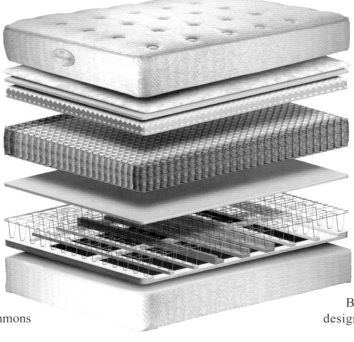

mattress. Considering all the tossing and turning that goes on between sleeping partners, and the resultant motion transfer, you can see why Beautyrest® is the ideal mattress for couples, especially because both partners can benefit from peaceful, undisturbed sleep. Alertness, productivity, happiness, and slowing the aging process are just some of the health attributes associated with improved sleep.

For people who suffer from stiffness or morning back pain, Simmons BackCare has been designed in a way that the company believes alleviates back pain. Its patented five-zone construction provides the ideal lumbar support, so the spine stays correctly aligned during sleep.

The Simmons Olympic Queen is another example of Simmons' creative thinking in designing the kind of sleep consumers desire. This ingenious mattress adds six inches to the traditional queen size; the Olympic Queen sleeps like a king, but still fits a queen-sized foundation. It's the ideal solution for consumers who want a larger mattress but already own queen-size furniture. The Simmons Olympic Queen fills the need by delivering not only 10 percent more space, but also a better quality of sleep.

If better sleep is the goal, Simmons has the products for it. From the luxurious DreamScape and partnerships with noted New York designers to new generation coils in Deep Sleep® and Adjustable Beds, Simmons continues to reinvent the way Americans sleep.

RECENT DEVELOPMENTS

Now is an exciting time to be involved in the science of sleep. While updating its product line with the latest technological advancements, Simmons continues to pioneer sleep research and product development. Working with noted sleep experts, authors, and researchers, the company is always testing and exploring the possibilities of improved sleep. The beneficial results are apparent both in stores and on line.

On the company's Web site, *www.simmons.com*, consumers are invited to experience the ultimate resource for better sleep. Interactive activities include a Sleep Research Center, on-line sleep analysis, and the opportunity to design the perfect bed for their individual sleep needs. You can also take a sleep deprivation test and learn all about sleep disorders, tips, and strategies.

Plans for the future include continuing sleep education for consumers and the ongoing development of products to help people everywhere achieve or enhance quality sleep.

PROMOTION

With a product line that's differentiated from the rest of the industry, the need to demonstrate unique benefits is almost irresistible. Over the years, Simmons has created advertising and promotions that are as distinctive and memorable as their products.

The 1920s saw one of the most high-profile testimonial campaigns ever launched in the United States. Well-known personalities like Henry Ford, Thomas Edison, and Eleanor Roosevelt all extolled the virtues of their Beautyrest. In the 1940s, glamour prevailed, with stars like Dorothy Lamour and Maureen O'Hara enjoying sumptuous comfort and support. Bill Cosby and Arthur Ashe promoted Simmons bedding in the '60s, and more recently, John Madden went to the videotape in sizing up the benefits of the Olympic Queen mattress.

Elephants, celebrities, and politicians have all helped demonstrate the Simmons difference over the years. U.S. Olympic athletes also benefited. They slept on Simmons mattresses during the 1980, 1988, and 1996 Games.

One of the most memorable mattress icons of all time is the Beautyrest "Bowling Ball," an imaginative way to illustrate how independent Pocketed Coil® construction promotes undisturbed sleep. Like all Simmons advertising, the core concept is carried on down through the retailer and consumer levels.

BRAND VALUES

The Simmons® name has become synonymous with sleeping innovation, and brand development today rests on three passions. First is "Better Sleep Through Science.®" Simmons is committed to helping consumers achieve healthier sleeping habits as well as higher levels of quality sleep. Second is a strong belief that not all mattresses are the same. Simmons strives to make superior mattresses with discernible differences that produce unique benefits. Third, knowing consumers want better sleep, Simmons provides solutions.

Can a mattress really impact sleep quality? Simmons believes so. They believe their Beautyrest®, BackCare®, and Olympic Queen® mattresses all contribute to better sleep. Are consumers getting the message? Yes. As it has for over 130 years, Simmons continues to lead the way with solutions to better sleep and smarter sleep routines.

THINGS YOU DIDN'T KNOW ABOUT SIMMONS

- ○ Simmons was also first with the brass bed and the wall bed.

- ○ Another industry first is the Environments Collection, a partnership with New York designer Joseph Abboud. This offering features intricate designs, luxurious fabrics, and exquisite tailoring.

- ○ Simmons Beautyrest Adjustable beds have innovative features, such as remote controls that wake you with a gentle, soothing massage.

- ○ Another innovation is the no-rotate mattress, heralding a new maintenance-free era of convenience.

- ○ The *www.simmons.com* Web site is the first in the industry to help consumers better understand sleep and sleep products so people can make more informed buying decisions.

- ○ The company leads the industry with some 40 registered patents promoting better sleep.

SONY®

THE MARKET

Sony Corporation is a leading manufacturer of audio, video, communications, and information technology products for the consumer and professional markets. Additionally, the company's music, motion picture, television-production, game, and online businesses make Sony one of the most comprehensive entertainment companies in the world.

ACHIEVEMENTS

Today, Sony employs almost 170,000 people worldwide, with almost 22,000 working in the United States. For fiscal year 2001, Sony Corporation had total sales of more than $56.9 billion, with the electronics segment making up more than two-thirds of the revenues.

Sony Electronics Inc. (SEL), formerly known as Sony Corporation of America, was established in 1960 to oversee Sony's sales and marketing activities in the United States. Today, Sony's U.S. operations include research and development, design, engineering, manufacturing, sales, marketing, distribution, and customer service.

Sony has become not just the market leader in consumer electronics but through research and development it has made considerable inroads in the areas of professional broadcasting, mobile communications, personal computers, storage, media, and now, the Internet.

As a corporation, Sony has convergence at its very heart. Driven by an integrated business model, the company is positioned to bring new benefits to consumers by combining hardware, software, content, and services.

HISTORY

Sony founders Masaru Ibuka and Akio Morita complemented each other with a unique blend of product innovation and marketing savvy.

In 1950, in postwar Japan, Ibuka and Morita created Sony's first hardware device: a tape player/recorder called the G-TYPE recorder. Materials were so scarce that the first tapes were made of paper with hand-painted magnetic material.

Ibuka was a practical visionary who could foretell what products and technologies could be applied to everyday life. He inspired a spirit of innovation in his engineers and fostered an exciting working atmosphere and an open corporate culture.

Through Ibuka's persistence, the magnetic tape recorder evolved into the Model P (for "Portable"), which became the company's first profitable product.

When the company obtained licensing rights to the transistor from Western Electric in 1953, Ibuka urged his engineers to improve production methods with the goal of creating a transistor radio. The introduction of the TR-55, Japan's first transistor radio, in 1955 led to Sony's 1957 launch of the world's first pocket transistor radio, establishing a market leadership position for the company.

Akio Morita was a true marketing pioneer who was instrumental not only in making Sony a global brand but also in creating the name itself. With the firm establishing itself in the United States and other foreign markets, he suggested to Ibuka that the original name of Tokyo Tsushin Kogyo be changed to one that was easily pronounceable and recognized. "Sony" was created to evoke simultaneously the concepts of the Latin *sonus*, "sonic," and "sonny," meaning little son. The combination conveyed the reality of Sony as a very small group of young people with the energy and passion for unlimited creation.

This passion and creativity eventually led to the development of Sony's Trinitron TV in 1968, which set the world standard for high quality in home theater products.

As a proponent of global operations based on a local presence, Morita set up manufacturing plants all over the world. Its Trinitron® color television assembly plant in San Diego, California, built in 1972, was the first consumer electronics manufacturing facility built in the United States by a Japanese-based company.

Morita's deep confidence in another legendary Sony product, the Walkman® personal stereo, was the key factor in its ultimate success. While retailers were initially resistant, the Walkman stereo's compact size and excellent sound quality attracted consumers, ultimately igniting the personal audio revolution.

Kazuo Iwama was a detail-oriented person, admired for his scientific knowledge and discipline. He was made president of Sony in 1976, and became thoroughly involved in developing the "charged coupled device" or CCD, which paved the way for the camcorder and digital still camera. While he was president, Sony launched the Betamax® video cassette recorder and the compact disc player, another Sony innovation that changed the way people listened to music.

THE PRODUCT

Throughout its history, Sony has demonstrated an ability to capture people's imaginations and enhance their lives. The company has been at the cutting edge of technology for more than 50 years, positively impacting the way we live. Further, few companies are as well positioned to drive the digital age into homes and businesses around the world for the next 50 years and beyond.

Sony innovations have become part of mainstream culture. Today, Sony continues to fuel industry growth with the sale of innovative products, as well as through the company's convergence strategy.

Sony's approach is to make it possible for consumers to enjoy various forms of content — both on "home networks," consisting of connected electronic devices, and "mobile networks" that are accessible through mobile terminals.

Sony's vision is to give consumers easy, ubiquitous access to entertainment and information anytime, anywhere. The concept of seamless connectivity and interaction between products and the network has been termed as the "Ubiquitous Value Network." This technology platform aims to offer customers content and services that match their unique lifestyles and values.

In the future, look for Sony to create entirely new forms of entertainment, blending movies, computer-generated worlds, games, and music. Sony has the vision, technology, and content to forge a direction in consumer entertainment that no other company can match.

RECENT DEVELOPMENTS

Norio Ohga was responsible for bringing Sony into the modern age and injecting it with a unique sense of style through product planning, stylish product design, and innovative marketing. During his tenure as president from 1982 to 1995, Sony was transformed from an electronics company into a total entertainment company through the establishment of the music, pictures, and gaming business.

Sony acquired CBS Records in 1988 and Columbia Pictures in 1989, which today are Sony Music Entertainment (SME) and Sony Pictures Entertainment (SPE), two of the world's largest content producers.

Through Ohga's persistence, the Sony PlayStation® game console was launched in Japan in 1994 and worldwide in 1995 in a market dominated by Nintendo® and Sega® game systems. With the PlayStation game console and, more recently, PlayStation2, Sony has become the most successful game manufacturer ever.

Nobuyuki Idei, current chairman and CEO, played a key role in moving Sony into the digital network era by emphasizing the integration of audiovisual and information technology. He

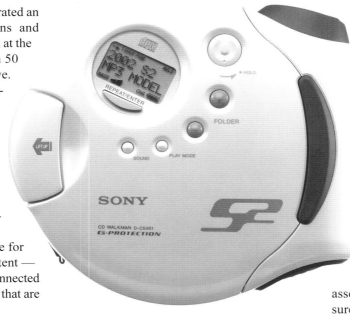

was responsible for Sony's image campaign, "Do you dream in Sony?" and helped coin the term "digital dream kids." The premise of the campaign was to provide shareholders, customers, employees, and business partners who come into contact with Sony with the opportunities to create and fulfill their dreams.

Sony has also given consumers reasons to visit the Internet with *SonyStyle.com*, a one-stop-Sony consumer product shop within a unique, world-class Sony shopping experience.

PROMOTION

In 2002, Sony Electronics launched an innovative marketing strategy designed to educate consumers about Sony products by analyzing their purchasing preferences. After extensive research, Sony is focusing on the following consumer segments: Affluents, Alphas or early adopters, Gen Y, Young Professionals (Gen X), Families, "Zoomers" (empty-nester baby boomers 55 years and older), and SOHO (small office, home office). Based on these target segments, products were grouped together to reach consumers more efficiently as they explore their passions and hobbies.

The quick evolution of digital technology has made it difficult to maintain product differentiation in the market. As Sony Electronics President and COO Fujio Nishida stated, "Times are changing and we need to change with them. We need to combine our power of technology with the power of marketing, to make Sony a company that stands apart from the competition." The market segment approach will shift efforts from product-centric to consumer-centric.

Sony will utilize a more "U(ser)-centric" marketing strategy by developing innovative products that meet the needs of consumers in each segment.

Using an unprecedented approach to Sony Electronics advertising, each segment created an ad campaign targeted to their audience. Through print ads, television commercials, direct mail, and the Internet, Sony educates consumers on how to integrate technology into their everyday lives.

BRAND VALUES

In the company's annual welcoming ceremony for new employees, Chairman of the Board Norio Ohga cited Sony's strength in these words: "We have many marvelous assets here. The most valuable asset of all are the four letters, S-O-N-Y. Make sure the basis of your actions is increasing the value of these four letters. In other words, when you consider doing something, you must consider whether your action will increase the value of Sony, or lower its value."

Sony's brand equity is rooted in product innovation. To ensure the future of the brand, part of the company's role is to foster a common understanding of the Sony brand among employees, retailers, and consumers. A well-known phrase among Sony employees is: "The Sony brand is central to everything we are and everything we do."

The company's desire is to establish a new Sony — a customer-centric entity centered around broadband entertainment, yet driven by the venture of Sony's founding days.

THE MARKET

Once known primarily as a long-distance carrier, the Sprint name today represents innovation throughout the telecommunications field, from voice and data transmission to wireline and wireless solutions. And as Internet and wireless technologies fundamentally change the way people and businesses communicate, the field keeps growing. In fact, the telecom sector is forecast to grow at more than a 4 percent compounded annual rate through 2005 — a rate faster than most other segments of the economy.

Sprint's customer base incorporates a vast range of communication needs, encompassing individuals, families, small business owners, Fortune 500 companies, and the U.S. government. As these customers become more techno-savvy and demanding, Sprint has responded by transforming itself into a high-growth, data-driven company committed to offering total, on-demand access to communications.

ACHIEVEMENTS

Sprint's reputation for high-tech quality and customer care has made the brand a powerful leader in the telecommunications industry. Sprint views the market in terms of total access solutions — all distance, wireline and wireless, voice and data. Having built a strong standing in the fastest-growing segments of the industry, Sprint is poised to enhance its leadership position.

And Sprint's leadership position is well recognized within the industry. The company has been named *Information Week*'s number-one information technology innovator in the telecom industry for three years in a row. In June 2001, *SmartMoney* rated Sprint PCS number one in customer service in the wireless industry, and Sprint received the 3G Industry Achievement Award at the 3G World Congress in 2001. Also in 2001, facilities-based carriers ranked Sprint as the number-one wholesale carrier. Sprint was also chosen as one of the top five brands that most consistently meet consumer expectations by a Brand Keys study of 146 brands (*Brandweek*, May 28, 2001).

HISTORY

Sprint began in 1899 as the Brown Telephone Company, a local company determined to bring the residents of Abilene, Kansas, an alternative to the phone monopoly of the day. Decades of expansion created a diversified "United Telecommunications," which provided more than 3.5 million local telephone lines in states from coast to coast. In 1984, plans were announced for the first nationwide 100 percent digital fiber-optic network, which was completed in 1987. In 1992, United Telecom adopted the nationally recognized identity of its long distance unit, changing its name to Sprint Corporation.

In 1995, with its partners, Sprint acquired PCS wireless licenses in 29 major trading areas. By 1998, Sprint had acquired its partners' interests and had full management control of Sprint PCS. Today, Sprint's PCS division serves the majority of the nation's metropolitan areas, including more than 4,000 cities and communities. The service offered by the PCS division and its third-party affiliates now reaches more than 247 million people.

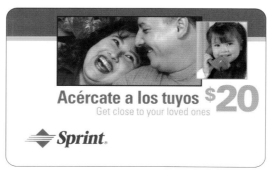

From its small-town roots, Sprint has evolved into a global communications company that serves 23 million customers in more than 70 countries. With 80,000 employees worldwide and an unmatched portfolio of telecommunications products and services, Sprint is continuing its legacy of leadership and innovation in the 21st century.

THE PRODUCT

Sprint is preparing for the future by investing in growth areas such as:

Internet — Sprint operates a Tier 1 Internet backbone, carrying high volumes of traffic for thousands of businesses, Web sites, and Internet Service Providers. Sprint also is deploying its Internet backbone in 35 cities in Europe and Asia. Sprint has built Internet centers across the country to target the Web hosting and managed services market. For those always on the go, Sprint PCS service allows customers to browse the Internet, get news, entertainment, and information, and make purchases on their Internet-ready PCS phones.

Wireless — Sprint operates one of the fastest-growing all-digital PCS wireless networks. Sprint's wireless network technology and existing capacity make it better positioned to move to third-generation (3G) high-speed data services. Beginning this year, third-generation technology will double network capacity and increase data transmission speeds tenfold, allowing Sprint to provide higher capacity for voice and data to customers.

Local Broadband — Sprint provides local service in 18 states and has targeted DSL (Digital Subscriber Line) expansion in its local markets. Sprint has provided last-mile network infrastructure for more than 2,000 sites in 115 markets in support of its Sprint FastConnect DSL product.

Sprint products and services are built to provide complete, integrated solutions. This commitment to

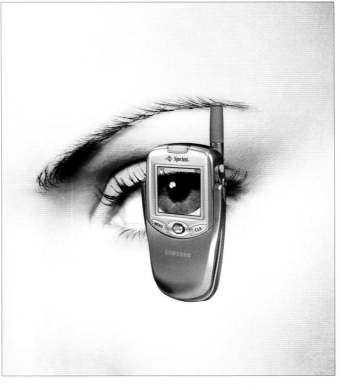

total solutions extends to the way Sprint products and services are packaged. Customers prefer bundling their communications services, so Sprint offers packages of local service, network features, long distance, local broadband, and wireless.

RECENT DEVELOPMENTS

Customer preference for anywhere, anytime communications persists today and will continue in the future, particularly among business customers. The area of wireless data, for example, is opening a broad new market for services, which today is only in the nascent stage. Technological advancements, in particular third-generation wireless and wireless local area networks, will prompt new applications and services that business customers demand and that Sprint can provide. Over the next four years, business is expected to account for about two-thirds of new revenue growth. In 2003, an estimated 90 percent of e-commerce transactions will be business-to-business. Sprint is poised to capture a solid share of this growth. The company has a long history of leadership in data communications services, operating the fastest-growing local telephone business, leading the industry for 15 consecutive quarters in wireless growth, and expanding its Internet services business. Sprint offers a complete portfolio in the fastest-growing segments of the industry.

PROMOTION

When customers think of Sprint, they think of the pin drop — that simple reminder of Sprint's commitment to clarity. This widespread recognition has been cultivated with a long-running broadcast presence, as well as the extensive print advertising, growing retail presence, and strong sponsorship program that round out Sprint's promotional strategy. Sprint's aggressive sponsorship

strategy has brought strategic alliances with some of the top sports properties in the nation —Petty Enterprises, the US Ski and Snowboard Association, American Skiing Company (ASC), Vail Resorts, and PGA of America. Partnerships are also a key part of Sprint's retail approach, creating a niche for the Sprint Brand inside RadioShack, Best Buy, Circuit City, and Staples stores.

BRAND VALUES

According to *The New York Times* (Oct. 5, 1999), "One reason the Sprint corporate identity is perceived as so strong is because the brand's variegated advertising and marketing campaigns have resonated deeply with the consumers. The image perhaps most familiar is the 'pin drop,' initially included in commercials to convey that a Sprint long distance call was quiet and thus high-quality."

Sprint has always been different — not a faceless corporate bureaucracy, but an independent-minded, slightly irreverent company that talks straight and delivers what it promises. Today, the Sprint pin drop represents more than just a clear connection. It's the Sprint commitment to making the whole world of communications clear, simple, and accessible for real people every day.

THINGS YOU DIDN'T KNOW ABOUT SPRINT

○ To complete construction on the country's first nationwide fiber-optic network, Sprint battled floods and landslides in California's Feather River Canyon, dodged alligators in the swamps of Georgia, and scuba dove to research an endangered species of fresh water mussel before crossing the St. Croix River.

○ At the time of its construction, 1997–2002, the Sprint World Headquarters in Overland Park, Kansas, was the largest building project in the history of the Midwest, using over 7.5 million bricks.

○ Sprint serves more than 94 percent of the Fortune 500.

○ Sprint's Internet backbone carries one-quarter of the world's Internet traffic.

○ Sprint has led major carriers for the sixth straight year with the fewest FCC-reportable outages.

○ Sprint was the first to build a transcontinental all-digital fiber optic network, the first to build an all-digital nationwide wireless network, the first carrier to provide commercial Internet access, and the first to complete a 10 Gbps transatlantic IP network connecting Europe and Asia.

○ The Sprint Brand has a staggering 95 percent brand awareness rate.

○ Sprint PCS technology runs on the same fiber-optic network that made Sprint famous in 1987.

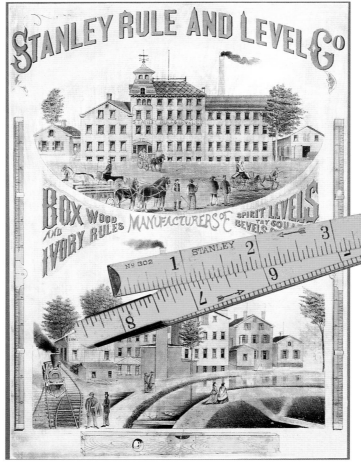

STANLEY

MAKE SOMETHING GREAT™

THE MARKET

Whose life has not been touched in some way by a product bearing the Stanley® name? From the hammer housed in your toolbox, to the hinges used on your microwave, to the level and plane employed to make your kitchen table, to the tools that assembled your car, to the automatic doors that you walk through at the grocery store, to the mirror doors you see as you enter many hotels...Stanley touches more people on a daily basis than can ever be imagined.

The name Stanley is synonymous with quality and reliability. Stanley is a worldwide producer of over 50,000 tool, hardware, and door products for professional, industrial, and consumer use. The company is known globally and receives nearly 20 percent of its revenue from Europe, where the Stanley brand is stronger than anywhere else in the world.

ACHIEVEMENTS

As one of the oldest tool manufacturers in America, Stanley believes in the power of a strong brand.

Since the brand was introduced 160 years ago, Stanley's ingenuity and excellence have led to numerous firsts, from patents for new products, to design improvements on existing products, to what may have been the industry's first patent issued for ergonomically designed tools. Stanley's solid heritage has not only gained the loyalty and trust of consumers, but it has also won the praise of many industry leaders for advertising creativity and the innovation and design of its products.

From engineering research to design excellence to new product innovation, Stanley has received awards and recognition across all of its product categories for its distinctive and quality items. Add to this one of the greatest awards of all: the fact that antique Stanley® tools have become valuable collectors' items. That recognition is a testament to both the superior quality of the products and the long, impressive history of the company.

HISTORY

In 1843, an enterprising businessman named Frederick Trent Stanley established a little shop in New Britain, Connecticut, to manufacture door bolts and other hardware made from wrought iron. Stanley's Bolt Manufactory was only one of dozens of small foundries and other backyard industries in a town struggling to succeed by producing metal products.

While the manufacturing shop epitomized the storied Yankee virtues of enterprise and craftsmanship, Stanley himself also possessed a special innovative spirit and an uncommon passion for doing things right. Although he employed a few skilled craftsmen, Stanley often made the products himself, fashioning door bolts with his own hands and then riding into the country on his horse-drawn buggy to sell them to farmers. He carried a screwdriver and personally installed the bolts on barn doors and farmhouses, thereby establishing customer service as a company hallmark.

In less than 10 years after starting his small bolt business, Stanley had built a strong reputation for quality and received sufficient product demand to warrant the opening of a second shop to make hinges and other hardware. He joined with his brother and five other investors to incorporate The Stanley Works with a workforce of 19 men.

The Stanley Works flourished under the leadership of several great presidents, and a diverse group of products were produced under the Stanley name. With the acquisition of the Stanley Rule & Level Company, another New Britain–based business which had been cofounded by a distant cousin of Frederick T. Stanley, The Stanley Works boasted a broad line of rules, levels, and planes, as well as hammers, carpenter squares, and other hand tools.

Emerging new American markets allowed for new territory for Stanley's products. Capitalizing on the advent of the automobile age, Stanley introduced hardware sets for home garage doors in 1914. To counter the Great Depression, which practically paralyzed the building industry, the company created new markets with products such as portable electric tools and the "Magic Door®" product, which, to the astonishment and convenience of those who passed through it, opened automatically in response to a signal from its photoelectric cell.

Today, 160 years after the company's founding, The Stanley Works continues to be an innovative developer, manufacturer, and marketer of tools, hardware, and specialty hardware products for home improvement, consumer, industrial, and professional use. The company still bears not only Frederick Stanley's name but also the spirit and passion that drove him to succeed in a business where others had not.

THE PRODUCT

The Stanley Works provides a comprehensive line of world-class, professional-grade, industry-specific products. These products fall into eight product groups, which are in turn classified under two business segments: Tools and Doors.

The Tools segment includes carpenters, mechanics, pneumatic, and hydraulic tools as well as tool sets. The Doors segment comprises com-

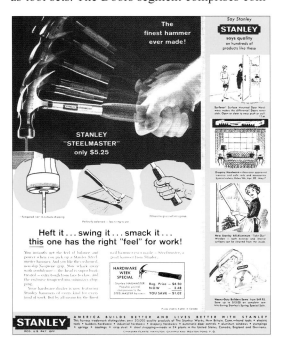

mercial and residential doors, both automatic and manual, as well as closet doors and systems, home décor, and door and consumer hardware.

RECENT DEVELOPMENTS

A "great brand" is a brand that shows performance improvement year after year and is built through consistent excellence in products, people, customer service, and financial returns.

Stanley's brand vision and strategy comes down to three words: Growth, Positioning and Competitiveness.

Growth. Stanley's commitment to continuous innovation has created a steady stream of new products and business opportunities worldwide. Innovative new products have been developed to make the professional's job easier and more productive, and a push into new or previously untapped market segments has created additional needs and demand for Stanley products, both old and new.

Positioning. Stanley has realized that the key to winning a strong retail position is to merchandise stores effectively with innovative products. Targeting the professional user,

Stanley complemented this strategy by repositioning the brand with one look and feel, which was achieved through consistency of both colors and packaging.

Competitiveness. Stanley believes that the key enablers of growth are competitiveness and exceptional customer service, both of which depend upon simplicity, standardization, and systemization.

In 1997 and 1998, the company began the introduction of electronic technology to Stanley® tools: the IntelliTools® product line comprises 18 models of electronic sensors, laser levels, and electronic measuring tools, offering a technically advanced array of electronic builder's tools.

The introduction of the FatMax® product line included the FatMax® tape rule — which features a standout of 11 feet, the longest in the industry — and has gathered praise and press coverage for its original design.

Continuously diversifying, Stanley also created AccuScape® Garden Tools, a line of more than 60 products designed for both the landscape professional and the avid home gardener, from shear and hand pruners to hedge clippers and loppers.

Among Stanley's most recent innovations is a cordless roofing nailer, part of a new line of Bostitch® finish and framing nailers. More than 400 new products have been introduced over the past four years, and Stanley's industry-leading licensees continue to bring new and innovative products to market on a regular basis.

Appropriately representing this exciting period of new product innovation, Stanley unveiled a bold brand campaign and tagline — "Stanley. Make Something Great." — which defines the end result from using Stanley® products.

PROMOTION

The slogan "Stanley. Make Something Great." also defines what Stanley does all over the world. One of the world's most trusted names, Stanley's commitment to its customers goes well beyond providing a wide range of products; through continuous product innovation and strong product support, the company encourages and enables every professional to do his or her very best on every job.

Stanley's commitment to people is expressed in its longtime support of Habitat for Humanity. Stanley volunteers have helped to build thousands of homes for the needy. The company has also

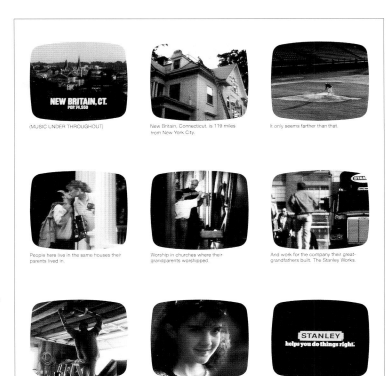

sponsored the TeamWorks Competition at the SkillsUSA Championships, an event that teaches students the importance of team-building skills in business and tests their technical skills in the masonry, carpentry, electrical, and plumbing trades.

BRAND VALUES

Stanley's strength lies in its heritage of quality, innovation, knowledge, and integrity. The world-class brands that Stanley has built have been designed for professionals and for those who think like professionals. Stanley's brand vision is to inspire and motivate consumers to fully realize their skills, vision, and creativity, and by doing so, to be the leadership brand of the hardgoods industry.

THINGS YOU DIDN'T KNOW ABOUT STANLEY

○ Stanley® Hardware is used in some of the most prestigious buildings in the world, including the White House, the Empire State Building, Buckingham Palace, Windsor Castle, and the Petronas Towers in Malaysia, the tallest building in the world.

○ Stanley® Air Tools are used to build nearly every car and truck made in North America.

○ Stanley® tools have been used in constructing virtually every home, school, church, and hospital in America.

○ Eight out of 10 wood manufacturing plants use Stanley® Bostitch® Pneumatic Tools.

○ Millions of people worldwide pass through Stanley® Automatic Doors every day.

○ Stanley® is a leader in residential Steel Entry Doors sold through retail outlets.

○ Stanley® Jensen® is the leading tool supplier to electronics technicians.

THE MARKET

State Farm® is the leading insurer of cars and homes in the United States, protecting one out of every five insured cars and one out of every five homes. State Farm Life Insurance Companies is ranked fifth in paid-for volume for ordinary life insurance among all U.S. companies. State Farm also offers customers a wide variety of financial services. State Farm and its more than 16,000 agents serve households in the United States and three provinces of Canada with nearly 70.4 million auto, fire, life, and health policies in force.

ACHIEVEMENTS

In 2002, State Farm Mutual Automobile Insurance Company celebrates its 80th year in business and its 60th year as the largest U.S. auto insurer. State Farm has also been the largest U.S. insurer of homes since 1964.

The company has consistently been recognized with the top ratings for financial strength and claims paying ability.

State Farm Mutual is a mutual company, meaning there are no shareholders. State Farm is the only company in the top ranks of the Fortune 500 that is not publicly traded.

In 1995, State Farm became one of the first major insurers to establish a Web site on the Internet. *Statefarm.com*® has grown from an informational site to an interactive site that helps customers find a State Farm agent, get a quote, and in some states, purchase a policy. State Farm has been able to combine the convenience of the Internet with the knowledge and service of the dedicated State Farm agent.

The company has also achieved exceptional customer service through its 24-hour customer response center. Even when an agent's office is closed, customers can receive service around the clock. State Farm also has a completely bilingual call center that helps customers both in English and Spanish.

Headquartered in Bloomington, Ill., the company is known for involvement with local communities around the nation. The company provides a wide variety of educational materials to schools and community groups. These programs offer instruction on topics ranging from insurance basics to fire safety. State Farm Companies Foundation provides grants that further the company's

commitment to higher education. Various organizations such as the National Council of La Raza, the United States Hispanic Leadership Institute, and the Korean-American Coalition have recognized State Farm's community commitment.

Latina Style and *Hispanic* magazines, among others, have showcased the quality of State Farm's working environment.

Ed Rust Jr., the company's chairman and CEO, has been very involved with education. He served as part of President George W. Bush's transition committee on education. State Farm encourages each employee to become involved in local community efforts to help improve the quality of education.

HISTORY

At age 22, George J. Mecherle started farming his own land near Bloomington, Ill. After he and his wife Mae Edith had farmed for 20 years, Mrs. Mecherle's health began to fail and the couple moved to Bloomington where George Mecherle

accepted a job selling insurance for a small company. He was successful as a salesman, but he did not feel the rates or business practices of the company suited the needs of farmers.

Mecherle believed that farmers should pay less for insurance because they drove less and had fewer losses than folks in cities. When he informed his employer of this approach to insurance pricing, his employer laughed and said, "If you think you've got such a good idea, why don't you start your own company?"

Mecherle started State Farm in 1922 as a mutual automobile insurance company owned by its policyholders.

In 1924, some farmers in Indiana asked if they could buy policies, and in 1925 State Farm began selling in Indiana and other states. In 1926, State Farm began selling to people living in cities and on farms.

In just 80 years, State Farm Insurance Companies has grown from a small farm mutual auto insurer to one of the world's largest financial institutions. Despite State Farm's growth, Mecherle's original philosophy of insurance coverage at a fair price coupled with fair claim settlement has remained.

THE PRODUCT

State Farm provides many different insurance products as well as financial services products.

Although known primarily for its property-casualty lines — such as auto, homeowners, boatowners, condominium unit owners, and renters insurance — State Farm also has a wide range of financial services products that focus on the various needs of the client such as investment options for retirement and college education.

Attractive rates and reputation for quality service are the primary reasons people choose State Farm for their insurance needs. State Farm handles more than 30,000 insurance claims a day with special programs that make the claim process faster. Discounts are available for safe drivers, good students, and customers with safety features in their homes or autos, as well as policyholders who have multiple policies.

RECENT DEVELOPMENTS

Over the past few years State Farm has made an aggressive move toward financial services by offering products to meet the needs of customers.

PROMOTION

In 1953, State Farm's logo was created, and with it came the creation of one of America's strongest brands. In 1971, the slogan *Like a Good Neighbor, State Farm is there*® was born; it has since become one of the most recognizable taglines in the advertising industry.

State Farm commercials are unique in showcasing real State Farm agents. State Farm's advertising is also focused on the customer. State Farm's marketing approach is to show how the company can serve the individual customer, whether he or she is just beginning to drive or preparing for retirement.

State Farm has had a keen interest in highway safety since the 1950s, when it helped found the Insurance Institute for Highway Safety. State Farm has worked with the institute on a number of safety efforts, including eliminating roadside hazards, encouraging the use of seat belts and the installation of air bags in cars, and pointing out the need to make head restraints more effective. State Farm sponsors the Advocates for Highway and Auto Safety, a group devoted to promoting a broad array of auto safety measures. State Farm also works with automakers on improving damage resistance and other safety features of cars. This approach demonstrates the company's desire to protect people and to do good within communities beyond its customers.

In 2001, State Farm compiled new lists of the most dangerous intersections in the United States and in many individual states, the District of Columbia and the Canadian province of Ontario. These lists were based on crashes that resulted in claims for State Farm policyholders in 1999 and 2000. State Farm performs these analyses to focus attention on a new way of evaluating intersection design by analyzing driver behavior and placing greater emphasis on safety-driven solutions to intersection problems. The company is making $5 million available to communities to study and, in some cases, make physical changes to enhance safety at specific intersections.

State Farm has also partnered with The Children's Hospital of Philadelphia to find out why and how children are injured in vehicle accidents. Besides funding the study, State Farm provides a link between hospital researchers and customers whose children have been in crashes and who are willing to share their experiences.

In a move that reinforces State Farm's commitment toward branding the company as an integrated insurance and financial services provider, a new advertising approach, *We Live Where You Live*™, was launched in 2002 to unify the brand across insurance and financial services product lines and market segments. The "We Live Where You Live" campaign does not replace the State Farm "Good Neighbor" slogan, but builds on its strength.

BRAND VALUES

State Farm's business philosophy is to be a good neighbor. People come to State Farm for solutions, not just insurance protection. State Farm takes pride in helping its customers move safely and securely through different stages of their lives.

State Farm is part of the American fabric. The company evolves with customers as they grow and understands its customers' needs. State Farm connects with customers not just as individuals and families, but through neighborhoods and communities of every kind. The promise of being a good neighbor is at the heart of State Farm's brand. The company is built on a foundation of shared values: quality service and relationships, mutual trust, integrity, and financial strength.

State Farm employees bring diverse talents and experiences to their work of serving the customer. The vision for the future is to be the customer's first and best choice in the products and services State Farm provides.

THINGS YOU DIDN'T KNOW ABOUT STATE FARM

○ State Farm has been the number-one insurer of cars in the United States since 1942 and homes since 1964.

○ In 1971, Barry Manilow wrote the music for the jingle "Like a good neighbor, State Farm is there," and the words were written by Keith Reinhard, ad legend and co-chairman, DDB Worldwide, State Farm's long-standing ad agency.

○ State Farm has given more than $100 million in loans to revitalize low-income neighborhoods.

○ Within 48 hours after the 1994 Northridge, Calif., earthquake, 600 claims specialists from across the United States and Canada joined local claims people. Two DC-8 jet freighters loaded with more than 217 tons of office supplies promptly arrived. Five mobile catastrophe offices handled 3,414 phone calls in the first two days of operation.

THE MARKET

As more women enter the workforce, two-income families have time pressures and less time to cook. Frozen prepared meals have become a necessity when people don't have the time to plan meals ahead, don't know how to cook, or don't have the time required to cook from scratch and clean up afterward. As a result, most home-cooked meals today now contain at least one item that is just warmed or heated. Consumers are no longer embarrassed to serve prepared items to their families or guests. In fact, 50 percent of consumers state that "convenience is most important in the foods I eat."

ACHIEVEMENTS

As the originator of frozen dinners in 1953, Swanson® offered the first frozen prepared meal created with busy housewives in mind. Fifty years later, Swanson is a $450 million brand — the second-largest brand of full-calorie frozen meals — and remains a powerful force within the frozen food industry. Swanson is a quintessential American brand, with virtually 100 percent brand awareness. Swanson continues to evoke fond memories of childhood among consumers who remember growing up with the brand.

HISTORY

In 1896, Carl Swanson immigrated to the United States, unable to speak any English. By 1949, he had built one of the nation's largest commodity food processing companies, packing and freezing poultry for General Foods' Birds Eye label. In the early 1950s, Carl's sons took control of the company and recognized two key factors that would change its course. First, in order to be successful, they would need to move away from competing only in commodity businesses. Second, in the post–World War II era, the demographics of the American family were changing dramatically.

The Swanson brothers introduced their first frozen food product in 1951: the chicken pot pie. Although Swanson was not the first company to manufacture a chicken pot pie, Swanson introduced a higher-quality product with a better-tasting crust, more chicken, and higher-quality ingredients than its competitors. The brothers experienced instant success.

By 1952, America was recovering from the effects of the war years. Price controls were removed from fresh and processed vegetables and meats. The employment of women was the highest in history, and families were moving from radio as a form of entertainment to television — with about 10 percent of homes sporting eight-inch black-and-white sets prominently displayed in the living rooms. The Swanson brothers were desperate to find a way to capitalize on these changing trends. Women in the workforce still needed to provide high-quality meals for their families, yet had less time available to prepare them.

Returning from a business trip, one of the key Swanson sales representatives was faced with a business problem. The demand for Swanson turkeys, the company's primary product, did not meet supply. The Thanksgiving holiday had passed, and the company had ten remaining railroad cars of turkey, each weighing 52,000 pounds. The company couldn't sell the turkeys and not enough warehouses were available to store them.

The enterprising sales rep shared with management an idea he devised while on a recent airline trip: a frozen prepared meal. Pan-Am Airways was experimenting with serving warm meals in a tray to their customers, a step up from cold sandwiches. His suggestion was to take the excess supply of turkey and use it for frozen prepared meals for the retail market. He showed them a drawing of a three-compartment aluminum tray, which would hold the staples of a turkey dinner: turkey with cornbread stuffing and gravy, sweet potatoes, and peas. This idea forever changed the frozen meal category with the introduction of the "TV dinner," born in December 1953. The product name was developed to link the very contemporary television appliance that was hitting the scene with the observation that a good deal of pot pie consumption was already occurring in front of the TV set.

In 1954, the trademarked TV Dinner® went into production, made by hand. One of the first customers was Safeway in Oakland, Calif., which bought 100 cases. Winn Dixie bought 50 cases. The product, with a suggested retail price of $1.29, was a success. Within two years, the Swansons had added fried chicken and sliced beef. Many more products came to market over the years to respond to changing consumer demands.

In 1954, Swanson had a 100 percent share of the frozen dinner market. By 1955, the company sold 25 million dinners. This success of this brand led to the Campbell Soup Company's purchase of the company. Campbell's was certainly interested in having a piece of the fast-growing frozen foods market.

THE PRODUCT

Swanson has built a reputation of excellence, quality, and trust by evolving to meet ever-changing consumer needs:
• Swanson recognized that the breakfast meal occasion was another opportunity to deliver balanced meals for the family. Swanson Frozen

Breakfasts were introduced in 1969 and are still the leader in frozen breakfast entrees.

- In 1973, Swanson addressed the heartier appetites in the family. Swanson Hungry-Man®, larger portions of the stick-to-your-ribs foods, was introduced. Today Swanson is the number-one brand of hearty frozen meals.

- Capitalizing on a growth trend in comfort foods, Swanson provided innovation into the pot pie category, introducing a line of Potato-Topped Pot Pies, combining two of America's most popular foods, pot pies and mashed potatoes.

While fried chicken and turkey are still Swanson's heritage, the Swanson line includes many other varieties. Swanson ships approximately 150 million frozen meals into American homes each year.

RECENT DEVELOPMENTS

After creating and ruling the frozen food industry for years, Swanson struggled in the 1980s and 1990s as Campbell Soup Company shifted their focus away from frozen foods. Eventually, Campbell's decided to spin off the Swanson brand to a newly formed Vlasic Foods International, which eventually went bankrupt.

Pinnacle Foods Corporation, backed by the leveraged buyout firm of Hicks, Muse, Tate and Furst (HMTF), recently purchased the brand out of bankruptcy. HMTF's stated goal is to reinvest in Swanson to restore it to a solid leadership position within frozen foods.

Upgrading Swanson product quality was the first step taken to restore Swanson. Co-branding agreements were developed with high-quality suppliers such as Tyson Foods, Inc., to reinforce Swanson's quality image. Package graphics were overhauled for the first time in ten years, also reinforcing Swanson's quality and contemporary image. Most significantly, Swanson Hungry-Man was advertised for the first time in many years to remind consumers of a brand that was not top-of-mind.

While much of the brand's recent success has come from growth of existing products, new products figure prominently in the future. Product variations on Hungry-Man, Swanson Dinners, and Great Starts Breakfasts are hitting the market to reflect current food trends. Consumers will always find new items to try from Swanson.

PROMOTION

Throughout the years, Swanson has been promoted as the brand to trust. Associations with leading TV shows like *Lassie*, *Donna Reed*, and Johnny Carson's *Who Do You Trust* supported the notion that Swanson was meant for families.

"Have a Swanson Night" and "Have Dinner with the Swanson's" were popular themes of Swanson dinner advertising. Swanson was also known as the brand that was a special treat for parents' night out. Kids had liberty to choose their favorite meal — and to eat the dessert first — and Mom knew that they were having a wholesome meal.

Over the years the brand has been promoted as one that allowed busy moms to spend more time with their families yet still provide their families with balanced high-quality meals. The message to moms was clear: When you're not home cooking, Swanson is.

Hungry-Man tackled hearty appetites and built a strong association with NFL celebrities including Mean Joe Greene, Charles Mann, Randall Cunningham, and Roger Craig. This affiliation lasted for 15 years. Regional TV spots featured local talent, and national sweepstakes sent consumers to Fantasy Football Camp. Hungry-Man sponsored the development of "Hungriest Men in the NFL" videos that spotlighted key plays of leading role models who, of course, ate Hungry-Man dinners.

Promotional activity waned as Vlasic International struggled to gain financial security. While most brands would have broken under heavy competitive onslaught and reduced marketing activity, the strength of the brand was solid enough to weather the storm. In 2001, after 10 years of being off the air, Swanson returned with a vengeance, investing heavily behind the advertising. Returning to the TV airwaves by supporting the new and improved Hungry-Man products caused a major turnaround in the business trends. Swanson recaptured the hearts of hungry men. A new campaign in 2002 featured Swanson American Recipe Dinners.

BRAND VALUES

From its very inception, Swanson has been committed to delivering products that were of the highest quality. One of the guiding principles for the originators of Swanson frozen meals was to provide a meal of the quality that could be found in a restaurant. This emphasis has convinced consumers to trust Swanson for over 50 years. Parents value it as a brand that is always there to serve the family when they do not have time to cook. Family members value it as a special treat. Growing up with Swanson evokes warm family memories and product experiences from metal TV trays, family TV shows, eating dessert first, and, of course, special moments with the babysitter.

Swanson® is a registered trademark of CSC Brands, Inc. Hungry-Man® and TV Dinner® are the registered trademarks of Pinnacle Foods Brands Corporation.

THINGS YOU DIDN'T KNOW ABOUT SWANSON

- Desserts did not become part of the dinners until 1960, six years after the brand was introduced
- Swanson dinners were sold in aluminum trays until 1986, when the entire dinner line was reformulated and repackaged for the new microwave ovens.
- The original Swanson dinner tray was placed into the Smithsonian Institute (next to Fonzi's jacket) in 1986.
- Swanson is truly an American icon brand. Ninety-eight percent of all households are aware of the brand and 86 percent have ever bought it.
- The celebration of Swanson's 45th anniversary was celebrated on TV in 1999 with over 500 news stories delivered across the country. National coverage spanned four months and generated over $5 million in media coverage, with key celebrities like Jay Leno spreading the Swanson story.
- An imprint of the TV dinner tray was put on the Walk of Fame outside Grauman's Chinese Theatre.

TBS Superstation ®

THE MARKET

More than 106 million households have television, and of those, more than 89 million have basic cable or satellite service. What was once a minor blip in the television marketplace is now a dominating force, as basic cable accounts for an average of 45 percent of all television viewing, a figure that has steadily increased from year to year.

Basic ad-supported cable channels are cropping up everywhere, with an average of five new channels entering the marketplace each year, making competition for advertising revenue and viewers fierce. In addition, commercial television itself faces increased competition from other fast-growing leisure activities, such as Internet usage and the booming home video industry. But television viewing still remains America's number-one leisure activity, and that statistic will not likely change anytime soon.

ACHIEVEMENTS

TBS Superstation, television's first-ever basic cable network and the most widely distributed to date, is available in more than 88 million households (82 percent of

all television households; 99 percent of all cable/satellite homes). One of the most popular basic cable networks among key adult demos, TBS Superstation dominated the marketplace in 2001 by ranking as the number-one basic cable network among adults 18–34 and 18–49 in both prime time and total day, as well as among adults 25–54 in prime time. The Superstation also claimed the number-one theatrical movie presentation on basic cable for the year (*Rush Hour*), as well as eight of the top-ten theatrical movies in household rating and delivery of adults 18–49 and 25–54.

HISTORY

TBS Superstation began life as a small independent television station in Atlanta, when R. E. "Ted" Turner bought WJRJ and renamed it WTCG (Turner Communications Group). Immediately, Turner began buying up programming for his station to make it more competitive in an already

crowded Atlanta market. Among his earliest acquisitions were Atlanta Braves baseball and Atlanta Hawks basketball.

In 1976, Turner realized that his local independent could be beamed nationwide via satellite, thus creating the "superstation" concept. On December 17 of that year, the soon-to-be-renamed TBS Superstation was "up on the bird," as Turner put it. Not only could it be seen in Atlanta, but also in 24,000 homes on four cable systems, a humble but promising beginning. Within five years, that number would explode to more than 20 million homes.

But Turner and his network were not content to sit on their laurels. In 1986, TBS Superstation's parent company, Turner Broadcasting System, Inc., bought the MGM film library, setting into motion a series of acquisition deals that would provide the Superstation and its future sister networks a virtually endless library of programming.

During its first 15 years as a cable network, the Superstation's primary original programming ranged from high-profile environmental programs from the Audubon and Cousteau societies to World Championship Wrestling.

In the 1990s, TBS Superstation embarked on a number of original

programming concepts, including a multi-network Native American initiative and several Peabody Award–winning documentaries. The Superstation also began to debut contemporary blockbuster hits, which made their world broadcast premieres on the network. Among those, *Dumb and Dumber*, *The American President*, and *As Good As It Gets* all set ratings records, putting TBS Superstation in the same league as the broadcast networks.

Hosted movie franchises also found their way to the Superstation during the late 1990s, with *Dinner & a Movie* redefining not only how movies can be packaged, but also how advertising can be sold during the hosted segments. Since then, the Superstation has added such movie showcases as *Movies for Guys Who Like Movies* and *The Man-Made Movie*, with plans to add three more hosted franchises by 2003.

TBS Superstation ventured into original movie territory in 1999 by producing popular, action-oriented fare that would draw young adult audiences and help to better brand the network. During its first year of making original movies, the Superstation broke a basic cable ratings record with its premiere of *First Daughter*, a Secret Service thriller that has since spawned two sequels.

In 2000, TBS Superstation expanded beyond original movies by planting its foot firmly in the original series arena. *Ripley's Believe It or Not!*, which enters its fourth season in 2003, set a basic cable record with its premiere episode.

THE PRODUCT

TBS Superstation is a general entertainment network that specifically targets key adult demos. To that end, the network's movies, sitcoms, and original programming are all designed or packaged with adults 18–34, 18–49, and 25–54 in mind.

To continue increasing its prime-time audiences, the Superstation launched the "Non-Stop Comedy Block" in Fall 2002, an unrivaled line-up

No wonder they call it the Superstation

of prime access comedies. The block includes such sitcom giants as *Seinfeld*, *Friends*, *Home Improvement*, and *The Drew Carey Show*.

Within prime time, TBS Superstation focuses on original programming, high-profile movies, and sports. Original series include *Ripley's Believe It or Not!* and the new *Worst-Case Scenario*, both of which make up the "Unbelievable Wednesdays" programming block.

Movies on the Superstation range from blockbuster comedies and action films, many making their network television debuts, to tried-and-true hits from such stars as Clint Eastwood and John Wayne.

Superstation Original Movies, which are produced at a rate of four to six per year, are a major part of TBS Superstation's programming strategy. These movies are generally action thrillers featuring popular young stars and fast-paced storytelling.

The final piece of the Superstation programming puzzle is sports. The Atlanta Braves have been a fixture on the Superstation schedule since the network began, and in 2002, their audience saw dramatic increases across the board. Also that year, the Superstation began airing college football on Saturday nights.

RECENT DEVELOPMENTS

One of the most popular recent developments to hit TBS Superstation is the original series *Worst-Case Scenario*, a combination reality/magazine series based on the ultra-popular book *The Worst-Case Scenario Survival Handbook*. This show, which airs as a companion series to the network's *Ripley's Believe It or Not!*, debuted in July 2002 to strong ratings success among key adult demos.

College football, which had been a part of the Superstation's schedule more than 10 years ago, returned in September. Through a five-year sub-licensing deal with Fox Sports Net (FSN), TBS Superstation presents one PAC-10 or Big XII game each Saturday.

With the popularity of its hosted movie franchises, the Superstation has embarked on a mission to add three new showcases by 2003. They include *Movie & a Makeover*, a female-skewing movie

franchise offering "chick flicks" and complete with some type of makeover; *The Movie Break*, for the hip crowd into what's hot in entertainment; and *The Movie Bowl*, which leads out from the Superstation's college football telecasts in a programming block called "Big Play Saturday."

PROMOTION

TBS Superstation's tag line, "No Wonder They Call It the Superstation," reflects the very essence of how the network is able to promote itself. Everything on TBS Superstation is "supersized," from movies that are expanded to include hosted segments, to original series and original movies that take viewers places they've never been before.

The Superstation focuses its energy on attracting a young adult audience, specifically a range that includes adults 18–34 and adults 18–49, two of the most valuable demographics for advertisers. As a result, the Superstation not only topped basic cable among those two groups in 2001, but also attracted and continues to deliver more men than ESPN and more women than Lifetime.

Attracting the Superstation's target young-adult audience involves innovative on-air graphics packages combined with hip, popular music. It also involves incorporating added value to the network's programming through its hosted movie franchises, special contest promotions, and live events, such as 2001's Atlanta Braves stunt that sent former players Sid Bream and Jose Cabrera from city to city.

Of course, one of the best ways to reach young adults is through new technology, which is where the TBS Superstation Web site (*TBSsuperstation.com*) enters the picture. This site both complements and expands upon the Superstation's programming through hi-tech games, contests, and other innovative elements.

As part of the AOL Time Warner family, the Superstation is able to explore new ways to take advantage of the company's assets to promote the network in a way that reaches key adults directly through the products they buy. Earlier in 2001, for example, the network was able to extend its *Dinner & a Movie* brand into the new DVD marketplace

through a partnership with Warner Home Video and one of its biggest advertisers. Recently, TBS Superstation was granted unprecedented access to the stars of *Rush Hour 2* to help promote the network television premiere of *Rush Hour*, as well as to the stars of *Austin Powers in Goldmember*, to help promote the network television premiere of *Austin Powers: The Spy Who Shagged Me.*

BRAND VALUES

Dennis Quinn, executive vice president and general manager for TBS Superstation, explains that the value of the network lies in its pure-entertainment programming and an attitude that encourages both innovation and excitement. "The secret of our success is our brand and our attitude," he says. "We started out as an independent station bent on becoming a national force in television by consistently providing great entertainment for mainstream America."

The success of the Superstation lies in its ability to connect directly with viewers by meeting their entertainment needs. "First and foremost, TBS Superstation is pure entertainment fun," Quinn says. "It's not stuffy, not educational, not cynical or self-serious. We know our audience turns on their TVs to relax and escape. So we've put together a schedule that gives them more of what they want."

Giving viewers more of what they want, giving advertisers the key demographics and promotional opportunities that they seek, pushing the industry forward through innovation and a maverick attitude: these are the benchmarks TBS Superstation has set and will continue to set. As the slogan says: No Wonder They Call It the Superstation.

THINGS YOU DIDN'T KNOW ABOUT TBS SUPERSTATION

❍ When TBS Superstation first went up on satellite in 1976, it was distributed to only 24,000 households on four cable systems. Today, TBS Superstation is also seen in Canada, Puerto Rico, and the Virgin Islands.

❍ TBS Superstation's August 2000 premiere of the movie *As Good As It Gets* delivered more than 5.4 million households, the largest audience for a theatrical movie in basic cable history.

❍ In 2002, TBS Superstation expanded its broadcast of Atlanta Braves telecasts to include a Spanish-language feed available for retransmission in the SAP (second audio programming) format. This feed goes beyond simply being translations of the English broadcast. It features live, Spanish-language announcers covering the game in their own language and style.

The New York Times

THE MARKET

The core purpose of *The New York Times* is "to enhance society by creating, collecting, and distributing high-quality news, information, and entertainment." *The Times* is read nationwide by those seeking the most complete, compelling, and thoughtful report on news and trends in a single package. Leaders in every profession and the intellectually curious and discerning seek out *The New York Times*.

In recent years, *The Times* has expanded both its home delivery and retail access to areas of the country where it had not been widely available before. It has extended its national availability in part by forming alliances with other companies, such as local papers (willing to offer delivery of *The Times* to readers who wish to purchase it) and retailers (such as Starbucks Coffee, which made *The New York Times* available in more than 2,000 of its locations). Increased national circulation has led to increased national advertising in *The Times*, which now exceeds local advertising.

According to the leading marketing and media study of the U.S. adult population, Mediamark Research Inc. (MRI), the weekday/Sunday *New*

Tall Ships Render a Stately Tribute to Independence

York Times has a net readership of over 7 million (7,089,000) (source: MRI Spring 2002). And *Times* readers are known to have an exceptionally intense relationship with their newspaper.

"In over 25 years of researching loyalists in virtually every product or service category," says Bonnie Goebert, president and owner, The Bonnie Goebert Company, a marketing research firm, "I have rarely encountered such a dedicated group. Without *The Times*, there seems to be an absolute gap in their lives that no other paper, indeed no other medium, can fulfill."

ACHIEVEMENTS

The New York Times is one of the most honored names in journalism, the recipient of 88 Pulitzer Prizes (among many other journalism awards), far more than any other newspaper. In 2002 alone, *The Times* won an unprecedented seven Pulitzers.

In 2000, publisher Arthur Sulzberger Jr. was named newspaper publisher of the year by *Editor & Publisher* magazine, the leading publication on the newspaper industry, and *Working Mother* magazine recognized The New York Times Company as one of the best companies for working mothers. In 2002, *The Times* was ranked number-one in the publishing industry in *Fortune* magazine's survey of America's Most Admired Companies. Among all the companies on the list, *The Times* was ranked number-one for the

quality of its products and services and for community responsibility.

HISTORY

Henry Jarvis Raymond and George Jones founded *The New York Times* in 1851. Its exposé of widespread corruption of the Tammany Hall Democratic organization, run by "Boss" William Marcy Tweed, in New York City, helped to end Tweed's hold on city politics and became a landmark in American journalism.

In 1896, Adolph S. Ochs, a newspaper publisher from Chattanooga, Tennessee, bought *The Times*, which was then having severe financial difficulties. He took *The Times* to new heights of achievement, establishing it as the serious, balanced newspaper that would bring readers "All the News That's Fit to Print" (a slogan that he coined and that still appears on the paper's front

page). His publication would do so, he added, "without fear or favor." Mr. Ochs introduced such features as *The New York Times Magazine* and *The Book Review*.

On his death in 1935, Ochs was succeeded as publisher by his son-in-law, Arthur Hays Sulzberger, whose grandson, Arthur Sulzberger Jr., is the publisher today. In its extensive coverage of world events throughout the 20th century, *The Times* came to be known as "the newspaper of record." In 1971, the Supreme Court ruled in favor of *The Times*' right to publish the so-called

Pentagon Papers, government documents concerning the Vietnam War. In 1996, *The Times* entered the dawning digital era, launching its acclaimed Web site, *nytimes.com*.

THE PRODUCT

The New York Times is a seven-day newspaper, with daily coverage of world, national, and New York–area news, business, and sports, daily weather, news summaries and, of course, the crossword puzzle. *The Times* has been hailed as "easily the best, most important newspaper in the country" by *Time* magazine. "If it's in *The New York Times*, it's news," *U.S. News & World Report* has written.

The daily newspaper features special coverage of the media on Mondays, a Science Times section and fashion coverage on Tuesdays, food-related content on Wednesdays, the Circuits section and home-related articles on Thursdays, a two-part Weekend section and the Escapes section (introduced in 2002) on Fridays, and extra cultural coverage on Saturdays. The Sunday *Times* includes the Arts & Leisure section, *The New York Times Magazine*, *The Book Review*, the Week in Review, Travel, and Money & Business sections.

The Times publishes three editions: New York, Northeast (serving the Washington and New England areas), and National. *The Times* also publishes online, at *nytimes.com*, which includes The Learning Network, a special component for

educators, students, and parents (*nytimes.com/learning*). The New York Times Electronic Edition, an exact digital replica of the newspaper, was launched in 2002.

The New York Times makes content of the paper available to other national and international customers, offers photo reprints to consumers, and also offers such special publications as *The New York Times Large Type Weekly*. *The Times* is especially valued not only for its extensive coverage but also for the careful analysis and context it provides.

RECENT DEVELOPMENTS

In 2002, The New York Times Electronic Edition, an exact digital replica of the newspaper, was launched. This edition makes it possible for the first time to read the paper anywhere in the world on the date of publication from a computer with Internet access. Also in 2002, *The Times* introduced the Escapes section in its Friday paper (reporting on a broad range of weekend destinations, automobiles, second homes, and retirement communities) and Arts & Leisure weekend. Arts & Leisure weekend has become an annual program, during which cultural institutions offer special discounts to *Times* readers, and *The Times* holds Critics Choice panel discussions, featuring notable figures in the arts and moderated by *New York Times* journalists.

As 2003 began, *The Times* was extending its presence on television with the new Discovery Times channel. It has also become the sole owner of the *International Herald Tribune*, formerly operated in partnership with *The Washington Post*.

PROMOTION

The New York Times is widely promoted in markets across the country and throughout the New York area. It especially strives to reach "like-minded non-readers," whom *The Times* has identified as sharing many of the characteristics of its most loyal readers: intellectually and culturally curious, concerned about social issues, career, and their own as well as their children's education.

Among the broad range of promotional tools that *The Times* uses are image advertising (including its "Expect the World" television campaign, print ads, and billboards) and direct response (including television and direct mail).

The Times has also developed special programs to various segments of the population, including Chinese-Americans, Hispanics, Asian Indians, and the gay and lesbian communities.

BRAND VALUES

The Times has a long-standing reputation for integrity and depth of reporting. Many feel that *The Times* has long set the standard for quality journalism. Readers value *The Times* because they know that the paper's editors and reporters strive to provide them all the most important news, as well as their prized insights, every day. In an era of ever-more media choices, readers know they can rely on *The Times* for both substance and style. Advertisers value *The Times* because of the closely read, esteemed, and timely editorial environment in which their messages will appear, and because of the influence and purchasing power of so many *Times* readers.

THINGS YOU DIDN'T KNOW ABOUT THE NEW YORK TIMES

○ The editorial staff of *The New York Times* consists of more than 1,000 people. They report, write, and edit from three floors in *The Times*' current building on West 43rd Street in New York City or work in the eight news bureaus reporting to the metropolitan desk, a bureau in Washington, D.C., 11 other news bureaus covering national news, and in 26 news bureaus reporting news from outside the United States.

○ Times Square was named for *The New York Times* after the paper moved to the neighborhood in 1905; previously the area was known as Longacre Square. The first Times Square New Year's Eve ball dropped from the Times Tower on December 31, 1907. Plans for a new state-of-the-art *Times* headquarters in the Times Square area are being completed as this book goes to press.

○ *The New York Times* was the first newspaper to publish a story, and a correct one at that, about the sinking of the *Titanic* in 1912.

○ The first Sunday crossword appeared in *The New York Times Magazine* in 1942. The first crossword in the daily paper appeared in 1950.

○ *The Times* first popularized the Op-Ed page, which it introduced in 1970, running opinion pieces by outside writers on the page opposite its editorials: hence, "op-ed."

○ Food critics for *The New York Times* spend about $200,000 a year in restaurant bills (tips included).

3M

THE MARKET

3M is a diversified technology company with vast technological, market, brand, and geographic reach. The company is known throughout the world for high-quality, innovative products that respond to customer needs. 3M is a leader in the health care, safety, electronics, telecommunications, home and office, and industrial markets. With operations in more than 60 countries and customers in nearly 200 countries, 3M's focus remains constant: to create practical and ingenious solutions that help customers succeed.

ACHIEVEMENTS

3M (NYSE: MMM), formerly Minnesota Mining and Manufacturing, is a $16 billion company with 69,000 employees worldwide. 3M is one of 30 companies whose stock compose the Dow Jones Industrial Average and is a component of the Standard & Poor's 500 Index.

Known for its innovative products, 3M has exhibited remarkable resiliency over the past century. By exercising creativity and initiative through its diverse technology platforms, 3M expands and combines technologies to create products that meet customers' needs. For example, 3M's early products were based on three technologies: abrasives, adhesives, and coatings. These technologies led to the development of sandpaper, which the automotive industry used for metal finishing, and masking tape, which was created in 1925 as a solution for painting two-tone automobiles. Scotch® masking tape set the stage for thousands of other products that 3M would introduce. Today, Scotch brand tapes continue to reinvent themselves, from the original masking tape to cellophane tape to the recent addition of Scotch Pop-up Tape.

3M adhesive technology also led to the development of Post-it® Notes, which revolutionized communications. 3M's adhesive expertise expanded into the medical and surgical markets, initially developing medical tapes and disposable surgical drapes and more recently bringing consumers Nexcare™, a family of first-aid products.

3M also applied its understanding of coatings and adhesives to the transportation market, and created 3M™ Scotchlite™ Reflective Sheeting, which helps to make highways safer by increasing visibility. This same technology is also used in fabric to increase pedestrian visibility.

3M's more than 30 technology platforms are the core of the company's innovation. These technologies range from adhesives, abrasives, and precision coatings to fiber optics, drug delivery systems, and fuel cells. The entrepreneurial spirit on which the company was founded continues as 3M's scientists and engineers combine and apply its core technologies to design solutions that solve everyday problems and make life easier for its customers.

HISTORY

3M celebrated its 100th anniversary in 2002. In 1902, five Minnesota businessmen thought they had discovered corundum, and they believed it could rival garnet, the widely used abrasive found in furniture manufacturers' grinding wheels. By 1907, they learned what they thought was corundum was actually an inferior, low-grade mineral. They modified their plans and secured funding to make sandpaper. Their new

plant collapsed and the quality of the paper was poor; still 3M persevered.

In 1907, 3M hired William L. McKnight, an assistant bookkeeper who eventually became president and CEO. He supported freedom in the workplace and fostered a spirit of adventure and challenge.

Under McKnight's leadership, 3M declared its first dividend in the last quarter of 1916 and has paid dividends every quarter since. By 1919, annual sales topped $1 million. The company was poised for rapid growth.

McKnight believed that diversification was the key to building superior technologies and exploring new applications. During the first years of his tenure, 3M developed 3M™ Wetordry™ Sandpaper, a product that could be used with water to create smoother surfaces while reducing the dust hazard to workers. And as the popularity of automobiles grew, 3M's researchers developed another practical product, Scotchlite reflective sheeting. When a car beam shines on it, Scotchlite sheeting reflects the light back, making night driving less hazardous.

In the mid-1940s, 3M acquired the rights to a process for creating fluorochemical compounds. The investment paid off in 1952 with Scotchgard™ Fabric Protector. At this juncture, 3M began to promote the "cross-pollination" that fueled the company's continued growth. Researchers were encouraged to collaborate with colleagues in other divisions to see what their combined efforts might produce. By 1951, this practice was well established among 3M's scientists and engineers.

From the late 1940s through the 1950s, several breakthroughs distinguished 3M as a diversified technology company, including the development of the adhesive-backed surgical drapes that started 3M's health care business. 3M also continued to strengthen its home and office business with tapes, adhesives, sandpapers, and scouring pads. By the mid-1950s, the company's annual sales exceeded $1 billion.

The 1950s were an important part of 3M's history. In addition to the development of new products, 3M began its international operations. 3M International was born in 1951 with the creation

of companies in seven countries: Australia, Brazil, Canada, France, Germany, Mexico, and the United Kingdom. Today, 3M holds fast to its goal of keeping resources close to its customers. As a result, the company has laboratories in 32 countries and operates manufacturing or converting operations at nearly 90 sites worldwide.

Throughout the next half-century, 3M grew at an unprecedented rate, becoming a category leader in each of its businesses with familiar brands, such as Scotchgard™, Post-it®, Scotch-Brite™, Filtrete™ and Nexcare™. In 2000, America's highest award for technical achievement — the National Medal of Technology — was given to 3M, recognizing its unique culture that promotes research and collaboration among its diverse technologies and allows its employees and businesses the freedom to respond to the emerging needs of their customers.

THE PRODUCTS

3M is probably best known for inventing two of the most ubiquitous products of the 20th century: Scotch® Transparent Tapes and Post-it® Notes. However, 3M is much more. As a diversified technology company, 3M has developed products in a variety of markets, including aerospace, transportation, graphic arts, pharmaceuticals, entertainment, and textiles. The diversity of 3M's products illustrates its commitment to using its technologies to develop practical solutions that help customers succeed.

Since 1964, 3M has been the leader in the graphics market, creating the first vinyl film that replaced paint for automobiles. 3M's glass bead technology sharpens colors and makes graphics more durable. Today, Scotchprint® Graphics are seen in stores, and on buses and cars, advertising some of the worlds' favorite brands.

3M's nonwoven technology has contributed to the development of several of the company's well-known products, including Scotch-Brite® Scrubbing Pads, 3M™ Nomad™ Floor Matting, a family of surgical tapes, and Filtrete™ Filters.

Also using nonwoven technology, in the 1960s 3M began developing super-lightweight fabrics to help keep people warm and dry. Within 10 years, Thinsulate™ Insulation was introduced.

3M has also succeeded by combining dissimilar materials, like ceramics and polymers, for practical applications. Using nanotechnology, 3M developed a dental composite that has aesthetic properties almost identical to a tooth's natural structure. These nanocomposite fillers provide strength and wear-resistance, and yet have a more natural appearance than traditional fillers. Today, 3M supplies more than 2,000 products to the dental market.

In its 100-year history, 3M's products have followed a similar path — from challenges to opportunities to discovery to practical applications — using technology to change the everyday lives of people around the world.

RECENT DEVELOPMENTS

3M's diversified technologies easily adapt to the digital age. As laptop computers, flat-panel displays, cell phones, and PDAs develop into a standard means of global communications, consumers have a growing need to enhance the performance of their electronic displays by improving their brightness and clarity. Today, Vikuiti™ Display Enhancement Films are widely used to increase screen brightness, reduce glare, and secure viewing privacy. In addition, car navigation systems, rear-projection televisions, and the rapidly growing touch-screen market are among the film's newer applications.

Another 3M breakthrough is its immune response modifiers (IRMs) — a new class of pharmaceuticals that stimulate the body's immune system to fight virus-infected cells. 3M's first IRM — Aldara™ — was launched in 2001 as the only patient-applied treatment that combats the virus that causes genital warts. Already, Aldara is the leading prescription treatment in its category. 3M continues to research several other promising IRMs.

To capitalize on its culture of ingenuity and discovery and to develop its operational excellence, 3M recently introduced Six Sigma into its operations. By creating a common language and measurement tools to reduce variation and deliver consistent results, the Six Sigma methodology has taken hold throughout 3M's global operations. From product development and manufacturing to sales and marketing, many projects already have achieved targeted improvements. Employees and customers alike are seeing even higher-quality products and faster response times, and shareholders are seeing 3M's renewed focus on growth.

PROMOTION

People around the world recognize and trust 3M. The company has achieved this position through major national and international programs, including advertising campaigns, public relations, in-store promotions, and trade shows. 3M has also sponsored the Olympics and continues to be involved in NASCAR.

3M supports its major brands through consumer advertising and public relations. Post-it, Filtrete, and Command have had very successful advertising campaigns. To improve awareness of Scotch Pop-up Tape, 3M created the annual Scotch® Brand Most Gifted Wrapper™ Contest. Each year, professionals and amateurs alike face off in popular venues, like New York's bustling Penn Station or Rockefeller Center. With ribbons, scissors, and Scotch brand tape in hand, they wrap hatboxes, skateboards, and giant rocking horses for a $10,000 grand prize. Major media including CNN, *New York Times*, NBC's *Today* show, and CBS' *Good Morning America* have covered the event.

In 2002, 3M captured global media attention with its Century of Innovation celebration. 3M locations around the world seized the opportunity of the company's 100th anniversary to increase awareness of the breadth of 3M products and technologies.

Each location used consistent graphics and messages, while customizing the activities to fit the local culture. Activities included a media campaign with billboards, advertising in local publications, and radio programs on the company's history. The program resulted in extensive coverage in local and national publications.

BRAND VALUES

Throughout its long history, 3M has delivered on its reputation as a practical problem solver. 3M focuses on delivering ingenious solutions that help customers succeed, winning their confidence and trust. Customers associate 3M with superior products, thus improving their incentive to try new products.

Earning this trust isn't the result of happenstance. From the beginning, 3M has focused on creativity and practicality, which time and again have been exhibited in 3M's long history of solving everyday problems and producing results for people throughout the world. The company excels in its combination of products, people, and systems and consistently delivers original solutions that work.

THINGS YOU DIDN'T KNOW ABOUT 3M

○ Neil Armstrong walked on the moon wearing space boots with soles made of synthetic material from 3M.

○ 3M was one of the first American companies to establish a global presence.

○ In 1984, 3M became the first American-based company in modern history with a wholly owned subsidiary in mainland China.

○ 3M developed the first refastenable diaper tapes in 1985.

○ Michael Johnson won a gold medal in the 2000 Olympics' 400-meter sprint wearing shoes made from 24-carat Gold Scotchlite™ Reflective Fabric developed by 3M.

WE KNOW DRAMA™

THE MARKET

With over 200 channels in the current television universe, viewers have more choice than ever. As a result, television networks must define their brands to let viewers know what to expect as they navigate this vast universe of choice. In 2001, TNT left behind its "general entertainment" identity to become the first and only network dedicated to drama. TNT is creating a home for a core group of viewers: drama lovers, who are drawn to television that engages their hearts and minds and rewards them with a whole range of emotions.

Drama lovers prefer one-hour drama series, dramatic movies, and championship sports over other viewing choices; this group is mainly composed of college-educated, higher-income adults who are married, have families, and live in large cities and suburbs. TNT is building a home for drama lovers, as conveyed in its tag line/mission statement: "We Know Drama."

ACHIEVEMENTS

TNT has become cable's number-one destination for drama, accounting for more viewing of drama

series and movies than any other basic or premium cable network. The focus on drama has led TNT to become basic cable's number-one network among adults 18–49 and 25–54 in prime time for 2002. TNT has also become the number-one basic cable entertainment network in delivery of key upscale demos for adults 18–49 including professional/managerial, living in "A" counties, household incomes of $75K+, $100K+, $150K+, and 4+ years of college.

TNT's focus on satisfying drama lovers has led the network to unprecedented success as a movie creator and presenter. The all-weekend-long movie strategy has not only created a highly rated movie destination, it has established a launching pad for TNT's successful run of original film dramas. TNT Originals such as *The Mists of Avalon*, *James Dean*, *Crossfire Trail*, and *Door to Door* have generated record-breaking ratings (often out-drawing broadcast network competition) and a track record in Emmy, Golden Globe, and SAG Award honors that leads the basic cable category.

HISTORY

Created by Ted Turner, TNT launched in 1988 as Turner's challenge to the broadcast networks. Just two years later, TNT was in more than 50 million cable homes, making it the fastest-growing cable network in industry history.

In the early days, TNT was known for quality and variety with a strong library including MGM classic movies and Hanna-Barbera cartoons. As the network grew, TNT presented professional sports like the NFL and the NBA. Production of original movies became a centerpiece of programming, earning big ratings and critical acclaim.

Throughout the 1990s, TNT consistently delivered some of cable's highest ratings and garnered numerous honors including Primetime Emmys as well as Screen Actors Guild and Golden Globe awards. In 2001, to further differentiate itself from the competition, TNT officially unveiled its new positioning as the first and only network dedicated to drama.

THE PRODUCT

Living up to the promise that "We Know Drama," TNT has assembled a first-rate lineup of dramatic series, blockbuster theatrical movies, and championship sports, and TNT continues to create powerful original films and drama series.

In its mission to meet the needs of drama lovers, TNT invests in original dramas with top talent and production values. Major Hollywood filmmakers and actors continue to make original films for TNT, with upcoming productions

dra′ma (drǎ′mə) n.
A compelling series of events involving action, suspense, romance, humor and/or excitement; Storytelling that touches the heart and engages the mind. *Syn:* TNT

WE KNOW DRAMA™

TNT is also committed to championship sports as live dramatic programming, led by its exclusive coverage of two sports known for intense drama: NASCAR and the NBA. In a landmark six-year deal with the NBA beginning in the 2002/2003 season, TNT's exclusive NBA coverage includes 52 regular-season games and approximately 45 NBA playoff games. TNT is also proud to have exclusive coverage of the NBA All-Star Game as well as the entire NBA All-Star weekend of events.

TNT's Web site, *www.tnt.tv*, is building a community called The Drama Lounge for drama lovers to share their enthusiasm for specific programs and drama in general via entertaining and interactive features and applications.

including the sweeping Western *Monte Walsh* (starring Tom Selleck and Isabella Rossellini, from the director of *Lonesome Dove*), Simon Wincer, the thriller *Second Nature* (executive produced by and starring Alec Baldwin), and the multipart epic *Caesar* (with an all-star cast that includes Chris Noth).

TNT is the drama lovers' weekend destination for movies. Friday nights on TNT are home to blockbuster theatricals like *The Perfect Storm*, *Gone in 60 Seconds*, *Erin Brockovich*, and *Proof of Life*. Saturday nights are dedicated to the "New Classics," featuring a lineup of Hollywood's most memorable films including *Backdraft*, *The Mummy*, *Jerry Maguire*, and *The Matrix*.

Dramatic series are a cornerstone of programming for drama lovers. Weekdays, TNT is the home for Primetime in the Daytime — a stellar daytime lineup of television's best dramatic series, including *ER*, *Law & Order*, *NYPD Blue*, and *The X-Files*. By combining all these favorite dramas together in one exciting daypart, TNT gives viewers more of the top-rated dramatic series they love and want to watch.

NASCAR is the ultimate professional sport to pay off TNT's promise of delivering 100 percent dramatic entertainment. From July to November, TNT is the exclusive cable home for live NASCAR Winston Cup and Busch Series racing.

RECENT DEVELOPMENTS
In October 2002, TNT announced that it will develop a diverse lineup of dramatic original films as part of the network's $300 million investment in original programming. This new development slate complements TNT's commitment to drama while bringing viewers entertaining, quality original movies from some of the top filmmakers in the business. TNT's new slate includes adaptations of *Night Over Water*, the number-one national bestseller by author Ken Follett, and *Pleading Guilty*, based on Scott Turow's number-one best-selling novel. Academy Award®–nominated and Emmy® Award–winning writer Neil Simon will write and executive produce a contemporary turn on his beloved piece *The Goodbye Girl*. Also in development are *Where Is the Mango Princess?*, starring Emmy®-winning actress Julianna Marguiles; *I, Jesse James*, executive produced by John Woo; and *SWAT*, a Jan de Bont action-adventure movie.

TNT has blazed new trails in how a television network can share its brand landscape with sponsors. In April 2002, TNT and Johnson & Johnson announced a multi-year collaboration for the development and production of original films, a significant collaboration between a national television network and a national advertiser.

PROMOTION
In addition to a new on-air look, logo, and tagline, TNT introduced an advertising campaign as a vital part of its branding initiative. TNT's "Drama Is…" image campaign features dramatists including Whoopi Goldberg, Ashley Judd, Tom Selleck, Dennis Hopper, Patrick Stewart, Martin Short, Allison Janney, Richard Schiff, Joan Allen, Martin Scorsese, William H. Macy, Dennis Franz, Noah Wyle, and Sam Waterston offering their personal insights and anecdotes about drama. TNT extended this campaign to include special promotional spots that put a focus on major studio releases. The spots demonstrate TNT's appreciation for movies and for drama by showing audiences what's new from Hollywood. So far, "Drama Is…" spots have been created for major studio releases with stars including Meg Ryan, Denzel Washington, Harrison Ford, Cameron Diaz, Catherine Zeta-Jones, Renee Zellweger, and Richard Gere.

BRAND VALUES
TNT promises to engage the hearts and minds of viewers with dramatic programming that offers a powerful combination of compelling stories and interesting characters, mixed with excitement, action, suspense, romance, and humor.

THINGS YOU DIDN'T KNOW ABOUT TNT

❍ TNT's weekday daytime drama lineup, which includes *Law & Order*, *NYPD Blue*, *ER*, and *The X-Files*, boasts a combined 60 Emmy® wins.

❍ The "Drama Is…" image campaign is completely unscripted. The actors share candid, extemporaneous insights about drama.

❍ TNT Originals have earned a combined 128 Primetime Emmy nominations; in 2002, TNT earned 23 nominations, the most ever for a basic cable network in one year.

❍ In its first time on TNT, the 2003 NBA All-Star Game earned a 9.8 overnight rating, making it the most-watched basketball game in cable history, and the #1 cable program for the year.

TOYS Я US

THE MARKET

According to the Toy Industry Association, Inc., consumers spent more than $34 billion on toys in the United States in 2001, compared to $31 billion in 2000.

While many of the same toys parents played with as kids are still on the market today, the toy industry has broadened and expanded over the years to include new and exciting toys — such as interactive, high-tech toys — and the explosion of the learning/educational toy category. The rapid growth of the Internet had a substantial impact on the toy retail business as more and more consumers choose to shop online.

But whether consumers shop online or in stores, the fact is that the toy market is unique. More than half of all toy sales occur during the fourth quarter, driven primarily by holiday season spending. Furthermore, only a few of the hundreds of thousands of toys sold actually become hot sellers. Fewer still remain popular for more than one or two years.

As one of the world's leading retailers of toys, children's apparel, and baby products, Toys "R" Us, Inc. has more than 1,600 stores worldwide, including Toys "R" Us, Kids R Us, Babies "R" Us, Imaginarium, and Geoffrey stores, and Internet sites at *www.toysrus.com*, *www.babiesrus.com*, *www.imaginarium.com*, and *www.giftsrus.com*.

ACHIEVEMENTS

On November 17, 2001, Toys "R" Us opened its international flagship store in the heart of New York City's Times Square. The 110,000-square-foot, multilevel store offers families a vast array of toys, dramatic retail attractions, and

distinctive feature shops. The centerpiece of Toys "R" Us Times Square is a 60-foot indoor Ferris Wheel, which includes 14 individually themed cars, each inspired by a favorite children's toy character.

The store also features more than 20 attractions including a 4,000-square-foot, two-story Barbie Dollhouse; a Jurassic Park Exhibit with a 5-ton, animatronic T-Rex dinosaur measuring 20 feet high and 34 feet long with a mighty roar and realistic moves; Baby Land General Hospital — the official adoption site for Cabbage Patch babies and kids — with a 17-foot-high tree and tree house; a Candy Land Shop, which is like walking into the actual children's board game and finding yourself among tempting aisles of chocolate, candy, and other colorful confections; plus much more.

The store's entire external façade consists of glass panels that reveal an expansive scrolling billboard system that unveils timed toy and branding messages for the 1.5 million guests who travel through Times Square every day. The billboard, consisting of 165 six-foot-by-five-foot scrolling panels, changes appearance in a matter of seconds. In addition to the large external billboard system, the store also has a Geoffreytron™ video display, which is a 20-foot LED screen that entertains passersby by displaying toy trivia highlighting the hottest toys and special events in the store.

The international flagship store has received many awards since opening. Toys "R" Us received a Gold Clio award for the exterior design of the Times Square scrim system. In addition, Toys "R" Us Times Square was named "Store of the Year" in *Chain Store Age*'s 2001 Retail Store of the Year design competition. The store also earned the publication's two First Place awards for "Best Exterior" and "Hard Lines Store Greater than 30,000 Sq. Ft.," and *Business Week* featured Toys "R" Us Times Square as a winner of its 6th Annual *Business Week/Architectural Record* Awards in November 2002.

HISTORY

In 1948, 22-year old Charles Lazarus transformed his father's Washington, D.C., bicycle repair shop into a baby furniture store to meet the needs of the postwar baby boom. When customers told him they were also looking for baby toys, Charles listened and added toys to the products he sold. That policy of determining customer needs by simply listening was to become a key ingredient in Lazarus' success.

By 1957, Lazarus' baby furniture store was transformed and christened Toys "R" Us, complete with its distinguishing backwards "R." Nine years later, Lazarus had four toy stores posting sales of $12 million per year. To expand his business, he sold the stores to a large retail conglomerate, Interstate Sales. Lazarus continued to run the Toys "R" Us stores, which prospered. When Interstate filed for bankruptcy in 1974, Lazarus took over the entire company. Four years later he led Interstate out of bankruptcy and renamed the company Toys "R" Us, Inc.

Toys "R" Us, Inc. has grown and expanded significantly since then. In 1983, Toys "R" Us, Inc. added a children's clothing division when it opened the first Kids R Us clothing store. Global expansion of Toys "R" Us stores followed a year later with the opening of toy stores in Canada, England, and Singapore. Expansion continued into baby products when the first Babies "R" Us store opened in 1996. A year later, Toys "R" Us acquired Baby Superstores and merged it with Babies "R" Us, becoming the leader in the juvenile industry.

Toys "R" Us moved into the cyber world in 1998 when it established *www.toysrus.com*, the company's first online toy store. The online site gained significant momentum two years later when it entered into a strategic partnership with *Amazon.com*, becoming a premier online toy, video game, and baby products store. With a customer base now rapidly approaching 6 million, *toysrus.com* was the most visited e-commerce destination for toys, video games, and baby products during the October 2001–July 2002 time period.

Today, more than 50 years after Charles Lazarus opened his first baby furniture store, Toys "R" Us, Inc. continues to meet his goals of providing customers with exceptional value and selection. At the same time, the company never forgets its founder's most important rule of business: listening to the customer.

THE PRODUCT

Toys "R" Us, Inc. is one of the world's largest retailers of toys, children's apparel, and baby products. The company's stores feature thousands of items that appeal to every guest: infants, teenagers, and even adults. The chain offers a wide array of products, including items that are exclusive to Toys "R" Us like Animal Alley plush, Home Depot tools for kids, Cabbage Patch Kids, Scholastic Products, Pavilion Games, and more.

Toys "R" Us stores stock toys and games for kids and adults, ranging from classic standards to the latest innovations. Vast selections of well-known brand names like Barbie, Hasbro, and LEGO share the shelves with the latest novelty toys. Toys "R" Us has an extensive selection of family recreational items, learning toys, action figures, and dolls.

RECENT DEVELOPMENTS

Exciting changes are taking place at Toys "R" Us. A redesign of the stores was completed in 2002. The new format focuses on delighting guests in a store that's more convenient, open, and easy to shop.

A number of the Kids R Us stores are also sporting a new look and feel. The new KRU stores feature clothes that are trend-right and affordable, along with a lifestyle shop that contains fashion accessories, bath and body products, cosmetics, home décor, and more.

In September 2002, the first of four stores called "Geoffrey" opened in Wisconsin. A new concept in children's retail, Geoffrey offers toys, clothing, baby items, Imaginarium products, and video game hardware and software, among other related items. The Geoffrey store features special attractions such as "Studio G," the centerpiece of the store, which offers daily activities. Children can celebrate birthday parties in the "Giraffic Party" section of the stores, and teens can visit the "R" Zone to test the latest video games.

Also in 2002, *Toysrus.com*, LLC launched several new sites that enhance the "R" Us family of brands on the Internet. The addition of *Imaginariumbaby.com* introduced parents to toys that teach or foster learning at every stage of a baby's development through different colors, textures, and sounds. *Collectors@Toysrus.com* (*www.toysrus.com/collectors*) features the most sought-after first-run collectibles, from action figures and dolls to die-cast models. *Giftsrus.com* (*www.giftsrus.com*) allows shoppers to create personalized gifts for all of their special occasions such as personalized baby blankets, stuffed animals holding a personalized heart, and much more.

PROMOTION

From the days when Geoffrey the Giraffe had both children and adults singing, "I don't wanna grow up, I'm a Toys "R" Us kid!" Geoffrey's never lost his appeal to children and families. In 1960, company executives chose the giraffe as their mascot because they liked the idea of having a large, friendly animal represent their large, friendly store. He was named Geoffrey when an associate suggested it in a contest in 1970.

Since that time, Toys "R" Us branding and marketing efforts have broadened to include in-store promotions such as sweepstakes, sponsorships, and movie tie-ins. Eager to reach families, Toys "R" Us seeks out marketing projects with world-class partners encompassing areas that include entertainment and sports such as Universal Studios and NASCAR.

In 2001, Toys "R" Us featured a new animatronic Geoffrey in the company's advertising campaign, which introduced consumers to the "new" Toys "R" Us. In 2002, Toys "R" Us commercials featuring Geoffrey were listed among Intermedia Advertising Group's (IAG) most effective advertising of the year; in fact, they were the number-one, number-three, and number-four spots out of 4,000 contenders. A spot called "Phone Call," which featured Geoffrey on the telephone with a competitor checking in-stock items, was the number-one-ranked commercial on the IAG list.

BRAND VALUES

The essence of the Toys "R" Us brand is all about "kids, families, and fun." You only have to watch a child's eyes light up the moment he or she sees the Toys "R" Us multicolored logo to understand the magic of one of retail's most powerful icon brands.

The revitalized Toys "R" Us brand values remain squarely focused on the special relationship the store has with children throughout the

world, while also working toward being attentive to a family's needs. This approach is evidenced by Toys "R" Us' increased concentration in the areas of learning and child development. The brand values include a firm belief that products should have terrific play value and help children develop their skills. Exclusive relationships with brands like Animal Planet, Scholastic, and Home Depot help the company achieve this goal.

THINGS YOU DIDN'T KNOW ABOUT TOYS "R" US

○ Toys "R" Us television commercials had the highest brand recall in 2002, according to Intermedia Advertising Group's research.

○ During the holiday season, Toys "R" Us, Inc. and ABC's *Good Morning America* launched "A Time for Smiles," a holiday toy drive benefiting The Boys & Girls Clubs of America. The event raised more than $3.5 million in 2002.

○ To kick off the holiday season, Toys "R" Us Times Square coordinates a toy procession that dazzles children as the world's best-loved characters march down the streets of New York City to their favorite destination, Toys "R" Us Times Square.

Marines
The Few. The Proud.

THE MARKET

As America slowly recovers emotionally from September 11, the economy's recovery continues to stall. The likelihood of facing combat increases for those 17- and 18-year-olds who are considering military service. Despite that fact, the military is becoming a more attractive option, in part because the job market has little to offer. College, however, remains the "gold standard." Both prospects and parents still view college as the ticket to a secure and successful future.

Nevertheless, a resurgence in patriotism following the September 11 attacks has resulted in an initial spike in interest for joining the services. The Army has begun to capitalize on this trend and is focusing its advertising imagery around it. As the Army moves in this direction, the Marine Corps is faced with the same recruiting goals and funding concerns, even though a pressing need remains to build America's elite fighting force.

As for prospects, Generation X has been replaced by a new generation: the Millennials. They are not loners or latchkey kids. They are a generation that looks up to their parents and trusts American institutions. They also believe in accomplishing tasks as a team and have a strong belief in the military. Their parents, however, have often had little exposure to the military, and are unfamiliar with what it does. Thus, the recruiting environment remains challenging.

ACHIEVEMENTS

Although budgets haven't increased and recruiting needs remain constant, the Marine Corps continues to meet its objective of 38,635 qualified recruits annually, even in a market where 70 percent of the prime youth target of high school seniors goes on to college. What's more, the quality standards to join the Marine Corps are among the highest in the Department of Defense.

Once again, the United States Marine Corps has secured its position as the only military service to meet its recruiting goals and maintain quality standards for the seventh year in a row, despite having the longest and toughest boot camp. The result is one of the lowest attrition rates among recruits in the military.

As the "War on Terror" grips America, the Corps has adjusted its recruiting message. Instead

of running blatant recruitment advertising, the Corps has turned to spots that focus on its heritage and deep traditions and the importance they play in securing and protecting America's freedom.

Public relations also is an essential part of the current communications program. Branded mailers are sent to national media and on-air personalities asking for their support. David Letterman invites Marines onto his set. TNT's NBA half-time show broadcasts from legendary Parris Island. A special Marine Corps Birthday car was developed and races in the NASCAR Busch Series.

The Marine Corps addresses the changing marketplace with appropriate but highly effective communication tools, which help the Corps exceed its quality recruiting objectives.

HISTORY

The Marine Corps was founded on November 10, 1775, in a place called Tun Tavern in Philadelphia. America was facing an oppressive English Crown and war loomed on the horizon. That date marked the beginning of the Marine Corps with a new military unit called the Continental Marines.

Captain Samuel Nicholas was commissioned to raise two battalions of Marines. Seventeen dollars was the standard enlistment incentive. The Marines fought valiantly in the Revolutionary War. They made raids on British soil, the first in 700 years. But when the Treaty of Paris ended the war in 1785, the Continental Marines faded out of existence. Fifteen years later, however, with France and the new United States preparing to fight, the United States Marine Corps was formally reestablished.

The War of 1812, the Mexican-American War, the battle of Belleau Wood, the bloody fight at Chosin . . . for 227 years, Marines have proven they are one of the toughest, most revered fighting forces ever established. Their forces are legendary, and their accomplishments are forever a part of American history. The sacred "Blood Stripe," the scarlet piping that appears on the trousers of Marine Corps noncommissioned officers, is a visible reminder of the blood shed in the capture of Chapultepec Castle.

The most famous battle of all, though, was the battle of Iwo Jima. This foreboding island was a fortress of volcanic rock that contained over a thousand fortified artillery and antiaircraft batteries. The Japanese believed the island was impregnable. The Marines fought for 36 hard and bloody days to secure this desolate island defense. Raising the American flag here was a significant moment in history that was later captured in the famed Iwo Jima memorial. The words "Uncommon Valor Was A Common Virtue" are inscribed on its base.

The Marine Corps has continued to courageously defend foreign soil the world over. From the Persian Gulf Crisis in 1991 to the current "War on Terror," the Marines have always been

"the First to Fight," the "Leathernecks," the "Devil Dogs," the legend that continues to live on in the hearts of the American people.

THE PRODUCT

The Corps has always been viewed as the toughest, most regarded fighting force in America. They are "Elite Warriors" who only admit people who have proven themselves worthy. Those men and women have endured the rigors of Marine Corps Recruit Training — a grueling 13-week boot camp that tests the mettle of all who attempt to complete it. If they do, they are awarded the respected Eagle, Globe, and Anchor, on which appears the time-honored motto of the Corps, "Semper Fidelis" — "Always Faithful."

The Corps is also America's first line of defense, or "the tip of the spear," against today's nontraditional enemies. The Marines have small, highly trained units that can be quickly and effectively deployed anywhere in the world. These units are trained to deal with terrorist-type activities such as chemical and biological warfare and close combat where the fight comes down to inches.

The Corps continues to be the smallest of the military services with 173,000 members, and is also the only service that stands guard at all of America's embassies overseas.

RECENT DEVELOPMENTS

As technology and weapons become more portable and available to enemies, the nature of threats in the world not only changes, but also comes closer to home. Conventional warfare is a thing of the past. Today's Marine must be prepared to fight in city streets, caves, and the halls and stairways of buildings, while confronted with the presence and safety of civilian populations.

Close, hand-to-hand combat is a reality. And because civilians may be present, many times the best weapon is the individual Marine. All Marines are trained in martial arts and taught to use only appropriate force in a hostile situation. The "Three Block Strategy," which every Marine learns, involves ways to handle different, escalating situations of conflict.

The Corps has also placed emphasis on "Forward Fighting," or being "Forward Deployed." Present-day battle calls for small, highly trained, expeditionary-type units that can deploy quickly and strike with proven effectiveness. The Marine Corps calls these units MEUs, or Marine Expeditionary Units, and they can be sent anywhere in the world, anytime.

The Marine Corps has also added a new uniform to its inventory: a new combat utility with a distinct camouflage pattern. Unlike the customary "camis" that the other military services use, this new uniform distinguishes the Corps in the field of battle.

PROMOTION

With the advent of the Millennials, a generation that supports longstanding institutions, the Corps' advertising and message required adjustment. "Elite Warrior" was and always will be the heart of the Corps' marketing strategy, but an element was added to strengthen its appeal.

The Corps' motto, "Semper Fidelis" or "Always Faithful," became part of all communications. In other words, the Corps is not only true to its values and heritage, but true to its Marines. "Once a Marine, always a Marine" is not just a saying, it's a promise. Once you become a member of the family called Marines, you are a member for life.

A new commercial, simply titled "The Climb," was conceived and produced to bring this strategy to life. A lone figure ascends a steep, rocky crag. It's a perilous journey, but this individual is determined to complete it. The towering rock formation symbolizes recruit training. Projected against the rock are overpowering images of Marine Corps icons. They stand as beacons of encouragement and inspiration. As the climber nears the top, the rock underneath his foot crumbles and he almost falls, but finds the determination to continue. He's welcomed to the Brotherhood by the spirit of a WWII Marine. As they exchange salutes, the transformation is complete. The young Marine is now one of the faithful, one of the Few.

CHOOSE A PLACE AMONG the few. *Marines*
THE FEW. THE PROUD.

This strategic point of difference was also incorporated into a revised *Marines.com* Web site and will soon be extended into an upcoming print and outdoor campaign. The Corps also wanted to create a public awareness of the organization because this target is so strongly influenced by parents, relatives, teachers, and coaches. The new message demanded new media. Powerful, moving billboards were created and placed on the sides of trucks, and a special car was designed and developed for NASCAR.

BRAND VALUES

For 227 years, the United States Marine Corps has represented the epitome of military virtue. It is a tough, elite expeditionary force whose members earn the right to belong. If everyone could be a Marine, it wouldn't be the Marine Corps.

Men and women who earn the title and wear the dress blue uniform uphold a history, a tradition, and a reputation that has been honored throughout time. They will always be the first to defend America's freedom. They will always be faithful to their country and to their Corps. They will always be "The Few. The Proud. The Marines."

THINGS YOU DIDN'T KNOW ABOUT THE UNITED STATES MARINE CORPS

○ Since Franklin Roosevelt's presidency, Marines have provided security for the president at Camp David.

○ Marines are the only service members who fly and maintain the helicopters ("Marine One") in the presidential helicopter squadron.

○ The origin of "A Few Good Men" came from a recruitment advertisement that appeared in the *Providence Gazette* on March 20, 1779.

○ The Marine Corps' mascot, the English Bulldog, is the result of a name German soldiers called attacking Marines during WWI: *Teufel-hunden*, or "Devil Dogs."

us bank
Five Star Service Guaranteed

THE MARKET

U.S. Bank is the principal subsidiary of U.S. Bancorp, the eighth-largest financial holding company in the United States. U.S. Bank serves more than 10 million customers, principally through more than 2,100 full-service branch offices in its 24-state primary footprint; additional specialized loan, trust, and brokerage offices across the country; more than 4,600 ATMs; telephone banking; and Internet banking. From the Midwest to the West Coast, from the Great Plains to the Pacific Northwest, U.S. Bank operates in an industry that is increasingly competitive — among banks and nonbanks — and in an era of accelerating consolidation and convergence.

ACHIEVEMENTS

In an industry in which competitors distinguish themselves with the service they offer, only U.S. Bank guarantees outstanding customer service by every business line and every employee for every transaction every day. The exclusive U.S. Bank *Five Star Service Guarantee* ensures specific performance standards that reflect customer expectations for quality, responsiveness, accuracy, and availability. The goal of the *Five Star Service Guarantee* is to bring customers the highest level of service they have ever experienced from a financial institution. Each department and line of business at U.S. Bank has a customized guarantee for its external and internal customers — more than 80 guarantees in all. Each quarter, a select few employees who exemplify outstanding service qualify for induction into the U.S. Bank *Circle of Service Excellence*. The inductees are honored with a number of recognition events and financial rewards.

U.S. Bank is a leader in assuring that its financial services and communications are easily accessible to the Hispanic population in its market areas. Launched in July 2001, U.S. Bank's Hispanic initiative centers around three core objectives: to increase the number of Spanish-speaking Hispanic employees in the branches and throughout the company, to become even more involved in Hispanic organizations locally and nationally, and to develop and communicate "best in class" financial products and services that meet the distinct needs of Hispanics. U.S. Bank partners with the Consulate of Mexico, the United States Hispanic Chamber of Commerce, the National Council of La Rasa, and the Latin Business Association, among other organizations.

Along with other materials that it publishes and distributes in Spanish, U.S. Bank has launched *espanol@usbank.com*, a Spanish Internet site that includes product information and the capability to apply for accounts online.

HISTORY

Today's U.S. Bank was forged during the 1990s from the combination of several excellent major regional banks, including Star Bank, Firstar, Mercantile, First Bank System, U.S. Bank, and Colorado National Bank. Those banks, in turn, had grown from the mergers of numerous smaller banks throughout the years. In the eastern part of the franchise, U.S. Bank traces some of its earliest roots to 1853 when Farmers and Millers Bank in Milwaukee opened its doors, growing into the First National Bank of Milwaukee and eventually becoming First Wisconsin and ultimately Firstar. In St. Louis,

State Savings Institution, with just $8,500 in capital and one teller, opened in St. Louis in 1855, later to become part of the Mercantile Trust Company, the forerunner of Mercantile Bancorporation. In Cincinnati, The First National Bank of Cincinnati opened for business in 1863 under National Charter #24 with the boom of Civil War cannons firing just across the Ohio, but it survived through many more decades to grow into Star Bank. About this same time, The First National Bank of St. Paul was chartered in 1864. A year later, The First National Bank of Minneapolis received its charter. These two First Nationals formed a holding company in early 1929, known as First Bank Stock Corporation, and they kept that name until 1968 when they became First Bank System. Across the Rocky Mountains in 1891, several prominent business leaders received a charter for The United States National Bank of Portland, Oregon, a *de novo* banking company.

From their largely unremarkable beginnings, these banks thrived as independent entities, each growing into a respected force (and usually the largest commercial bank) in their respective marketplaces. As opportunities arose, each participated in in-market mergers and acquisitions during the early decades of the 20th century and in more widespread expansions during the 1980s and 1990s — including the 1993 transaction that brought Colorado National Bank in Denver into the First Bank System, and West One Bancorp of Boise, Idaho, coming into the original U.S. Bancorp in 1995.

Of particular note, in 1902 the U.S. National Bank of Portland was merged into the Ainsworth National Bank of Portland, but kept the U.S. National Bank name. The decision turned out to be an auspicious one, as a 1913 federal law prohibited other banks from using "United States" in their names from that time forward. U.S. National was among the first banks to form a bank holding company — called U.S. Bancorp.

Since 1988 alone, mergers with and acquisitions of more than 50 banks, large and small, have helped form today's U.S. Bank. During the 1990s, Star, Firstar, and Mercantile merged to become the new Firstar, and First Bank System and U.S. Bancorp combined as U.S. Bancorp. On February 27, 2001, Firstar and U.S. Bancorp became today's new U.S. Bancorp.

THE PRODUCT

U.S. Bancorp and its subsidiaries, including U.S. Bank, provide a comprehensive selection of premium financial products and services to individuals, businesses, nonprofit organizations, institutions, and government entities. U.S. Bank products and services are distributed primarily through five major lines of business.

Consumer Banking delivers products and services to the broad consumer market and small businesses, and encompasses community banking, metropolitan banking, small business banking, consumer lending, mortgage banking, workplace banking, student banking, 24-hour banking, and investment products and insurance sales.

Wholesale Banking offers lending, depository, treasury management, and other financial services to middle-market, large corporate, and public-sector clients.

Payment Services includes consumer and business credit cards, corporate and purchasing card services, consumer lines of credit, ATM processing, merchant processing, and debit cards.

Private Client, Trust, and Asset Management provides mutual fund processing services, trust, private banking, and financial advisory services through four businesses, including the Private Client Group, Corporate Trust, Institutional Trust and Custody, and Mutual Fund Services, LLC. The business segment also offers investment management services to several client segments,

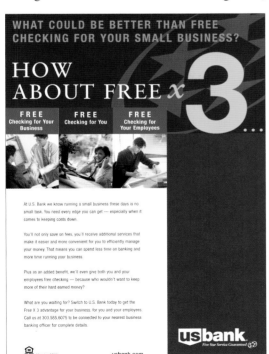

including mutual funds, institutional customers, and private asset management.

Capital Markets engages in equity and fixed-income trading activities through a network of brokerage offices, offering investment banking and underwriting services for corporate and public-sector customers and regionally based businesses.

RECENT DEVELOPMENTS

Through a new program called Checking That Pays, U.S. Bank is rewarding its customers for using their checking accounts. The program pays customers up to 1 percent of the amount of total purchases made with their U.S. Bank check card. U.S. Bank is the only bank in the country to offer Checking That Pays.

Gomez ranks U.S. Bank's *usbank.com* Web site in the elite top ten among financial institutions that provide Internet banking. Gomez is an Internet quality measurement group that analyzes the online customer experience at various Web sites. The ranking is a testament to the research and enhancement that U.S. Bank has implemented and offered its online customers.

U.S. Bancorp, through its predecessor companies, has increased its annual dividend rate in each of the past 30 years and has paid a dividend for 139 consecutive years. The most recent increase in the U.S. Bancorp common share dividend was announced on March 13, 2002.

In August 2002, U.S. Bank announced an agreement to acquire the corporate trust business of State Street Corporation. This transaction clearly established U.S. Bank as a leader in the corporate trust industry — the largest trustee in the area of municipal finance and the third largest in new corporate bond issuances and structured finance.

PROMOTION

U.S. Bank is always looking for channels to market the U.S. Bank brand in a way that raises the bank's reputation and status in the communities it serves. Also, U.S. Bank strives to enhance the brand's value by ensuring a positive personal experience for every customer, prospect, and community. The U.S. Bank brand is promoted continuously through a broad range of standard media channels including television, radio, newspaper, magazine, direct mail, and outdoor advertising; numerous sponsorships and events across the country; corporate giving and employee volunteerism; and programs that foster economic and community development. Equally important, U.S. Bank employees embody the brand through the service they provide to customers.

BRAND VALUES

Outstanding customer service is so fundamental a brand value that U.S. Bank employees, including the CEO, wear lapel pins with the inscription "Service Guaranteed," a visible symbol of the bank's commitment. The U.S. Bank *Five Star Service Guaranteed* brand communicates two key values: commitment to serving customers across the United States, and commitment to outstanding customer service. Both are critical, understandable, and deliverable benefits for virtually all

consumers in the financial marketplace.

The appearance of the brand reflects the way U.S. Bank does business with its customers: direct, clear, and specific about the brand promise and the scope of the bank's capability. The solid, stable shape of the U.S. shield element illustrates the company's solid performance and stability, important factors when a consumer or corporation is choosing a financial partner. At the same time, the sleek *Five Star Service Guaranteed* line and circle of stars communicates the commitment to service and the bank's progressive and innovative approach to doing business.

The bright, bold red, white, and blue of the bank's logo clearly underscores the company name, as well as the bank's pride in being part of the American financial services industry. The logo reflects U.S. Bank's recognition of the importance of banks in the nation's economic system.

145

THE MARKET

Skincare is a dynamic and exciting category as more people than ever before are interested in keeping their skin looking and feeling great. The U.S. market for hand and body lotion is competitive and growing — with dollar sales up around $1.5 billion in 2001. As the U.S. population inches towards 300 million, there is no shortage of bodies to care for — and hands and bodies both need care to feel healthy and look attractive every day.

American consumers buy their hand and body lotion products in a wide variety of marketplaces. Grocery stores, drugstores, mass merchandisers, category-busting retail environments, and high-end department stores are some of the options.

ACHIEVEMENTS

Vaseline Intensive Care Lotion has been the number-one selling body lotion brand in the United States for over thirty years (*AC Nielsen dollar share data*). Few products can claim similar success. Not only is the brand a market leader in skincare, Vaseline also has the highest household penetration in the body lotion category. Even with all the changes in American society since 1970 and with the seemingly daily parade of changing opinions on what's good for you and what's not, Vaseline Intensive Care Lotion has remained a favorite with Americans.

In addition to lotions, Vaseline Petroleum Jelly has been an excellent moisturizer since the

Stronger nails and **younger, healthier** looking hands in just **two weeks.**
New Healthy Hand Essentials. You might want to get your hands on it.

1870s. Today you can find Vaseline Petroleum Jelly in 80 percent of American households. It might be in the bathroom or the kitchen, or on the changing table or the nightstand — but in four out of five homes in the United States, there's a place for Vaseline Petroleum Jelly.

HISTORY

Petroleum jelly has been used for over 140 years. The starting point for Vaseline Petroleum Jelly can be traced to 1859, when Robert Augustus Chesebrough, a 22-year-old English-born chemist with an interest in the oil industry, noticed Pennsylvania oil field workers using rod wax — a petroleum by-product from the oil pump rods — to soothe and promote the healing of cuts and burns.

Chesebrough returned to his home in Brooklyn, New York, and spent years refining and testing the product he called "petroleum jelly." By 1870, Chesebrough was manufacturing the product. He traveled door-to-door marketing his wonder jelly, which provided protection for minor cuts and burns and soothed dry skin. In the early 1870s, Chesebrough received several patents on his petroleum jelly. Vaseline also became a registered trademark.

A full century passed between the time of Chesebrough's original creation and when Vaseline extended its franchise by putting the hallowed Vaseline name on another product. In 1970, the Vaseline franchise expanded to include the Vaseline Intensive Care Lotion brand — offering the Dry Skin Formula. Then additions to the product line came more frequently.

The Vaseline Intensive Care bath line was introduced in 1973. Vaseline Lip Therapy reached the market in 1985 with a tube applicator, and in 1987, customers found out about Vaseline Intensive Care Lotion Aloe Vera.

As the twentieth century wound down, Vaseline Intensive Care acknowledged the changing composition of American society. No longer was the United States an easily categorized palette of women staying at home and men performing largely physical labor, as it was when Chesebrough began his work. Vaseline in the 1990s expanded its product line to meet the skincare needs of all kinds of people with all types of skin.

Innovation continued in the new millennium. In 2001, Vaseline launched its first anti-aging body lotion, Renew & Protect, which helps bring out a healthy-looking, youthful glow. In 2002, Vaseline Intensive Care introduced two additional products: Healthy Hand Essentials — a complete-care solution for both hands and nails — and Healthy Body Complexion, a lotion that evens out skin tone and improves texture to reveal a radiant complexion.

THE PRODUCT

The Vaseline brand is widely recognized for its hardworking and effective moisturizing properties. Many elbows, knees, hands, and feet have been softened by Vaseline products. Today its lineup includes lotions, jellies, and bath products:

Vaseline Intensive Care Lotion
Dry Skin
Aloe & Naturals
Advanced Healing
Water Resistant
Renew & Protect
Healthy Hand Essentials
Healthy Body
   Complexion
Firming & Nourishing
   (to launch May 2003)

Vaseline Petroleum Jelly
Creamy
Dual Action

Lip Therapy
Advanced
Cherry

Vaseline Bath Line
Moisturizing Bath Beads line
Foaming Creme Bath line

RECENT DEVELOPMENTS

In the past year, Vaseline Intensive Care introduced two new advanced body moisturizers that meet consumers' desire for better skin:

- **Healthy Hand Essentials**, an Alpha Hydroxy lotion for the hands with Vitamin E and Keratin. Its special formula immediately hydrates skin, strengthens nails, and softens cuticles in two weeks, and in four weeks diminishes the appearance of fine lines and wrinkles.
- **Healthy Body Complexion**, an Alpha Hydroxy lotion for the body with Vitamins A and E. Its formula helps diminish the appearance of rough spots, dry patches, and blotches to reveal a radiant, healthy-looking complexion all over.

PROMOTION

The first advertising campaign for Vaseline Intensive Care Lotion launched in 1971 and featured a dry leaf, which symbolized dry skin. The "Leaf" advertising was highly memorable and drove the brand to market leadership. Another famous campaign was "Scratch Dry" (1986), where the Vaseline lotion provided visual evidence of its moisturizing properties through scratching the word "dry" on skin. This campaign helped to reinforce Vaseline Intensive Care Lotion's efficacy image and drove market share in a competitive environment.

Given its long therapeutic heritage, Vaseline Intensive Care Lotion evolved to an even more positive positioning in the 1990s. The "Take Good Care" advertising campaign launched in 1999 featured people of all ages and ethnicities taking good care of their skin with Vaseline Intensive Care Lotion. The campaign carried the brand's message of nurturing, caring, and skin intimacy. Vaseline Intensive Care is one of the only brands that appeals to both men and women (and children) of all ages, and the "Take Good Care" campaign focused specifically on the positive aspects of how everyone feels good when they have good skin.

In 2001, Vaseline Intensive Care won an Effie Award for "From Here On," a commercial for the product launch of Vaseline Intensive Care Lotion Water Resistant, a lotion with moisturizers that last through a hand washing. In 2000, the ad, which was within the "Take Good Care" campaign, had helped Water Resistant achieve a top-ten share ranking in the body lotion innovations category after only six months. Effie Awards are presented annually by the New York American Marketing Association in recognition of the year's most effective advertising campaigns.

BRAND VALUES

With so many uses for so many different types of people, the Vaseline brand represents a bundle of impressions that people have accumulated over generations of its use. The Vaseline brand is a contemporary classic — genuine, honest, and hard-working. For over 125 years, people have trusted Vaseline to take care of themselves and their loved ones. Families have found a multitude of ways to use Vaseline's products, which — oddly enough — emerged from an industrial environment.

Through its promotions, the Vaseline brand lets its loyal customer base know that the backers of the brand genuinely care about the customers' health and well-being. In turn, consumers depend on the Vaseline brand to deliver quality products that are effective in bringing forth their best skin. With promotions such as Vaseline Intensive Care Month and related events such as an essay contest in upbeat *Self* magazine, Vaseline educates others about the importance of skincare and promotes an image of the vitality and self-assuredness that come from taking care of one's own body.

Extraordinary women don't use ordinary lotions.

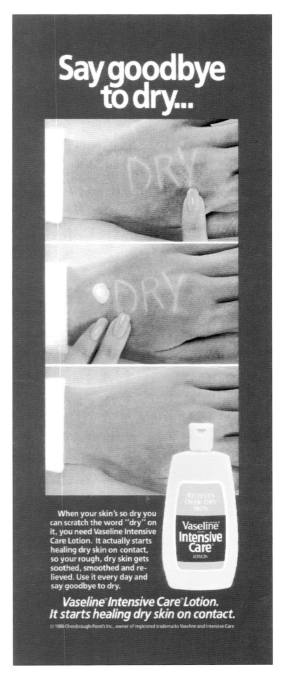

Say goodbye to dry...

When your skin's so dry you can scratch the word "dry" on it, you need Vaseline Intensive Care Lotion. It actually starts healing dry skin on contact, so your rough, dry skin gets soothed, smoothed and relieved. Use it every day and say goodbye to dry.

Vaseline Intensive Care Lotion. It starts healing dry skin on contact.

© 1988 Chesebrough-Pond's Inc., owner of registered trademarks Vaseline and Intensive Care

THINGS YOU DIDN'T KNOW ABOUT VASELINE

❍ Robert Chesebrough, the pioneer and an avid user of Vaseline, lived to the ripe age of 96.

❍ Vaseline Petroleum Jelly skincare secrets have been passed down from generation to generation. Celebrities reported to use Vaseline Petroleum Jelly include Yasmine Bleeth, Rachel Hunter, Bobbi Brown, Eartha Kitt, and Kim Alexis.

❍ More people use Vaseline Intensive Care Lotion than any other body lotion brand in America.

❍ Vaseline Petroleum Jelly can be used to remove makeup, soften cuticles, moisturize lips, and as an overnight hand and foot softener.

❍ Marilyn Monroe reportedly used to wear three shades of lipstick blended together and coated with a glossy mixture of Vaseline Petroleum Jelly and wax to make them look their fullest.

THE MARKET

The telecommunications industry is facing its toughest challenges to date. A weak economy, excess network capacity, waves of merger and acquisition activities, and new market entrants have created difficult market conditions.

There is good news, however, as the demand for telecommunications services remains strong. In fact, over the next five years the average monthly U.S. household expenditure on various forms of communications is expected to increase to just over $120.

As the nation's leading telecommunications company, Verizon is well positioned to leverage its particular strengths. Verizon understands the importance of staying focused on the fundamentals, and making the right promises and keeping them. For Verizon's customers, that means benefiting from all the innovation, features, and convenience that technology promises — as Verizon helps them make progress every day.

ACHIEVEMENTS

With the launch of Verizon Freedom[SM], Verizon now offers a comprehensive product package with fully integrated billing that is unique among its competitors, including long-distance carriers, competitive local exchange carriers, and cable TV companies. Verizon Freedom[SM] gives consumers the ease of one point of contact for all their telecommunications services, including local and regional toll calling, long-distance, wireless service, and a high-speed Internet connection with DSL — all together on one bill at a great price. With the added value of package pricing, consumers no longer have to choose between making a call on their wireless phone or their wired phone. And with identical long-distance calling plans for both wireless and wireline calls, consumers can choose the most convenient way to call, without worrying about costs. Verizon Freedom[SM] is now available in many of the states that Verizon serves.

HISTORY

Verizon Communications (NYSE: VZ), formed by the merger of Bell Atlantic and GTE, is one of the world's leading providers of high-growth communications services. This merger brought together two powerful telecommunication companies — each strongly committed to customer services, rich in management expertise and experience, and aggressive in its technological foresight — combining to form the ultimate telecommunications resource: Verizon Communications.

From day one, Verizon led the industry with more ways than any other company to touch customers and meet their requirements, more cash to fuel growth and innovation, and more investment capital to deploy the technologies of the future. Verizon's digital networks already include more fiber optics and more "first mile" assets than any other communications company. These networks, as they continue to develop, will give Verizon the premiere distribution platform for electronic commerce and delivery of a comprehensive suite of Internet-age services, including high-speed Internet access powered by DSL.

Today, Verizon companies are the largest providers of wireline and wireless communications in the United States, with more than 135 million access line equivalents and more than 31.5 million wireless customers.

Verizon is also the world's largest provider of print and online directory information. A Fortune 10 company with more than 236,000 employees and $67 billion in 2002 revenues, Verizon's global presence is felt in the Americas, Europe, Asia, and the Pacific.

And with more than 10 million long-distance customers in 47 states, Verizon has passed Sprint to become the third largest long-distance provider in the United States, according to independent surveys of long-distance customers.

To launch the brand in 2000, Verizon recognized that its new name and logo would be one of its most important and valuable assets for gaining immediate recognition and competitive advantage. An integrated name change advertising campaign was launched, and a complete brand identity system was quickly developed, covering hundreds of applications that included more than just advertising. The impact of the rebranding effort can now be seen across the entire corporation from Hawaii to Puerto Rico, and was one of the largest, most aggressive, and most comprehensive rebranding efforts in U.S. corporate history.

THE PRODUCT

With over 135 million access line equivalents in 67 of the top 100 markets in the United States, and nine of the top 10, Verizon reaches one-third of the nation's households, more than one-third of Fortune 500 company headquarters, as well as the U.S. federal government. Verizon also has wireline and wireless operations in 37 countries around the world.

Verizon Wireless is the nation's largest wireless communications provider with more than 31.5 million wireless voice and data customers. The company's footprint covers nearly 90 percent of the U.S. population, 49 of the top 50 and 97 of the top 100 U.S. markets.

Verizon Information Services is a world-leading print and online directory publisher and content provider. In addition to print directories, Verizon Information Services produces and markets *SuperPages.com*, the Internet's preeminent online directory and shopping resource. *SuperPages.com* provides Yellow Pages and directory services to AltaVista, MSN, Lycos, Excite, InfoSpace, Ask Jeeves, BigFoot, HotBot, Tripod, and Angelfire.

Bringing the benefits of communications to everybody also means doing so with convenience. Verizon's One Bill allows customers to consolidate billing for local, long-distance, and wireless services. Coupled with the launch of the Verizon Freedom[SM] service packages, Verizon customers now have the flexibility to bundle a host of Verizon products and services that fit their lifestyle and budget requirements while capturing significant savings.

RECENT DEVELOPMENTS

Since day one, Verizon's goal was to be the most respected brand in communications. Recent survey results indicate that the Verizon brand has grown stronger and continues to gain strength. Verizon is now considered the most respected, the preferred, and the most recommended brand in the markets that it serves. The results attained trace back to the commitment of Verizon's leadership team and the work of employees at every level, each and every day. Further, the use of a Master Brand strategy — using the single Verizon name and logo in all lines of business — has proven to be the right move. Verizon Wireless and Verizon Information Services advertisements contribute to overall awareness as well as the personality of the company.

Verizon wants to be known as contemporary, optimistic, forward moving, confident, and resourceful. Verizon has a long history of fostering confidence by being there for its customers — a key ingredient to making progress.

PROMOTION

Verizon has become one of the most powerful and recognizable brands in the world through a distinctive brand strategy and the effective implementation of a comprehensive brand identity system. But with that recognition came the desire to establish Verizon firmly in the minds of its customers with a solid, ownable positioning: "Progress."

What is progress? Progress is different things to different people. To some, progress may be coming up with "that one big idea" or completing all the daily tasks on their to-do lists. For others, progress is spending quality time with family and friends. At Verizon, making progress means helping its customers and communities move forward in ways that are important to them, whether holding a conference call on a project, finding a shop that carries the gift they want to buy, or doing online research. When Verizon customers accomplish any of these everyday tasks, it represents the progress they are making. Through the thousands of daily contacts with customers, Verizon's employees demonstrate a relentless desire to help customers move forward in a positive direction every day.

"Make progress every day" is Verizon's tagline, which expresses the brand's overall positioning. This theme of the company's brand advertising shows Verizon's commitment to its customers, shareowners, and communities, and represents the natural progression of the Verizon brand while offering a unique market positioning strategy.

BRAND VALUES

As Bell Atlantic and GTE merged to form the new Verizon, CEO Ivan Seidenberg was very clear about his objective for the new company: Verizon will become the most respected brand in communications. Progress, integrity, diversity, and confidence anchor that commitment. Today, Verizon employees are working harder than ever to make that goal a reality, helping customers move forward, get better, and make progress every day.

THINGS YOU DIDN'T KNOW ABOUT VERIZON

○ Verizon was commended with a unanimous resolution by the New York Public Service Commission — the first time all commissioners signed one resolution — for Verizon's efforts to restore the telecommunications infrastructure in lower Manhattan after September 11, 2001.

○ Laubach Literacy International and Literacy Volunteers of America have awarded Verizon the National Literacy Leadership Award two years in a row.

○ Aside from being recognized as a customer service leader, Verizon is also a great place to work. Verizon is placed on the lists of the 100 best U.S. companies to work for in *Hispanic* and *Working Mother* magazines.

○ Verizon's rebranding effort represented a huge undertaking. The array of branded assets requiring standards and rebranding was a fleet with more than 69,000 vehicles, a nationwide network of 250,000 payphones, ID badges, 6,000 buildings, directories, bill media, recorded greetings and announcements, product packaging, calling cards, and more.

○ Verizon has received many accolades over the last few years, including a number-one ranking by high-volume long-distance callers (J.D. Power & Associates Residential Long Distance Customer Satisfaction Study, July 2002), Excellence in Local Telephone Customer Satisfaction (J.D. Power & Associates Residential Local Telephone Customer Satisfaction Study, August 2002), Excellence in Customer Satisfaction in DSL Service (J.D. Power & Associates 2002 Internet Service Provider Residential Customer Satisfaction Study, August 2002), Most Reliable Network and Customer Service, for Verizon Wireless (*Wall Street Journal*, October 2002), and the highest rating for "Overall Satisfaction" for Verizon Long Distance (Yankee Group's annual Technologically Advanced Family Survey, December 2001).

YELLOW ®

ground service with same-day, next-day, and any-day service, featuring proactive notification and an industry-leading 100% satisfaction guarantee.

- **Definite Delivery™:** Guaranteed service with constant monitoring and proactive notification for standard transit-time shipments.
- **Standard Ground™:** The fastest, most reliable ground service with more direct points than any other national transportation provider.
- **Standard Ground Regional Advantage:** An advanced high-speed network that significantly reduces short-haul transit time between metropolitan areas.
- **Cross-Border:** Door-to-door transportation solutions between Canada, the United States, and Mexico.
- **Yellow Global®:** Fully integrated international solutions via air, ocean, and land, powered by the industry's first online instant booking, tracking, and tracing application.

Meridian IQ™: A global transportation management company that offers fast, flexible, and easy-to-implement solutions that are guaranteed to deliver on the promise of real return on investment (ROI). The company offers both transportation solutions management and shipment management services such as:

- **PowerTMS™:** A web-native transportation management system that can be implemented quickly and is easy to use. In addition to offering planning and optimization tools, TMS also provides order management, administration, and tracking, as well as settlement and reporting functions.
- **Solutions Design and Consulting:** Consistent and proven processes, Web-native technology, and experienced professionals who design, implement, and manage solutions that deliver rapid improvements and overall long-term value.
- **Global Services:** Integrated air, ocean, and land

services, including complete customs brokerage. Through a network of partners covering more than 88 countries, a seamless source for door-to-door services through major world markets.

- **Multi-modal Domestic Services:** Procurement of transportation providers to fit your service requirements at extremely competitive rates. This service is great for companies with truckload or specialized capacity requirements, or those with special or expedited shipping needs.

Yellow Technologies: Cutting-edge capabilities, resources, and expertise that deliver state-of-the-art

transportation solutions and services. This Yellow subsidiary's mission is to explore new technology and provide innovative information solutions and exceptional technology services to create a competitive advantage for Yellow businesses.

RECENT DEVELOPMENTS
Yellow is transforming itself, and in the process, transforming the way customers look at transportation solutions providers. After the company launched the Transformation Conference, the meeting quickly became a much-anticipated and highly regarded industry event, featuring such speakers as Rudy Giuliani, former President George Bush and former First Lady Barbara Bush, and best-selling authors such as Jim Collins, Jason Jennings, and Tom Peters. This award-winning business and logistics conference includes educational and professional development programs for senior-level executives. Attendees at previous conferences have called it "superb," "outstanding," and among the "best conferences" ever attended.

In March 2002, Yellow announced the launch of Meridian IQ, a non-asset services company that utilizes Web-native technology to provide customers a single source for global transportation management and improved return on investment through fast, flexible, and easy-to-implement solutions.

The year 2002 also marked the company's successful spin-off of small, regional trucking companies, a move that solidified the Yellow position as a global business and logistics partner and a one-stop shop for transportation solutions. Customers' regional needs are handled by Standard Ground Regional Advantage and other Yellow services.

PROMOTION
As a worldwide leader in transportation and logistics services, Yellow is one of the most recognized and respected transportation companies in the world. Advertising began in 1983, three years after deregulation, with the inclusion of institutional ads in trade and business publications. Before then, the industry and the company were accustomed to regulation and its influences, with little advertising or marketing effort allowed.

Yellow has recently focused on re-energizing the brand and making it more visible. In addition to print advertising in trade journals, the company has developed an innovative approach to communicating the company's brand proposition. The "Yes We Can" bobblehead only knows how to say "yes" to all customer needs, demonstrating the corporate-wide "Yes We Can" attitude.

In addition, Yellow sponsors a racing team in the NASCAR Busch Series. This association strengthens the brand's awareness through increased exposure to motorsports fans. Team Yellow Racing creates excitement and builds loyalty with both

internal and external audiences; it's a proven value in building customer relations.

BRAND VALUES
At the foundation of the Yellow mission are core values: exceed customer expectations, value employees and associates, work safely, demonstrate good citizenship, act with integrity, and embrace teamwork. Rooted in these values, the brand promises to do "whatever it takes" to more than satisfy the customer at every turn. Yellow delivers on that promise in offering the widest array of services, the broadest domestic network, and award-winning technologies to meet the ever-changing needs of today's transportation marketplace. At Yellow, "Yes We Can" is more than just an advertising slogan. It is a very real expression of the commitment of 24,000 employees to live by these brand values and exceed the customer's expectations in everything they do.

THINGS YOU DIDN'T KNOW ABOUT YELLOW

○ Yellow originally operated as a bus and taxi company serving central Oklahoma.

○ Yellow commissioned DuPont to determine what color was most visible from the greatest distance for the fleet. After careful research, DuPont presented a color, dubbed "Swamp Holly Orange." And so the company named Yellow gained its official, distinctive color — the safest color on the road.

○ Yellow supports many local and national organizations, such as the United Way, American Heart Association, Habitat for Humanity, Heart to Heart International and the National Center for Missing and Exploited Children.

zenith

THE MARKET

Americans love to be entertained, and they look to consumer electronics as the primary source of that entertainment. For more than 80 years, Zenith Electronics Corporation has established a proud heritage of leadership in consumer electronics products to provide an entertainment experience that surpasses all others. As digital technologies such as HDTV, DVD, and flat-panel displays gain momentum in the United States and around the world, Zenith is committed to helping consumers "Digitize the Experience" by making digital television more affordable and widely accessible.

ACHIEVEMENTS

A pioneer in electronics technology, Zenith has invented countless industry-leading developments, including the first wireless TV remote controls, the first portable and push-button radios, and the first high-definition television (HDTV) system using digital technology. In fact, Zenith developed the digital transmission system adopted by the Federal Communications Commission (FCC) for HDTV broadcasts. Today, together with its new parent company, global consumer electronics giant LG Electronics, Zenith is paving the way for the digital TV age.

HISTORY

Zenith's story began in 1918 when two wireless-radio enthusiasts set up a "factory" on a kitchen table in Chicago and began making radio equipment for other amateurs. Over the next decade, the infant radio industry began to grow as did the business, which sold radios under the name "Z-Nith." In 1923, Zenith Radio Corporation was born.

The young company's early accomplishments included the world's first portable radios, the first home radio receivers to operate on household current, and in 1927 the first automatic push-button radio tuning (when Zenith's famous slogan, "The Quality Goes In Before The Name Goes On," was first used). Zenith also pioneered developments in shortwave and multiband radios such as the famous Trans-Oceanic, first introduced in 1942. Zenith was on the leading edge of AM and FM radio broadcasting — including the invention of the stereo FM radio broadcast system used worldwide — and played a key role in developing broadcast standards for black-and-white and color television.

Television Pioneer. Early television developments included some of the first prototype television receivers in the 1930s and experimental TV broadcasts, which began in 1939 and, at the request of the FCC, continued during World War II. Zenith launched the world's first subscription television system in 1947 and introduced black-and-white TV sets in 1948, followed by a series

of innovations throughout the 1950s, including the industry's first wireless remote controls and 21-inch, three-gun rectangular color picture tubes.

Zenith introduced its first color TV sets for consumers in 1961 and quickly established itself as the leading brand. The 1969 introduction of the revolutionary "Chromacolor" black-matrix negative guardband picture tube doubled the image brightness of color television and established a new standard of performance for the entire industry. The "EFL" (extended field length) electron gun in 1976 and "System 3" modular TV chassis in 1978 also contributed to Zenith's continued strength in color television during the 1970s.

From "Zenith Radio" to "Zenith Electronics." Mounting competitive pressures in its core consumer electronics business led Zenith to use its broad engineering and marketing expertise to diversify in the late 1970s when the company entered the components and cable television products businesses.

In 1979, for example, Zenith acquired the Heath Company, the world's largest manufacturer of build-it-yourself electronics kit products for hobbyists. Capitalizing on Heath's entry into personal computers, Zenith formed Zenith Data Systems (ZDS) in 1980. Zenith's management built the computer business into a billion-dollar operation by the late 1980s and sold the Heath and ZDS businesses in 1989.

By the mid-1980s, Zenith Cable Products (later known as Zenith Network Systems) was a leading supplier of set-top boxes to the cable industry and a pioneer in cable modem technologies. The 1990s saw this business evolve into a supplier of digital set-top boxes for wired and wireless networks. Zenith sold its Network Systems division in 2000.

The company changed its name from Zenith Radio Corporation to Zenith Electronics Corporation in 1984, while remaining committed to audio engineering related to television. Zenith engineers co-developed the multichannel television sound (MTS) transmission system adopted by the industry for stereo TV broadcasts in 1984, and the company received an Emmy for pioneering work on development of MTS stereo TV in 1986.

A major Zenith advance of the 1980s was the patented "flat tension mask" technology for high-resolution color video displays with perfectly flat screens, glare-free viewing, and superior

performance, which earned the company a technical Emmy in 2001. Other noteworthy Zenith television innovations include TV receivers with "Sound by Bose" in 1986 and "Dolby Surround Sound" in 1988, as well as the first TVs featuring built-in closed caption decoders (1991), electronic program guides (1994), and track-ball-operated remote controls (1995).

THE PRODUCT
Zenith has been a leader in HDTV, or high-definition television, for 15 years, setting the stage for the broadcast revolution currently under way. As one of HDTV's earliest proponents, Zenith developed a number of key digital technologies, most notably the VSB (Vestigial Side Band) digital transmission system that the FCC adopted in 1996 as the centerpiece of the U.S. digital television broadcast standard. In 1997, Zenith earned a technical Emmy for pioneering developments behind the digital standard.

Today, as the transition to digital TV broadcasting continues to gain momentum — with local TV stations using Zenith's patented VSB technology to transmit HDTV programming to more than 90 percent of U.S. households — Zenith

offers for the home and professional markets one of the industry's broadest arrays of digital television technologies. They include direct-view and rear-projection HDTVs, plasma display panels and liquid crystal displays; digital set-top boxes; DVD, MP3, and CD players; and VCRs and other products designed to digitize and enhance the viewing experience for American consumers.

RECENT DEVELOPMENTS
By the mid-1990s, Zenith was seeking a global partner with complementary strengths that could help lay the groundwork for leadership in the digital age. The company found that strong partner in LG Electronics Inc. (LGE), which acquired a majority interest in Zenith in 1995. In 1999, after completing a broad financial and operational restructuring, Zenith became a wholly owned, independent subsidiary of LGE.

Ushering in the new millennium, Zenith began to reposition its famous brand by building on its distribution and technology strengths and the vast resources of its new parent company. The transformation into the digital leader accelerated in 2001 as Zenith dramatically reduced its analog product offerings and introduced a comprehensive family of digital television products. By 2002, Zenith had established the industry's most aggressive approach to digital television, with a product line comprising more than 80 percent digital products — reflecting the powerful combination of Zenith's longtime leadership in HDTV and LGE's display technology strengths.

PROMOTION
Calling on consumers to "Digitize the Experience®," Zenith's broad-based branding campaign is introducing Zenith to a new generation of consumers. Armed with its broad digital product lines, an updated version of its famous lightning-bolt logo, and an aggressive new marketing campaign, Zenith is targeting a younger, more affluent target audience.

High-profile partnerships such as the Sundance Film Festival and the New Museum of Contemporary Art also reflect the company's focus on bringing digital technology to technology-savvy consumers. Building on the success of its 2001–2002 marketing program (Zenith's first major national advertising campaign in 15 years), Zenith is further expanding its advertising presence in 2003 to reclaim its birthright in HDTV.

BRAND VALUES
Beginning with the advent of radio, the Zenith name has been synonymous with quality and innovation. The company's lightning-bolt logo is one of the most recognizable trademarks in the country, evoking feelings of trust, security, and familiarity in generations of Americans. With these core values as a foundation, and backed by the technological resources and marketing muscle of its parent company, Zenith has repositioned its famous brand as the digital leader.

THINGS YOU DIDN'T KNOW ABOUT ZENITH

○ Zenith invented and introduced TV remote controls: "Lazy Bones," the first wired TV remote in 1950; "Flash-Matic," the first wireless TV remote in 1955; and "Space Command," the first practical wireless remote control (1956), based on ultrasonic technology used throughout the industry for the next quarter century before being replaced in the early 1980s by infrared remotes.

○ Zenith invented the first baby monitor. "The Radio Nurse," introduced in 1937, which allowed parents to hear sounds from their children's rooms.

○ Other little-known developments from Zenith's laboratories over the years included innovations in hearing aids (the only Zenith consumer products built during World War II when production was devoted to communications devices for the war effort), as well as night-vision, laser discs, and subscription TV, to name a few.

○ Zenith pioneered the technology behind today's perfectly flat picture tubes for high-definition and conventional television—earning 137 U.S. patents for core research in flat CRTs for television and computer displays.

○ Zenith has more inductees in the Consumer Electronics Hall of Fame than any other company.

○ Zenith is a major supplier of televisions to hotels, hospitals, schools, military installations, and correctional institutions.

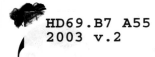

can Red Cross
r, we can save a life

AVERY

AVIS.

2008 01 09

BUICK
THE SPIRIT OF AMERICAN STYLE.

Callaway
GOLF

Carlsberg
Beer

Carrier

CATERPILLAR®

Century 21

Chiquita

Club Med

Coca-Cola
CLASSIC

comcast

Crest

CUNARD
The Most Famous Ocean Liners in the World

Domino's
Pizza

French's

Fritos

Gateway

Gatorade

GEICO
DIRECT

GUARDSMARK

GUESS
U.S.A.
?

Hanes   Hanes
Her Way

Honeywell

HOOVER

HUGGIES
BRAND

Hush Puppies

IBM

IKON
Document Efficiency
At Work.℠

ITT Industries
Engineered for life

JOCKEY

Kellogg's

KeyBank
Achieve anything.

LENNOX

m&m's
Milk Chocolate

McDonald's

THE
Meow Mix
COMPANY

MOEN
Buy it for looks. Buy it for life.®

NYSE
New York Stock Exchange

OSHKOSH
EST. 1895

Panasonic ideas for life

PitneyBowes
Engineering the flow of communication™

Polaroid

ROADWAY
Express

THE
ROYAL DOULTON
COMPANY

SBC

Scott
Products

Scotts

Simmons
Better Sleep Through Science

SONY

Sprint

STANLEY
MAKE SOMETHING GREAT™

STATE FARM
Auto
Life Fire
INSURANCE

Swanson

TBS
Superstation

The New York Times

3M

TNT
WE KNOW DRAMA™

TOYS Я US

Marines
The Few. The Proud.

usbank
Five Star Service Guaranteed

Vaseline
Intensive Care

verizon

YELLOW

zenith